James Bovell

The World at the Advent of the Lord Jesus

James Bovell

The World at the Advent of the Lord Jesus

ISBN/EAN: 9783743336292

Manufactured in Europe, USA, Canada, Australia, Japa

Cover: Foto ©Lupo / pixelio.de

Manufactured and distributed by brebook publishing software (www.brebook.com)

James Bovell

The World at the Advent of the Lord Jesus

TABLE OF CONTENTS.

Preparation for the Advent of Christ among the Jews	5
Preparation among the Jews and Greeks	12
The Jews and Greeks (continued)	17
The Influence of Rome in preparing the World for The Advent	27
Influence of Ancient Rome	38
The Triumvirate	47
Condition of the Jews 71 years B. C.	58
Further decline of Independence	67
The Government under Herod	78
Near Approach of Messiah	84
Government of the Nation A. D. 1	101
Casting away of the Jews	112
Christian Work	127
The Kingdom of Christ	138
Justification	162
The New Birth	170
Rejection of Christ	181
The Eucharist	195
God a Spirit and Man a Spiritual being	211
Concerning the Sacraments	241
The Eucharist a Spiritual Sacrifice	339
The Presence of Christ	386

This little Christmas offering is made to a few Christian brethren who have been accustomed to meet together at Christmas-tide, to enjoy social converse, and to speak of the results of work done through cottage meetings, held throughout the year in the houses of labouring men. At Christmas tide a meeting of Cottagers assembled in the family home of a gentleman from which flows continually the little bright stream of Christian charity, not the less bright and clear and refreshing because hidden beneath the shadow of unostentatious benevolence.

In venturing to bring these short papers before the public eye, the writer has no other object than that of doing good to his fellow men; and to induce others to devote some of their spare time to more frequent Christian intercourse between the various orders of society. One of the evils flowing from the upper to the lower strata of life has become known to us, since the institution of "The Cottage Lectures," an evil curable to a great extent by the mere kindness of visiting among the poor, and bringing the rich and less wealthy together. The love of extravagant personal adornment has a very bad effect and deters the poor from going to the house of God. There can be little objection to personal adornment and the gratification of the taste for the really beautiful in art, when that taste is gratified among equals. But there must be something wrong in the extravagant use of adornment, when all classes are required to meet at the foot of the throne of God, and only one class is found to obey, and that, the one whose apparel brings

PREFACE.

into painful contrast, the homely garb of poverty. These remarks are not written for censure: God forbid! they are written because as a general rule, good kind-hearted people will on knowing one of the causes of the exclusion of the poor from our churches, lend their great influence to encourage a more simple and chaste style of dress, at any rate, for the service of God's house.

Among the youth, attending the Colleges and Schools of Medicine and Law, in Toronto, not a few engage in the work of the Sunday School; and in a few instances social meetings are held for the purpose of conversation on religious and moral subjects. For such friends of truth and order also, this little work has been arranged, some of them having been pleased to request, that the subject treated on should be given to them in more permanent form. To some of those attending the writer's classes, the idea pervading these papers will be familiar as one strongly insisted on in the more systematic teaching of the College course, that, as in the kingdom of Nature, so in the kingdom of Grace, the footprints of the great I AM are everywhere manifest, preparing and perfecting a world for future joys.

The work is professedly a compilation from authentic sources, for the use of Sunday School Teachers and Cottage Readings; and the leading purpose of the whole is to portray the condition of the world at the Advent of the blessed Saviour, and the benefits flowing to man from this wonderful event in the history of the human race.

The papers themselves have been written at intervals snatched from the time usually occupied by the duties of a position requiring close attention. Imperfect as they must be, the writer yet hopes, that, they may subserve the purposes for which they are published, viz., to give to his brethren in brief outline the state of the World at the First Advent.

LAUS DEO.

PREPARATION

FOR THE ADVENT AMONG THE JEWS.

> "Thy holy cities are a wilderness;
> Zion is a wilderness;
> Jerusalem a desolation;
> Our holy and our beautiful house,
> Where our forefathers praised Thee,
> Is burned up with fire,
> And all our pleasant things
> Are laid waste."
>
> ISAIAH clxiv. v. 11, 12.

"Israel hath not obtained that which he seeketh for, but the election hath obtained it. Through their fall, salvation is come unto the Gentiles." It is this salvation that we all meet here together to read about, and to talk about. Jesus Christ is the author of it: He was born of human flesh, that He might effect it; He lived in humility on earth, that He might purchase it; and He died, that the penalty of death should be paid and life be secured to us, His sinful people. It is a great subject, worthy of a more vigorous pen, and truly Christian heart. May the Spirit bless the endeavour made to bring that great time before you.

Any thing that takes us out of the every day contact with the world, to place us at the foot of the cross, is grateful. There is a fullness of pleasure in meeting one another to talk of that wondrous and adoring love, which sought out the poor wretched fallen sinner, that he may hear and know something of the depth of the wickedness of sin, and of the freedom and peace that is in Christ Jesus. It is a great comfort to be able to realize a man of sorrows, one acquainted with grief, walking and talking with men; opening up to them the cause of all their misery, and explaining to them a way of escape from their trials and hard temptations.

It is indeed a happy privilege to meet together for the purpose of meditating on the benefits wrought by a merciful Saviour for us; to contemplate the boundless mercy which the Son of Man exhibits in becoming the head of a fallen race, in Whom that race is re-made. Yes, these words are written, that a band of Christian brothers and sisters may speak to each other of that great salvation, effected for us, whereby we are reconciled to the all holy Almighty Father and Spirit, through the everlasting Son.

The Christian year has closed upon us; and, like the rich and resplendent autumn mantle with which it enwrapt its departure, many-hued events have come and are gone into the storehouse of the past.

> "The year is gone beyond recall,
> With all its hopes and fears;
> With all its bright and gladdening smiles,
> With all its mourner's tears."

To some of us, no doubt, the passing hand of time has flung leaves sear and yellow, hopes blighted and dead. To others, it has wafted the brighter crimson of joys attained. To all we may be certain not evil or disquiet only; for that cannot be, but unmerited mercies: for—

> "New every morning is the love,
> Our wakening and uprising prove;
> Through sleep and darkness safely brought,
> Restored to life and power and thought."

Well, dear **brethren,** another advent-tide is on us; " Christ is near," **it seems to** say, and the "watchers on the tower" look down **upon** a world troubled and sore distressed. **There** is expectancy. Every where there is unrest; for already **the signal** note is heard in the streets, "Where is the promise of His coming?" and men, Baal-like, are turning to gods of their own invention, denying **The Saviour King,** and counting the Blood of the Covenant **a vain thing. We do** indeed seem to be drawing **nigh to** that **time, in the which it was** said, "Faith should be wanting on **the Earth."** How few, compared with the **vast** mass of baptized Christians, nourish the seed of **Grace,** implanted in them by the Holy Spirit; **how few live, as if** they believed, that, the Sacrifice of the Son of God, was still in continuous unending oblation offered for sinful man; how few believe, that, there is a sacrifice for sin, and that, *in*, that sacrifice, they have a part. **In the midst of this scene of desolation, stands** God's altar-**table** yet, and to the true Christmas-keepers these dark forebodings are lights; for when they see these things "they begin **to lift** up their heads, for they know that redemption draweth nigh." "As it was in the days of **Noe, so shall it be** also **in** the days of the Son of Man. They **did eat,** they drank, they married wives, they **were** given **in marriage,** until the day **that** Noe entered into **the ark, and the** flood came and destroyed them all." And so it was too when the very first Christmas-tide broke **upon** the world. What a wondrous time was that! how strange the condition, how marvellous the death-like hush of human energy! **From the day,** that the decree went forth, "The seed **of the woman** shall bruise the serpent's head," up to **the last pro-**phetic **warning** utterance of the Prophet Malachi, no **such** brooding time of thought had happened to man.

Through the long Judaic dispensation the All-Holy, Holy, **Holy,** Lord **God** Almighty, had **been** pleading with, and teaching man. Prophet after prophet had been sent, with sweet enticing words of love, of loving complaint, and with some, full of terrible and awful warning, to secure, if by any means could be secured, man's obedient and reverent remembrance of God. The Tabernacle had **been, and** the Temple was in the midst, as the true gate through which **was** revealed the glory **and** the greatness **and the majesty of Heaven.** God dwelleth **not in** Temples made with hands, yet **He has** been pleased to make known His will and pleasure, that, men must meet Him in that place, where he is pleased to set His name. The richness of the Tabernacle, therefore, need not surprise **us**, the magnificence and gorgeous beauty **of** the Temple and **its majestic** Ritual need not excite our astonishment. All that external glory, and material adornment, **was** demanded by **the Most High,** very much for our own sakes, to teach us by outward sign the majesty and might which are His.

Great as these gifts were, the hand of **God** was yet more open, for as the Jew was the guardian of the true worship, to **him was also** committed the law **and the covenant.** If the possession of all these great privileges brought with them great responsibilities, we know, that, God imposes no duties, nor requires any service, which willing hearts may **not, if** they please, render to Him. History is not slack in exposing the waywardness and obstinacy of the chosen people of **God.** Step by step it brings before us the providence of **God, ever** watchful and long-suffering, ever attentive to their cries, and active in His interposition for Israel's safety. How often would **He have** "**gathered them** under His wings **as a hen doth** gather her chickens, **and** they would not;" **how** frequent, was their wilful rejection of his commands, **and the** rejection of his loving kindness towards them. These truths are upon the broad face of history ; **they are** written for our learning; they tell us of lifelong disobedience, and enduring mercy; of perseverance in rebellion, and final rejection. We look back upon the records of Israel's sins, and we wonder at their folly, forgetting that to-day with the experience of their errors, and with brighter knowledge of God, our ways are treacherous and perverse. Israel, perverting the prophetic deliverances, had cheated themselves into the belief, that, their's was the Kingdom of God; that, to them Christ should come alone; and that, over them and through them, should He sit a King for ever. Were not to them the promises? Had not God fed them in the wilderness? Were not their fathers the Prophets? Was not Israel a chosen people—a nation loved of God? Such they were, truly! Yea! to-day, they abide a peculiar people, kept until the end, that, God's love to Israel may, after long, long years of withdrawal, burst forth again in a full flowing stream. Let us take heed.

You know, my Christian brethren, some of those mysterious and awful warnings which were boldly uttered by the voice of Inspiration; every student of God's Holy Word can call to mind, one or more of those word-paintings of woe and desolation, which in such vivid colour, depict the fall and dispersion of so loved and royal a people. False, capricious, stiff-necked, the Jew clung to the privileges of his race, as to something inalienable. He forgot the conditions under which such were to be enjoyed. Entrusted with all that God had in unmeasured abundance given to him, the Jew looked only to earthly grandeur and riches, and not to the pure and holy spiritual wealth, which he was bid to accumulate. Why was the earnest pleading unheeded: " Bring no more vain oblations; incense is an abomination unto me: the new moons and the Sabbaths, the calling of assemblies, I cannot away with; *it is* iniquity, even the solemn meeting?" "Oh!" said the mourning Jeremiah, "that my head were waters, and mine eyes a fountain of tears, that I might weep day and night for the slain of the daughter of my people." "Oh! that I had in the wilderness a lodging place of wayfaring men; that I might leave my people, and go from them! for they be all adulterers; an assembly of treacherous men." Could more alarming words of warning have been spoken?

If we would in some measure realize the depth of sin and its desolating effect on human nature, and the mercy of God in salvation, let us stand in silent awe with Ezekiel, and gaze on the dim valley of death, the sepulchre of the rebellious dead. There they lie, heap upon heap,—those dry bones, which are so very dry! There is no marrow of fatness left in them, even for the wild beast of the field to suck thereout nourishment. Those tenantless halls of thought, and life, and motion, are but the hideous, soulless skeletons of men who once were disobedient to the voice of God. Son of man, son of man, can these bones live? And as with Ezekiel of old the answer is returned, "O Lord God, thou knowest!" we look, and there is a voice, and behold a shaking, and the bones come together, bone to his bone: and lo! the sinews and the flesh come upon them, and the skin covers them above, but there is no breath in them. Then He said, "Come from the four winds, O Breath, and breathe upon these slain, that they may live. And the breath came upon them, and they heard, and stood up upon their feet an exceeding army." Recovery from the very death of sin was thus held up to the world for our encouragement. Might not Israel have trusted? Oh! why did they not list to the promises of the coming Messiah? Why did they sell themselves for nought, and refuse to be redeemed without money? All these pleadings and representations tell of a nation sunk in almost hopeless misery. Could any picture represent more truly the land of Judea and its people, than that which Ezekiel has so faithfully sketched? For four hundred years succeeding the death of Malachi, the very dew of religion had been sucked out of the heart of the Jew. A death-like stillness lay upon them; they were as dead men. Shut up until the time that Shiloh should come; they seemed but to wait, to fill up the measure of their wickedness. Yet even now it was not too late; their course of life had fitted them for all the evil that they were guilty of; but the cry was still, " Even from the days of your fathers, ye are gone away from my ordinances, and have not kept them. Return unto me, and I will return unto you. But ye said, wherein shall we return? Your words have been stout against me, saith the Lord. Yet ye say, what have we spoken so much against thee? Ye have said, it is vain to serve God, and what profit is it that we have kept his ordinances, and that we have walked mournfully before the Lord of Hosts?' Can language portray more distinctly the entire heart-destitution of a people, or set forth more graphically their alienation from that Almighty Father, who had led them through mighty tribulations? The very circumstances of the times were calculated to arouse thought, and to direct them to some of those stirring and soul-moving promises that prophets had declared.

The Word of God abideth; warnings may be unheeded, rebukes despised; but when the Lord saith, it is done—He does not count slackness, as man counts slackness. He had declared that the sceptre should not depart from Judah, nor a law-giver from between his feet till Shiloh come. God could wait until the appointed time, even until the time of preparation for the coming of the Christ.

PREPARATION

AMONG THE JEWS AND GREEKS.

It cannot be a matter void of interest to sketch even very briefly the state of the world at the first Christmas-tide, to learn something of that momentous period of the history of Human Life, whereat man was to be visibly assured of Salvation, by The Advent of the long promised Messias, through whom and in whom was to be effected the re-generation of fallen Human Nature.

It may be that a brief review of the decline and fall of a people called of God, may help us to understand somewhat that long-suffering and patience, which Jehovah had ever exhibited, and to the very latest moment did exhibit to His self-willed children.

In the possession of Moses and the Prophets, they had all that they really needed; but corrupting themselves more and more, God in his mercy was preparing for the world a kingdom which should be open to all believers.

God permitted nations great and mighty to arise, that His will might be done. He ever maketh the fierceness of man to praise Him and restraineth the remainder of wrath. Two nations stand out prominently before us. Greece and Rome. They developed two very important qualities of Human Nature and have displayed, and to this hour display, correspondingly important influences on the world.

Greece had from the very peculiarity of her position and her contact with early civilization, reached the highest point of intellectual power. It is to be questioned whether human intellect can, for it has never done so yet, surpass the mighty development it attained in Greece: and certainly no nation, ancient or modern, not even Britain, more successfully carried out the system of colonization. "It matters little," says a recent writer, "how much lay in the mind of Alexander, whether his Greek cities were to be links of commerce, or means of blending east and west into one, or bands of his dominions, or centres of civilization, any or all of these. Certainly his inquiry of Aristotle as to the best mode of colonizing, shews how deep the plan lay in his mind. His instantaneous perception of the value of the site of Alexandria, and his choice of a situation whose value the circumnavigation of Africa has not lessened, and the experience of 2000 years has confirmed, imply no ordinary scheme."

The main characteristic of this colonization is the evident purpose to establish Greek cities along all the lines of communication by land or water. It is marvellous to follow the march of that wonderful genius, and to observe him seizing each important spot, alike in Egypt, in the long civilized countries of the Euphrates and Tigris, and in lands but lately known to European energy or curiosity; conquering, not to *desolate*, but to *settle with fixed populations*. Nor did the followers of Alexander imitate him only in colonizing. The blending of races was continued; and very remarkably in part, through the position given to *the Jews* on the ground of their faithfulness to their sovereigns. The early Ptolemies and Seleucidæ multiplied as they thought faithful subjects, but prepared a seed-plot for the Gospel. Of this most extraordinary migration the Historian Merivale writes:—"As the Roman statesmen cast their eyes eastward, they might behold with curiosity and interest the increasing throng of strangers of this same nation (the Jews who had found their way to Rome) who maintained their own peculiar usages and worship and moral physiognomy throughout the continent and islands of Greece. As they extended their view beyond the boundaries of Europe, this infusion of the Jewish element among the native population, became still more strongly marked. Lydia and Phrygia had received a draft of two thousand families, transplanted thither from Judea by Antiochus The Great. The Jews spread in successive migrations over all countries of lesser Asia, and Ephesus, Pergamos, Tralles and Sardis, became celebrated for the resort of wanderers from Palestine. Before the date of Cicero's consulship, their numbers had become so great in the Roman province of Asia, that it was esteemed a good service to the State on the part of the Prætor Flavius, when he forbade them to drain the country of gold by sending their annual contributions to the temple at Jerusalem. At the same time, we hear of a multitude of Jews being employed by Octavius, in working the mines of copper in Cyprus. Great multitudes of Jews were settled by Seleucus Nicator in Syria and Palestine; and Antioch became a seat of famous resort."

To the east of Syria and Palestine, the dispersion was still greater. The ten tribes which had been transported beyond Euphrates, had never returned to the abode of their ancestors. The ceaseless pulse of emigration beat, we are assured, more faintly through Adiabene and Armenia to the Caucasus and the Caspian shore, and was not exhausted even on the borders of China. Whatever motive had induced each successive swarm to abandon the parent hive, whether it had been sold in captivity or transplanted at the caprice of a conqueror, it still clung pertinaciously to the outward symbols of its nationality. The annual tribute to the temple was a faint expression of this characteristic feeling.

Seleucus Nicator, in the then third city of the known world, Antioch, and in the other cities of his vast portion of the empire of Alexander, gave to the Jews equal rights with Macedonians. In religion only they were Jews; as members of a polity they had sometimes special privileges bearing on their law and their religion, else they were Alexandrians, Antiochenes, Ephesians. The blending of races begun by Alexander was continued by his successors to such an extent, that one-third of the population of Egypt consisted of Jews. Ptolemy Lagi, when he wished to have strong hold of Cyrene, and of the other cities in Libya, sent Jews to settle there. "This people," says Strabo, "hath now found its way into every city, and it is not easy to find a spot in the world, which hath not received this race, and which is not overpowered by them. Many other places have imitated Egypt and Cyrene—in this too, that they support especially bodies of Jews, and are enlarged together, using the hereditary discipline of the Jews. In Egypt at least a settlement has been assigned them apart, and great part of Alexandria has been set aside for this nation. They have an Ethnarch of their own, who administers the affairs of this nation, hears causes, takes charge of contracts and ordinances, *as if he were the ruler* of an independent polity." Nor was this intermingling only in large places. Josephus mentions decrees in favor of Jews not only at Ephesus, Laodicea, Miletus, Pergamos, Philadelphia, but in Delos also.

In this case Greece was the recipient. Actively it concentrated its energy of colonization chiefly on the lands around or within the Tigris and Euphrates: forty new cities can still be counted in Upper Syria, between Mount Taurus, Lebanon and the Euphrates. These were undoubtedly only a portion. The Ptolemies advanced southward on the coast of Abyssinia; and that so solidly, that far into Christian times, the Greek maintained itself together with the native element, rivaling too the advancing Arab.

In both Asia and Egypt, **Alexander** laid the foundation: in both, his successors built **on towards an** end in God's providence which they knew not. **But even** man's rough-hewing his ends, which God **so** shaped, **was no chance** work. **Letters** were the hereditary province of even **degenerate** Ptolemies. The Septuagint, the dialect which, uniting **the** depth of Hebrew with the intellectual precision of the Greek language, was to be the vehicle of the revelation of the Gospel. The Greek of Alexandria, modified by the Old Testament, were productions of the peculiar character of the third Empire, in **Alexander** and his successors. Alexandria and Antioch, **early** conquests of Christianity, chief Sees and schools of thought **were their joint production.** Lastly, to show the influence **of Greece,** Seneca **says,** "What mean Greek cities in **the** midst **of barbarian countries?** What means the language of Macedonians **among** Indians and Persians?" Even the barbarians who penetrated to India, had, as it seems, for above a **century, Greek letters or** words **on** their coins. In truth, the language in **which** the Apostles preached, was the language of **the world.** Further, Athens was the seat and centre of learning, the intellectual brightness of her philosophy **to** this day influencing with scarcely diminished power, human thought, and exercising **lasting** influence on the inner life of man. By her **search** after wisdom, Greece was thus preparing minds for the reception of that true wisdom which **was to** govern **man,** and be the very life of his soul. **In** those four hundred years before the kingdom of God was opened to believers, we witness the fierce struggle **of** Human Life, unaided and in its **own** strength, seeking to find **out truth.**

THE JEWS AND GREEKS.
(CONTINUED.)

From Alexander of Melitus, and Pythygoras, and the Mathematicians, six hundred and ten years before Christ, to Aristotle, three hundred and eighty-four years before Christ, a restless energizing spirit stirred up a host of intellectual gladiators, ever endeavouring to cut their way through the mazes of thought, and succeeded only in proving their weakness, and the truth of a better philosophy, "No one, by searching, can find out God." Yet their power has been immense, and it is not waste of time to note the influence such minds had in directing the advance of Christianity. The mere planting of colonies by a Macedonian leader would have availed but little, had the learning and philosophy of Greece remained pent up. The aggressive energy which planted those colonies was, in a way we can scarcely realize, equally effective in rousing the Greek mind to struggle with ignorance with a zeal and power which was resistless. When Learning walks forth from the closet to contend with Ignorance in the market-place, we may be certain as to which of the two will be overcome. With our settled colleges and schools of learning, whither men resort for instruction, we do not enter fully into the purpose of Socrates, who, early in the morning, frequented the public walks, the gymnasium for bodily training, and the schools where youths were receiving instruction. He was to be seen in the market-place, at the hour when it was most crowded, among the booths and tables where goods were exposed for sale. His whole day was usually spent in this public manner. He talked with any one, young or old, rich or poor, who sought to address him, and in the hearing of all who stood by. Not only did he never either ask or receive any reward, but he made no distinction of persons, never withheld his conversation from any one, and talked on the same general subjects with all. By this perpetual and indiscriminate public teaching, he became more widely known, and his vast influence reached a wider circle of admiring and sometimes opposing minds. That his teaching must have touched the hearts of the people whom he addressed, and was calculated to inspire them with wholesome thoughts, may be gathered from Xenophon, who says: "When he sacrificed, he feared not his offering would fail of acceptance in that he was poor; but, giving *according to his ability*, he doubted not but, in the sight of the Gods, he equalled those men whose gifts and sacrifices overspread the whole altar: for Socrates always reckoned upon it as a most solemn truth, that the service paid the Deity by the pure and pious soul, was the most grateful service." Again, what could have been more valuable to a heathen people sunk in gross superstition, than a discourse on the spiritual life?—words which even the hand of time has not cancelled, and which no doubt speak to us to-day with little less force than when they were first spoken to inquisitive Greeks. "It is not with respect to the body," he says, "alone that the Gods have shown themselves bountiful to man. Their most excellent gift is that soul they have infused into him, which so far surpasses what is elsewhere to be found; for by what animal, except man, is even the *existence* of those Gods discovered, who have produced and still uphold in such regular order this beautiful and stupendous frame of the universe? What other species of creature can be found that can serve and adore them? . . . These things being so, who seeth not that man is, as it were, a God in the midst of this visible creation?—so far doth he surpass, whether in the endowments of his soul or body, all animals whatsoever that have been produced therein; for if the body of the ox had been joined to the mind of man, the acuteness of the latter would have stood him in small stead, while unable to execute the well designed plan: nor would the human form have been of more use to the brute, so long as it remained destitute of understanding! But in the austodemus hath been joined to a wonderful soul a body no less wonderful; and sayst thou, after this, 'the Gods take no thought for me?' What wouldst thou more to convince thee of their care?"

A worthy disciple of a worthy master, Plato, wore the mantle which Socrates left. Following his teacher's method, he yet sought out truth for himself, seeking to enlarge the view which Socrates had opened out. Yet, unlike Socrates, he lived less among the people: the familiar and untiring intercourse which the master had constantly kept up with the people, had accomplished all that was necessary to infuse and inspire a love for the acquisition of knowledge. Plato, therefore, imbued strongly with the desire to know, withdrew himself for purposes of improvement. It is probable he travelled into Egypt. "While studious youth," says Valerius Maximus, "were crowding to Athens from every quarter, in search of Plato for their master, that philosopher was wandering along the winding banks of the Nile, or on the vast plains of a barbarous country, himself a disciple of the old men of Egypt." He returned at last, and eager scholars flocked around him. With a mind richly stored by foreign travel and constant meditation, he began to emulate his beloved master, and to devote himself to teaching. Like Socrates, he taught gratuitously. The Academia, a public garden in the neighbourhood of Athens, was the favourite resort of Plato, and gave its name to the school which he founded. His assertion of Objective Truth must have had a powerful influence on those **who** listened to him; and the no less **fearless** declaration of the limitation of human thought to grasp absolute Truth, had a wholesome influence on minds destined afterwards to be the recipients of wisdom beyond the reach of human discovery. "All *human* **knowledge**," he says, "is imperfect necessarily. Sensation **troubles** the intellectual eye; and only when the soul is free from the hindrances of the body, shall we be able to discern things as **they are**, in all the ineffable splendours of truth." He had been taught by Socrates that beyond the world of **sense was** that of **Eternal Truth**; that men who differed greatly respecting individual things, did not differ respecting universals; **that** there was a common fund of Truth, from which all human souls drew their share. And his very discourses on the origin of Good and Evil could not have fallen uselessly on the ears of his students. But no sooner does the personal intercourse of Plato cease, and his well-known voice no longer incite the minds of the listening throng, than behold his own pupil, Aristotle, "the Mind" of his school, is in the schools disputing some of the deep sayings and deductions of his master. If Plato undervalued Subjective, Aristotle cannot be accused of estimating over much **Objective** Truth; yet his influence has been, as that of his master's, **lasting**. The friend of Alexander, he was, under the liberal care of **that** great man, enabled to do more than either perhaps Socrates or Plato could do. Vast sums were placed at his disposal, and hundreds of men employed to facilitate his laborious researches. His constant and minute study of Natural History, pursued into objects from all parts of the world, must have brought him into contact with many and varied minds; and, ever thus seeking out the wonderful adaptation of and special peculiarities of structure, the relations of parts to each other, and of animals one to another, we cannot wonder that his mind would rest satisfied only in knowledge other than that which he assumed could only be subjectively attained. In him was the commencement of Positive Science. "But," says a learned writer (Blakesly), "the influence of this man was world-wide. Translated, in the fifth century of the Christian era, into the Syriac language by the Nestorians, who fled into Persia, and from Syriac into Arabic four hundred years later, his writings furnished the Mohammedan conquerors of the East with a germ of science, which, but for the effect of their religious and political institutions, might have shot up into as tall a tree as it did produce in the West; while his logical works, in the Latin translation, which Boethens, 'the last of the Romans,' bequeathed to posterity, formed the basis of that extraordinary phenomenon, the Philosophy of the Schoolmen. An empire like this, extending over nearly twenty centuries of time; recognised in Bagdad, in Cordova, in Egypt, in Britain; and leaving abundant traces of itself in the language of thought of every European nation, is assuredly without a parallel." Pyrrho, travelling in Alexander's train, brought Western civilization and philosophy in contact with the Eastern mind and its curious systems; and on his return, hopelessly dissatisfied with the uncertainty and doubts engendered by the failure of Platonism, and the equal uncertainty in the discovery of truth, as followed out by the Aristotelian, led to the development of Scepticism. REASON, assailed thus on all sides, and abandoned at best as as an uncertain guide to truth; and the Senses affording no more certain criterion of truth,—well may we believe that everywhere there must have been a longing for rest—for some sure anchor of the soul to which men might cling, **as to something** that should satisfy them. Well may Aristotle have said, "Rest, **rest, rest!—there** *is* rest in Eternity." With the Sceptics, Philosophy **ceased to** find a home in Greece. Macedonian influence, **through** Alexander and his **successors,** had done its work. Greek **colonies,** as we have seen, planted everywhere along **the great roads of** human abode, had been as many centres for the reception **and dissemination** of learning. "Exiled," says Mr. Lewes, "**from** Greece, Philosophy was a favoured guest in Alexandria **and** Rome. In both cases it was a stranger, and could **not be** naturalized. **In** Alexandria it made a brilliant display, and **the** men it produced gave it an originality and an influence which it never possessed in **Rome.** Roman philosophy was but a weak paraphrase of the Grecian. To speak Greek, to write Greek, became the fashionable ambition of Rome. The child was instructed by a Greek slave; **Greek professors** taught philosophy to aspiring youths. It was then that Cicero learned those ideas which he delighted in setting forth in charming dialogues." In **Alexandria the case was** different. There several schools were formed, and some new elements introduced into the doctrines then extant. Great thinkers—Plotinus, Proclus, Porphyry—made it illustrious; and it had a rival whose antagonism alone could confer immortal renown upon it. That rival was Christianity. We do not catch the full force of St. Paul's remonstrating appeal to the Athenians, nor understand his soul-moving address to the Corinthians **on** the resurrection of the dead, until we are brought to recognize the difficulties which Christianity encountered through "philosophy falsely so called." "In no species of grandeur," says Mr. Sarsset, "was the Alexandrian school deficient. Genius, power, and duration have consecrated it. Reanimating, during an **epoch of decline,** the fecundity of an aged civilization, it created **a whole family of illustrious** names. Plotinus, its real **founder, resuscitated Plato**; Proclus gave the world Aristotle; and **in the** person of Julian the Apostate, it became master of **the** world. For three centuries it was a formidable rival to the greatest power that ever appeared **on** earth—the power **of** Christianity; and if it succumbed in the struggle, it only fell with the civilization of which it had **been the last** rampart." Evil is ever waiting to mar the progress of good; and notwithstanding the influence **for** good which Greece was permitted to exercise, it is manifest that there came from her **an influence also for** evil, which has confronted that **Christian** truth, for which she had done so much to prepare the way.

The Mind of Man fully developed by the exercise of those powers which belong to it; illuminated by no other light than that which it received from kindred mind, had earnestly striven for some sure resting place on which to repose in the enjoyment of Truth discovered. The search proved a vain one. Philosophy, toyed with her devoted followers, luring them on by her enchanting coquetry. The highest pinnacle of the Temple of Fame was attained, leaving only for those who should follow, a record of the toil and weariness of the ascent, and of the barrenness of the view which burst on the vision when the giddy height was reached.

Opposition to objective truth is as **strong** now as it was in the days of Socrates, and at this very day, subjective **belief** is with too numerous a class put in the place of **that revealed** Faith once for all delivered. The history of Christianity testifies to the hostility, **which** men naturally exhibit to positive teaching; and a large class of learned men openly advocate a wide toleration of diverging belief on the ground, that, there must be great latitude given for the expression of *opinions*. The thoughtful Christian will find, that the ground left him for mere opinion, is relatively narrow, and contains only those points which refer to matters of indifference; while on all that relates to Truth, as set forth by the Holy Ghost through the Scriptures and the Church, there is the most positive teaching of Divine Truth, which is so unalterable, **that, even an angel** from heaven must not proclaim against it.

Amid all this uncertainty and disquiet the human **soul** is like a tempest tossed ship, driven every where on shoals and shallows, finding no haven, and no hand to guide **to** any sure harbour of refuge. To hear and learn something new was the only pleasurable excitement for the learned mind; this perhaps **in some measure** prepared those who **were** earnest seekers of truth for its reception, when as the consequence **of** the Mission **of Christ,** the Religion which was by him, began that conflict with the world which has been unceasingly carried on to the present time.

In all the journeyings of St. Paul we find him perpetually brought into contact with Greeks and Jews.—It **is in** Athens, that, he enters boldly into the spirit of the Grecian philosophy, and contends with it, not only disputing in the Synagogue with the Jews, and in the market daily with them that met him, but even with Epicureans and Stoics who encountered him. Publicly on Mars Hill, where the Philosophers had declaimed, he declared to them the Discovery of that Truth, which they **had never been** able to find. His labours seem indeed abundant; and as we read of his conquests over superstition and ignorance, and call to mind the nature of the struggle in which human intellect, for the first time, found itself engaged and before which it fell back wasted, we cannot but recognize the power of that Gospel, which, although to the Jews a stumbling block and to the Greeks foolishness, yet showed that God had a faithful few; for some consorted with Paul and Silas,—of the devout **Greeks** a great multitude, and of the chief women not **a few.** And, the Corinthians hearing him, many **of them** believed, " for God had much people in that city."

Christianity had thus, in its earliest hour to engage in fierce conflict. The learning of the Greek confronted, and the malignant opposition of the Jew rose up against it. So long as men propagate opinions they seldom excite **more** than animated controversy; but the moment a **teacher** delivers himself of what he affirms to be Truth necessary to be received, then **argument** and controversy cease, and violent opposition instantly rises to its reception. Socrates declared himself a teacher of Truth, not a deliverer of speculative opinions. He had transcended the sphere of sense and gazed on absolute Truth. For this the poisoned chalice was forced to his lips. Christianity was promulged **as a** divine revelation of Truth to man; it was declared to be a complement of truth already delivered, and as a necessary **result,** *it* has ever met with determined opposition, and still excites the bitter hostility of those whose lives rebel against that discipline which Christian doctrine demands. In order to comprehend **fully the** blessing bestowed on mankind by the Advent **of** the Lord and Saviour of **the world,** as a teacher of Truth, **we** have but to note the influence which the existence **of** His Church as **the custodian** of Truth, has had on the race of man. Complete in its organization, divinely taught by the Spirit of Truth, its authority declared **and its** doctrines taught by Holy Apostles, and from the **first, that** teaching and authority asserted and exercised by a ministry, named by Christ Himself, the ministry of reconciliation; **we see** a divine Institution, against which even the gates of Hell should **not prevail.**

We form but a poor estimate of the Church in early times, if we assent to the opinion that it was only at the Fifth Century, that its power as a Church awoke. It was because the Church had an existence, and was an organization perfect in all its parts, that at the overthrow of the Roman Empire, Christianity was preserved; and acknowledging the Divine superintendence, and not considering only the natural effects of natural causes, it is not difficult to see how the Church was enabled to withstand the rude shocks which so mighty a convulsion as the fall of the Empire caused. The Church thus commends herself to us, as continuing her Lord's work; and with M. Guizot, we too can say, "that it is not too much to aver, that in the fourth and fifth centuries it was the Christian Church that saved Christianity; that it was the Church with its institutions, its magistrates, its authority—the Christian Church which struggled so vigorously to prevent the interior dissolution of the empire, which struggled against the barbarian, and which in fact overcame the barbarians—it was this Church that became the great connecting link—the principle of civilization between the Roman and the barbarian world." It was the Church then in her Divine Power which saved the world to her Lord.

THE INFUENCE OF ROME,

IN PREPARING THE WORLD FOR THE ADVENT AND FOR THE RECEPTION OF CHRISTIAN TRUTH.

If we turn to Roman History, and seek to know the influence which Rome had and still has on the destinies of the Human Race, we shall find that that influence has been very great, yet peculiarly Roman.

From the very first, her influence was opposite to that of Greece. Every energy was bent in developing manhood, in perfecting institutions, and enacting laws, for the civil government of men. She had nothing to give, and cared not to give anything to the religious life of the world. To this very hour her influence lasts, all her developments are and were directed to the temporal condition of Human beings.

To the Jew we are indebted for the Faith, to the Greek for methods of Intellectual culture, to the Roman for civil Law and Municipal Institutions. Under the growth of Human Power, Rome was enabled to push her victorious arms East and West, until at length through conquest, she was in the position to hold the reins of power and tightly to curb the nations, that the voice of Him who should cry in the wilderness, might be heard. Greece conquered but to settle; Rome to aggrandise her power and satisfy her lust. There was nothing in her that was lasting, and, she leaves only now a caricature representation of her former human greatness, the fatal imitation of a municipal system and love of Imperial power which had outgrown itself at her fall. **It is indeed remarkable how** strangely Jehovah has brought down to our own day, the influences which both Greece and Rome exercised on the early world. To this very hour both peoples, continue to manifest the same peculiar tendencies which characterised their earlier states. Rome, as we have said, gave us institutions and laws; developing human life in all that relates to its temporal advancement. A few of her Statesmen were very unselfish and profoundly loyal to their country; and if we follow her, as she plays her part now in the great drama of life, we shall find that she is deeply concerned in building up a vast and cumbrous system of rule, and in consolidating a power whose vastness almost rivals that of her ancient days.

"In short," says Guizot, "the history of the conquest of the world by Rome, is the history of the conquest and foundation, of a vast number of cities. It is true that *in the East*, the extension of Roman dominion was somewhat of a different character; the population was not distributed there, in the same way as in the Western world; it was under a social system, partaking more of the patriarchal form, and was consequently much less concentrated in cities. But confining ourselves to the West we find,—in the Gauls in Spain, nothing but cities. At any distance from these, the country consisted of marshes and forest;" and a municipal corporation like Rome, might be able to conquer the world, but it was a much more difficult task to govern it, mould it into one compact body. Thus when the work seemed done, when all the West and a great part of the East had submitted to the Roman yoke, we find an immense host of cities, of little states, formed for separate existence and independence; breaking their chains and escaping on every side. This was one of the causes which made the establishment of Empire necessary, which called for a more **concentrated form** of government, one better able to hold **together** elements which had so few points of cohesion. **She** endeavoured to bind together this extensive and scattered society; and to a certain point succeeded. Between the reigns of Augustus and Diocletian, during the very time that her admirable civil legislation was being carried to perfection, that vast and despotic administration was established, which, spreading over the Empire **a sort of** chain-work of functionaries subordinately arranged; firmly knit together the people and the imperial court, serving at at the same time to convey to society the will of the government, and to bring to the government, the tribute and obedience of society. This system besides rallying the forces, and holding together the elements of the Roman world, introduced with wonderful celerity into society a taste for despotism, for central power. It is truly astonishing to see how rapidly this incoherent mass of little republics, this association of municipal corporations sunk into an humble and obedient respect for the sacred name of Emperor. **The** necessity for **establishing some** tie between all these parts of the Roman world, must have been very apparent and powerful, otherwise we can hardly conceive how the spirit of despotism could so easily have made its way into the minds and almost into the affections of the people. How much more marvellous to find the same spirit surviving the fall of the empire. At the close of the 4th and early **part** of the 5th Century, A.D., the Church had become a recognised power in the world. Triumphant over all opposition it stood compact, with a settled ecclesiastical polity. "**It** had," adds Guizot, " the rallying points suitable to a great society, in its provincial, national and general councils, in which were wont to be debated in common the affairs of society." And again: "Had it not been a Church, it is hard to say what would have been its fate in the general convulsion which attended the overthrow of the Roman **Empire." We** may well regret **that this** independence of councils and dioceses was invaded; that it should have been supplanted by an unlawful consolidation of **rule,** the end and aim of which was to bring under subjection **to a single** mind the reason and the will of all men. At the **present** moment the Roman Episcopate is reduced to the condition of a petty magistracy. Independence is so curtailed, as to reduce bishops to a subservient vassalage. And if the Roman Church has ever bestowed on Christianity benefits **for which we should never be** unmindful, our gratitude is painfully lessened by **the remembrance that** such benefits were never conferred but with the view "**to** develop that spirit of lawlessness" which even in apostolic times was declared to be already working. The assumption by an ecclesiastical potentate of imperial rule, and the subjugation of all ancient provinces and dioceses, is to engraft upon the Church a system of government as unlawful as it is contrary to ancient usage.

"I could," says M. Guizot, "cite numerous laws, in all of which this one **fact prevails,** viz., that between the Roman municipal system and that of the free cities of the middle ages, there intervened an ecclesiastical municipal **system.** The preponderance of the clergy in the management of the affairs of the city corporations succeeded to that of the ancient Roman municipal magistrates, and paved the way **for** the organization of our modern free communities." But what the Roman church once enjoyed in common with the state, she has continued to engraft into her own ecclesiastical system. The influence of Rome upon the progress of Christianity has been so far hurtful, as she has exhibited the Church in an ever-unsettled condition, liable to change both in doctrine and practice, and ever in process of development. Such is not the character of the Church as depicted in the inspired Book. There we learn of an organization complete in all its parts, possessed of the divine word, governed by an authorised body of officers, who exercised an authority which they did not hesitate to declare was by divine right. With the whole weight of ancient authority against him, it is more than a mistake, when so able a writer as Guizot commits himself to a doctrine which, false in itself, leaves the whole ground occupied by Rome perfectly impregnable. What, for instance, can be more unhappy than the following declaration of M. Guizot: "In its infancy, in its very babyhood, Christian society presents itself before us as a simple association of men possessing the same faith and opinions, the same sentiments and feelings. The first Christians met to enjoy their common emotions, their common religious convictions. At this time, we find *no settled form of doctrine, no settled rules of discipline, no body of magistrates.* Still it is obvious that no society, however young, however feebly held together, or whatever its nature, can exist without some moral power which animates and guides it; and thus in the various Christian congregations there were men who preached, who taught, who morally governed the congregation. Still there was no settled *magistrate*, no discipline: a simple association of believers in a common faith." Now, how entirely untrue is all this! Of course there was "no settled magistrate," but there were *several magistrates*—apostles, priests and deacons. Of course there *was* discipline, and exercised fully by the apostles, of whom St. Paul more than once administered it. "Extremes meet." The Presbyterian Guizot advances the doctrine of Development with all the earnestness of Father Newman: neither **can** prove the correctness of his position, except that doctrine be conceded. Both belong to systems which have gone far away from primitive practice and truth; both alike believe the organization of the Church to have been progressive. The Anglican Church, falling back **from the** errors of Rome, rests her claim to be a true branch **of the Vine on** her apostolic descent, and her firm adhesion to the Scriptures, as interpreted by the One Holy Catholic Church, **which,** founded on Jesus Christ, and built on apostles and prophets, continued one and undivided, until the grievous errors of **Rome forced** a separation between the East and West; and **until** in the West again, by her course of systematic adulte**ration of truth, she brought** further division and discontent on mankind. It is deeply to be regretted that so able a man as M. Guizot should for one moment have lent the weight of his great name to support doctrine so essentially vicious and opposed to truth; for if it were possible to prove the theory of development correct, then the alternative is disastrous to all who have felt Rome to be unauthorized in her proceedings. The protestant action of the Greek Church, **and the** determined opposition of the Anglican to any departure from ancient customs, assumes a very grave aspect. The Right Rev. the Bishop of Western New York, in his "Criterion," has taken safe ground; and it is to be deeply lamented that a work calculated to lead many to think seriously of the position of the Church, in its true relation to the primitive Church, should **be so** painfully marred by harsh and bitter invective. Yet we feel that the Bishop is right; and if ever the union of Christendom is to be effected, it can only be by a return to "the good old paths"—to those ancient doctrines which at Nicea were formularized and promulgated as the truth, received of the whole Church, **always and everywhere.**

There can be no manner of doubt that **we** of the Anglican fold are required **to manifest a** more active living faith to show **forth that** faith by our works; to exhibit the **doctrines** of Christ, committed to the keeping **of the Church, in all** their fulness and energizing power. But **in order to do this, we** have no need to look to any model of post-Nicene date; still less may we, without grievous sin, **seek to** clothe even truth itself in garments which **would** tend **to confound** the wearers with those servants who no **longer serve at their** Master's Table. **Thus the danger to the Church is very great.** She has, on the one **hand, to resist the** perpetual **encroachment of Roman development, and on** the other to stop the disintegrating effects of that equally dangerous ultra-Protestant theory, the abuse of private judgment. Our only safety **is in** following apostolic teaching. It calls upon us to pray with the understanding; to give a reason for the faith that is in us. Yet, we are also informed, that "the Church **is the** pillar and ground of truth"—"the keeper **of Holy Writ**"—"the Lord's Bride"—**an** organization whose **voice we** are to hear, and **to which, if we** have **cause, we are to** make complaint;—a body having **a** corporate existence, and in which corporation the Holy Spirit continually dwells. Bishops, priests **and deacons are** that threefold **ministry** which the Church has perpetuated, having received **it from** the holy Pentecostal outpouring of **Grace. Blessed Sacraments** she has, instituted as divinely appointed means for ensuring to the spirits **of** men, the outflowing of that ener**gizing** power, which **is of** the glorified humanity of the **crucified** Saviour; and which, to the faithful soul, is the very reception, the very engrafting of the Word. She bids us read, mark, **learn** and inwardly digest the Scriptures, that we may the better understand them and judge their import when she explains them to us. In the English Church how fitly is this done! The Book of Common Prayer is the tongue of the Church, revealing to us the will of God and the way of God. In it, and through it, she reveals to men the whole council of God, rightly dividing the Word. Gathered from time-honored liturgies, the Church of England speaks not in the language of those who engaged in reformation of doctrine and removal of error, but she speaks in the very words, and bids her children seek for pardon and grace, through the use of those very prayers, which found age after age, acceptance at the great mercy-seat of the living God. It is because the English Church, firm in apostolic order, and impregnated by divine truth, continues to manifest the power of a living Church, keeping before the world the oracles of God, that we should trust to her as to the true teacher sent of God. We lose sight of the true spirit of the Reformation, if we suppose that it was the intention to develop some new phase of religious belief or life. The great and good men who in England were instrumental in freeing the Church from error of doctrine and practice, knew too well that the only course open to them, was the return to primitive truth, and that, to set forth once again that truth, they must take their stand on the councils of the undivided Church; and if no other result had followed on the Pan-Anglican Council, held at Lambeth, 1867, the Church has still gained immensely, by the reaffirmation of the declaration, that she is firmly one with the ancient Church, as determined by the first six General Councils. With the English Prayer Book in our hands, we need not fear the promulgation of untruth; for a right exercise of reason will approve our judgment, in condemning by it the utterances of error. We scarcely appreciate the privilege we possess in the Book of Common Prayer; and they only can know how safe a guide it is to the understanding the

Word of God, who make it their book of common prayer, and fulfill all the duties of daily devotion and practice which it so imperatively sets forth. So, when the Romanist says to you, "See what private judgment has brought forth!" answer him, "The right use of private judgment has taught me, to hear that Church which has given me the key to her own mind, and to a right understanding the Word." And if the Non-conformist twits you with your subjection to rigid formalism, explain to him that such formalism has at all events kept alive in the world the truth once for all delivered to the saints; and in the face of unceasing and uncompromising hostility has preserved the Catholic and Apostolic Church these more than eighteen hundred years, a witness to the glorious work of Redemption. It is this Church which now, suffering and hindered in her progress, mourns as a dove, but hereafter shall be presented to her Lord without spot or wrinkle, or any such thing. Not yet triumphant, she is the Church militant. As such, her unceasing energy must be devoted to the entire conquest of a world lying in sin.

My judgment approving, my reason tells me to correct my own errors, and to school my mind by the law of God, as explained and taught by His Church: Justification by a living faith, fruitful in good works; salvation in and through that ONE LIVING, continuous sacrifice, to which we are joined, and in which we must ever offer ourselves living sacrifices; daily renewal by the Holy Spirit, the All-holy Sanctifier and Guide and Teacher, through whom is the Gift—He who takes of the things of His Son, and shows them unto us; reconciliation to an offended Father Almighty, to whose favor and love the lost are restored through the Blood of the cross. Such are the truths set before us by the Church of God, from the Scriptures of God.

To set forth these, and to perpetuate the Faith undimmed by the fitful changes of human thought, the Anglican Church has by forms and ceremonies symbolized that Faith. It is her stern duty to prevent an undue manifestation of excessive ritual borrowed from an unstable communion, and to maintain inviolate, with a loyalty sincere and based on genuine love of the truth, that form of sound words which nerved the whole army of Martyrs for the conflict they endured, and which has perfected Saints for their entrance on that rest, which Christ has promised to all they who, with hearty repentance and true faith turn to Him.

At the command of Her Great and only High Priest, the portals of Salvation are opened; ministering Priests are bidden to proclaim the one Baptism for the remission of sin, to all who have the gift of repentance: they are to declare the glad tidings of Forgiveness of sin, and to every repentant soul, they are commissioned to proclaim pardon in Christ's name, and ever as ministering Priests to present the one only sacrifice to God as their own and their peoples claim to pardon. There are no other terms of salvation. The blood of Christ is the price that is still paid, deep unwavering faith in the efficacy of that blood, is the condition required of every truly repentant sinner. Such is the teaching of the Church of Christ.

It is quite true that the Church in Asia and Africa fell before the advance of the accursed Mahommedan, that is, *ceased to advance*, with the energy with which the Roman Branch has done to power and solidity. But if we look a little below the surface, it cannot be questioned but that the Greek Church is to-day in a far more Catholic position, and more largely blessed with the true Spirit of Life, than her sister, against whose unlawful corruptions of doctrine and practice, she too has ever nobly protested. When

Guizot says, the Church *fell* in Asia and Africa, he uses a word that conveys more than the truth. The Church of Greece still lives and has braved bitter persecutions, her Bishops and Priests have, under circumstances we can hardly understand, kept burning the lamp of truth; and surrounded by a horde of base and utterly depraved infidels, battle for the kingdom of Christ with a zeal which makes one blush to think, finds but little response in more highly favoured Europe.

This digression which could hardly be avoided, serves not only to place before us the abiding influence which two nations have had on Christianity, but also shows how both have contributed to the advancement and retardation of the Church, and will enable, we hope, a clearer view to be caught, of the state of the world in its social and political life, when the old was ready to make way for the New Covenant; that time in which Rome busied herself to let loose her eagles that they might flesh themselves to the full.

INFLUENCE OF ANCIENT ROME.

Ancient Rome had been all along deeply concerned in the acquisition of territorial possessions. The time at length arrived when, stimulated by lust of conquest, she, through the dissension engendered by lust, entered on a course of turbulence which, while it served but little to advance the real happiness of the people, in the end contributed to the solid advantage of the world.

Brutus and his confederates had struck down Cæsar, but they did not see that their daggers had penetrated the heart of the commonwealth, and made the way open to the establishment of another phase of Roman existence. The ill-digested plans of the conspirators, the want of any proper motive to justify their act, the absence of that deep-rooted prejudice which, inflaming the passions, overruling the reason, and taking possession of the popular mind, enables the leaders of opinion to carry out their designs, soon unnerved hands which had not been slow to embrue themselves in gore. In slaying Cæsar, his party was not destroyed. If the destruction of Cæsar was justifiable, then the liberators should have buried their swords in the body of Antonius, which some of Brutus's party were wise enough to see should be in the tomb with that of Cæsar. The assassination of the usurper had opened, not closed, the question, how the state was to be governed. Availing himself of the uncertain temper of the popular mind, Antonius, with wonderful readiness and tact, obtained the confidence of the bereaved Calpurnia. In the course of the night, she had conveyed to Antonius' house four thousand talents and Cæsar's private papers. Antonius, thus armed, and liberally supplied with money, increased by sums secreted in the Temple of Ops, it was not long before Brutus learned how impossible it is that, even the purest motives should succeed, when once resort to violence is had to ensure success, if the violent do not hold by force that which they have seized. Reason is silenced when passion reigns supreme. Cicero saw the mischief of the temporizing policy of which his party was guilty; but, just as irresolute himself, he failed either to influence the popular mind or to secure the soldiery. The hesitancy of the liberators and their friends involved them more and more in difficulty, until their incapacity was finally made manifest in their assent to the proposition for a decree for a *public funeral to Cæsar. The decree went forth, that the body should be honored with magnificent obsequies, and solemnly reduced to ashes in the Field of Mars. Fortunately for Antonius, Cæsar unsuspicious of any treachery on the part of the assassins, had left some of them in his will, executors to his family and estate. Antonius but too easily snatched the opportunity, which such facts gave him, in a funeral oration to wither the character of men whose overthrow he in turn was plotting. The magnificent bequests which Cæsar made to the people—gifts both of land and money—could not but give to the address of Antonius, delivered with all the skill and polish of a finished orator, the power which was needed to bring over to him a populace swayed, not by hatred or violent passion, but by the base and corrupt policy of misguided men. Cæsar had left no children, but had adopted Octavius. Octavius, now left master of the field, was not slow in making his position secure. Meeting promptly his bitterest opponents with a spirit of graceful concession, he foiled them at every point; and when himself proposed that the name and office of Dictator should be abolished, the assembled Senate rang with hearty acclamations. "We are," said Cicero, "delivered, not only from kingly rule, but from all apprehension of kingly rule."

Octavius, receiving copies of decrees of the Senate, and Cæsar's Will, at once assumed the name of Caius Julius Cæsar Octavianus. With singular prudence, he repressed the indiscreet zeal of the veterans, and advanced Romeward from Apulia with few attendants. Cicero welcomed him as a rival to Antonius. The nobles, as was their wont, had failed to provide for the festival of Parilia, an epoch of interest in the career of Julius Cæsar. Young Octavianus sent on to his friends, and ordered the festival to be kept at his expense. He advanced slowly to Rome. Alive to the influence which would be aroused, on the appearance of the heir to the man whose memory and whose character he had so passionately vindicated, Antonius absented himself from Rome. On the morning of the entrance of the new idol of the people into the city, the appearance of a radiant effulgence around the sun was taken as a happy omen. Throughout his whole life, omens ever and again attended upon his career; and his father, Octavius, said that an astrologer, Nigidius, had declared that "the Lord of the World was born." Nobles and people seemed infatuated. A deliverance from oppression and uncertainty seemed at hand. Senators dreamed; Cicero saw the King of gods and men place a scourge in his hand, while he was yet unknown either to himself or Catulus by sight. In the camp at Apollonia, Cæsar was moved to adopt him by a portent which he saw on the field of Munda. In the camp at Apollonia, Octavius consulted, with his friend Agrippa, the soothsayer Theogenes. As soon as he had disclosed the hour of his birth, and of his nativity, Theogenes leaped from his seat and worshipped him.

This was the popular character Antonius affected to despise. Successful in his intrigues against the liberators, already Brutus, Cassius, Decimus and Cicero were driven away from Rome. In the person of Octavius, he was boldly confronted by one who was becoming more and more the man of the hour. The nobles and the Senate, as well as most of the thoughtful citizens, dreaded the power of Antonius. Assigned to the province of Macedonia by the Senate, which he had himself chosen, Antonius soon made the demand to be appointed to the Cisalpine government, and coveted the command of legions destined for the Parthian war. In these intrigues Antonius was partially successful. The Senate became alarmed. Octavius quickly availed himself of the growing unpopularity of Antonius; and by constantly exposing his designs against Cæsar's policy, and charging him with misappropriation of Cæsar's funds, induced an inevitable rupture with Antonius, giving himself an excuse to pay greater court to the veterans, and to extol the worth of Cæsar, and the unreality and hollowness of Antonius's defence of him. By such action Octavius was enabled to seize the opportune moment to surround himself with armed attendants.

Antonius, too wise not to see and to feel his position, instantly set about seeking a reconciliation with Octavius. A false truce between them was established. It is interesting to trace the career of two such characters, as they stand out in history, the actors and promoters of events which shaped in a remarkable way the destiny of the human race. Very imperfectly did the astrologer understand the import of his own words, when he attributed to Octavius a career full of significance; and in marking the career of Antonius, it is no less important **to note the results** which followed his every **act, tending as they did in the end to** bring about results never thought of, never intended by **himself.** The moment his reconciliation with **Octavius seemed to** be effected, he intrigued for the command of Gaul; and after **much** alarm and vacillation, the Senate failed to defeat the plan in not accepting a proposition to admit the whole of the Cisalpine Gaul within the bounds of Italy. Octavius, seeing the difficulty, took the bold step of advising the Senate to agree to **the** request of Antonius. Thus a constant game for preeminence was carried on **by these** two men, involving expensive movements of troops, and **the** maintenance of large forces; each in turn availing himself **of the** mischievous combinations which the provincial commanders effected, to subserve their own ends, bringing on at length the frightful misery of civil war.

Decimus, in the Alpine valleys, did nothing that was **likely** to excite hostility; but in Gaul he was a thorn in Antonius' path. Octavius equally dreaded his position as the enemy of his house. Antonius demanded an exchange of provinces,—Macedonia to be transferred to his brother Caius, and Gaul to himself. The exchange was decreed, **but not** without provoking that which the circumstances of **Roman** intrigue rendered inevitable. Antonius now more and more encroached on the powers of the Senate and people, and assumed a command to which his position did not entitle him. It was at this crisis of affairs that Cicero fulminated his phillippics against the Antonians. All these plots and counterplots served more the cause of Octavius than Antonius. The policy of the former was to precipitate nothing, propose but little, and to wait the development of the schemes of his wily opponent. Antonius, strengthened as he supposed himself to be, by the transference of provinces, after the most assiduous and bold measures, prepared to bring Decimus to terms. But the friends of the liberators, now truly alarmed at the progress of events and the partial uncovering of Antonius' policy, took steps to defeat his plans. Decimus was warned of Antonius' designs, and prepared to resist them. Accordingly, Antonius marched against Mutina to assail him. Cicero's noble demand before the Senate was made in the true interests of the State: "Let him retire, forsooth, from Mutina; let him desist from assailing Decimus; let him withdraw from the province! Surely we are not to entreat him with words; we must compel him by arms." Words which produced an effect. Three of the gravest senators—Piso, Sulpicius and Philippus—were charged with the commission to demand the retirement of Antonius from the province. Insolent demands made in return were the only answer Antonius condescended to give to the message conveyed by the ambassadors of the Senate.

With the commission which he held from the Senate to drive out any pretender from the Cisalpine, Antonius had at his back powerful forces, amongst whom were veterans. Lepidus was in Spain; Plancus, with three legions, in Further Gaul.

Octavius had not been idle; aided materially by the declamations of Cicero against Antonius, and seizing every opportunity to unmask the intentions of his rival, he drew to himself citizens of all classes, and by his address brought over many who had been loud in their praise of Antonius. The critical moment had arrived, and Rome was about to be impelled a stage onward in her destiny; an unseen power was shaping events, the effects of which could **not** be foreseen nor understood. "They would," says **the** Historian, "**have preferred** another leader to Octavius, but even him the **Senate were now** prepared to listen to, and blindly and eagerly to adopt as a counterpoise to Antonius. Such was the vacillation or such the bewilderment of the nobles. Yet again the Senate was *insincere*, they still **hoped** to play these characters one **against the other.** Through the Consuls Hertius and **Pansa** they **desired that command** should be wrested from both, **trained as these Consuls** had been amid the veterans of Cæsar. **Brutus and Cassius** were in the East in the provinces to which **they claimed to** have been appointed by Cæsar. **Dolobella had rushed to Syria,** Tribonius was in lesser **Asia, Decimus awaited attack, and** Cassius was preparing himself against the advance of Dolobella. Brutus was in Macedonia, where he had displaced C. Antonius, his rival. A proposal **once more to bring Antonius to reason by sending** to him **four** respectable messengers, failed. **Pansa's levies** were hurried on, and he joined Octavius with four legions. **Beneath the walls** of Mutina, Decimus looked **down on the force which** was about to initiate not his ruin, but **the series** of hostile encounters which were to end in the overthrow of the republic, **and** establish the reign of that imperial power which enabled Rome to consolidate her own, and **subdue the** authority **of every other government. Actions before** Mutina were fought. Antonius worsted **but** not **defeated,** retired **from** the city. Again jealousy and suspicion seized the Roman Senate, and with the overshadowing of Antonius' ascendency, there **came the** distrust of **Octavius.** Decimus might have **struck** a blow for the safety of the republic, but contented himself with vain marchings and counter-marchings in his own province, too late joining his forces to those of Plancus; a union which might for a time have paralysed Octavius' movements. Decimus deserted Octavius just as much as the latter may be said to have deserted him. Cicero, the still hesitating leader of public opinion at home, turned his eyes once more on Brutus and Cassius. Cassius marched his forces against Dolobella, the murderer of Tribonius, and overthrew him.

This achievement revived the drooping spirits of the republican party in Rome. Thinking themselves tolerably safe from Antonius, the Senate determined to humble Octavius. A decree of thanks was issued in which Decimus only as commander was named. Octavius' name being omitted, Sextus Pompius was placed in command of the Navy, and all officers from the Ionian to the Euphrates, were to place themselves under the command of Brutus and Cassius.

Forgetful of the former hollow truce between Antonius and Octavius, the Senate did not anticipate an alliance between such natural foes, in consequence of desperate and dangerous political blunders. But Octavius denied the demands which he insolently made, to be appointed to consular dignity, marched his forces on the city, and, supported by his cousin Quintus Pedius, routed the Senators, most of whom fled. By the remnant that remained, Octavius was nominated; the tribes assembled in the Comitium; there were no consuls, two persons were appointed by the prætor of the city to take their place. Octavius was selected with his cousin Q. Pedius as his colleague. The Senate bent before this last revolution.

Antonius and Octavius, the two creatures of revolution, now again confronted each other. Each well understood the other's designs, and prepared to arrange a meeting, which was at length effected at a conference on an islet in a river at Bononia. As they drew near, each watched the other, and at length demanded whether either carried secret arms. Lepidus, who according to agreement was to be with them, had crossed the **river**. **He was, or** pretended to be, friendly **to** Antonius. Octavius seated between **them, a** debate on **the** state and relative position of parties **commenced,** which **lasted** three days; ending **in the** commission **of three;** a triumvirate self-constituted, and intended to settle the **affairs of** the Commonwealth. Utterly regardless of the national voice, they proclaimed their office to be tenable for five years, appointed officers of government for the whole term, **and** partitioned among themselves all the western provinces of the Empire. **It was** not long ere the Triumvirs threw **off** the mask, and **now prepared to** wend their way to security through a river of blood. Three hundred senators and two **thousand** knights soon **fell, and some** of the finest districts were given to the **soldiery. A thirst for blood** spread through the masses, and a bitter and fierce persecution reigned. Among the victims was Cicero.

THE TRIUMVIRATE.

The Triumvirs had changed the complexion of the government; they had not obtained the submission of the provinces. Brutus was in Macedonia, where he had seized the government. Cassius still was in Syria. These chiefs had been successful in overthrowing the power of Antonius' Lieutenants; and now at the head of twenty legions met once more in Asia. Sextus Pompius, who still held the fleet, they expected would distract the triumvirs. The latter crossed a large force into Macedonia, into which the Antonian forces penetrated even unto Thrace, closing the defiles of the Rhodope against Brutus and Cassius, the republican leaders. Octavius followed more tardily than he would have done, had not sickness detained him. However, he was carried along with his soldiers, and effected a junction with the other legions encamped between Amphipolis and Philippi. Eighty thousand legionaries on the one side, and one hundred and twenty thousand on the other, contended in the mortal combat.

Then perished the republic. The miseries of these years is incredible. Brutus and Cassius had submitted all their hopes to the arbitrament of war, and were utterly undone. Oppressors and enemies of the people, they had drained the provincials of supplies, and in their cruel exactions, cost the unfortunate people not less perhaps of blood and suffering, than the ravages of Mithradates, and swelled the cry of the miserable nations for peace, **at any price.**

The self immolation of Cassius and Brutus, completed the destruction of their party, resulting in the desertion of large portions of the republican army over to the legions of the Triumvirs. Antonius and Octavius, now divided the command between them; the former going to the east, the latter taking the western provinces, and superseding even Lepidus in his home command.

Antonius commenced his career in Asia by the most exorbitant demands. As a first instalment he required money to sustain 170,000 men, besides cavalry—and yet he says, he only required " the same sum they were accustomed to contribute the last two years to Brutus," only the money was to be paid within one year. Amongst the places on which his wrath fell with severity, was Cilicia. Here he met with one, who had at a former period in her visit to Rome, proved her capacity for intrigue. Using arguments to excuse her apparent want of zeal in the Cæsarian cause, Cleopatra presented herself before the Triumvir, or rather invited him to her presence, as she reclined in her bark under a spangled canopy, attended by Cupids, Graces and Nereids, the air around perfumed as with the odours of Olympus. Antonius' fate was sealed, and from that fatal moment all his power as a Roman was gone.

Meanwhile let us see how Octavius fared. A man of much more cool and deliberative judgment, he was never moved by those violent impulses which so often placed his rival in danger. By his assiduity and unswerving devotion to the cause he had at heart, and perhaps chastened, or at all events deterred from grosser vice, by illness, which attacked him severely on more than one occasion, Octavius really devoted himself to the settlement of questions requiring the exercise of ability, and all the tact of which he was possessed. Antonius had sent no funds to Italy and difficulty of course arose in meeting the payments of the army, and the task of carrying out the re-distribution of the lands would **not lessen,** but serve to increase the complications which the creatures of Antonius were ever fomenting. **An** insurrection was the result at length of their intrigues, **which** Octavius overcame when Perrugia fell beneath a **siege.** Vainly wasting the strength **of his** country and vexing Octavius with incessant and fatiguing **war,** the Treaty of Tarentum again patched up a false truce **between** Antonius and Octavius, **renewing the** triumvirate for five years more. **Yet there could be no** permanent peace so long as either **of these men remained** at the head **of** powerful **forces.** Octavius still kept up his armaments, and although most unsuccessful at sea, yet set about to improve the condition of his Navy, by placing Agrippa, born in the same year as himself, in full command. After some disaster on the part of Octavius' division of the fleet, Agrippa obtained a signal victory. Sextus fled. A common pirate, he had nothing to serve but the advancement of his own private interests, and he deservedly met death at the hands of one of Antonius' officers.

Antonius was still **in** the East, his mind becoming more and more corrupted and poisoned by the influences which surrounded **him there.** Thus an opportunity was given for the remnant **of** the really better-thinking classes, wearied by the succession of disasters ever occurring, to concentrate their hopes quite on Octavius, who alone represented power **in** their midst. While Antonius had marched to attack Octavius, as we have seen, at Perrugia, Ventidius, with **legions** devoted to Antonius, attacked the Parthians, and after **three** successful attacks was victorious. His other lieutenants were no less successful. The Armenians were defeated, **and** Roman standards were once more planted at the foot of the Caucasus.

4

But the licentiousness of Antonius increased, as the extent of his military **power decreased**. Giving himself up to every idle indulgence, his **fatal passion** for Cleopatra became irresistible, and, jealous **of the position of** Octavius, and the **undoubted popularity he had obtained at Rome,** Antonius **took** the harsh step of dismissing Octavia his **wife,** ultimately following that dismissal by a decree of divorce. Antonius **now** openly entered into negociations **with the Egyptian** queen, and on his way to Syria he invited her **to come to** him. She but too eagerly set out to meet him, sacrificing all her womanhood in the hope that a wide and future world of conquest and grandeur lay before her. They met at Lycaonia, and there she obtained from Antonius gifts of territory **and treasures immense;** and, as the first step towards the **realization of that dream which dwelt** most upon her mind, **had the proud satisfaction** of having her twin children, which **were, as she said, born to** Antonius, acknowledged before those of Octavia. **Parthia was,** however, giving **him trouble, yet, by** awakening him from his life of **low debauchery, afforded a** chance of escape from **the** hold **of Cleopatra.** The Parthians had taken some **Roman standards and** prisoners from Crassus. These Antonius demanded should be given up. After a useless delay, spent idly with Cleopatra, Antonius moved with 100,000 men against the Parthians, and encamped on Euphrates, reluctantly sending Cleopatra to her own territories. **The effects of a bad** life evidently had already become apparent; **less resolute,** wavering in **his judgment, and** but little **inclined to activity,** his capacity as a great leader was declining: passing into Armenia to avoid the hostile deserts, **and** deficient in **siege** and **other** machines, and his rear **being** cut up; he destroyed his magazines and siege batteries, **and commenced one of the** most disastrous retreats a Roman army ever attempted. For twenty-seven days, through the most intense cold and driving sleet, and having but scanty supply of food, and after a march of three hundred miles, he crossed the boundary of Armenia. Again, inaction and a prolonged indulgence in dissolute life, paralyzes the life of the Roman. Once did Octavia fly to his relief; for, on hearing of the defeat he had sustained by the Parthians, she hurried to him with men and money. She was refused an audience.

In the spring of 720, he again suddenly advanced and attacked the Parthian, Artavades, advancing even to his city. Leaving a few garrisons to exact the tribute levied, Antonius returned to Egypt with immense booty and a train of noble captains, among whom was Artavades, who was led in the triumphal parade in chains through the streets of Alexandria, and to the disgust of every Roman, was even made to do homage to a paramour. Summoning the people of Alexandria in festive assembly, Antonius sat on a throne, with Cleopatra seated by his side on another, equal to his own, with their children at their feet, and, in an oration, bequeathed to the queen and her children Roman provinces, declaring her Queen, not only of Egypt, but of these newly added territories also.

The gross and licentious depravity of the court at Alexandria exceeded that of every other. Nothing was too vile, nothing too wicked and immoral, to hasten the downward tendencies of two such infamous characters.

At this time the population of Alexandria consisted of a heterogenious collection of men from all nations, "combining," says one writer, "the pride of the Greeks, the stubbornness of the Jews, and the sullen and acrid passions of the Coptic race." One-third of the free population were Jews. They connected themselves with the upper classes, cultivated the Greek language, and even translated the Scriptures into Alexandrian Greek.

Whilst Antonius was thus inextricably woven in the toils of a lewd Egyptian queen, Octavius was winning golden opinions in Rome. The Roman people, feeling themselves outraged by the lascivious conduct of Antonius, were inclined to mark their displeasure by an exhibition of increased and increasing respect for a colleague, who was never weary of ministering to the welfare of his command. Ably seconded in his efforts by the faithfulness and loyalty of Agrippa, the people had not only had their natural comforts increased, but the whole city was adorned and beautified by the erection of magnificent buildings, among these a noble library, and a large number of baths, for the free use of citizens.

Feeling secure in the affections of the people, Octavius now prepared to set Antonius at defiance. It was no easy task which he had undertaken. Antonius still had friends in Rome; and with no little boldness did they endeavour, not only to defend the absent triumvir, but sought to defame Octavius. Antonius had deposited his will in the hands of the Vestal Virgins. On no pretext should the seals have been broken; but Octavius, with little regard to the sanctity of the deposit, produced the will, and publicly informed the people of its contents. Inflamed beyond endurance, the people would at once have declared Antonius a public enemy; but Octavius, wishing to place him in as unfavorable a position as possible, desired that war might be declared against Egypt, so that Antonius would thus, in defending Cleopatra's dominions, become the assailant of Rome. Octavius himself, dressed in the garb of a Fetial herald, and standing at the portals of the Temple of Bellona, surrounded by a dense throng of citizens in military garb, made the necessary proclamation.

This step aroused the **dormant** energy of Antonius. **With all the** skill of **which he** was master, he made rapid **disposition of his** immense forces, naval and military, and through **lavish** expenditure sought to corrupt the Cæsareans at Rome. **A year of** positive inaction passed; no blow had been struck. **Both** parties, however, labored to strengthen their positions, little suspecting that they both were actors in a drama which represented not only the immediate scenes of shifting **Roman** policy, but agents **in the preparation of** the world for **events** which **should affect the** deepest interests of the human family. We now contemplate the period A. U. 723, or 31 B. C.

Such a character as Octavius becomes most interesting **to us**; and with the memory of the popular stories current with reference to his birth it is not a little remarkable that Virgil should have in ecstasy, painted a character so far transcending that of man, as to seem an almost unconscious prophesy of the life of one, who was so shortly **to be in very** deed the king of kings. It is very likely that Jewish travellers, who, we have seen, were everywhere, had in some way spread their ideas among the people in whose midst they tarried. Speaking Greek themselves, and their books translated into Greek, **a** language with which educated Roman youth was familiar, it is very probable **that Virgil** learned from the prophetic writings and through Jews, **of the** supposed advent of a great and spotless **Being,** the description of whose character he thus **transferred** to Octavius. Be this as it may, Octavius stands out in history one of **its great** and most prominent characters.

The winter was spent in mere idle skirmishing, **but** the **delay was** mischievous to Antonius; his large navy suffered severely from being shut up in ports and from numerous desertions, leaving the place unguarded. Octavius seized the opportunity to cross his troops to Torune on the coast of Epirus. Attended by the principal Roman citizens, he steered for Corcyra, which was abandoned to him without a blow, and passed on to Ambracia at the mouth of which the great armaments of Antonius were assembled.

The army disembarked at the foot of the Acrocerannia, marching to meet Octavius at the place where his fleet had anchored. Encamping on the eminence on which was afterwards erected "the city of victory," he looked on the lines of Antonius with the Ionean sea on his right, and the splendid bay of Ambracia on his left. On a strip of land within the lines of Antonius, which was marshy, stood a temple sacred to Apollo, the Actium, or chapel of the point. Octavius threw up fortifications to defend his camp, connecting it with his fleet by entrenchments. At Comarus the ships rode at their moorings. Antonius left head-quarters at Patræ, as soon as he knew of Octavius' movement, and crossing the straits from his camp at Actium, entrenched himself in front of the Cæsarean lines. Antonius' profligate conduct now began to bear fruit, and in a short time serious defections aroused him to a sense of danger. Agrippa had already discomfited him, cutting up his fleet at the island of Leneas, and again under Sosius, while Antonius had suffered in an out-post skirmish. Defections continued, and Antonius was obliged to destroy several of his ships.

His own courage even gave way, and he fell a prey to irresolution.

Octavius was thus victor before a battle had been fought. At length the fleets met—the heavy galleys of Antonius still formidable, both in size and number, seemed as if they must crush the lighter and less bulky vessels of the Cæsarean fleet. The result was soon made known. The lighter and more active fleet manœuvered with the most consummate skill. The heavy ships of Antonius could not be broken, but harrassed and crippled, they seized the opportunity which a favorable breeze afforded, and led by Cleopatra in her gilded galley, and Antonius in his own, the once proud fleet steered away in flight. With indomitable perseverance the Cæsarean fleet followed, and by throwing combustible material on the ships, drifted burning masses amongst them, until a conflagration raged, destroying numbers. Thus was settled the question, which of all others most deeply affected the interests of the world for all time.

The East and the West had met in deadly conflict. Possessing and liberally giving all it had to bestow, we shall soon see, that subjection to the West was not to result in an annihilation of those stupendous gifts, which had been intrusted to it for the benefit of a whole race, but that on the contrary, as had happened before, the East was to be again the medium through which "tidings of great joy" should be disseminated throughout the world. Thus was decided, thirty-one years before the advent of Christ, a battle which terminated the government of the Roman Republic, and inaugurated that empire which was henceforth to be the agency, by which a greater and a mightier empire over the hearts of men should be raised.

The victory at Actium gave Rome all the Eastern possessions over which Antonius had exercised usurped power, and of course threw Egypt at the feet of the conquerors. The self-destruction virtually of Antonius and Cleopatra, removed from the path of Octavius two formidable foes. Triumphant and in power, Octavius sheathed his sword, but not before he had stained his honor by useless and vengeful murders. In the East all was Eastern, the Roman mind had made no impression there. Octavius saw this, and in it saw his way to introduce one element of Eastern thought into the west.

The time had arrived when power must be centralized, therefore, instead of delivering the Eastern conquests over to the Republic, Octavius retained the power in his own hands. Egypt could easily be held, and her rich stores of grain would find their way to the Roman markets.

Octavius garrisoned his acquired possessions, and made disposal of the Parthian Kingdom. But there is one kingdom whose interest for us is great. Among the potentates prostrate beneath his power, and earnest for his good will, was the chief whom Antonius had established on the throne of Judea. Herod the Great, a half Jew, being an Idumean, was in possession of Sovereign rights only by favour of the Roman people. The same power may undo what it had done, but Octavius deemed it to be for the interest of his government, that Herod should be continued in his position.

To Herod the battle of Actium brought great gain. Having adhered to the cause of Antony, he became alarmed for his own safety; laying aside all state, he sailed to Rhodes to meet Cæsar, to whom, concealing nothing, he addressed himself in candour and submission. "O Cæsar, as I was made King of the Jews by Antony, so do I profess that I have used my royal authority in the best manner and entirely for his advantage: nor will I conceal this farther, that thou hast certainly found me in arms, and an inseparable companion of his, had not the Arabians hindered me. However, I sent him as many auxiliaries as I was able. Nay, I deserted him not after the battle of Actium, but gave him the best advice I could, when I was no longer able to assist him in the war." Cæsar, in answer to this, confirmed Herod in his kingdom and added to his territories considerably.

At this time, says a learned writer, the relations of Judea to the Republic were remarkable, for in Judea there arose that extraordinary development of political enthusiasm which at a later period shook the empire; and in the streets of Galilee were sowed the seeds of a moral revolution which undermined, in their appointed time, the foundations of ancient society, establishing Christianity upon the ruins of the common heathenism.

Throughout all the years of Roman rule, we see nothing done directly for the elevation of human thought. Following in the wake of Grecian civilization, Rome was but the imperial mistress of a world requiring to be held by the strong arm of power, until, from the throes and agony of social and civil discord, humanity should be elevated by the only power adequate to accomplish its regeneration, and free man from the thraldom of a life which had become hateful, unbearable, and unsatisfying.

Such are the judgments of the Almighty. "His ways are on the sea, and His paths in the great waters, and His footsteps are not known." He led his people like sheep by the hand of Moses and Aaron, to the completion of the work he intended them to fulfil: of this people let us now briefly seek their condition about the time of the advent, and try to discover the influence they exercised over the events which tended to prepare the world for the coming of the Lord of all the earth.

CONDITION OF THE JEWS,

SEVENTY-ONE YEARS BEFORE THE **ADVENT OF CHRIST, THE LORD.**

By treating in a special manner of the condition of the Jews shortly before the coming of our blessed Lord, their exact connection with the circumstances of that period, will be more clearly apparent. One hundred and fifty-three years B. C., they, as a nation, had recovered their freedom, when they had been enslaved by THE MACEDONIANS. The evil disposed among them who deserted the faith, delivered up their faithful leader Judas, a son of Mattathias the Armenian, to the apostate Bacchides. A grievous persecution followed, till Jonathan assumed the command of the Jewish army. Mattathias, an old man of the line of the Priesthood, and a devoted servant of God, resisted the edict which Antiochus had issued against the Jews. By the aid of his sons he stirred up the people, calling upon all who were zealous for the law to follow him. Numbers were caught on the Sabbath in a cave and slain. Hid in the mountain fastnesses, they poured down upon the town, punishing apostates and heathens alike, even defending themselves on the Sabbath: for the first time admitting the lawfulness of defence on the Sabbath. Their ranks were filled by zealots for the law, who were then called Chasidins, for these with the Zadikins, sects who arose after the return from Babylon, divided the people. From the former, says Millman, sprang the Sadducees, from the latter the Pharisees. Mattathias was old, for such toil shortened his days, and to his son Judas was bequeathed the command. Cautiously the new commander disciplined and tried his forces, until confidence in themselves as well as in himself was secured. Attacked by Samaria, he met and defeated her forces.

Antiochus, by his folly and extravagance, had exhausted his resources. He was obliged to divide his forces. Going himself to the East, he left Lysius to crush an insurrection in Judea. The progress of Judas had alarmed him. The Syrian governor in Jerusalem sent for relief. The vanguard under Nicanor marched with a large army into the province, consisting of 40,000 and 7,000 horse. Judas had only 6,000 men at Mizpeh. Performing their religious duties, Judas issued a stirring appeal to the people, even offering to those who, from being heads of families, might naturally fear a contest, the privilege of retiring. His force fell to 3,000. With these he fell suddenly on the enemy's camp, utterly routing the Syrians, who fled to Gazera, and into Idumea and Azotus. Restraining his victorious little army, he waited until Gorgias, the lieutenant of Nicanor, who had been in command of the force just defeated, had returned from his search for the Jews, among the mountains. Gorgias found his camp deserted and burnt. The Syrians fled without striking a blow. With similar enterprise and daring, Judas gained other victories for his people, and in the following year met Lysias near Hebron, who, with a large force, was encamped to attack Judas. This great host was met and defeated by Judas, who had only 10,000 men. Victorious on all sides, Judas led his army into ruined and desolate Jerusalem. Shrubs and brushwood had taken possession of the Temple; every part of the building had been defiled. With enthusiasm they sang praises to, and worshipped God, this outpouring of their hearts accompanied by the **solemn ritual and** music they loved so well.

Thus were the house of the Maccabees the means of raising once more **the Jewish people to be a** powerful people in Judea. But neighbouring **tribes would not** patiently submit to the rising influence of **Judea. The Syrians and** their allies attacked the Jews scattered **in Galilee and the** near provinces. Judas and his brothers **in command crossed** the Jordan, himself with a force of 8,000, Simon **with 3,000, into** Galilee.

Again triumphant, he determined to consolidate **the** government, and with that view, removed all the Jews beyond Jordan, to the **more** defensible province of Judea. **In the conduct of affairs by** this able man, and his illustrious **father, we are carried back to the time of Israel's** prosperity. **Obedient to the Law, and illustrating** their faith by implicit **trust in the promises of Jehovah, success accompanied** their every step. **It seemed that** God "waited **to** be gracious," and was ready **to help, so soon as they turned to Him.** Antiochus the oppressor had just died **in Persia, of a foul** disease. Lysias who commanded in Syria, immediately proclaimed **Demetrius** the rightful **heir to the** throne. Antiochus had left the kingdom to his son named after him. The **garrison in** the citadel of Jerusalem, **with apostate** Jews **who had** adopted the **religious worship, which** had been commanded **by Antiochus Epiphanes,** made a brutal assault on the Jews going **up to the Temple to worship.** Judas led a force to punish these **bad men,** when some **of the** escaped appealed **to young** Antiochus for protection.

Marching hastily out **of Antioch** with Lysias, who was in command, they besieged Bethsura, **a strong city.** Judas raised the seige of the citadel, and met King Antiochus; **a**

hard contested battle ensued, **Judas being forced to return
to Jerusalem and await a** seige.

It was a Sabbatical year.* A year full of importance, as

---

* I am indebted to my friend Mr. Little, the **respected Teacher of the
Grammar** School at Acton P. O., for the following:—

This Table extends from the first Sabbatical **year to the building of the
second** temple.

NOTE.—*a* means that **the event took place in the Julian year before which
it stands, and** *b* that it **occurred in the Julian year which it follows.**

The division of **the cisjordanic** territory amongst the **western tribes in the
seventh year of the occupation** of Canaan. (Josh. iv. 7, 10.)
B. C. (*a*) 1546–5.

From this sabbatic year to the end of Samuel's judicature, St. Paul reckons
450 years. (Acts xiii. 19, 20.)

The eighteen years of anarchy (Jos. Ant. v. 1, 29), during which the events
recorded in the last five chapters of Judges took place, began in the
S. Y. .... (*a*) 1518–7.

Ehud delivers Israel from the oppression of Eglon, king of Moab, and
begins to judge Israel in the sabbatic year................ (*a*) 1434–3.

His judgeship ends in the sabbatic year................ (*a*) 1427–6.

Shamgar delivers Israel from the Philistine invasion in the sabbatic year.
1427–6.*(*b*)

**Jabin's oppression begins immediately after the preceding S. Y. and ends in
the S. Y.** .... (*a*) 1406–5.

Barak **and Deborah begin to judge after their victory over Sisera, at Mount
Tabor, in the S. Y.**................................ 1406–5. (*b*)

Tola's judicature **begins in the S. Y.** after the death of Abimelech.
(*a*) 1315–4.

and ends in the S. Y...................................... 1294–3. (*b*)

Jephthah puts **an end to the** tyranny of **Ammon in the 300th year of the
occupation of Canaan (Judg. xi. 26). and begins to judge in the succeeding S. Y.**................................... (*a*) 1252–1.

Samson begins to deliver Israel from the oppression of the Philistines in the
S. Y .... 1203–2. (*b*)

He destroys the temple of Dagon **and puts an** end to the oppression **of the
Philistines in the S. Y.** .... (*a*) 1182–1.

After Samson's death, Eli begins to judge.................... 1182–1. (*b*)

Samuel's **judicature of 45 years and the 450 years of the** judges end in the
S. Y.. 1098–7. (*b*)

It is probable that **Saul was anointed as the first king of Israel** in this year.

almost all, if not all, the most marked and the greatest

David began to reign in the S. Y. .... (a) 1056-5.

He removed from Hebron to Jerusalem in the eighth year of his reign, in the S. Y. .... (a) 1049-8.

Solomon lays the foundation of the temple in the fourth year of his reign, in the S. Y. .... 1014-3. (b)

The 480 years counted from the first year of Othniel, the first judge, end in this sabbatic year.

Solomon dedicates the temple in the 11th year of his reign, in the S. Y. 1007-6. (b)

Shishak, king of Egypt, invades Judah in the fifth year of the reign of Rehoboam, in the S. Y. .... (a) 972-1.

A solemn covenant made with God in the fifteenth year of Asa (2 Chron. xv. 10.), in the S. Y. .... 944-3. (b)

Freedom from war until the 35th year of Asa, the S. Y. .... (a) 923-2.

Baasha, king of Israel, invades Judah in the 36th year of Asa, in the S. Y. 923-2. (b)

Jehoshaphat, in the 17th year of his reign, associates his son Jehoram with him on the throne, in the S. Y. .... 902-1. (b)

After the assassination of Ahaziah of Judah and Jehoram of Israel, Athaliah and Jehu begin to reign respectively over Judah and Israel, in the S. Y. .... (a) 888-7.

The priests had not repaired the house of the Lord in the 23rd year of Joash, king of Judah .... (a) 860-859.

Amaziah associated with his father Joash on the throne of Judah, in the second year of Joash, king of Israel, in the S.Y. .... 846-5. (b)

Joash of Israel died in the 15th year of Amaziah of Judah, and was succeeded by his son Jeroboam II. in the S. Y. .... 832-1. (b)

Fifteen years after this S. Y., Amaziah died, in the S. Y. .... 818-7. (b)

After the death of Jeroboam II., which seems to have been a violent one (Amos vii. 9, 11), an interregnum of 22 years began in the S. Y.
(a) 790-789.

and ended in the S. Y. .... (a) 769-768.

Zachariah's reign of 3 months in the S. Y. .... 769-768. (b)

Uzziah wished to force himself into the priests' office, and was smitten with leprosy, in the S. Y. .... 755-4.

Jotham, his son, was set over the house, judging the people of the land, in the same S. Y. .... 755-4. (b) events occurring in history, occurred in Sabbattical years.

Isaiah's heavenly vision, in the year king Uzziah died.......... 755–4. (b)

Pekah assassinates Pekahiah in the S. Y...................... (a) 755–4.
and begins to reign the same year............................ 755–4. (b)

Interregnum of eight current years after **the assassination of** Pekah by Hoshea, begins in the S. Y...................................... (a) 734–3.

Hoshea terminates the interregnum **by ascending the throne in the S. Y.**
(a) 727–6.

Samaria destroyed by Sargon **in the 9th year of Hoshea, and Israel carried into captivity** in the S. Y. .... 722–719. (b)

The great passover, **in the 18th year of Josiah, celebrated in the S. Y.**
632–1. (b)

Josiah slain at Megiddo, by Pharoah Necho, **in the S. Y**......... (a) 608–7.

Jerusalem taken and destroyed in the 11th year of Zedekiah, in the 12th year of Jehoiachin's captivity, and in the 19th year of Nebuchadnezzar, in the S. Y... 587–6. (b)

The hand of the Lord on Ezekiel, in the 25th year of Jehoiachin's captivity and the 14th year after the city **was** smitten, in the S. Y........ 593–2.

Babylon taken by Darius and Cyrus **in the S. Y.**.............. 539–8. (b)

Temple re-built in the 6th year of Darius (Hystaspes) (Ezra vi. 15) in the S. Y. .... 518–7. (b)

Haman's proposal **to** destroy the **Jews, made in the 13th year of** Ahasuerus (Darius Hystaspes). (Esther iii. 7.).... .... B. C. 510.

Practice **of usury reformed** by Nehemiah **in the 32nd year of Artaxerxes I.** (Longimanus.) **(Neh. v. 14.)**

The wall of Jerusalem **finished. Neh. vi. 15.**
A sure covenant made with **God. Neh. ix. 38.**
These vents belong **to the S. Y**............................. B. C. 433.

It was, no doubt, in consideration of the **recent** occurrence of the S. Y. in B. C. 335, that the Jewish high-priest **requested** Alexander the Great to remit the tribute of the seventh year. (**Jos. Ant.** xi. 8, 5.)

Antiochus Epiphanes, in the 145th year **of** the era of the Silucidae, **in the** cliii. Ol., took Jerusalem by treachery. (Jos. Ant. XII. v. 4, **and xii.** 7, 6.).. B. C. 167.

In accordance **with the request of** the Samaritans, the temple on Mount Gerizim is named " the **temple** of Jupiter Helleuius." Same S. Y.

Food therefore was less abundant and the Jews less prepared for a siege.

Antiochus (Eupator) beseiged Judas Maccabaeus in the temple, and took it. Josephus distinctly says this happened in a S. Y. (Ant. B. xii. ch. 9, sect. 3, 5, compared with ch. x. sect. i.).................... B. C. 160.

Alexander (Bala) made Jonathan high-priest in the 160th year of the era of the Salucidae. (Jos. Ant. xiii. 2, 1.)..................... B. C. 152.

Simon being made high-priest by the multitude, set his people free from their slavery under the Macedonians *after* 170 years of the kingdom of the Asyrians. He then spent three whole years in demolishing the citadel of Jerusalem, and the mount on which it stood, because the temple was in danger in time of war. This brings down the time to the S. Y. (Jos. Ant. xiii. 6, 7.) .... B. C. 139.

In this year also Antiochus Sidetes gave leave to Simon *to coin money* for his country, and with his own stamp; and declared that *Jerusalem and the sanctuary should be free.* (1 Mac. xv. 6, 7.)

Antiochus Pious began to beseige Jerusalem in the fourth year of his reign. (Jos. Ant. xiii. 8. 2.) The seige was lengthened to the sabbatic year (J. A. xiii. 8, 1), so that it was not taken till the clxii. Ol. (J. A. xiii. 8, 2.).......................... .... B. C. 132.

Hyrcanus began his priesthood in the 3rd year of the clxxvii. Ol. (J. A. xiv. 1, 2.)... B. C. 69.

Jerusalem taken by Pompey in the clxxix. Ol., when Caius Antonius and Marcus Tullius Cicero were consuls.............·............ B. C. 62.

Herod took Jerusalem in the clxxxv. Ol. Marcus Agrippa and Caninius Gallus. Coss. and put an end to the government of the Asamoneans, 126 years after it was first set up. (J. A. xiv. 14, 4.) In B. xv. 1, 2, Josephus distinctly says that Jerusalem was taken by Herod in a S. Y. B. C. 40.

The 13th and 14th years of Herod were sabbatic years. (Jos Sat. xv. 9, 1.) Prob. B. C. 27-26.

Christ's public ministry began in the S. Y...................... A. D. 30.

Decree of Claudius in favour of the Jews in the fifth year of his reign. (Jos. Ant. xx. 1, 2.)... A. D. 45.

Terrible famine in Judea at this time, as foretold by Agabus. (Acts xi. 28.) (Jos. Ant. xx. 2, 5.)

The Jews revolt in the 12th year of Nero, on account of the ostentatious wickedness of Gessins Florus. (Jos. Ant. xx. 2, 1.) Romans defeated. (Jud. Bel. ii. 19, 9.)... A. D. 66.

Bethsura was pressed into a surrender by famine, but the skill with which Judas retired, and shut himself up in Jerusalem, caused great distress in the Syrian host, which in like manner began to suffer from want. News of no pleasant character from Antioch, induced Antiochus to conclude a treaty, giving to the Jews full liberty of religious worship, and the right to live according to their own laws.

Demetrius the son of Seleucus had fled from Rome, and with a force which he had collected, took Tripoli. Here as often happened before, recusant Jews flocked to him, raising cries against Judas.

Demetrius was the lineal heir to the throne. He was very wroth, and sent Bacchides a friend of Antiochus Epiphanes with a large force against Judas, and demanded the high-priesthood for Alcemus. Through deceitful promises, some of the Jews were won by Bacchides who wished to avoid a battle. Alcemus speaking them fair, and by winning speeches seducing them, soon gained a large following: with these he began the work of slaughter. Finding notwithstanding that he could not cope with Judas, he sent against him Nicanor. With the most dastardly treachery, Nicanor, under a pretended truce endeavoured to take Judas, who only in time discovered the base intentions of Nicanor, and with his army retired beaten, once more to the citadel of Jerusalem. Some of the priests met Nicanor and saluted him, as he came to the Temple. He demanded of them the surrender of Judas, and shocked them by his profanity and blasphemy. Judas however was not in a mood to surrender, and meeting Nicanor with the remnant of his forces which remained true to him, he addressed a soul-stirring speech to the thousand who were true, and engaged boldly the enemy. After a fierce conflict he fell. Simon and Jonathan his brother, removed the body of

5

Judas Maccabees burning it at Medin, where his father's body lay; the Jews who were faithful to him making great lamentation. Before his death he had entered into correspondence with Rome for a formal treaty of alliance, another step forward in Jewish degradation. The party led by Alcemus the base, now triumphed, and by the aid of Bacchides inflicted dire punishments on the party of Judas. Jonathan, brother of Judas, had retired to the wilderness of Tekoa, where, abiding his time, and skilfully disciplining followers as they came to him, he made only some forays to harrass Bacchides' force.

FURTHER DECLINE OF
JEWISH INDEPENDENCE.

Some years passed away, and Jonathan became master of Judea, although Jerusalem and many of the towns were still garrisoned by Syrians and rebel Jews. An adventurer now laid claim to the throne of Antiochus; a claim which Rome favored, as it suited her policy. Once more the Jews are suddenly placed in a favorable position, courted both by Balas and Antiochus, claimants to the crown of the Seleucidœ.

The impostor Balas was successful. He overthrew Demitrius (B. C. 150), mounted the throne of Syria, and formed an alliance with the Egyptian Court. Jonathan supported Balas, and marching against the army of young Demetrius, led by Apollonais, defeated it. Balas not satisfied with his position intrigued against Ptolomy, by whom he was overthrown, and caused to fly into Arabia, the chief Zabdiel beheaded him. Ptolemy Philometer, who had won the crowns of Syria and Egypt, died of the wound which he had received in the battle. At this juncture Jonathan laid siege to Jerusalem, held by apostate Jews. Demetrius, called Nicator, had ascended the throne of Syria. No time was to be lost, therefore. His opponents endeavoured to win assistance of Demetrius; Jonathan, however, leaving his troops before Jerusalem, repaired to the court of Demetrius, and being received with much honor, concluded a treaty with him. To Jonathan, Demetrius was largely indebted for the occupancy of his throne, and in turn he was confirmed in his office of High Priest, and made fresh treaties with Rome and Lacedæmon.

Demetrius and Jonathan soon parted, and the former deprived of the support of so powerful an arm, soon succumbed to Antiochus. Alexander, the son of Antiochus Epiphanes, went into Syria, and received Ptolemais, betrayed into his hands by the soldiers. Under Alexander, Jonathan was formally appointed High Priest, being sent a purple robe and golden crown, the garb of the Pontificate. Alexander, desiring to form an alliance with Ptolemy, demanded his daughter in marriage, a demand gladly acceded to by Ptolemy. Jonathan was summoned to Ptolemais, and when the wedding was over, Alexander took a purple robe and put it on Jonathan, and made him sit by him on his throne, and caused proclamation to be made of the dignity conferred upon him.

The victorious career of Jonathan was cut short as we shall see. But what we especially note at this period is the painful division amongst the Jews, and we learn somewhat of the depth of meaning which are in our Lord's words, "A house divided against itself cannot stand." Party lines were ever widening, until even rival temples were erected. At Gerizzim and in Egypt the apostates endeavoured to supplant Jerusalem. The Pharisees, the Sadducees and Essens constituted the chief sects. Of the opinions held by these Josephus gives a terse account: "The Pharisees say, that, some actions, but not all, are the work of fate, and some are in our own power, and that they are liable to fate, but are not caused by fate. The Essens affirm that fate governs all things and determines all things. The Sadducees say there is no such thing as fate, that human affairs are not at its disposal, that all our actions are in our own power, so that we ourselves are the causes of what is good and receive what is evil from our own folly." From this time the Jews suffered all the consequences of a divided house. Under the leadership of Jonathan, however, they procured some advantages, especially over Demetrius or Nicator, as he was also named. Antiochus the son of Alexander had, through the influence of Typho (an Apamian by birth) over the Jewish deserters, and "other wicked men," obtained the kingdom. His first endeavour was to secure the friendship of Jonathan; a friendship requited by the basest ingratitude, punished in the end by the consistent and courageous conduct of Jonathan. Demetrius dead, Typho began to plot against Jonathan. Going to Bethshan to meet Jonathan, he found him with forty thousand men. Unable to cope with such a force, he pretended submission and friendship, and enticing Jonathan, got him away into Ptolemais, where being with his own followers, he shut the gates and murdered Jonathan. His career was short, for Simon rallying the alarmed Jews, they at once appointed him their leader. Under Simon, the High Priest, the Jews recovered their freedom from the Macedonian yoke. Simon assuming the government deemed it necessary to attach Ptolemais; this fruit of his ill-advised measures tending only to provoke hostility, for ultimately Ptolemy overran Judea, committing the most horrible atrocities against the Jews.

Cleopatra, jealous of the progress of the arms of Ptolemy, entered a treaty, offensive and defensive, with Alexander, enabling the latter to make an expedition into Celesyria, for the punishment of Gaza and other refractory cities.

Again did the Jews revolt against their leader, dishonoring Alexander by insult and reproach. Getting into war with the King of Arabia, Obedas, he fell into ambush, and narrowly escaped to Jerusalem. Insulted by the Jews for this, for six years he carried on an incessant fight with them, killing numbers. At length the Jews appealed for protection to Demetrius Eucerus, who, marching against Alexander, defeated him. Simon fell; first through the baseness of Antiochus, who harrassed the Jewish nation, and immediately through the treachery of Ptolemy, his son-in-law, who threw him and his family into prison. However, retribution was at hand. When Hyrcanus escapes to Jerusalem, where he informed the people of his father's fate, he is made highpriest, and commences a war against Ptolemy, which only ended in trouble; for it happening that the siege being prolonged into a sabbatical year, Hyrcanus had to desist, and so gave Ptolemy the opportunity of injuring his family.

Antiochus now invaded Judea. Hyrcanus was defeated, but, through the great moderation of Antiochus, was spared, and all his people, they only paying tribute for the city, and Joppa and other cities bordering on Judea. Contrary to the conduct of his father A. Epephanes, who offered swine's flesh on the altar, the son sent to Hyrcanus golden cups, and bulls with their horns gilded, and in every way exhibited reverence for the religious opinions of the Jews. Soon after Hyrcanus, hearing of the death of Antiochus, slain in battle against Arsaces, King of Parthia, attacked Syria, taking several cities, subduing Idumea. He now turned his attention to a league of unity with the Romans, which the Romans as readily entered into. Hyrcanus, averting the dangers which ever and again were springing up, lead his people to successes, and was soon engaged in resisting the attacks of Antiochus Cyzianus, whom he was punishing in Samaria, having set over the army his two sons, Antigonus and Aristobulus. He says, " I was in the temple offering incense, when a voice declared that his sons had just won a victory." "Now," says Josephus, "at this time the whole Jewish people were in great prosperity."

And now again began one of those fatal divisions to which Israel was so continually given. Hyrcanus was exciting their envy. The Pharisees raised up opposition against him, and, endeavouring to wound his personal feelings, taunted him with being the son of a woman who was captive to Antiochus Epiphanes. Hyrcanus, resenting the false assertion, threw himself into the arms of the Sadducees.

Administering the government satisfactorily for thirty-one years, he died. His son Aristobulus, as the eldest of his sons, took the government. Cruel and treacherous, he slew his brother, and put his own mother in prison because she disputed with him his right to rule. He perished miserably at the end of a year, and was succeeded by Alexander, the despised son of Hyrcanus, who had been brought up at Galilee; but more of these by-and bye. Alexander, after further contests, closed a turbulent reign, leaving his wife Alexandra in power.

Profiting by past experience, he gave her advice which he had not himself followed, *i. e.*, to please the popular party; advice very generally recommended at the present day, and very generally followed. Throwing herself into the hands of the Pharisees, and loading them with compliments, she made them her confidential advisers. She thus commenced her reign, in which she was enabled to accomplish some very excellent things. Of the two left by Alexander, Hyrcanus and Aristobulus, the latter only was active and bold. Hyrcanus, therefore, was made high priest, and, caring not for politics, let the Pharisees do as they pleased. Aristobulus, restless and ambitious, but without real talent, was entrusted by his mother to lead an army against Ptolemy, who was a bad neighbour to the city. He gained no advantage, and returned home. Shortly after, on occasion of the illness of the Queen, he intrigued with some old friends who were settled about in the fortresses, and instigated a rebellion, through which much trouble fell upon the nation. Hyrcanus and Aristobulus appealed to Pompey, who condemned Aristobulus of course, as less subservient.

This period is one of the most important in the history of the Jews. "An enemy," says Mr. Merrivale, "more fatal than the Greek was at hand." The rivalries which sprang up within the family of the Asmonean Princes led to an invitation to the Romans to take part in the national divisions. Pompey decided in favour of Hyrcanus as the most pliant tool in his hands, and kept up a rigid watchfulness over the new government, by the proconsuls of Syria; a watchfulness intended to crush the national spirit and familiarize them with the idea of complete subjugation.

A very lamentable picture of the Jewish race is now apparent. The Greek language and ideas had penetrated the people. Thus observes Merrivale, at Tyre, at Sidon, and at Ascalon, the Romans published their decrees in the Latin and Greek idioms. The prevalence of the Greek language even at Jerusalem itself, is marked by an interesting circumstance, recorded in the Acts of the Holy Apostles. On the occasion of a riot which was excited in the city between the Oriental and Greek Jews, St. Paul addressed the multitude; when they heard that he spoke in the Hebrew tongue they the more kept silence, "from which it appears that if he had addressed them in Greek they would have understood him."

But a deeper and important influence had passed upon them in the infusion of Greek ideas. Among the educated and higher classes an extensive influence had been exercised. The revolution to which allusion has been made, by which

John Hyrcanus changed the form of government into a royal dominion, at once drew accurately party lines, throwing into strong contrast, the opinions which characterised the Pharisees and Sadducees. The Pharisees holding fast the traditions they had received, strongly maintained the theocracy or divine government. They beheld with alarm the falling away from the faith, and the corruptions and perils of society around them. To avert those dangers, they magnified the importance of the strict observance of ceremonies, and endeavoured to strengthen the law, by interpretations derived from sources, as corrupt as the Greek Theosophies which they combated. The Sadducees, on the other hand, seem to have imbibed, on the contrary, from the Greek philosophies those principles which so materially affected their religious belief, and belonging for the most part to the higher classes, they were indifferent to the great religious questions of the day.

It would seem that party spirit had so entirely entered in to divide and separate them, that no reverses or warnings had the slightest effect upon them. Divided, they became a prey to contending political intriguers, who ever and anon played one party against the other. Their history is wonderfully preserved for our instruction, and perhaps we may not be far wrong when we say that in the Church of Christ to-day, safety is sacrificed to a wretched contention between the Pharisees and Sadducees of Christianity.

On the death of Alexandra, Hyrcanus had obtained the Priesthood, 71 B. C. Soon attacked by Aristobulus, who had massed a large force, he engaged in conflict which was decided at Jericho. Aristobulus delivered from prison his wife and children who had been shut up at the instigation of the Pharisees, and forced Hyrcanus to yield. The Asmonean family was in imminent peril, from a foe far more dangerous than the Pharisees. Hyrcanus' friend, the Idumean Antipater, a bad man, was a determined enemy of Aristobulus, of whose power he was jealous. The timid Hyrcanus was worked upon by Antipater; his fears greatly excited on account of the supposed designs of Aristobulus against his life, Antipater persuaded him to fly to Aretas, king of Arabia, now a man of might and influence. Aretas won over by large concessions of territory and bribes, marched against Jerusalem and defeated Aristobulus. During this seige, Josephus narrates an instance of faith and prayer, which even in these latter days, many know to be effectual. "There was one whose name was Onias, a righteous man, and beloved of God, who in a certain drought had prayed to God to put an end to the intense heat, and whose prayers God *had heard, and had sent them rain.* This man had hid himself, because he saw that this sedition would last a great while. They brought him however to the Jewish Camp, and desired that as by his prayers he had once put an end to the drought, so he would in like manner make imprecations on Aristobulus and those of his faction. Forcing him to speak against his will, Onias stood forth in the midst, and with a loyal patriotism to his people, and with fidelity to God, said: O God, the King of the whole world! since those that stand now with me are Thy people, and those that are besieged are also Thy priests, I beseech Thee, that Thou will neither hearken to the prayers of those against these, nor bring to effect what those pray against those." Upon this the Jews standing by stoned him. God, continues Josephus, punished them for their cruelty to Onias, and for subsequent insult to His own Majesty. While the priests and Aristobulus were besieged, it happened that the feast called the Passover was come, at which it is our custom to offer a great many sacrifices.

Those that were with Aristobulus wanted sacrifices, and desired that their countrymen without would furnish them with such, and assured them that they should have as much money for them as they should desire. Large sums were let down in baskets over the wall. It is said that swine were returned for the money. A vehement storm of wind arose, destroying the fruits of the country around, rendering provisions so dear that a modus of wheat was bought for eleven drachmœ. While Hyrcanus and Aristobulus were thus wasting the strength and life of the nation, Rome was ready to advance her own power. Pompey engaged himself in Armenia, sent his active and able Lieutenant Scaurus, who had seized Damascus. With little delay he went into Judea, where ambassadors from Hyrcanus and Aristobulus met him. Aristobulus offered him 400 talents; Hyrcanus the same. Aristobulus being in possession of the public treasury and of the temple was deemed the more eligible by Scaurus, so he induced Aretas to retire, and so raised the seige. On the retirement of Scaurus, Aristobulus with his army pressed Aretas and Hyrcanus, defeating them at a place called Papyron. The contest between the factions was not yet ended, as the unfortunate Onias had predicted. Soon after Pompey went to Damascus and marched over Cœle-Syria, kings and ambassadors from all Syria, Egypt, and out of Judea, conveyed to him rich presents and immense wealth. Antipater from Hyrcanus, and Nicodemus from Aristobulus, came making charges against those who had taken bribes. Pompey ordered all who had controversies to meet him in the beginning of the spring, when, bringing his army out of winter quarters, he marched into the country of Damascus, subduing, as he went along, the various countries. It was at Damascus he heard the causes of the Jews, and of their governors, Hyrcanus and

Aristobulus, who were at difference one with another, as also of the nation against them both, "which *did not desire* to be under kingly government, *because* the form of government they received from their forefathers was that of subjection to the priests of that God whom they worshipped; and they complained that, though these two were of the posterity of the priests, yet did they seek to change the government of their nation to another form, in order to enslave them." Neither Hyrcanus nor Aristobulus gained by their procedure; for soon after Pompey led his army against Jerusalem, 64 B. C.; and after fearful suffering, the city was won by Pompey. "All this misery," says Josephus, "came upon Jerusalem through Hyrcanus and Aristobulus, the one raising a sedition against the other. *We now lost our liberty*, and became subject to the Romans, and were deprived of that country which we had gained by our arms from the Syrians, and were compelled to restore it to the Syrians. *Moreover the Romans exacted of us*, in a little time, above ten thousand talents, and THE ROYAL AUTHORITY, *which was a dignity* formerly bestowed on *those that were high-priests by the right of their family*, and which now *became the property of private men*."
B. C. 48. The Jews became confederate with Cæsar, Pompey being dead, and afforded, through Antipater and Hyrcanus, material aid to Cæsar. They received from the Romans and Athenians in return very great honors. Hyrcanus was appointed high-priest and Antipater procurator of Judea. Gallilee was committed to HEROD, his eldest son, being governor of Jerusalem. The rapacity and wickedness of Antipater soon showed itself, for purloining the gifts which Hyrcanus sent to the Roman Emperor, and guilty of other acts of baseness, the Jews became alarmed. Discovering the evil character of Antipater, they cried out to the

high-priest, "How long wilt thou be quiet under such actions as are now done? Or dost thou not see that Antipater and his sons have already seized upon the government, and that it is only the name of a king which is given to thee?"

The Jews made such complaints, and the mothers of those who had been slain by Herod so constantly appealed to him, that Hyrcanus was moved to cite Herod before the Sanhedrim for what he had done. Through the influence of Sextus Cæsar, president of Syria, Hyrcanus was ordered to clear Herod, who, appearing before the Sanhedrim with an armed retinue, awed his accusers into silence. There is reason to believe that one just man protested against so flagrant miscarriage of justice. Sameas, in a noble address, warned the Sanhedrim of their folly in giving heed to the threats of Sextus Cæsar, concluding his spirited remonstrance in the memorable words, "I do not make complaint against Herod himself; he is to be sure more concerned for himself than for the laws; but my complaint is against yourselves and your king, who gave him license so to do. However, take you notice, that God is great; and that this very man, whom you are going to absolve and dismiss, for the sake of Hyrcanus, will one day punish both you and your king himself also." A prediction fulfilled: for no sooner did Herod receive the kingdom, than he slew all the members of the Sanhedrim and Hyrcanus, saving only Sameas.

THE GOVERNMENT UNDER HEROD.

Forty years before Christ, Cæsar was slain by Cassius and Brutus in the senate house. Cassius went from Rome into Syria, to raise the siege at Apomia; having effected which, he went over the cities gathering together soldiers and levying heavy taxes upon the cities. He heavily oppressed Judea, and exacted of it many hundred talents. Antipater, when he saw the condition of affairs, divided the collection of the sum, and set his sons to collect it. Because Herod exacted what was required of him from Galilee before others, he obtained the favour of Cassius, a favour which he thought would ingratiate him too with the Romans, however much the steps he took to gain their good-will would be at the expense of others. Antipater's murder by Malichus, and the death of Malichus by Cassius, an action commanded by Hyrcanus, seemed an act of retributive justice. Herod, raising an army, displaced Antigonus, the son of Aristobulus, whom Ptolemy the son of Medusus had brought back into Judea. He had already raised an army, and had by money made Tobias to be his friend. Ptolemy had been left by Cassius to tyrannize over Syria. When Herod came, he took all from him. Beating Antigonus, he drove him out of Judea. Going to Jerusalem, Hyrcanus and the people crowned him with garlands, for he had already contracted an affinity with the family of Hyrcanus by having espoused a descendant of his, and for that reason Herod was kind to him. Antonius and Cæsar had beaten Cassius near Phillippi. Cæsar went into Gaul, and Antony into Asia. Arriving at Bythenia, the principal men, also of the Jews met him, accusing Herod and Phasælus. Antony had received from Herod a handsome bribe, which, as usual, was successful in ensuring his friendship. Antony, however, gave heed to the other complaints of the Jews, and set those of the nation free, considering their complaint, and restoring them that country, which in the days of Cassius had been taken from them. Antony's friendship for Herod continued, so that he made himself and his brother Phasælus tetrarchs, and committed the public affairs of the Jews to their care. Herod did not remain at ease, but, attacked by Parthian friends of Antigonus, he was brought to great straits, until rescued by Antony; and as protector, Cæsar hesitated not to raise Herod's dignity, for through Antony's influence with the Senate, a decree was passed making Herod king. After much opposition, Herod, three years after he had been made king at Rome, came near to Jerusalem and pitched his camp, besieging it, and went himself into Samaria to celebrate his marriage with Mariamne. Returning after his marriage, he, by the assistance of Sosius, took Jerusalem by force. By his judgment and forethought, the city was saved from ruin, the savage soldiery being rewarded out of his own funds.

After a series of most eventful encounters and wars, Herod escaping the machinations of his family, was treated by Antonius with marked respect, who seating him on a throne beside himself, added to his former territory, Celœsyria, Entering into a war to enforce tribute over Malchus, King of Arabia, Herod, crafty and selfish, avoided the danger of taking sides in the contest between Antonius and Octavius. Securing the friendship of Octavius Cæsar, Herod was ordered to retain the diadem which he had obsequiously laid aside; returning to Judea in full possession of his sovereignty. Jealousy inflaming his mind against Mariamne, he suffered all the agony of so evil a passion, and sacrificing her, he became gloomy and his temper wicked. Herod himself miserable, his house ever distracted, his mind on the watch for danger, and fired by suspicion, was destined to close a sad life amid scenes which must have been very full of horror and pain. The two sons of Mariamne brought up at Rome had returned to Jerusalem. The Jews were favourably disposed towards them because of the Asmonean blood which flowed in their veins. Herod married them, Alexander to Claphyra, the daughter of Archetaus, King of Cappadocia; Aristobulus to Mariamne, daughter of Salome. They were celebrated for their elegance and beauty, praise which excited the envy of Salome. The cruel fate of their mother was evidently buried deeply in the minds of the youth, and ever and again painful memories would seem to have arisen, and to have found expression in careless words, which prudence should have forbid them to utter. Salome and her friends gave to such expressions wings, which very soon reached the popular mind. Herod for some time refused to listen to what he thought were mere idle rumors; but going to the Bosphorus to be with Agrippa, who was engaged in war, he heard much that changed his spirit. Ever ready with some counterplot to foil his opponents, he instantly sent for Antipater, an elder son, borne to him by Doris, a wife whom he had divorced to marry Mariamne. Antipater too eagerly entered into the plan, and tried every device to alienate his father from his two other sons. Inflamed at length by reiterated reports of his sons' designs to avenge their mother's death, Herod determined to accuse his sons before the courts of Augustus.

Herod, with his sons, appeared before Augustus, at Aquelei. He charged them with being disobedient, unnaturally obstinate, and of entertaining criminal designs against his life. Humiliated and distressed beyond measure, they stood awed and silent before Augustus, unable to speak, lest they should criminate their father. Augustus, with his usual tact and good feeling, instead of proceeding to punish, brought about a reconciliation. Adding to his former difficulties, Pheroras, Herod's brother, sowed the seeds of jealousy and hate between the father and his sons again, by the most unnatural and infamous charges. At length the whole Court became the scene of intrigue and plot, until no one could trust another. Archelaus, King of Cappadocia, hearing of the trouble, repaired to the court of Herod, and by dexterous management succeeded in reconciling Herod to his son Alexander. Again, through the wicked intrigues of Antipater, Salome and Pheroras, Herod's wrath was roused against Alexander and Aristobulus. At once the tribunal of Augustus was appealed to, who, vainly trying to soothe the father, allowed the accused sons to be cited for trial at Berytus. By the immediate accusation of Herod, they were condemned, and finally put to death. The cruelty of this sentence evoked from Augustus the bitter saying, "I would rather be one of Herod's swine than one of his sons."

Retributive justice overtook all engaged in these diabolical plans, and Herod lived to discover that his son Antipater for whom he had imbrued his hands in the blood of his own sons, had conspired to poison the father who had elevated him to interests and to a position, which those unfortunate sons should have enjoyed. Herod, seized with mortal disease, now determined to re-write his will. Antipater was under condemnation. He therefore left the kingdom to Antipas, passing over Archelaus and Philip, suspected of collusion with Antipater. These events bring before us characters which have become familiar to us through the sacred writings.

In the case of Antipater, Herod had ample cause for those fears which the treachery of his son called forth. Antipater was already proved to have conspired with Pheroras to poison his father. The wife of Pheroras confessed the whole plot. Mariamne, Herod's wife, daughter of Simon, high-priest, was implicated. Repudiating her, Herod deposed Simon, and elevated Mattathias to the high office. Antipater returning from Rome, whither he had gone, landed at Cæsarea, where, from the silence and aversion of the people, his suspicions that his designs were discovered, seem to have been awakened. It was too late to fly, so on he went to Jerusalem. Cited before Herod, who sat on the judgment seat, aided by Varus, the Roman governor of Syria, Antipater had all the proofs of guilt made known to him. The evidence was conclusive. Antipater was condemned. The sentence could not be executed until confirmation of the decree was received from Rome. At length, just before Herod was stricken by the hand of death, the decree arrived. Herod, in the pangs of acute suffering, had attempted suicide. Antipater, hearing he was dead, tried to bribe the keeper of the prison to release him. Herod, learning this, had just strength enough to order his execution, and once more altering his will, fell into the arms of death.

The unenviable notoriety to which this man attained, is not to be lost sight of by us. Utterly reckless of mercy to the members of his own family, he could cajole when it suited his purpose. The most cold-blooded of murderers, he yet did some good to his country. In proportion to his own misery, the prosperity of the country increased. He seems to have been a politic king, and did many good things for his people. Once he fed, at his own expense, 50,000 people, importing corn to avert the horrors of the famine. And to mark the influence given Rome by the government of Herod, Cæsarea was built, having standing in its centre a vast temple, dedicated to Cæsar, with two colossal statues, one of Cæsar, the other of Rome. Before his death Rome had become virtually mistress of the East, for Herod, no longer a Jewish king, but truly a vassal of Rome, had sent his two sons to be educated in Rome, where they were in the palace of Augustus. This of itself was an offence and direct injury to the Jews. Roman greatness was to the Jew but evidence of his own degradation; and when at length the smothered disaffection became openly apparent, Herod tried to purchase their good-will by an apparent act of generosity and respect for their religion. The Pharisees and Essenes had opposed him in some of his measures. He determined to restore the Temple to its former pride and magnificence. The dilapidated structure of Zorobabel had stood many a siege, and was to the Jews a structure of too sacred and hallowed associations. Herod, to convince them of his sincerity, collected the material requisite for its restoration before he removed the decayed structure. Soon (17 B. C.) the Jews saw with the utmost pride the new fabric, stately and magnificent, crown the brow of Moriah, its pinnacles glittering in gold, and its masses of purest marble standing out in all the majesty of art. Herod meant nothing by his restoration of the Temple but the pacification of his Jewish subjects. He was, with much more real zeal, intent upon the entire subjection of his kingdom to the Cæsar, and hence even paternal affection did not deter him from placing the very lives of his sons in the hands of the Roman. Nevertheless he wrought on to an end.

NEAR APPROACH OF THE MESSIAH.

What a wonderful undertaking was the restoration of the Temple at this time! Who amongst the mass of infatuated Jews foresaw that the Lord was to be in that holy temple, coming truly to His own house? Who understood that even the restorer of that Temple would tremble, when, on the completion of his work, he should hear from "wise men" that the King of the Jews was born?

It is now that the sacred narrative becomes to us so movingly interesting. In the midst of power, backed by all the influence of Rome, Herod seemed secure. In the midst of this security, events occur which change the history of the world, and manifest the true destiny of the human race. From the Message of Truth, recorded by St. Luke, we hear of the holy life of one of the priests of God, whose daily office it was to minister in the Temple: it was his duty to offer incense. We also learn that there was still a multitude who daily resorted to the Temple for Prayer. While executing the office of priest, the holy man, who had led a long life of devout and earnest prayer, was answered by an angelic messenger announcing to him at the altar of incense, that God had chosen him to be the father of a son, who should be filled with the Holy Ghost from the womb; and that he should turn many of the children of Israel to the Lord. It is to be remarked that God at the time did not speak through any prophet, or through any other means than those ordinarily used, viz., the law and **the Priests.** He now **sent** an angel with His message **of joy.**

That the worshippers in the Temple might believe the **truth and** reality of the message, God was pleased to deprive Zacharias of speech. Five months after the event, the Word of God, as it had been declared to the aged **priest,** was fulfilled. We read of the apparent punishment **inflicted on** the holy servant of God, and seldom recognise the deep significance of **this miraculous closing of the good man's mouth,** as one of **the means of** keeping from the mass of the people, and **from the stern and** jealous **Herod, the** knowledge **of events which** would have moved them, as they were moved **afterwards, to** deeds of violence. The people knew that he **had seen** a vision, but what the vision was, it was not intended then that they should know. While these occurrences had taken place in the Temple at Jerusalem, another event of far deeper consequence happened in the little city of Galilee called Nazareth. There lived in the quiet of **an** humble home, a family of the house and lineage of David, which, nevertheless, occupied no exalted position in the country. Like good Zacharias, they were unknown to men; but to God, they were servants raised up to do his will. Joseph and Mary were these. It must have been a strange circumstance to a young maiden of no mark in human life, to receive the strange salutation which greeted the lowly Virgin, as the angel came in unto her with the words, "Hail, Mary! thou that art highly favored, the Lord is with thee! Blessed art thou among women!" Well, indeed, **may she have been** troubled, and wondered what the salutation could mean. She was vouchsafed an answer: "Thou shalt conceive **in thy womb,** and bring forth a son, and thou shalt call his name Jesus;"—satisfying her that the Holy Ghost would bring this to pass. The angelic messenger also informed her that her cousin Elizabeth was to be the mother of a son. What fullness of holy **resignation is** now exhibited for our instruction; what **humility, and** patient waiting for more light; what conflict **of mind in those few** spoken words, "Behold the handmaid of the Lord; **be it unto me** according **to** thy word." Instantly recognising **herself** as an instrument in God's hands for a **great work, which she may** not fully have understood, she is prepared **to accept it; she** is submissive, is trustful that God, who could **do his will** through her, would guard her from reproach, from misery and ruin. **As** soon as the angel had departed, the Virgin **lost no time,** but hastened to Elizabeth. From the narrative, **it would seem that she did no more than** is done every day **amongst ourselves, when we go to a dear** friend's house, unceremoniously and with **the love of** friendship, entering the door, calling **out our salutation; for when** Elizabeth **heard her the** babe **leaped in her** womb. She herself, **by** the Holy Ghost, **gave words to the** holy feelings of her **heart,** in **that** hymn **of praise,** chanted **by** millions of Christian voices through these long years of grace and love. After **three months, passed** in happy fellowship, the youthful maiden returns **to** her home in Nazareth. From an **expression** in the Sacred Word, **we catch a** slight glimpse **of her** present distress. She was espoused to a **man named** Joseph. He, it is said, was minded **to** put her away **privately, when her state was** known to him. Being a **just man,** he would **not be harsh to** her, whose life hitherto had **been as** faultless as human life could be. Yet, not understanding the glory **to be** reflected on **him, he seems to have known** nothing of the great truth **revealed to the Virgin** blessed. He either did not or could not understand **her** story.

Just at this time a decree is issued by Cæsar Augustus **from Rome,** that **there** should **be a** general **census taken** of the people, each man and household being required to go up to their own city to be enrolled; and it is said, "all went, each to his own city." Evidently no exceptions were made in favor of those who, from infirmity, sickness or age, might be sorely tried in obeying so arbitrary a decree. The immense travel on the roads leading to various cities and towns, must have been wonderful. Among those obliged to move from their place of abode, was the family of Joseph, who, being of the house of David, was forced to go up to a little city called Bethlehem, his native city, to be taxed, taking with him Mary his espoused wife, being great with child. Amid so vast a throng, who were they, that honor should be shown to them, or charity open her door to receive them? Leaning heavily on the tender arm, to which she clung for support, the heart-distressed Mary must have deeply pondered over the angelic declarations. Had she any fears, lest, through her, the promise should fail? Did her heart doubt, when she, to whom an angel had been sent with so awful a message, found herself in a crowd, destitute of shelter, and of that common solicitude so almost necessary to the female heart at her hour of anguish? No room is found for them in the inn. Herod is in his palace; the Temple at Jerusalem is resplendent in its new beauty; the priests are there; but a Greater than Herod, the Lord of the Temple, is come to Bethlehem, and is cradled among beasts; rejected of men!

The conviction, **extending far and wide,** that a Mighty Prince should come, had already dreamily passed before the Western mind. In the East, that expectation had become intensified into certitude. We know not intimately how certain wise men were influenced, or how their minds were satisfied, but that a star appeared moving and inviting them to follow. It matters not to us what that star was; we only know that it was, or must have been, a wondrous star, differing from all other stars in glory, as it attracted attention, and moved in one special direction. To man it was a guiding light, prefiguring the Church with the lamp of God's truth, His holy word, leading men to the Saviour King. Not only learned, but wise, those Eastern men came to see the great thing that had come to pass. They kept no secret of their mission, but openly asked, "Where is He that is born King of the Jews?" From His earthly house, the Temple, one faithful voice had blessed His name; but now that He appears and comes to His own, His own receive Him not. The Temple rang not with Hosannas to the Prince of Peace, the High-priest chanted forth no welcome to the Saviour King. Wrapped in the embrace of Roman power, and crushed beneath the foot of faction, Palestine lived on the past. His coming expected, looked for, none of his race recognized the King of Israel in a carpenter's son. Who believed that Nazareth should send forth, or Bethlehem, the least of the cities, be the inhospitable birth-place of, the Mighty One? If Jews were silent, other mouths proclaimed Him.

From the far-off East the prophetic sayings had made their way. Wise men, who had been looking forward with restless expectancy, alone with humble shepherds do Him homage, and worship the New-born King.

If the first advent of our Lord and Saviour had been prophetically announced in general terms, such as those used by Balaam, or in one or two of the prophecies of Isaiah, there would have been less interest for us in the closing scenes of the Jewish dispensation. It is the very minuteness and carefulness of detail, which makes the scriptural account of our Lord's birth so intensely interesting for us. In the Holy Gospels we hear of persons, and find precise accounts of events having reference to the political condition of countries and to the policy of rulers, which are of considerable importance, because intimately associated with the advent of the Saviour. It is thus we become desirous to know something of the state of the Jewish people, when the wise men came from the East to Jerusalem; when Herod was king, he who was so soon deeply interested in events which nearly affected both himself and his country. As was but natural, an inquiry made by men who had such a reputation as to be called "wise," was enough to startle a king who was familiar with the past history of the land he governed. He could not have been ignorant of the rumour, which, like the rising and falling of the waves of the mighty sea, ever and again rose and fell upon the ears of men. He could not despise the saying of the Eastern Magi as the raving of fools; for he must have felt some distrust of the security of his position, when, with all the earnestness of interrogated men, they added to the mere question, "Where is he?" the singular reason for the visit, "for we have seen His star in the East, and are come to worship him." With zealous steps they wound their way, and, led by the unerring light, found in Bethlehem Him they sought. All this was noised abroad, and all that the wise men did became known. They found Him, and, offering their gifts, declared their belief that He whom they sought, and had found cradled in an ox's stall, was The King. Beneath the shelter of the humblest roof, lay the Virgin Mother and her Infant Child. How did she understand, now these wise men had come, the divine outpouring of Elizabeth's heart! "Whence is this to me?—that the mother of my Lord should come to me! For lo! as soon as the voice of thy salutation sounded in mine ears, the babe leaped in my womb for joy." The Blessed Virgin could answer, "My soul doth magnify the Lord, and my spirit hath rejoiced in God my Saviour." Was this neglected maiden, who, through toil and weariness of travel, had, at the command of an earthly king, been forced to leave her quiet home to sojourn in a city which had no room to shelter her, the mother of the Saviour? She must have been indeed cheered by the visit of the humble shepherds. Doubts which we may suppose to have arisen naturally in her mind would somewhat be settled, although the mystery of her present apparent humiliation, must have been intensely strange and perplexing. As a daughter of Eve, she knew she shared the lot of Eve, and her young heart must have yearned for the safety of her Child. Fears, not unnatural, must have come upon her; for she was soon to learn that against her child the rage of hate would arise, rendering all care necessary for his safety, a duty too stern to be neglected. She was indeed to be perfected through her suffering Son. In all those tender years of His infancy, she must have watched with an intensity beyond our appreciation, the gradual unfolding of that holy life which was His alone. She must have been awed by filial love so pure, obedience so ready, goodness so unalloyed. Woman, blessed but tried beyond measure, we give thee all our human love. The more we think on Jesus, as He was with His mother, the more do we realise the gradual revealing of Himself to the human heart, as He "increased in wisdom, and stature, and in favor with God and man:" we can indeed but very imperfectly imagine the deep outpouring of maternal love which drew forth the remonstrance, "Thy father and I have sought thee sorrowing:" What that wisdom was, which in Him became manifest, we may well conjecture. The holy life of such a mother would be elevated, quickened, intensified by the daily converse and actions of such a son. Day by day, convictions must have grown stronger, hopes more certain, and adoring love deepened as the opening manhood grew more and more conspicuous. She well knew who her Son was said to be; yet her own recorded words and actions seem to prove that she only could have gradually understood the depth and fullness of that perfect Life, which came to give Life and Immortality to man.

She had already expressed her faith in a truly sublime hymn of thanksgiving. Her sojourn with Elizabeth must have been passed in frequent conversation concerning all the very mysterious events which so lately had happened to them. The salutation of Elizabeth must only have confirmed the angel's message, yet it is clear that the Blessed Virgin did not fully understand the Saviour's mission. Is not this written for our learning? The Church, in its early morn, after His death, received Him and accepted Him, as the Church in the stable of Bethlehem received Him: so apostles followed, and declared Him the Messias, when as yet *they* knew not all the truth. They required to be taught the fullness of the riches in Christ Jesus. So too with the individual Christian: first comes belief, then action on belief ever deepening. The devils believed and trembled, but they acted contrary to their belief, and not on it.

The love of His mother was as the love of the Church. It was the deep, lowly, awful resignation of her soul, not only to her own son, but to the Son of God. Her human affection was not lost; it must have been merged, enlarged, in that most devout and holy love which would welcome him to her innermost heart as her most blessed Saviour. "Whatsoever He saith unto you, do it!" is full of deep, hidden meaning. The mother of our Lord knew that he could bless, if he pleased; and this her confidence found expression in the command, "Whatsoever He saith unto you, *do it.*" So says His bride, the Church. Do not only say, I believe, but *do* the will of Christ. In this language of the Virgin mother, we have, too, a confession of her belief in His divine power, and we are prepared for her quiet, patient, submissive love, when she receives the answer, "What have I—(in such a divine manifestation)—to do with thee? Mine hour is not yet come." And we but love her the more when we note all absence of complaint or disappointment, when, once again, He, looking round, said, "Behold my mother, and sister, and brother."

The Nativity is in truth a deep mystery. Try as we may, we cannot realise the event in all its depth and fullness. Looking back these nearly two thousand years on that first Christmas day, we sink with shame before that lowly door, and dare not lift our eyes, had not the wise and holy in heart have knelt in adoration before the new-born Babe. Of the throng who filled the streets of Bethlehem, and sought with pressing need the shelter of Bethlehem's homes, not one of all the house of Israel was found to make way for their King. We cannot linger by His mother's side; we need not seek to know the anguish and strange conflicting thoughts which must have moved her human heart. We, in her tender care, her watching and her sufferings, see too well the foreshadowing of that anguish of the Son, too keen for mere mortal to have endured. Bright, glorious, pure, divine, the incarnate Son draws to himself all the deep adoring love that mortal hearts can pay. The Infant on his mother's knee, or lying nestled on her breast, alone receives the homage and the worship which are due to Him. From Bethlehem to Gethsemane, from thence to Pilate's hall, and from it to Calvary, she, the mother of such a Son, is content "to follow his most blessed footsteps," and to wait until the bitter hour should come when the Sword which should pierce her own soul, should have its keen edge broken by the salvation which the suffering Son should purchase for His suffering mother. As at Bethlehem, so on Calvary, how few are near to bless! Yet what home like hers? Who was ever so blessed? Where find so dutiful, so filial a child? In what other family the divine perfection of love so unselfish, the voice of truth so powerful? The worship paid by Eastern strangers to the Lamb of God, must have been an act of singular significance to the Holy Family. In it the Blessed Virgin must have seen no vague foreshadowing of the greatness of that Holy Child of which she was the human mother. But ere these wise men had come to offer the tribute of true wisdom to the new-born King, others had been to the humble abode, and given evidence that He who lay in the manger-bed was not only Joseph's son. The visit of the shepherds must have been a startling one, and must have awakened strange thoughts in those who heard them describe the angelic visitation. These things could not have been known to all; for it was only after some days that Joseph is directed to take his family into Egypt, to escape the outburst of jealousy and fear with which the heart of Herod had become filled. Then, soon was the bitter cry of lamentation heard over the land. "Rachel wept for her children, and would not be comforted, because they are not." The arm of heartless persecution was uplifted, and the blood of innocents was the first sacrifice which the children of evil offered at the birth of Him who came to crush their power.

What an Advent! The Temple, restored in its magnificence, and still in possession of its ancient ritual, had had within its sacred walls, through the voice of pious Zacharias, the nigh fulfillment of the promise announced. He, the father of the proclaimer of glad tidings, was still a priest of

God, ministering in the holy Temple; through him was there a warning of coming events. It is true that God's mercy was manifested in preventing the utterance of what must have been in the good priest's heart; but it is nevertheless true that in all the earth not one voice was raised to bless the King of Peace; no human tongue was loosed to hymn " peace! good-will to men." The advent had alone filled two hearts with life and light. We have their songs, and thousands of voices at Christmas tide still sing them.

The Birth at Bethlehem was the birth of Humanity regenerated and begotten anew. It was the reconciliation of God and man; the resurrection of life from the grave. As death was the penalty of sin, inflicted on each individual descended from Adam, so the restoration is individual. Marvel not when He saith, " Ye must be born again," and born of Him by " water and the spirit;" not by water only, for *it* is but the outward sign of that outflowing of inward grace, through which sinful flesh is buried into the death of Christ, that it may rise in His flesh and blood. Well may we, at Christmas tide, turn all our thoughts on Jesus; well may we open the flood-gates of our love and holiest emotions, that all the deep adoration of our souls may gush forth, and bathe the feet which tears of penitential sorrow once wetted. We look not on Him as the son of Mary only, for then we know not all He is. No! We look upon him, through all the tender days of infancy and the years of suffering manhood, as the incarnate Son. That sweet smile of innocence which dimples the cheek of childhood, playing like the softly sighing breeze on the placid waters, was in Him the smile of triumphant joy for victory already begun. The unfolding of His mysterious nature filled willing hearts with love and awe which we can but faintly realise. Faithful Simeon; the aged Elizabeth, who wondered that " the mother of her Lord should come to her," must have gazed on the Holy Child, not with the dim eye of age, but with the eye of faith, deep, clear, penetrating, and all illumined with the glory they saw revealed. The watchers of his early years discovered in all the manifestations of his life somewhat of that "hidden might veiled beneath the flesh." To them he was what he is to us—" the Son of God." In all that he did, they must have seen the working of a spirit not of this world; they must have gazed with ever increasing wonder on the growth of the Child "set for the fall and rising again of many in Israel," and who waxed strong in spirit filled with wisdom, the grace of God being on him. The prophetic promises must indeed have resounded in their hearts, moving them to echo back to heaven the triumphant alleluias, which, reverberating through earth from seraph voices, rang through the vault of heaven, choirs of angels taking up the words of sweet redeeming love, " With His own right hand and with His holy arm hath He gotten himself the victory. Alleluia! Peace, good-will to men!" "Mine eyes have seen thy salvation, have seen the Lord's Christ!" What glory! His presence then worked in believing souls with a power, not greater than that, with which for these nearly nineteen hundred years it has worked; maintaining, enlarging, strengthening His kingdom on earth. Beneath the few brief words, " they worshipped him," there lies a profundity of meaning which the cold heart knows not. Such worship could only mean the outgoing of the soul to gaze on the mystery of the new birth—the advent of the second Adam. It was the soul of man looking beyond the gloom and darkness in which sin had enwrapped it, into the brightness of that pure light whose shining is "like unto a stone most precious, even like a jasper stone, clear as crystal." And ought not we, who are now called to worship in spirit and in truth, to draw near by faith, and with adoring love gaze upon the incarnate One, until we are transfixed by the awful majesty of that incomprehensible mystery, the Son of God and the Son of Man, offering an atonement for us. We do not realise our sinfulness as we ought, until we place ourselves beside the wise men, and try with them to magnify the Holy Name. Let us endeavour to bring ourselves into the Holy Presence; let each one, in his spirit, stand before the Son of Mary; let us try for a moment to veil His divinity, that we may look on Him as the friend and brother we have wronged; and then let us honestly confess that worship does not gush forth from hearts so foul, until they have first cried out in bitter agony of spirit, "Thou Son of David, have mercy on me!" Each one of us has been baptized into His death; we have put on Christ, because He hath by the Spirit given us the adoption of sons. Is it not our duty to live in Him? We are to be sanctified, as He himself was sanctified, through trial. He may call us to bear and to suffer much; it is ours to submit, and in that suffering, to see our Lord enduring and waiting for the end. We cannot now see why, in God's method of working, we should be called to suffer anguish; perhaps from our earliest years to enter on a life of disappointment: it is enough for us to know that He requires we should suffer. To some there are trials which the heart must endure in silence: the heart knowing its own bitterness, and forbidding the stranger to intermeddle. An error of youth may be the stone of offence, bringing down a life-long punishment. The cry of sorrow may go up, the folly may be as chains to our hands and fetters to our feet; there may be no present help. Are we the less sons of God? No. We may even yet be sons, if in the spirit of the Lord Jesus we say, "Not my will, but Thine be done." He was perfected through suffering, who knew no sin; and who are we, that we should refuse to be chastised? The trials and sorrows, the utter bereavement and desolation of heart, to which some are **called**, are endurable sufferings only, as they are endured **and** suffered in Christ. It is thus that, in some sense, we may ask God to see in our sufferings the great propitiatory suffering of the only true sufferer, Jesus Christ; that He may abide with us to teach us and help us to endure, through the sufferings which **he underwent for us;** thus making our sufferings His, **since nothing of ours is of worth, but as it comes of Him, and is in Him; nor can we endure but in Him.** St. Paul felt that he bore in **his body** the marks of **the Lord Jesus, and** he could forbid us to crucify **the Lord afresh. He knew** well enough that there could be no efficacy in any suffering which we suffer, but he did know that there **was** One who had suffered for all mankind, the Just for the unjust, and that He would place His all-effectual **agony in** the stead of our well-deserved miseries, worthless and **ineffectual,** but as taken upon himself. He suffered for **us. We** have **sinned, and** must suffer. **He** is our **representative.** What Christ **did** for us, was to suffer, that, through Him, our suffering **might be** accepted. Repentance, **sorrow for sin,** self-denial, abasement, must be accompanied **by true suffering;** yet **such** suffering is nothing, but as **in relation to** Christ, and **borne in** Christ. Humanity **in Him was lifted** up; all joy, all **sorrow in Him was fuller and deeper than** was possible to fallen man. **Holy prophets dwelt** with rapture on the glory of His coming, for they saw the bright**ness and** express image of the Father. His glory **and** His **suffering was** the burden of estatic song. "Who **is** this that cometh **from** Edom, with dyed garments from Bozrah? *This* **that is g**lorious in His apparel, travelling in the greatness of His **strength?"**

In all these outpourings of prophetic truth, the true **greatness of the** Saviour is seen only by the Spirit given to man. He only will earnestly **need** a Saviour, who feels a void in his own heart which nothing can fill, nothing satisfy, save the Person of the Son of God. He must be to us a Friend, a Man whose heart **can be touched by our** infirmities; who **knows our sorrows, and can carry them in** His own bosom. He must be the pitying, **loving Saviour, who will hear** His childrens cry—

> When the mourner, weeping,
> Sheds the secret tear,
> God his watch is keeping,
> Though none else is near.
>
> **God will never leave thee;**
> All thy griefs He knows;
> Feels the pains that move thee;
> Sees thy cares and woes.
>
> Jesu, meek and **gentle;**
> Son of God most high;
> Pitying, loving Saviour,
> Hear Thy children's cry.
>
> Pardon our offences;
> **Loose our captive chains;**
> Break down every idol,
> **Which our soul** detains.

Jesus came; the Remedy provided in the purposes of God for sin. In our fall, *i. e.*, in the corruption **of** our nature through sin, our separation from **God** was necessarily effected. Perfect purity could have no sort of affinity with impurity; for the pure must naturally separate and be wide apart from the impure. God is not of like passions with man; He neither curses in hate, nor punishes in hate. He loves the sinner, and would save him. *It is sin* which hates Him, and keeps the sinner from Him. The only way by which the remedy for sin could be effectual, was by the application of the remedy to the soul of man, wherefore Christ came and took our flesh and blood, that, being cleansed by union with the Son of God, humanity may be imparted to us from the Second Adam through sacramental grace. "The wind bloweth where it listeth, and ye hear the sound thereof; but ye cannot tell whence it cometh, nor whither it goeth: so is every one that is born of the Spirit." Marvel not that he said unto you, ye must be born again. The first advent was and is to each human being the remedy for sin. The God Man is the true Tree of Life set in the midst for the healing of the nations. We know neither of remedy nor healing, but by direct application. Supernatural Power has declared that there is a method of healing, and has appointed the conditions under which the application is made, FAITH! which is the very substance of things hoped for; and Repentance. Through his own appointed institution, the Church, He causes the tree of life to flourish and the river of His love to flow, that the poor, weak, wretched sinner may find renewed life and comfort and rest. To enjoy the benefits of this rest, we must pass "through the waves of this troublesome world." Can we forget our forefathers' journey? Were not they all called? But with some of them God was not well pleased. What then? He overthrew them in the wilderness. Beware, oh! beware, Christian pilgrim! The Son of God has struck with His own Blood the very door of our hearts; His Cross, in His own Blood, is stamped upon us; His own Flesh has been given to us as the remedy for sin—the heavenly food, to stay us on our path. Beware then lest we tempt Him, and in the withdrawal of His love there be let in upon us that flood of anger, which cut off the rebellious aforetime, and sank them beneath the very waters which had been salvation. Well may we lay these remembrances to heart and walk sincerely, never trusting ourselves, but seeking the guidance **of the ever blessed** Spirit. **If Christ** cannot **save** the impenitent, the Church cannot do it. **God has not set** His Church for the hypocrite and unbeliever; it is the source of His grace only to the faithful followers of the Lamb. **It is** the Ark to him who carries in his forehead, the unfaded sign of the Cross, and on whose heart is still fresh **and** bright **the precious** sprinkling of the Blood of Jesus.

GOVERNMENT OF THE NATION

SHORTLY AFTER THE ADVENT.

The will of Herod had designated the sons of Malthace his successors. To Herod Antipas were assigned Galilee, and Pœria; to Archelaus, Idumea, Samaria, and Judea. Archelaus entered the Temple after he had celebrated with great pomp the obsequies of his father, and was received by acclamation. The Jews, however, made great demands for restoration of a legitimate successor to the High Priesthood; and in an outburst of fury demolished a golden eagle, which Herod had set up over a gate of the Temple. Archelaus tried to pacify them; but not before a river of blood had flowed was the tumult stayed. Meantime Herod Antipas appealed to Augustus, against what he considered the usurpation of Archelaus. Augustus took time to consider: and instantly intrigue was busy. Archelaus set out for Rome, accompanied by Nicolaus of Damascus to plead his cause, and by the false and wicked Salome, sister to Herod.

Archelaus met with serious opposition. His younger brother Antipas was in Rome maintaining his own rights; on the plea, that his father in a former will and in saner moments had named him successor.

Pending the settlement of these disputes, Sabinus the procurator of Syria, had, on the death of Herod, intended marching into Judea, for the purpose of seizing the **treasures left by Herod, and to obtain military possession. He was at first stayed by Varus, prefect** of Syria, but as **soon as Archelaus set sail and Varus had left** for Antioch, Sabinus **entered the place. All those in charge** refused to comply with the demands of Sabinus **until they had** orders from Rome. Through, however, **the continued wicked** irritation **and** insolence of Sabinus, the Jews broke out **into open insurrection.** Varus was obliged to advance and **restore order.** Instead of removing Sabinus, he left him still **in charge; as a consequence** another rebellion again broke forth. The **outer** courts of the Temple, built of wood and gilded, forming **a** splendid range of building, were set on fire; and in the conflagration many Jews perished. The whole country was one scene of confusion; the Roman government now exercising the most despotic tyranny. Left a prey to bands of marauding soldiery, the **land was laid waste, and the** people frightfully scourged. The Jews now made one more effort for the re-establishment of their ancient constitution. **Five** hundred arrived at Rome for this purpose, and were joined by eight thousand resident in Rome. Alarmed at this, the family of Herod ceased to maintain their own differences, and united to thwart the ambitious designs of the Jews.

It was at this juncture Augustus gave **his** decree. Archelaus was appointed to the sovereignty **of** Judea, Idumæa, and Samaria, as Ethnarch; Herod Antipas **obtained** Galilee and Peræa; Philip, Auranitis, Trachonitis, Panear, and Batanea. The chief cities of Archelaus were Jerusalem, Sebasto (Samaria), Cæsarea and Joppa. Gaza, **Gadara** and Hippo, **as** GREEK TOWNS, were added to the prefecture of Syria. Augustus gave the money Herod left him to two of Herod's daughters, and retained only some plate as a memento of him. Archelaus was thus in possession of Judæa, and commenced a reign which was characterized by cruelty and the most wicked injustice. Accused by his brothers and his subjects of infamous cruelty, Augustus condemned him. He was banished to Vienna, in Gaul, his estates confiscated, and Judæa became a mere Roman Province. Thus nine years after he commenced his reign, the sceptre finally passed from Judah. The kingdom of David and of Solomon became a dependency.

Professor Rawlison truly remarks—" the tone and temper of the Jews at this time, their feeling towards the Romans and towards their neighbours and sects; their confident expectations of a deliverer, are represented by Josephus and other writers in a manner which strikingly accords with the account accidentally given by the Evangelists. The extreme corruption and wickedness, not only of the mass of the people, but even of the rulers and chief men, is asserted in the strongest terms; while, at the same time, testimony is borne to the existence among them of a species of zeal for religion—a readiness to attend the feasts, a regularity in the offering of sacrifice, an almost superstitious regard for the temple, and a fanatic abhorrence of all who sought to change the customs which Moses had delivered." Josephus' own account is—" that time was fruitful among the Jews in all sorts of wickedness, so that they left no evil deed undone; nor was there any new form of wickedness which any one could invent, if he wished to do so. Then they were all corrupt both in their public and private relations; and they vied with each other who should excel in impiety towards God and injustice to men. The more powerful oppressed the common people, and the common people eagerly sought to destroy the more powerful; for the former class were governed by the love of power, and the latter by the desire to seize and plunder the possessions of the wealthy."

If we turn from this picture of Jewish corruption and **ask** what the condition of **Rome was,** history is not slow **in** furnishing us with **an answer. Already it** has been pointed out that Romans, who boasted so much of **their** honourable status, were as accessible to bribes as the poorest wretch whom they subdued. But the depth of moral degradation may be more readily discerned in the lives of the so-called **Roman** celebrities. The haughtiness of Roman pride **brooked no** restraint; a conqueror of men, he was the veriest slave of passion; unbridled license was dignified by him with **the sacred name of Liberty.** Enough is recorded of the violence and rapacity of Roman Proconsuls, Procurators and Governors to illustrate the entire disregard and apparent ignorance of justice. To satisfy the lust of power, and to provide for the fullest and most reckless indulgence **of their** passions was the only aim of life. Who can read the history of the lives of Antony and Cleopatra, of their intrigues and debauchery without immediately seeing **in such** lives a reflection of the lives of the people whom they ruled. The ever swelling tide of iniquity flowed on, and we shrink **from** its contemplation with dread, knowing something of its unfathomable depth from that withering, scathing salutation of the Holy man;—" Oh, generation of vipers, who hath warned *you* to flee from the wrath to **come,"** afterwards addressed to a corrupt people.

It has been already shown how entirely Rome had obtained power over the world; a power exercised with that dexterous caution which cajoles until its hold is safe and firm. "Look," says Dr. Pusey, in his Lectures on Daniel the Prophet, " at the state of the Roman Commonwealth 164 years B. C., the year when Antiochus Epiphanes died.

A generation (only thirty-seven years) had passed since **the second Punic war had** been carried to its own gates; **Carthage, its rival,** still stood over against it. It was **felt by Romans to be a** formidable foe. Witness the "delenda est Carthago," and the unscrupulous policy adopted in encouraging the aggressions of Massinissa. Enriched by the commerce of the west, Carthage was recovering its resources, and fell through its intestine divisions. Egypt and Antioch had lately mustered powerful armies. Perseus, King of Macedonia, **had been but recently defeated, and might have** repelled **the Romans, but for his timidity and** avarice. They **had defeated** Antiochus **the Great,** and by their **enormous fine for** the expenses of the war had crippled him. But true to their policy of dividing and conquering, supporting the weak whom they feared not, against the strong whom they feared, they had diminished the empires which were their rivals, by giving a portion of their possessions to **the** weaker, to be taken at their own will hereafter.

Who should foresee that all these nations should remain blinded by avarice; that common fear should never bind them in one; that they should never see until their own turn came, that Rome used her instruments successively, and flung each aside, and found some excuse **of** quarrel against each, as soon as she had gained her end. To us **it** seems unconceivable that no experience should have opened men's eyes until it was too late. Each helped in turn to roll round the wheel which crushed himself. Rome had, at that time—B. C. 164—no territory East or, except Sicily, **South** of Italy. Massinissa held the Throne of Numidia. **Rome had** not a foot of ground in Africa. In Spain she only **held** so much as had before been in the power of Carthage. **The** Western and Southern Provinces, now Valencia, Murcia, Andalusia, Granada: Gaul and Germany were almost unknown countries. Even Cis-Alpine Gaul had not been formally made a Roman Province; Venetia was friendly; Carniola unsubdued; Istria recently subdued —B. C. 177—Illyricum had now been divided into three, yet left nominally free. The battle of Pydna had destroyed the Kingdom of Macedon four years before—B. C. 168— but it seemed as if Rome knew not how to appropriate territory. She took nothing which she could not at once consolidate. Macedonia was only divided into four independent Republics. The territory which Antiochus was required to cede was given to Eumenes; Lycia and Caria, were taken from the Rhodians and made independent. Such was the impenetrable mask which she wore; every where professing to uphold the weak and maintain justice; every where unjust as soon as the time came; setting free in order to enslave; aiding in order to oppress. Lastly, we have two *Jewish documents*, one a little after the death of Antiochus Epiphanes, the other not later than B. C. 105, with two very different aspects of the Jewish mind toward Romans, the one in Alexandria, the other in Palestine. Yet in neither is there the slightest apprehension of Roman greatness. Again, in another place—" The Prophecy of Malachi is probably contemporaneous with the second visit of Nehemia, 400 B. C. Then prophecy ceased to act. It was exceptional while it lasted. For those five centuries, in the first instance, The Book of Daniel was written. God no longer willed to interfere visibly. Israel, a petty nation, hated, envied, on account of its magnificent claims, that its God was the God of the Whole World, was placed in the highway of the earth, to be trampled on by each in turn. Forerunner of the Christian Church, and destined very shortly to pass into it, it lay for the time, resting on the unseen Providence of God, and awaiting with keener expectation the Deliverer of Itself and the World. It was no longer to have single prophets raised up, to explain to it or to point out God's dealings with it, to preach submission, or to promise mitigation of suffering or deliverance on repentance." THE SHAME OF THE CROSS IS THE TRIUMPH OF PROPHECY. The time came, and then there was general expectation. All men's minds were stirred; the pious were waiting—men were on the look out—there was no doubt among them that Christ was coming; they were like men in a city when some great one is expected. As the time drew nearer they watched each token, that it might be He. "*Art thou He that should come, or do we look for another.*" " If thou be the Christ tell us plainly." The poor Samaritan woman said, " I know that Messiah cometh which is called Christ; when He is come He shall tell us all things." And yet with expectancy so strongly aroused, and longing for the wished for Deliverer, they could not discern the signs of the times, for which they were looking. The Prophet's warning, and the songs in which they hymned the greatness and the glory of Messiah's Kingdom, an empire declared to be Spiritual, were interpreted by decaying Israel as referring to the institution of earthly rule by an earthly king. Accustomed to the ostentatious display of power and magnificence of the Great Princes of the World, they supposed that a Majesty which should pale the dazzling brightness of such crowns, would alone comport with the dignity of a Heaven-born King. The forms of worship which had been given to the Jew, when faithful to the God who blessed him, with the rule and holy treasury of Truth, seemed now only the single political bond, uniting them, keeping, however dimly, in their minds the remembrance of their former national greatness. The interference of political chiefs in the appointment of their own partisans to the High Priesthood and priesthood only tended to lower the tone of religion. Trodden under foot by Roman oppressions, forgetful of the Hand which had so constantly delivered them, they dreamed not that a child of lowly birth would ever be to them a Deliverer.

The decay of their own political position withdrew their thoughts from their true relation to their God. They forgot the reason of their elevated position, and looked only to the maintenance of that position as the all important work of their lives. When He had come, whose character they understood not, nothing gave greater offence than the constant teaching which fell from the Divine lips, leading them to the recognition of those deep and inner meanings of the law, which to them were sacrificed to the very letter. The rumor of the birth of Him who was born King of the Jews, seems to have distressed Herod far more, and to have awakened his suspicions much more than it did even the curiosity of the Jews. To them He had no form nor comeliness, and when they saw Him there was no beauty that they should desire Him. "He was despised and rejected of men." Now, about this time, as we have seen, Rome sat a queen among the nations. Her Sovereign Lord now called "Augustus" a mighty temporal prince. Well might the world wonder at his power, and his subservient subjects say, as did abject Jews, "We have no king but Cæsar." No monarch less powerful; no king less exalted, would restore to the Jew his departed glory. No doubt they looked for one whom they might, in triumph, carry to the Temple; the glorious chant rising up to heaven as the thronging multitude sang out—"Lift up your heads, oh, ye gates, and be ye lifted up ye everlasting doors, that the King of Glory may come in." He came, but this was not the manner of His coming. The world could not understand the depth of His humiliation; how could it know the shame and the degradation which spotless purity was enduring in its contact with sin. Who can measure the agony of that conflict with the author of man's fall, which began even before the young child lingered in the Temple, hearing and asking the doctors questions which it was hard for them to answer. The "Wist ye not that I must be about my Father's business," from a boy twelve years old, must have sounded strangely in the ears of those who could not know, as He knew, the nature of that business which He had to do. Surrounded by no state, the infant of parents from a humble city, who was He, that Jews should accept Him as their king. Yet there were, as we know, circumstances about His advent, that might have satisfied the expectations of those who, from the signs of the times, had been looking for change. The decay of their own national power, the disruption of the religious unity which once bound them so strongly together, the dispersions, that made them citizens of governments which, in their hearts, they did not themselves recognise as having claims on their loyalty, such as they instinctively paid to their own High Priest in their own land; their abject condition, and more affecting still, their social and political state, should have directed their attention to the promises held out to them of a Deliverer. How often had they experienced the truth of the saying, "the battle is not to the strong, or the race to the swift." They knew God often triumphed by means which to them seemed small, and although the words of Isaiah as to the promised Christ were all fulfilled, yet saw they not their fulfillment.

Who but the Jew would utter the lamentation so expressive of deep wretchedness:—"Judgment is far from us, neither doth justice overtake us: we wait for light, but behold obscurity; for brightness, but we walk in darkness." Dependent as they were on an alien ruler, they had become the victims of an oppression, which ever and again provoked resistance. No longer had they perfect control over that, which to them was as their very life, viz.: their Religion; for the very office of the High Priesthood had become politically important to their foreign masters, and even the Temple itself was not free from unwelcomed and uninvited intrusion. We do not wonder that the unostentatious Babe who lay in Bethlehem, should have escaped the notice of the Jewish High Priest and the ever disputing Pharisee and Sadducee of the day. They may have thought the inspired song of the good old Priest, Zacharias, the phantasy of a religious enthusiast; the shepherds' visit and the eastern Magi's oblation, may have appeared to them acts of heathen extravagance. But who can cease to be surprised that the blindness which overtook Israel should have been so great as to have so entirely eclipsed faith in Jesus, as the Christ, since by His sinless life, and in His divine fulfillment of the law of perfect obedience, and by His acts He testified that He was indeed the Christ who should come into the world?

The political condition of Palestine—says Rawlinson—at the time to which the New Testament narrative properly belongs, was one curiously complicated and anomalous. It underwent frequent changes, but retained through them all certain peculiarities, which made the position of the country unique among the dependencies of Rome. Not having been conquered in the ordinary way, but having passed under the Roman dominion with the consent, and by the assistance of a large party among the inhabitants, it was allowed to maintain for a time a sort of semi-independence, not unlike that of various native states in India, which are really

British possessions or dependencies. A mixture, and **to some extent an** alternation, of Roman power with **native, resulted from this** arrangement, **and a** consequent complication **in the** political *status*, which must have made it very **difficult to** be thoroughly understood by any **one who** was **not a** native and a contemporary. The chief representative of the Roman power in the East, **the President** of Syria, the Local Governor, **whether a Herod or a Roman Procurator, and the High Priest, had each and all certain rights, and a certain authority in the country.** A double system of taxation, **a double administration of justice, and even in some degree a double** military command, **were** the natural **consequence;** while Roman customs, Jewish **and** Roman **words,** were simultaneously in use, and a condition of things existed full of harsh contrasts, strange mixtures, and abrupt transitions.

Within the space of fifty years Palestine was a single united kingdom under a native ruler; a set of principalities under native ethnarchs and tetrarchs; a country in part containing such principalities, in part reduced wholly to the condition of a Roman province; a kingdom once more under **a native sovereign; and a** country reduced wholly under **Rome, and governed** by Procurators dependent on the President of Syria, but still subject in certain respects to the Jewish monarch of a neighbouring territory.

CASTING AWAY OF THE JEWS.

"Thus saith the Lord, Where is the bill of your mother's divorcement, whom I have put away? or which of my creditors is it, to whom I have sold you? Behold, for your iniquities have ye sold yourselves, and for your transgressions is your mother put away."

Once again is the bitter lamentation poured forth :—

"There is none to guide her among all the sons whom she hath brought forth, neither is there any that taketh her by the hand of all the sons that she hath brought up. These two things shall come upon thee; who shall be sorry for thee? Desolation and destruction, and the famine and the sword; by whom shall I comfort thee?"

How surely this came to pass is but too painfully evident, and as the hour drew nigh in the which the glory of Israel should be done away, it seems as if the corruptions, political and moral, which surrounded them, increased in depth and violence. The political parties in a government, or of a country, may be disgraced by the offensive immorality of a leader or chief of state; a sovereign may corrupt his court, and bring discredit on the better class of society, yet if the vast mass of the people are penetrated with true morality and love of religion, the ill is comparatively small. Such was not the case with the Jews; their religious belief had waned, and was but a hollow pretence. Long custom had inured them to the observance of religious rites and ceremonies, but religion, as they once enjoyed it, as the deep and energizing principle in their very souls, was gone.

While angry disputations concerning religious ceremonies divided the House of Israel, the authorities of religion saw not the destructive influence which the diffusion of the Greek language and Greek ideas was exercising on the nation; and it is very probable, urges the historian, that the fusion of races had proceeded to a considerable extent, even while they affected to draw the strongest lines of demarkation between one another. Intercourse was mainly between the wealthier and educated classes; and the people saw with some alarm the decadence of their own customs and modes of life. The Pharisees, to avert the loss of national life, vainly endeavoured to retain in the minds of the people the ancient love which they bore to their religion, by insisting upon a rigid adherence to the very letter of both their written and traditional law; and maintained the necessity of ceremonial observances with such vigor, that at length the form was the important, and the spiritual life the unimportant object of all their care and devotion. Discussions on man's immortality, free will, and the non-interference of the Deity with the concerns of the world, were ever engaging the mind of the learned class, and Grecian philosophers contested with the ancient books of the law, supremacy over the mind of Israel. The antagonism raised up between the Pharisees and Sadducees, was but a necessary result of that departure from spiritual religion, which had once been the glory of the Jew. There was nothing in their observances, to withdraw them from the true meaning of that holy worship, which had been divinely established; and it was only when they had emptied ceremony of that, to preserve which ceremony was instituted, they fell into such grievous sin. It is plain that in rites and ceremonies there is no meaningless pantomime; ceremonies either mean a great deal, or they mean nothing; and it is because they are important, that Jehovah was so careful in instituting by his servant Moses, what the exact ceremonial for His worship should be. It was the corruption and exaggerated importance given to ritual, over doctrine and practice, which drew from the Saviour of men His denunciation of the hypocrites who cheated His once chosen people. Had the Pharisees returned to the ancient usages of the Temple service, and have taught the observance of the law of God, rather than the traditions of men, it would have been well for their people. As it was, their gorgeous displays, their long prayers, and their exhibitions at the corners of streets, and in the market places, were better fitted, better adapted to the followers of Socrates, than to the Disciples of the Prophets.

To a people so undone, the vicious life of Romans must have been a fatal example to have had before them. Verily, to a people so circumstanced, it is no wonder their decline should be rapid, and the eclipse of religious truth so complete, that although for a long time the keepers of the truth, yet when the time came, in which it was revealed in all fullness, that "gross darkness was upon them" none could be found to understand that evil days were upon Israel.

"How hath the Lord covered the daughter of Zion with a cloud in his anger, and cast down from heaven unto the earth the beauty of Israel, and remembered not his footstool in the day of his anger.

"The Lord has accomplished His fury; He hath poured out his fierce anger, and hath kindled a fire in Zion, and it hath devoured the foundations thereof.

"The kings of the earth, and all the inhabitants of the world, would not have believed that the adversary and the enemy should have entered into the gates of Jerusalem."

In the midst of such times of rebuke, and blasphemy, and darkness, the dimness was not such as in her vexation, when he afflicted lightly the land of Napthalim and Zebulun, and afterwards did more grievously afflict her "by the way of the sea beyond Jordan in Galilee of the nations." Never but once again may the world witness such disruption of old ideas, such disquiet and looking forward to change. Yet God had not left himself without witness. "I am," said he, "sought of them that asked not for me; I am found of them that sought me not; I said Behold me! unto a nation that was not called by my Name." So, when the Sanctuary, and the name of the Most High, were dishonoured by those who had been, and were even yet, His covenanted people, there were found those who waited for the promises of God. How this expectancy was at last satisfied, is related in the Word of Inspiration.

It must have been a painful period to the faithful remnant, who yet clung to the true glories of Israel. We know what a hard matter it is to serve the World and God at the same time. The more public morality declines, the greater the laxity in religious duty; the more indifferent men become to the calls to holiness and to communion with God, the less energetic, the less deep, the less fervid our love of Him. Hard and bitter temptation fell upon Israel, and it was a punishment to them. We, therefore, with thankful praise in our hearts to God, bless Him for that he permitted even a few faithful and holy ones, to exhibit to us the power of His grace, in the midst of so incredible wickedness.

With the close of the old began the new dispensation. The Jew was not suddenly cast off; on the contrary, he was entreated, pleaded with. The Temple worship was the worship which had been divinely instituted, and was that form of worship offered by our Lord himself, as man to God. In Him was closed the offering of bloody sacrifice by his death, but nowhere do we learn of our Lord's avoidance or condemnation of the worship of the Temple. Yet the Temple was removed, and as the Holy Spirit was pleased to guide and direct, so holy men, immediate followers of our Lord, were inspired to guard the Church of the New Covenant, reconstructed on the old foundations of God's truth and order. The Priesthood was changed from the Aaronic to the Melchisedeckian, of which latter our Lord continues Himself the High Priest. Sacrifices involving shedding of blood ceased, that the One Sacrifice offered may be in perpetual offering before God for men.

Seeing, then, that we have this Priesthood, what manner of persons ought we to be? If the Jew was required to keep himself from pollution of the flesh; an immediate indication of that inward purity which was required of him of God; how much rather should the Christian strive to keep himself from sin. No longer may an inferior animal represent Christ slain for *us;* no longer may we pour out the blood of a brute, as representing satisfaction for sin. We, human beings, baptized into the nature of Christ, *into* His death, are required, each in his own person, to present himself before the Lord, dead unto sin, and; in the place of the bull, the goat, and the heifer, to stand at His most Holy Altar-Table and do that which Jesus did, and desired should be done—present the soul and body to be a Living Sacrifice in Him. Inasmuch as we are unworthy to offer any sacrifice, the Lord Jesus having taken our nature, put away and concealed all its defects, in His own human nature, and having become the Head of Our Race, through suffering, now bids us come to Him, *i. e.*, to present ourselves before God, having in our hands the signs of the Blood of Sprinkling, and about our bodies the marks of the Lord Jesus. Verily, verily the Cup of blessing is the Communion of the Blood of Christ, and the bread which we break is the

Communion of the Body of Christ. This is a solemn thought; as awful as solemn. God requiring of us loyal, devout, holy service, provides for us means whereby we may come acceptably; not that He may send us away empty, but filled with His Grace and Heavenly benediction. He, therefore, plainly tells us, no longer to come with the blood of bulls and of goats, or the ashes of an heifer, but to come with the symbols of the Body and Blood of Christ in our hands, in order that we may, through the power of the Holy Ghost, receive the Body and the Blood of Christ, to the salvation of our souls and bodies.

The Holy Communion is thus, in a very high sense, a Sacrifice, and no Christian man can refuse to receive less than our Lord and Master teaches. It gives man a precious interest in this duty and service; it brings us to a knowledge of the truth, that the gift of Christ will not be bestowed unless we have sacrificed ourselves for Him, *i. e.*, crucified ourselves to the World, given up all our evil ways, and turning to God for pardon, implore the gift of the Body and Blood of Christ, that eating and drinking we may live by Him.

When we read of Israel's fall, we almost all of us, assume the Pharisee's self-complacency. We very seldom think that, practically, Christ is rejected to-day under circumstances of deeper wickedness, than that of which the Jew was guilty. We look upon the suffering, and upon the work of the Lord Jesus, as something done 1800 years ago. It seldom enters into the mind, that the Lamb of God that TAKETH away the sins of the world, is He who, dying on the cross, yet liveth to make intercession for us; and that He pours out from His wounded side that blood, by which alone the dead in trespasses and sins are even still re-animated with life.

> Here, at Thy Cross, my dying God,
> I lay my soul beneath Thy love,
> **Beneath** the droppings of Thy blood,
> **Jesu, nor shall it e'er remove.**

A **cold** and heartless worship is **destructive** of all true, **vital** religion. **God, in bestowing upon us** reason, also gave us emotions, **and** passions, **and senses, all of which are** to be employed to His glory. Above all, **He has promised to us** Faith, the Eye of the Spirit, that we **may see and adore** Him. He bids us come unto Him, and we are bidden with different **objects** in view. At one time, that He may hear our prayer and receive **our** praises, and accept our thanksgivings. At another, that He may hear our supplications. And **more gracious,** more condescendingly merciful than we **know, He bids us come, that our souls and** bodies may be **made clean by His most precious body and blood.** Faith **alone reveals** all this **to us; with carnal sight we** see naught; **with bodily sense we apprehend naught; yet, as He has said, so we must** receive, that, **the Lord Jesus, on the same night** on which He was betrayed, **took** bread, and when **He had given thanks He brake** it, and gave **to His** disciples, **saying, "Take, eat;** this is My Body;" likewise, after supper, He took the cup, saying, **"Drink** ye all of this, for this is my blood **of the** New Testament, which is shed for you, and for many, for the remission of sins."

As the sun is the source of light and warmth **to** this world, so, in a higher, truer, and better sense, **is** the Sun of Righteousness the source of life to **us.** He is the Lamb that was slain **and is alive again, ever making** intercession for us; and when **we** make on earth the representative sacrifice of His death, **He,** actually **in Heaven, is** THE propitiation **for** our sins, and **the only source** from whence is derived to **us** the spiritual **food of His** own most blessed Body and Blood.

> Calvary's mournful mountain climb;
>   There, *adoring at His feet*,
> **Mark that** miracle of time,
>   **God's** own sacrifice complete.
> " It is finished;" hear the cry;
> Learn of Jesus Christ to die.

To the sacrifice of the Son of God, the most wretched sinner must look for salvation. None are too vile to be saved by such a sacrifice. **It is** only they who will **remain** vile that it cannot reach. **There is no other way of salvation.** Christ **alone is the** Saviour. Do not, therefore, say you are too wicked **to serve Him**; but only say—Lord rid me of **my wickedness,** that **I may serve** Thee.

Repentance **is a** gift from God. To Him we are indebted **for that great** gift, that which characterises us from His **mere** brute creation, CONSCIENCE: He has set this **mirror** in our spirits, that it may reflect back upon us, and affright us with, the evil which we suffer to enter in. There are but few diseases which do not give pain; none which sooner or later do not manifest decay and impending ruin. **Sin** is in the spirit of man, disease, and for *its* removal man possesses *no remedy*. He is utterly **powerless to heal** his own infirmity. **Yet there is** salvation. **From first** to last it is salvation effected by another. God, through the pain of a disquieted mind, allows no rest to the wicked soul; and if, haply, the poor wretched outcast, feeding on the husks and garbage of the world's base lusts, is brought to remember his Father's home, let him follow the guiding of conscience, and go to his Father; for here is just the turning point of life or death.

> Just as I am, without one plea,
> But that Thy blood was shed for me,
> **And** that Thou bidst me come to Thee,
> Oh! Lamb of God, I come.

Faith must **concur** with repentance; **it** is involved in repentance; is concurrent with **it**. **The** prodigal had faith that a once kind, good father would even yet be kind **if he went to him** confessing his errors and offences. It is evident that he was sorry for his sins; yet they were still on him. He was not forgiven, and could not be, until he had sought his Father and confessed his sins, and even then he might have been required **to wait forgiveness.** His Father might have thought it necessary **to keep** him **under trial**; it might have so happened that his offences **had** been **oft** repeated; that he had stubbornly gone on in sin, and needed stern rebuke. If so, his Father might have deemed discipline essential to his son's safety. The load of sin is not always **taken off at** once. Repentance first, and then forgiveness. God's ways are just, and he deals with us, as He has disposed an earthly father generally to deal with his children. In one way our Heavenly Father is far more to us. High above all earthly parents, he requires our true, heartfelt humiliation, and He would have us feel that no power less than His, suffices to lift the burden of sin from us. **We** cannot lay it down ourselves, and He means us to feel **that** we cannot. Why? We all must have experienced the physical difficulty of setting down some very heavy weight which **had been put upon us, or** which we had foolishly taken hold of. **In** countries where burdens are carried on the head, we see illustrated the positive inability of **a man to** rid himself of his burden. It must be taken off him. He *desires* to get rid of it, but cannot, so he seeks help. Just so with the crushing weight of sin which we have pressing **us down.** "Come unto ME all that labour and ARE HEAVY LADEN"—this is the cry of Mercy. It is the man weary and worn out with fatigue, who feels his burden heavy. It is **to him that** the offer is made.

In every age **the agent** of sin is busy. We forget **that** there is outside of us a living personal being, who, unseen, is yet ever on the watch to lure us into error. If in the world of nature, matter acts on matter by presence, it has been clearly revealed to us that in the spiritual world spirit influences spirit. It is because most of us have lost sight of the great truth that there is an agent of Evil, while we look only on evil as to something springing up in ourselves, that we have learned to think too lightly of sin. It was not thus that our most blessed Lord was assailed. *No evil* could possibly be *in* Him who knew no sin; therefore the Author of evil attacked Him. If Him, how much more readily sinful, fallen man!

"Satan has desired to have thee, but *I* have prayed for thee, that thy faith fail not." These were the words of Him, who knew better than we can know, the power of the Prince of this world. If we would realize the truth everywhere taught in scripture, that sin is as an impenetrable cloud which shuts us out from the presence of God, hiding Him from us, so that not one ray of love and peace can flow to us while the consuming fire of evil flows in upon us; if we could understand this, we would more earnestly seek in prayer deliverance from the power of Satan.

Temptation is the lot of all men; it is not sin. When we yield to the temptation we have sinned. Temptation is a trial very bitter, very hard to resist. We are told to pray to be kept from falling into it. Whenever, therefore, we are tempted, it is our duty to recognise that it is another power than that of God who is attacking us, and that God has warned us that with the temptation He will make a way of escape. When, for instance, men know that the unnecessary consumption of intoxicating drinks leads to drunkenness, and they wilfully give way to indulgence, and to their abuse; such men not only fall into temptation, but they put themselves into that position from which recovery may become physically impossible. In man such physical weakness **means,** too, moral imbecility. As with drunkenness, so with **every habitual sin; with** the moral there comes the physical **disorder, complicating recovery** and facilitating death. Emotions, passions, the senses, are all good gifts, and are **awakened to action in us through** physical agencies, **or the remembrance of pleasures** which are far more frequently physical **than** mental. **Immoral ideas,** awakened in the immoral by mere passing physical states, are nurtured **and allowed** to remain **in** the mind, in place **of being banished** by voluntary effort and the habitual practice of **keeping** evil **from the mind,** the inculcation of good thoughts, the prayerful **habit,** and the practice of virtue. A good man **will** pass down the street and see not the evidence of evil, **because unaccustomed to hunt it, while** the eye of the sensualist sees it everywhere. **Satan soon** understands us.

The young of the present day **are sorely tried.** Religious liberty is a great blessing, but **it is a dangerous one. To the** *young*, it has been often the source of irretrievable ruin. **We are** no advocates for the restoration of the Roman confessional, but we are advocates for the restoration of that **close** intercourse between priest and people, which the Bible commands. Medical men are now the recipients of confessions made frequently too late. Their ears have poured into them tales of suffering and horror which, at an earlier time, should have been related to some wise counsellor, who may have prevented, by timely advice, great evil, **by** giving to the victim of ungodliness the knowledge of error. It is not wise, it is not right, it is very wrong, to commit the correction of evils which too easily track the footsteps of the young, to those whose office is not to minister about holy things. It is better to prevent an evil than to cure it. We, therefore, honestly say that the ministers of God's Word **and** Sacraments are guilty of most unfortunate, although it may be unintentional, neglect, in not seeking out the young and inexperienced, to explain to them the fearful dangers to which they must inevitably be exposed. We beg not to be misunderstood; we have not said a word concerning the **value of** discipline; individually we may desire it, as directly **bringing** about the close intercourse between pastor and people, which should be restored to the Church. We believe that to the young especially it would lead to a deep conviction of the heinousness of sin, and to a clearer recognition of God's mercy in **forgiveness**. But, quite irrespective of all ministerial absolution, there is need that ministers of religion, as Moral **Educators of** the World, be ready to instruct and reprove, **with all the authority** which is given to them. **We** shall **say no more.**

We are called upon as spiritual beings to contemplate the Birth of Redemption. Dear Christian people, there be **some** among us who now, for the first time, are ready to yield to the movement of the Spirit, as the still small voice calls us to Jesus. To us this beginning of renewed life in Christ, **is as the beginning of** the World's Salvation. We, as He did in the **flesh, must grow in** grace and to fullness of stature. His *ordinary* **method** with us is not from weakness at once to strength; from death to the full vigour of life. St. Paul **was not ashamed to address his** Corinthian **converts** "as unto carnal, *even* as unto babes in Christ." The milk of the Gospel *first*, then the strong meat. **It is thus** God works; every *part* of His work *is* perfect. He pleases to work in part. This earth, and all that **is in it**, was not at **once** prepared, but a long time preparing for man: our forefather fell: salvation was not denied, but the Author of it came **only** in the fullness of time. Do not be disheartened then, **if, after conviction of sin,** your conversion **to** God be slower than **you expected.*** There may be bitter groanings

---

* Holy **Gospel by S.** Luke, lxxii. v. 32.

of spirit, hard trials, sore temptations yet in store. How else can God prove us. We must wait patiently, for *we cannot get salvation of ourselves.* What may we give in exchange for our soul? Nothing. Let us leave that alone. But, bad as we may have been, great as our sins may have been, turning to God with faith in the efficacy of the atoning blood ever flowing from the wounds of the Son of Man, and with nought but true sorrow in our heart for all the evil of our lives, Christ will give pardon. Well may we tremble at the mystery of His cleansing. Christ will heal, let us not reject his method of healing. There was one on whom the power of Christ first fell; who first saw men as trees walking, but who saw all things perfectly on an additional outpouring of Divine Love. The Devil tempted the Divine Lord of Heaven and Earth, not one day, but for forty long weary days and nights did the Holy, Spotless, Blessed Jesus submit to the awful presence of the author of sin. He alone could bear the presence of evil and be unspotted. How can we suppose that Satan will leave us alone, who are so prone to be his willing slaves.

If, then, we are truly in earnest, if sin is felt to be hateful and oppressive, let us think of salvation as it is by Jesus, and in Him alone. No man has seen God at any time, yet God was manifest in the flesh and came among men, that they may be assured that God was, through the Son of Man, reconciling the world unto Himself. If, then, you would draw comfort from the only fount of comfort, look to Jesus as He was with us on earth. Think of Him as the infant lying on his mother's breast: the power of God, and the glory of God, concealed in human weakness. Think of Him as a youth living in a human home, surrounded only by that which the poorest home may possess, the peace of God, and the love of God. Think of Him as a man seeking to fulfil all righteousness; answering Himself the Baptist's call, and on

Jordan's banks, receiving the anointing which His Godhead openly poured on His manhood, self-anointed for the work which He came to perform. Think of Him as a man among men, their brother, ever labouring to open up to them the cause of all sorrow, and shame, and death. In the broad time of day looking out the distressed, that He might heal the sick, that He might cure the leper, and console the poor, that He might claim them as His own, not freed from suffering, but as suffering and enduring in Him. As the great and only High Priest, see Him offering up to God THE SACRIFICE by which, and through which, His work was finished. As the life of Jesus passes before the mind, it is only by meditating on each wondrous stage, that we are able to bear the blaze of glory, which ever and ever shines forth. As the Church brings before us His Advent, it is enough for human weakness that, like the Magi, we fall on our knees and worship Him who is our righteousness; who has come, that men may know how their salvation is secured, and be permitted to look on God and not die. In His humility, in His lowliness, in His submission to the will of God the Father, He is our ensample. He as man, from the manger in Bethlehem to the Mount of Calvary, suffered as no other man could suffer. If we will but follow Him in his life, ours may be more hallowed than it is. How follow Him? The Holy Spirit declares the way. He guides into all truth. Does temptation come upon us, turn to Jesus tempted; turn to Him as the Christ, whose heart so yearned to save fallen man, that agony incomprehensible seized upon Him; His life-giving blood welling forth in great drops of sweat, already the prelude to that overflowing river of life which He came to open, in which man might wash and be clean. Think of Him, gentle, kind, pitiful; now blessing the tender babes; presently loosening the bonds of death. Stand with Him before Pilate's judgment seat, and in every scoff and jeer let us hear the echo of our own insults. Let us walk with Him to the Hall of Pilate, and in the spitting and smiting, recognise **our own** unhallowed deeds. But God grant **we turn not back! Lead us** on, lead us on, all Holy Spirit! even to the **Sacred Mount, and** there lay us down exhausted, **and weary, and faint.** The forgiven Thief is there.

> "See, from His head, His hands, **His feet,**
> Sorrow and love flow mingled down;
> Did e'er such love and sorrow meet,
> Or thorns compose so rich a crown?"

Behold the Lamb of God, who bore
Thy **burdens on the** tree:
He died **the captives to** restore
His blood is shed for thee.

Look to Him till the sight endears
The Saviour to thy heart;
His pierced feet bedew with tears,
Nor from **His Cross depart.**

The habit of meditating **each** day on some portion of the life of Jesus, is one which brings untold comfort to the soul. It **must bring, when we** have done wrong, intense suffering. Yet **it is much better to endure such** suffering, rather than fly from Him?

In temptation **or in trial,** let us learn to think **of the Passion of Jesus;** to look to the five sacred wounds, **and** with them fully in our sight, ask if **we dare pierce Him** afresh. Look on them, and see forever and forever **flowing that** River of Life, to **be washed in which, is to be indeed** cleansed. By those sacred **wounds, may our wounds be** healed; by His agony, **may our sufferings be relieved;** by the outpouring of His most precious **blood, may the** outflowing of our **corrupt and impure** lives be borne away.

CHRISTIAN WORK.

There is a peculiar reticence in the New Testament on the subject of death. The denunciations of the law seem to be suppressed, that the depth and majesty of Christ's Life may shine forth in all its richness and fullness. His Second Advent to claim His own redeemed, is the burthen of the song of the holy ones who live in Him. Death is so swallowed up in His victory over the grave, that nothing else is held before the Christian but the joy of His coming again. Hence Christmas-tide in the Holy Church has ever been a season of great joy and comfort. From age to age, these nearly 1,900 years, Christians have celebrated the first advent as the Day of days; now as then, the Angels' song is hymned, and million voices echo back to heaven, "Glory to God in the Highest." The earth seems full of the goodness of God, and heart answers heart, as Christ's Nativity is named. To enter into the fullness of joy which such hallowed love for Jesus awakens, we are required to lead a life of watchful care, of self-denial and charity. To be a Christian is no easy victory over death. It implies "*duties performed*," not sentiments or belief uttered. "Not every one that saith Lord! Lord! but he that doeth the will of my Father which is in heaven." To feed the hungry, to clothe the naked, to pity the distressed, to visit the widow and orphan in their affliction, these are some of the works which He hath given us *to do* until His coming again. Where these works abound, faith is likely to abound. We cannot discharge these trusts by deputy. No amount of public charity, as it is called, no delegated nursing and care of God's sick poor, will deliver the Church of God from the sin of disobedience, which He will condemn in His own fore-spoken words, "Inasmuch as ye *did it not* unto the least of these, ye did it not unto me." Remembering that His Church is His body corporate; each member of that body has a Christian duty to perform; and as He has given divers gifts, and has set each member in its place in the body, so most assuredly will He require at our hands, the work those hands should have performed. We have two words in our language which are unfortunately indifferently used—benevolence and charity. A government may be benevolent; *its* benevolence cannot stand in stead of the charity required of the members of Christ. Those who cannot worship together as the body of Christ, but worship apart, divided and estranged, may unite for works of benevolence and humanity; but they cannot discharge the offices of acceptable charity *in* Christ. Is Christ divided? Again, do not let us deceive ourselves; Christianity does not consist in going to church to say prayers once a week, and through the rest of the week to get money, and despise works of charity. At present we nowhere see Christianity exercising itself in this our own land, in visible strength and vigour. A house divided against itself, we are in danger of falling; one is of Paul, another is of Apollos, and so true Christian work is hindered, and God's vineyard defaced. Yet we may pray and strive to put away these hurtful things; at the Sacrifice of Praise and Thanksgiving we may remember Zion. There is an earnest now stirring men's hearts that cannot be stilled. For 300 years and more, the Church of England has been contending and disputing. The time has come in the which she must work **if she is to live.** In England **the poor, the sick, and** the outcast, are now looked for, and **the arms of Christ,** through His Church, are carrying the **little ones He loves.** No longer abandoning the poor alone to **the** benevolence of the state, alarmed at the frightful miseries which they suffer in the state **Bastiles called** poorhouses, conscious of the neglect **of works of charity,** the earnest and zealous of the **Church in England,** labour to mitigate wretchedness **too horrible to** be allowed **to continue.** There **is Christian work for** Christian hands everywhere. It cannot **be that God will suffer His poor to be** neglected.

That the people have been estranged **from the** Church of **England is a** truth **not** to be denied. In America she is making her way, but among what classes? The easy-going accumulators of wealth. Where are the **poorer classes?** Almost to a man the better-to-do, among *them*, are not with **her.** Why is this? The answer is—She said but did **not!** With a clearer recognition of duty, a change **is passing over her condition;** with a true, loyal devotion to Christian duty, **men and women now devote themselves to** works, the fruit of a living, energising **faith.** The more wealthy **cease to** waste means on frivolity, and female labour finds **occupation,** while numbers devote their time **to** intercourse **with** the less wealthy and afflicted. Above all, **religion is being** made more a habit of life than a sentiment. **Its duties are more** palpably demonstrated, **and not** only its compati**bility** with, but its necessity to, **true** happiness rendered **more** apparent. For the full effect **of** this awakening **we** must **wait and** pray. "**Shew me** thy faith by thy works" is the demand **made on Her** by those who would **enter** into her fold. Disintegration will stop and **vigorous** health return when **the battle** for **truth** shall have been **won.**

There are works of pressing need. They must be begun. If the Church, in her corporate capacity, is not yet prepared to undertake neither the education of her children, nor the care of the sick, individual members are required, in the several states of life to which they are called, to fulfil the duties of their respective stations. Christianity is not a mere speculative belief; to be a Christian is to be, in however remote a degree, a follower of its Author and Founder.

His life was one of unwearied toil, instant in season and out of season. He went about doing good. Obedient to the law, he fulfilled all its requirements. Seeking not His own, He sought to glorify His Father. In His ministration on earth, the well-being of men was His aim. To win souls to Himself, and to draw all men unto Himself, was the incessant labour of days, and the prayerful intermediation of night-long vigils. "I pray not for these alone, but for those that shall believe through them." "I will pray the Father for you, and He will send you another Comforter, that He may abide with you forever." What a wonderful outpouring of Divine love is that xvii. chap. of St. John! There the triumph of the Cross is declared by Jesus Himself. He is glorified in them whom He has redeemed. He asks nothing amiss; nothing incompatible with God's justice. He asks not for the world, but for them which were given Him. Over and above all this incomprehensible condescension on our behalf, are His mighty acts. Now, in manifestation of His divine power, He stoops to be the guest of publicans and sinners; to-morrow He makes known to an outcast woman that her sins are known; again, He restores to a bereaved mother, and she a widow, her dead son. Day by day He patiently is with His disciples, instructing, exhorting, revealing Himself. Thus Christ was the Worker. He came *to do* His Father's will, not to think what His Father's will was.

Now, each member of Christ may ask, as was very naturally asked of old, "Lord, what wouldst thou have me to do?" But one answer can be returned: Believe only on the Lord Jesus, and thou shalt be saved. Here explanation is necessary, in order to know the results which should follow on the declaration of such belief. Faith without works *is dead*. If you believe that Jesus is the Christ, then you can no longer be dead in trespasses and sins; you are alive in Christ Jesus. If alive, then that life must be manifest in good works. The body is dead because of sin, but alive in Christ Jesus our Lord.

> "If in our daily task our mind
> Be set to hallow all we find,
> New treasures still, of countless price,
> God will provide for sacrifice.
> The trivial round, the common task,
> Will furnish all we need to ask;
> Room to deny ourselves; a road
> To bring us daily nearer God."

Now our works are in themselves nothing. At best we are unprofitable. But see how kind and good God is. Whatever work we may do, as the result of the Life of Christ working in us, God accepts that work on account of His own most blessed Son. What are some of the works we have to do? Prayer, the prayer of faith, and the worship of God; obedience to the will of God; denying ourselves for the sake of Christ; restraining our evil passions, evil thoughts, evil desires; relieving each other's distress; comforting the poor and needy; visiting the sick; contributing to the necessities of the saints; taking care of the fatherless and widow. Now suppose this very Christmas, or at any time, the poorest person in our midst was to say, which of these works may I, poor sinful being, undertake for Christ my loved Master's sake? My dear brother, we would answer, any one you please: but to satisfy your question we will select one for you. Take up, heartily, for Christ, one only, as your work for the coming festival: "Contribute to the necessities of the saints." Why do you ask me to do this, the most impossible work of all for me, a poor, humble cottager, to accomplish? My friend, poor as you may be, if you please you may enrich others. Pray for the kingdom of Christ, for in-gathering of the harvest. Has it never struck you that you may, by your own prayers, if not by your own exertion, do much? yes by exertion, and by inducing others to aid in the work, you may very materially help on the missionary cause of the Church. Do you not know that twelve pence, given by every member of the Church in Canada, would put her in possession of funds to send the sacred ministry to every parish in the land? Here the widow's mite thrown into God's treasury becomes wealth indeed. A drop of cold water given to a disciple in the name of the Master, is not to go unrewarded. Work, Christian, work! and shew your faith by your works. Do not for a moment stop to question the result, but work. Do not be forever saying Lord! Lord! but do the will of God. Have you a sin which tracks your every step? Be persuaded to seek the sinner's Friend, and, resolving to be free, meekly sue for strength to be free; not once, not twice, but go on to "seventy times seven." Strive and work, work and strive.

"My Saviour, as Thou wilt!
　　Though seen through many a tear,
　Let not my star of hope
　　Grow dim and disappear.

"Since Thou on earth has wept,
　　And sorrowed oft alone,
　If I must weep with Thee,
　　My Lord, Thy will be done!"

Is there any one too poor to do that which their Lord did? Take young children upon their knees, put their hands upon them and bless them? May not the poorest Christian man or woman, in this day of rebuke and misbelief, call children to them and instruct them in the sure mercies of Jesus? Now, if ever; Sunday Schools are most important aids to true religion. Why not work a work for Christ through them, and diligently give yourselves up to teaching the little ones the truth as it is in Jesus? There is something very pleasing in the instruction of the young, which compensates for the trouble inseparable from teaching. If we enter upon the task, with an eye to the glory and love of Christ, the duty becomes one of pleasure and profit. In preparing for such work with a true and loyal spirit of devotion, the pupil will soon understand that his teacher "has been with Jesus." It is impossible prayerfully to read His Sacred Word, and to meditate thoughtfully on His blessed life, without feeling, through the influence of the Holy Spirit, the impress of that life on us. Here, then, is another widow's mite which may be thrown into the treasury of God.

Are any too poor but that they may find some spare time to wait by the couch of sickness, and even for a brief space to pour into the ear of the burthened soul, some of those soft sweet words which fell from Him, Who wept at the distresses of His poor servants. To those whose circumstances may permit a larger devotion of time to Christian works of charity, let the words of the holy St. Paul linger in their memories: "the women who laboured much in the Lord." There are many hundreds who yearn to do something for Christ, and would gladly (in His poor) minister to Him. In large towns and populous cities, many souls are perishing for want of common care.

Infirmity, want, sickness, evil example, and most awful pollution, hurry immortal souls onward to destruction. Single-handed, the clergy cannot contend effectually against the surging sea of vice and misery. If God should move the hearts of faithful men and women to give themselves to the work of winning these for Christ, help on the work, and deter it not. Again, women of the Church of England, keep in your minds "the women who LABOURED much in the Lord." Work is a duty, it is not of merit. We are too apt to run away with the notion that we can do something to please God; that is, to do something *of ourselves*. Now we must just give that notion up. We can do nothing at all of ourselves well pleasing to God; but we may do a very great deal that He *will accept*, because it is done in the Name and for the sake of His dear Son. If this be so, how much brighter our task. "Work while it is now called to-day, for the night cometh when no man can work." Resolve that from henceforth our work shall be daily and nightly to pray to, to praise, and to bless God; to be kindly affectioned one to another; to live soberly and chastely; to swear not; to curse not; to labour diligently to get our own living; and to live in unceasing expectation and hope of the coming of the Lord. Little ones in Christ! Jesus is your Saviour and friend. The stern aspect in which religion is generally represented to the young, is not that which the blessed Saviour represented in His contact with you. The " Suffer the little children to come unto me, and forbid them not," indicates the deep yearning of His heart to have such tender objects of love near Him. His denunciation of those who would injure them—the declaration that their angels do behold the face of His Father—His imperative command "Feed my lambs"—and lastly, the declaration, "Whoso doth not receive the Kingdom of Heaven as a little child, shall not enter therein"—all point to the interest which Jesus takes in the welfare of the young. It is certain that the young are capable of understanding the meaning of religious service at an earlier age than is generally supposed. Very often they enter with deep interest into the nature of events which older persons pass by; and if the instruction in religion be made pleasing by representing the gentle Saviour as the author of all love, and joy, and happiness, and as ever pleased to see them happy, you cannot but love Him; and as a rule children will learn to love Him. To the elder ones who are more advanced, the young, who are at that dangerous age when animal life is bursting into power, there is need that you should know of the existence of an author of Evil, who dared to tempt even your own Lord; a Being, personal, active, evil-disposed to man and the children of men, He is emphatically called in scripture "THE TEMPTER." Base suggestions spring up in the mind; fatal desires and evil passions struggle within us; how resist these? By the memory of the existence of One, and the seeking help from that One, who came to seek and to save lost and fallen man; One who does not put before man false hopes, delusive pleasures, and misconceived happiness; but One who exemplified to man that in this life there is probation, and trial, and sorrow; that in this world the prince of the power of evil, afflicts and assails the children of light, as even he assailed the Son of God. To this hour the malignity of Satan's power is exhibited in his detestation of youthful purity. The moral condition of the children both of the rich and of the poor,—the depravity which no longer hides itself in narrow streets and lanes,—the ever-increasing number of children abandoned to vice,—but too plainly testifies that it is here the ever-active enemy of man gathers in the victims of his wiles. "Even the sea monsters draw out the breasts;

they give suck to their young ones. The daughter of my people is become cruel, like the ostriches in the wilderness. The tongue of the sucking child cleaveth to the roof of his mouth for thirst; the young children ask bread, and no man breaketh it unto them." Yes, this is so, and what are we doing to save these unfortunate children of sin?

How, then, may we keep Holy Day, and make no effort to win these lost ones for Christ? To oppose a personal enemy, we must personally exert ourselves. Education, as it is carried on, does not reach the truly poor; Sunday Schools seldom succeed in bringing them within their influence. Christian men and women, study to remedy the evil ere it be too late. There is to be a time of desolation, in the which iniquity is to abound. Let this hallowed season of Christmas be passed in offering up prayers to God, that He may give us wisdom sufficient to work for the cure of this great evil. In the Holy Commemoration, supplicate Him who, as a little child, lay neglected and despised, that He would give to His people the ability and the will to minister to the wants of the poor despised children of the streets. Wise men brought to Him gifts of gold, frankincense and myrrh. Why should we refuse to offer Him the acceptable service of bringing to Him the child from whose brow Satan was effacing the Cross. Is it impossible to institute one factory school in which some of the children may be taught, not the art of reading and writing only, but in which they may be instructed in those holy truths, and taught to walk in those godly ways, which may alone save them? It is said that money is to be saved to the revenue of this Country by cessation of grants to Collegiate institutions. Money is provided for our Common Schools, in which the poor find no room. Why not establish boarding factory schools for the vagrant class, to which children should be sent, under compulsion? We have begun at the wrong end. A Reformatory is now necessary because we are false to the poor: it would in very few years be useless if in its place, and at the same cost, we had two or three large boarding schools for the young of the class to which allusion is made. The Common School system stops short at the very point where it might be useful. We do not think that children at present excluded from the Common Schools should be admitted there, nor do we believe that day schools would be productive of real benefit. Children who have base parents, unable to guide themselves or their children, should have such children taken from them for education. It is the law now, only the law is set in motion against the criminal child, and not against the parent. We take the child too late, and often make him ten-fold more the child of the Devil. Familiarized with evil from earliest infancy, witnesses of profligate and dishonest life, how are they to flee from the Sodom and Gomorrah which consumes them, unless some hand, for Christ's sake, pluck them from the burning? We boast ourselves in the possession of a pure faith; we point with intense satisfaction to the effects of the Reformation on the character of Englishmen; would to God we could point with equal pride to works correspondent to that faith! What Xavier will arise, to take these babes in his arms and lay them gently, a Christmas offering, at the foot of the Cross?

BABE OF BETHLEHEM, HEAR!

THE KINGDOM OF CHRIST.

"The people that walked in darkness have seen a great light: they that dwell in the land of the shadow of death, upon them hath the light shined.

"Thou hast multiplied the nation, and not increased the joy: they joy before thee according to the joy in harvest, and as men rejoice when they divide the spoil.

"For thou hast broken the yoke of his burden, and the staff of his shoulder, the rod of his oppressor, as in the day of Midian.

"For every battle of the warrior is with confused noise, and garments rolled in blood: but *this* shall be with burning and fuel of fire.

For unto us a child is born, unto us a son is given: and the government shall be upon his shoulder, and his name shall be called Wonderful, Counsellor, The Mighty God, The Everlasting Father, The Prince of Peace.

"Of the increase of *his* government and peace *there shall be* no end, upon the throne of David, and upon his kingdom, to order it, and to establish it with judgment and with justice from henceforth even for ever. The zeal of the Lord of hosts will perform this."

The slaughter of the innocent children by Herod was the first act of violence which wrung the hearts of bereaved mothers, whose babes were, unknown to themselves, baptised in the Saviour's blood. The violent outcry raised by the priests against the new-born King, so soon as He began to demonstrate the love and purity of His life; the quiet, unostentatious exercise of unlimited kindness and mercifulness to the poor, the halt and the blind; the scathing rebuke and exposure of hypocrisy, soon drew around the wonderful Son of Mary a companionship and fellowship on which was laid the foundation of divine power and goodness in the kingdoms of the world.

Our most **blessed** Lord and Saviour proclaimed not His advent to be **the** establishment of the earthly throne of David; no heralds, trumpet-tongued, demanded for Him the homage of **men.** He came to conquer Hell and Death, by the irre**sistible** majesty of His nature, and to demonstrate the innate **power of** Virtue over Evil. It is said **of** Him, "He went about doing good;" and **this but the confirmation of the** assertion made in His boyhood: **"Wist ye not that I must be** about my Father's **business?"** With no imperious demonstration of authority, He **yielded** himself **up in perfect obedience to accomplish His Father's will. Submitting to every** requirement **of the law, he failed not in one jot** or tittle **till all was fulfilled.** He never denied his Sonship, **nor** did **He ever fail, when** questioned as to His office, **to** intimate **or to declare that** His Kingdom was not of this world. For thirty-three years He was the Missionary Labourer, **incessant,** courageous, abundant in His efforts **to save** Israel and **to open the** Kingdom of Heaven to all **believers. But for men's opposition, Eden might have been new-planted among them.**

He came, however, "not to bring peace, but a sword."

"Who *is* this that cometh **from Edom, with** dyed garments from **Bozrah?** this *that* is glorious **in his apparel,** travelling in the greatness of his **strength?** I that speak in **righteousness, mighty to** save.

"Wherefore *art thou* red in thine apparel, and **thy garments like him that** treadeth in the winefat?

"I have trodden **the winepress alone; and of the people** *there was* none **with me:** for I will tread **them in mine anger, and trample them in** my fury; **and their** blood shall be **sprinkled upon my garments,** and I will stain all my **raiment.**

"For the day of vengeance *is* **in mine heart,** and the year of **my redeemed** is come.

"And **I looked, and** *there was* **none to** help: and I wondered that *there was* none to **uphold: therefore** mine own arm brought salvation unto me; and my fury, it upheld me."

And I will tread down the people in mine anger, and make them **drunk** in my fury, and I will bring down their strength to the earth."

Coming to His own, they received Him not. Perverting the sayings of prophets and teachers, corrupting the law of their God, and by their traditions setting aside His word, they looked for the advent of an earthly king, not their Lord from heaven. Long before, they had been warned of their apostacy; from age to age their defection was made known to them; and now that it *was* upon them, they knew not the time of their visitation.

"Who hath believed our report? and to whom is the arm of the Lord revealed?

"For he shall grow up before him as a tender plant, and as a root out of a dry ground: he hath no form nor comeliness; and when we shall see him, *there is* no beauty that we should desire him.

"He is despised and rejected of men; a man of sorrows, and acquainted with grief: and we hid as it were *our* faces from him; he was despised, and we esteemed him not.

"Surely he hath borne our griefs, and carried our sorrows: yet we did not esteem him stricken, smitten of God, and afflicted.

"But he *was* wounded for our transgressions, *he was* bruised for our iniquities: the chastisement of our peace *was* upon him; and with his stripes we are healed.

"All we like sheep have gone astray; we have turned every one to his own way; and the Lord hath laid on him the iniquities of us all.

"He was oppressed, and he was afflicted, yet he opened not his mouth: he is brought as a lamb to the slaughter, and as a sheep before her shearers is dumb, so he openeth not his mouth.

"He was taken from prison and from judgment: and who shall declare his generation? for he was cut off out of the living: for the transgression of my people was he stricken.

"And he made his grave with the wicked, and with the rich in his death; because he hath done no violence, neither *was any* deceit in his mouth."

It was impossible that "the Prince of the Power of The Air" should abate aught of His Malice or withdraw his deceivableness, incapable as he was of knowing who it was he contended with. He knew full well that there was a Person living with men, moving among them, influencing them, and drawing them from him. He could discover the mysterious meekness, the spotless innocence, the unsullied purity of Him whose presence in this scene of his temporary triumph troubled him. He knew not the Son of God. No wonder, then, that Satan should put forth all his might to dethrone Him who was born King of the Jews.

The corruption of Israel, only too ready to be corrupted, is summed up in a few words: "My house *is* the house of prayer, but ye have made it a den of thieves."

To repair the waste places, to heal the broken-hearted, and to reclaim the misguided lost sheep of the fold was the work which the Son of man undertook.

To ease the burthen, and to let the oppressed go free, He fulfilled the law, and, as man, for man came to purchase salvation. Born of God, He came not after the will of the flesh, but from God, in order that man might be re-constructed, not in the image of the flesh of man who had fallen and was corrupt and become abominable in God's sight, but after the likeness of the Lord Christ Himself, who was born of God, and took on Him flesh of the Virgin. It was to bring new life, to work a change in man's nature, to put into his weak, sin-cursed spirit the *capacity* to be like Himself, and from whose Nature and by whose nature that capacity is bestowed. Christ so coming in The Flesh, called Himself The Second Adam, The Quickenning Spirit, The God-man. The Fountain of Life, The Lamb of God that taketh away the sins of the World, The Head of His body The Church. This is The Eternal Being, who alone could free men from the terrors of the Law and bring them perfect freedom by the establishment of The Kingdom of Grace. No longer bound down to a slavery in the flesh, Christ set us free, that The

Spirit, rising in imparted strength, might serve Him without fear. No longer of the world, but for a while left in the world, His chosen ones, His elect are to yield up their members to His Spirit, and to make preparation for another and a better country.

To lead them on the way, and to keep them in the way, He faltered not, but amid cruel desertion, heartless rejection, perpetual rebukes and blasphemies, His cry was one unceasing call to repentance and to promised happiness in The Father's love.

"Awake, awake; put on thy strength, O Zion; put on thy beautiful garments, O Jerusalem, the holy city: for henceforth there shall no more come into thee the uncircumcised and the unclean.

"Shake thyself from the dust; arise, *and* sit down, O Jerusalem: loose thyself from the bands of thy neck, O captive daughter of Zion.

"For thus saith the LORD, Ye have sold yourselves for nought; and ye shall be redeemed without money.

"For thus saith the LORD GOD, My people went down aforetime into Egypt to sojourn there; and the Assyrian oppressed them without cause.

"Now, therefore, what have I here, saith the LORD, that my people taken away for nought? they that rule over them make them to howl, saith the LORD; and my name continually every day *is* blasphemed.

"Therefore my people shall know my name: therefore *they shall know* in that day that I *am* he that doth speak: behold, *it is* I."

A remnant was saved. Mourning, weeping over Jerusalem, The Holy City, He saw it crumbled into dust not one stone left upon another. The Temple was destroyed, and in three days there arose a Temple not made with hands, not of this building, but the true Temple of God into which He has taken our Flesh, that all they whom He should call and draw unto Himself, might worship God in Spirit and in Truth.

In Christ, the true Temple, the tribes now worship, nay, nay, they dwell in Him, and must needs worship Him; for they as lively stones are built up a spiritual house, built upon the foundation of apostles and prophets, Christ being the Chief Corner Stone.

Christ has become thus our Redeemer. Experience, **fully** coinciding with revelation, attests the inability of **human** nature to satisfy its end, without the necessary **means.** The discovery of these necessary means, by man was impossible, and he had therefore revealed **unto** him, that will of his Creator, **how he may** best satisfy **the** object or end of his **creation.** The whole object of **this revelation** is to **explain the** relation which man has to his **God**, and to declare **those** obligations under which his **nature** places him. **What has been** lost, and what has to be regained, and **how it is to be** regained, is revealed and manifested. **Disobedience in Adam,** obedience in Christ—Human nature ruined, the ruin repaired.

Well may it be said: "They were astonished **at His** doctrine: for his word was with power." For **with such** doctrine as salvation in Jesus Christ, man as an animal has **only a secondary interest.** The exhibition of such profound **agonizing love as is exhibited in** the character of the second **Adam, can only be understood by a** being whose nature is undying, **spiritual, and which** being spiritual he cannot if he would, **change. Man is a** living spirit, and **must ever and** for ever **live; live in** the nature which Christ **restores to** him, or in Adam's nature, blasted and undone. By revelation from God, **we learn of** the **consequences of the** Fall, and of the glorious **and merciful** promises immediately subsequent thereto; and from **that** instant, the promise was and is, the recovery of mankind through a recoverer.

Age after age mankind has joyed in this truth, because it has been **felt by the universal** world, that there is a universal need **of happiness, and it is found** that by **no other** scheme than that **declared by God can true** happiness be attained.

"Ho! every one that thirsteth, come ye to the waters; come buy and eat: yea come, buy wine and milk without money and without price. Incline your ear, and come unto me and your soul shall live; and I will make an everlasting covenant with you, even the sure mercies of David." "Behold, I have given him for a witness to the people, a leader and commander to the people."* "For Moses truly said unto the fathers, a prophet shall the Lord your God raise up unto you of your brethren like unto me, him shall ye hear in all things whatsoever he shall say unto you." And, elsewhere: "Arise, shine; for thy light is come, and the glory of the Lord is risen upon thee. For, behold, the darkness shall cover the earth, and gross darkness the people: but the Lord shall arise upon thee, and his glory shall shine upon thee. And the Gentiles shall come to thy light, and kings to the brightness of thy rising." "For Christ our Passover is sacrificed for us; therefore let us keep the feast, not with the old leaven, neither with the leaven of malice and wickedness, but with the unleavened bread of sincerity and truth."—1 Cor. c. v., vs. 7-8. "Rend your hearts, and not your garments; and turn unto the Lord your God; for he is gracious and merciful, slow to anger, and of great kindness, and repenteth him of the evil."—Joel, c. ii., v. 13. "Circumcise yourselves to the Lord, and take away the foreskin of your heart, ye men of Judah and inhabitants of Jerusalem."—Jeremiah, c. iv., v. 4. "Incline your ear, and come unto me: hear, and your souls shall live."—Isaiah, c. lv., v. 3. "For thus saith the high and lofty One that inhabiteth eternity, whose name is holy: I dwell in the high and holy place, with him also that is of a humble and contrite spirit, to revive the spirit of the hum-

---

* Isaiah lv.

ble, and to revive the **heart of** the contrite ones; for I will not contend **for** ever, neither will I be wroth; for **the spirit** should **fail** before me, and the souls which I have made."—Isaiah, c. lvii., v. 16. "Thus saith the Lord that **made thee,** and formed thee from the womb, which *will help thee:* **Fear** not, O Jacob, my servant, and thou Jeshurun whom I have chosen; for I will pour **out water upon him** that is thirsty, and floods **upon the dry ground; I will** *pour out my spirit upon thy seed*, and my blessing upon thine offspring."—Isaiah, c. xliv., v. 3. "Turn ye from your evil ways, and keep my commandments and my statutes, according to all the law which I command your fathers, and which I sent to you by my servants the prophets."—2 Kings, c. xvii., v. 13. "**For** verily I say unto you, till heaven and earth pass, **one** jot or one tittle shall in **no** wise pass from the law till all be fulfilled. Whosoever therefore shall break **one of these** least commandments, and shall teach **men so,** he shall be called least in **the** kingdom of heaven; but whosoever shall *do* and teach them, the same shall **be called great in the kingdom of heaven."—St. Matthew, c. v., v. 15. And in the New Testament some of the** qualifications for this **state of blessed rest from sin to which** man is called are given in the words of the Lord of that kingdom:

"Blessed *are* the poor in spirit, for theirs is the kingdom of heaven. Blessed *are* they that mourn: for they shall be comforted. Blessed *are* the meek: for they shall inherit the earth. Blessed *are* they which do hunger and thirst after righteousness: for they shall be **filled.** Blessed *are* the merciful: for they shall obtain mercy. Blessed *are* **the** pure in heart: for they shall see God. Blessed *are* the peacemakers: **for** they shall be called the children of God. Blessed *are* they which are persecuted for righteousness' sake: for **theirs is the** kingdom of heaven. Blessed are ye, when men **shall revile you, and persecute you, and** shall say all manner of evil against you **falsely, for** my sake; **rejoice and** be exceeding glad: for great is your reward in heaven: for so persecuted **they** the prophets which were before you. Ye are the **salt of the earth: but if the** salt hath lost its savour, wherewith shall it be salted?

It is thenceforth good for nothing but to be cast out, and to be trodden under foot of men. Ye are the light of the world. A city that is set on an hill cannot be hid. Neither do men light a candle and put it under a bushel, but on a candlestick; and it giveth light unto all that are in the house. Let your light so shine before men, that they may see your good works, and glorify your Father which is in heaven. Think not that I am come to destroy the law, or the prophets. I am not come to destroy, but to fulfil. For verily I say unto you, till heaven and earth pass, one jot or one tittle shall in no wise pass from the law, till all be fulfilled. For I say unto you, that except your righteousness shall exceed the righteousness of the Scribes and Pharisees, ye shall in no case enter into the kingdom of heaven."

Except as a revelation to man from a divine source, we cannot understand the full meaning of the great principles contained in the concise and emphatic promises thus drawn up for our comfort and assurance of eternal rest. Certainly in none of the systems of philosophy do we find a standard of excellence so pure, so lofty, so truly declarative of the dignified position to which human nature must attain; well, indeed, may the best of us say, "such knowledge is too wonderful for me: I cannot attain unto it." Nor is it a false conception of our own power which induces the utterance of so humiliating an acknowledgment. Man as a heathen, as an alien from the commonwealth of Israel, can of himself know nothing of God's perfect law, nor can he of himself understand how to minister to his own true wants. It is only when by God's free grace he *is* chosen, and elected, into the Covenant of mercy, it is only when he has been buried by baptism into Christ's death, and has received that one baptism for remission of sin, whereby he may cry Abba! Father! and by fulfilling all the requirements which that sacrament of responsibility imposes upon him, that it is possible for him to know and to believe and to receive unto active obedience the unsearchable riches of Christ. So it is not that we are left in doubt: no man can go to Christ except the Father draw him; and God has been pleased to appoint ways to draw men: through the Holy Ghost, speaking by the ministry of his word, by the gift of the Holy Ghost regenerating us in baptism, and by the renewing of our weak and wavering spirit, through his Word by the Blessed Sacrament. He promised to accomplish this, for he said: "I will pour upon the house of David and upon the inhabitants of Jerusalem the spirit of grace and supplication; and they shall look upon him whom they have pierced, and they shall mourn for him, as one mourneth for his only son, and shall be in bitterness for him, as one that is in bitterness for his first born."—Zec., c. xii., v. 10. "Ye are the children of the prophets, and of the covenant which God made with our fathers, saying unto Abraham, and in thy seed shall *all the kindreds of the earth* be blessed."—Acts, c. iii., v. 25. "For we are his workmanship, created in Christ Jesus unto good works, which God hath before ordained that we should walk in them. Wherefore remember, that ye being in time past Gentiles in the flesh, who are called uncircumcision in the flesh made by hands, that at that time were without Christ, being aliens from the commonwealth of Israel and strangers from the covenant of promise, having no hope and without God in the world. But now in Christ Jesus ye who sometime were far off are made nigh by the blood of Christ:" Such is the Christ. "I am Alpha and Omega, the beginning and the ending, saith the Lord, which is and was and which is to come, the Almighty."—Rev., c. i., v. 8. "I am that I am," and being so, thus shalt thou say unto the children of Israel: "I am hath sent me unto you."—Exodus, c. iii., v. 14. Isaiah, in c. lxi., proclaims Christ as the great deliverer and source of man's life:

"The Spirit of the **Lord God** *is* upon me: because **the** Lord hath anointed me to preach good tidings **unto the** meek; he hath **sent** me to bind up the broken-hearted, to proclaim liberty to the captives, and the opening of the prisons to them that are **bound**. To proclaim the acceptable year of **the** Lord, and the day of vengeance **of** God; to comfort all that mourn. To appoint unto them that mourn **in Zion, to** give unto them beauty for ashes, the **oil of joy for mourning, the garment of praise for the** spirit of heaviness; that they might be called trees of righteousness, the planting of the Lord, that he might be glorified. **And they shall build the old wastes,** and they **shall raise up the former desolation, and they shall repair the** waste cities, **the desolations of many generations. Strangers shall stand and feed** your flocks, and the sons of the alien *shall be* **your ploughmen and your vinedressers.** But ye shall be named the Priests of the Lord : *men* shall **call you** the Ministers of our God: ye shall **eat the** riches of the Gentiles, **and in their** glory shall ye boast yourselves. For your shame *ye shall have* double : **and** *for* confusion they shall rejoice in their portion : therefore in their **land** they **shall possess double :** everlasting joy shall be unto them. For I **the Lord love judgment, I hate robbery for** burnt offering ; and I will direct **their work in truth, and** will make an everlasting covenant with them. And **their seed shall be known among the** Gentiles, and **their** offspring among the people: all that see him shall acknowledge them, that they *are* the seed **which the Lord hath** blessed. **I will greatly rejoice in the** Lord, my soul shall **be** joyful in my **God; for he hath clothed me with the garments of** salvation, he hath covered me **with the robe of** righteousness, **as a bridegroom** decketh *himself* with ornaments. **For as the** earth **bringeth forth her bud, and as the garden causeth** the **things that** are sown in **it to come forth ;** so **the Lord God will cause righteousness and praise to spring forth before all the nations."**

St. Paul, to shew the reality of the reclamation of human nature through Christ, and **the** superiority of the Spiritual Kingdom which He **came to** establish, in which he **was to be** represented not by **meats, and drinks,** and divers **washings, but in which he** was **to be the meat and drink, and the eternal fountain,** accessible **to all who would** receive him ; **St. Paul, we say,** did most emphatically explain to his hearers, **(the Galatians,) that** if they continued to look to the old exploded **Jewish law** for salvation, Christ is become **of none** effect, for we through **the** Spirit wait for the hope of righteousness by **faith,** for in Jesus Christ neither circumcision availeth any thing, **nor** uncircumcision, but **faith** which worketh by love. The great elevation then **which** men **now** receive through Christ is this, that the Apostle **could freely** address them, as responsible beings entrusted with a great gift, by which they could walk as Spiritual beings, for, "These, I say, walk in the spirit, and ye shall not fulfil the lust of the flesh." In the whole argument contained in the fifth and **sixth** chapters **of** St. Paul to the Galatians, the **Apostle is proving the vast superiority and efficacy** of the **Covenant of Grace over that of Works, and** the dignity **of man as a spiritual being**; and forcibly explains not that circumcision *had been* a useless sacrament, but that under the new dispensation it had become useless, being replaced by another: and therefore he most truly says, "for IN *Christ Jesus* neither circumcision availeth any thing, nor uncircumcision, but a *new creature*." That the Galatians must have understood St. Paul to address them as men **who** were under the gift of **the Holy Spirit** is clear, for he **addresses them as** "**O, foolish Galatians, who hath bewitched you, that ye should not obey the truth, before** whose eyes Jesus Christ has been evidently **set forth**, crucified among you. **This** would **I learn of** you, *received* ye the spirit **by** the works of the law or by the hearing of faith? and ye *are all* the children of God by faith in Christ **Jesus.*** **They** certainly then had received some gift,—for as many of you "as have been baptised into Christ have put on Christ." The same apostle addressing the Ephesians says: "And you hath he quickened who were dead **in** trespasses and sins. But now in Christ Jesus ye who sometimes were far off are made **nigh by the** blood of Christ." "For through him we both

---

* The **Apostle** evidently alludes to the Holy Eucharist by which Christ had been set forth and by which they had been fed with the Spiritual Christ.

have access *by one spirit* unto the Father." "In whom ye are also builded together for an habitation of God, through the Spirit." In the same sort St. Paul addressed the Colossians, in the second chapter, urging as a strong reason for steadfastness, the reality of that gift of Christ which they had received, for he tells them, "in him dwelleth all the fullness of the Godhead bodily. And ye are complete in him who is the head of all principality and power. In whom also ye are circumcised with the circumcision made without hands, in putting off the body of the sins of the flesh *by the circumcision* of Christ: buried with him in baptism, wherein also ye are risen with him through the faith of the operation of God, who hath raised him from the dead:" and as a consequence of all this actually done for them, St. Paul appeals to them: "If ye then be risen with Christ (*i. e.* become spiritual and ceasing to be carnal) seek those things which are above. Lie not one to another, seeing that ye have put off the old man with his deeds, and have put on the new man." And so also the other Apostles constantly appeal to men to recognise the stupendous work of redemption and its individual application through baptism, as a sign of Christ's effectual operation on their fallen nature; for then is man's spirit regenerated by Christ through the Holy Ghost. That human nature has imparted to it by baptism, in the name of the Father, of the Son, and of the Holy Ghost, a special and peculiar gift we cannot doubt, for how else can we understand the strong language of scripture: "He that believeth and is baptised shall be saved." If belief in Christ *were* enough, why have the latter condition?

Thus does Christ restore our lost purity by giving to us that gift of Life by which we have the capacity to be in His likeness. We can no more help being Christ's than we can being citizens of the state. "So then seek ye the Lord while he may be found, **call upon him** when he is near; let the wicked forsake his **way, and the** unrighteous **man his** thoughts; **and** let him return unto the Lord and he **will have** mercy upon him, and to our God, and he will abundantly pardon."—Isaiah, c. lv., vs., 6, 7. "Behold the Lord's hand is not shortened that it cannot save: neither his ear heavy that it cannot hear; for he saith, **call unto me and I** will answer thee and shew thee great **and** mighty **things** which thou knowest not."—Jer., c. xxxiii., v. 3. "And it shall come to pass that before *they call* I will answer, and while they are yet speaking I will hear."—Isaiah, c. lxv., v. 24.

"Behold, it is come, and it is done saith the Lord God, this is the **day whereof I have spoken.** Verily, verily, I say unto you, He that believeth on **me hath** everlasting life. I am that bread of **life.** Your fathers did eat **manna in** the wilderness, and are dead. This is the bread which cometh down from heaven, that a man may eat thereof, and not die. I am the living bread which came down from heaven; if any man eat of this bread, he shall **live** for ever: and the bread that I will give is my flesh, which I will **give for the life of** the world."

As much as to say; Your bodies are not what those bodies shall be, for you shall be changed, your nature shall be regenerated and renewed. Verily it is your spiritual nature that I am dealing with now, it quickeneth your bodies now and is immortal, the flesh passeth away: but my flesh and my blood are more; I am the quickening spirit dealing with you as spiritual beings. How truly did St. Paul realize this in his epistle to the Philippians: "For to me to *live is* Christ, and to *die is* gain. But if I live in the flesh, (in this earthly tabernacle of flesh) this *is* the fruit of my labour: yet what I shall choose I wot not: for I am in a straight betwixt two, having a desire to depart (out of this fleshly house) and to be with Christ; which is far better." Such was the conscious superiority of spirit over flesh, which declares, "*I live* in the flesh."

Behold "God is a spirit: and they that worship him must worship him in spirit and in truth."* "For ye are all the children of God by faith in Christ Jesus, for as many of you as have been baptized **into** Christ, have put on Christ."† "Know **ye** not that **your bodies are the** members of Christ?"‡ Verily, verily, **we must now**—as they of old time—worship God in spirit **and in truth,** for even under the law it was really in spirit that men worshipped, **for to be** carnally minded is death.

What a mystery! what profound love! Of his **own will** begat he us, brought us to a true knowledge of himself **and** put into us the principle of eternal life, even the life which is of **Himself**; for throughout these scriptures where do we find **any reference** to man **except** as a being having a spiritual nature, an immortal being, who having lost himself, **is** reclaimed at enormous cost, and immense labour. By symbol and by sign, and by law openly declared the restoration of our lost nature is set forth : the shadows of things as seen in the church visible on earth **are really** and truly the reflection, the evidence of realities, **which** supranaturally exist.

The whole system of religion is designed to teach man **obedience, and purity,** as the proper state of pure being.

"Speak unto Aaron, saying whosoever ***he be* of thy** seed **in** their generations that hath any blemish, let him not **approach to offer** the bread of **his God.** For whatsoever man *he be* that hath a blemish, he shall not approach." ‖

Let no man who is blemished with sin, with his sins upon him, come. Such is the law, and it is to enable man so to seek God, that Christ came as the second Adam. Let no man deceive himself; the carnal man, the man who is not

---

* John, c. iv., vs. 23, 24, and Hebrews, c. iii., v. 1 to 14.
† Galatians, c. iii., vs. 27, 28. ‡ 1 Corinthians, c. vi., v. 15 to 20.
‖ Lev., c. xxi.

living as a spiritual being, is not accomplishing his end; he is like untimely fruit, withered or withering: none but the perfect man, **that is,** the man who is developing his *whole* nature, **can** be free to satisfy the end of his creation: for if, **under** the law it was Spirit, what shall we say of the Kingdom of Grace? There are a number of enactments to set forth this truth, and in all of them is the spiritual **kingdom,** and man, as a spiritual inhabitant of that kingdom. None but the contrite **may** worship, **none** but the **spiritually** minded may approach acceptably to God. So,—

"Jesus saith, **Woman, believe me, the hour cometh** when ye shall neither in this mountain, **nor yet at Jerusalem** worship the Father. Ye worship ye know not what: we know what we worship: for salvation is of the Jews. But the hour cometh, and now is, when the true worshippers shall worship the Father in spirit and in truth: for the Father seeketh such to worship Him. God is a spirit: and they that worship him must worship him in spirit and in truth. The woman said unto him, I know that Messiah cometh, which is called Christ: when he is come he will tell us all things. Jesus saith unto her, I that speak unto thee am He."

And another scripture saith, **that we are "under grace:"** and we stand **"in** this **grace,"** which is Christ's nature, wherein we were planted by the Holy Ghost in baptism.

"For the law of the spirit of life in Christ Jesus hath made **me free from the law of sin and death. For what the law could not do, in that it was weak** through **the flesh,** God sending his **own Son in the likeness of sinful flesh,** and for sin, condemned sin **in the flesh:** That the righteousness **of the law** might be fulfilled **in** us, who walk **not** after the flesh, **but after the spirit. For** they that are after the flesh do **mind** the things **of the flesh; but they that** are after the spirit the things of the spirit.* For to **be carnally minded is death:** but to be spiritually minded is life and **peace. But if the spirit of him** that raised up Jesus from the dead **dwell in** you, he that raised up **Christ** from the dead shall also quicken your mortal bodies by his spirit that **dwelleth in you."**

For the Apostle says again:—

"Know ye not, that **so many** of us as were baptized into Jesus Christ were baptized **into his death? Therefore** we are buried with him by baptism into

---

* They that have been born of water **and of the** Spirit.

death: that like as Christ was raised up from the dead by the glory **of the Father, even so we also should walk in newness of life."**

It is thus abundantly clear that the whole Word of God is addressed to and comprehends man, while yet in the flesh, as a spiritual being, and it is derogatory to man, and dishonouring to God, to suppose that it can comprehend him as any thing else. A man must either be a bad or a good man: as a human being he has a higher life than that of the brutes, for his is a spiritual life, and, therefore, either a bad spiritual life or a good one; either a spiritual nature which is becoming wholly evil, or is ever becoming wholly good: in the former case assimilated to that of demons, in the latter regenerated and daily renewed through the Spirit by the imparted Nature, and saved by the imputed righteousness of him who alone is the life-giving Spirit.

"God said, let us make man in our image, after our likeness: and let them have dominion over the fish of the sea, and over the fowl of the air, and over the cattle, and over all the earth, and over every creeping thing that creepeth upon the earth. So God created man in his own image, in the image of God created he him: male and female created he them."

St. Paul declares that, by the coming of Jesus Christ as our restorer, we are re-made in him, "For what man knoweth the things of a man *save the spirit of man* which is in him." "Now we have received, not the spirit of the world, but the spirit which *is* of God, that we might know the things that are freely given to us of God." "We have the mind of Christ." Yes! great is this mystery of love, for as Adam having the spirit of God yet fell, and was not altogether forsaken, so we having received of Christ the spirit of adoption, he to the last strives with our spirits that we may live in him.

In God's eternal image man was made, and breathed upon by the breath of immortality, he is a living soul:—fallen, corrupt, gone as far as possible from original righteousness, he is reclaimed through **Christ's human** nature, and saved **if he continue therein.**

Created once in our first parents perfect, knowing no sin, **and** enjoying the blessed privilege of immediate communion **with** our Father, we were indeed in the likeness of God. **But** as from this holy estate man fell away, in great mercy God's outstretched arm interposed to save him, **from the** consequences of **that grievous fall. No longer pure, but** tainted and corrupted, **unclean, vile, shut out from the presence** of God, **man always** inclines to evil, and no good thing **can he do. Cain, personifying sin,** slays the righteous Abel **who was keeping alive** God's truth, and is reprobated **and** turned from God by his wickedness: a life of vagabondage **is assigned to him**; a type of the life-long punishment of the wicked. Noah is saved, a preacher of righteousness, but he too finds sinful sons and daughters to conspire against God's truth: who in their turn are cast away. **Sin prevails; the prince of this world, who deceived mankind in Adam, seeks to keep his slaves in bondage. God, mightier than all, wills to save his own creatures from destruction.** Abraham **is** chosen **"as the Father of the Faithful," in whom all** the nations **of the** earth should be blessed. **God determines** to keep his Holy Name before his creatures, and to **establish** his pure worship before them, **and from Abraham's loins** came a people, and many people have **sprung from thence:** the God of Abraham, of Isaac, and of Jacob has, through the operation of his own will, established a kingdom and peoples, **zealous** of good works. In his dealings with them he hath **taught how, that he is** a Father, loving, caring **for,** teaching, saving, **his children; suffering** long their weakness, pitying their many **sins, forgiving their sins.** Who can read of the enormities **of** backsliding Israel, and **not** wonder at the endurance and loving kindness of their Father who made them to serve him? Who can cease to be astonished at their wickedness when the salvation which was wrought for them is remembered? What soul but melts with self-abasement when the cry of this very Israel is heard from the house of bondage and their prayers answered? How wonderfully did God provide for his people, chosen to keep his blessed truth alive in the earth? Unable, because they were of Adam's fallen race, to offer unto God the honour due unto his Name, they were immediately instructed how fitly to come to him who made them, and to fall down before his footstool who had redeemed them: the pattern of all things fit for holy worship was shewn unto them, and the law of God for the regulation of their lives in accordance with that worship and service was clearly revealed. In the fore-front of this high and holy worship "stood the Lamb, as it had been slain from the foundation of the world." The lesson imprinted on the very first title-page of God's revalation to man was, "that there was the Name written above every name." "The Lamb of God which taketh away the sins of the world." There was then, as now, "none other name given under heaven by which we must be saved." Thus did God declare himself in the Jewish polity to the world. The worship of God then, as now, was repentance and self-abasement, and prayer, the seeking for pardon and peace by the redemption of fallen man through the coming of the second Adam, by whose nature we are regenerated; and in whose Person was a perfect and acceptable sacrifice.

Whether it be Jew or Christian, the service which God demands of us is a reasonable service, and the only mode of access with Him was, and is, through the blood of the covenant which he made with our forefathers, and which he openly enlarged and set forth in his Son. "Will I eat the flesh of bulls or drink the blood of goats? Offer unto God thanksgiving, and pay thy vows unto the most high!" "I delight not in the blood of bullocks, or of lambs, or of he-goats." "Wash you, make you clean, put away the evil of your doings from before mine eyes. Sacrifice and offering thou wouldst not, but a body hast thou prepared me."

"And in that day thou shalt say, O Lord, I will praise thee: though thou wast angry with me, thine anger is turned away, and thou comfortedst me. Behold God is my salvation; I will trust, and not be afraid: for the Lord Jehovah is my strength and my song; he also is my salvation. Therefore with joyfulness shall ye draw water out of the wells of salvation. And in that day shall ye say, Praise the Lord, call upon his name, declare his doings among the people, make mention that his name is exalted. Sing unto the Lord, for he hath done excellent things; this is known in all the earth. Cry aloud and shout, thou inhabitants of Zion; for great is the holy one of Israel."

Accordingly God was pleased to demand of us obedience, and gave us commandment to set forth openly our dependence on him. "Ye shall observe this thing for an ordinance, to thee and thy sons for ever, and when your children shall say unto you, what mean ye by this service, ye shall say, it is the sacrifice of the Lord's passover." Sacrifice is then, in its true meaning, the giving up ourselves to God, wholly and devotedly in the name and in the person of Christ. It is the offering up ourselves in the Son of God continually. But how? As he offered! First, he was essentially holy, without spot, sinless, pure, he offered up his whole life to do His Father's will, was crucified to the world, and fulfilled all righteousness: he was love, and in his love and charity for his race, he verily offered himself up a full and perfect sacrifice for those fallen ones who had nought to offer, but who might have him to offer; and in act gave his life a ransom for ours by the death of the cross. If then he is the second Adam, and we are grafted into his body according to the election of grace, by the which we are called unto salvation, we then as regenerate, and grafted into his body must live in Him and do that which he did. We must walk in his likeness, so as to be clothed with his righteousness; our life must be hidden that Christ's life may appear in us. In such a state, rooted and grounded in love, may we continue to do that which Christ commanded us to do, "live in him." We who are unworthy to offer any sacrifice, must even take the sacrifice which Jesus made and yet offers,—"the rich banquet of His flesh and blood"—and pleading Him before God, shew the signs of His death as the representation of the price by which we are bought, and claim to be pardoned and reconciled to the Father of all.

Even as they of old who were all baptised unto Moses in the cloud and in the sea, and did *all eat the same spiritual meat*, and did all *drink the same spiritual drink*, for they drank of that spiritual rock that followed them, and that rock was Christ, so do we now. But with many of them God was not well pleased; for they were overthrown in the wilderness, and for doing that which is yet done, "crucifying the son of God afresh, and putting him to open shame, "eating and drinking their own damnation, not discerning the Lord's body." Representative sacrifice was ever God's appointed mode of prevailing intercourse between Himself and His people: while the sacrifice of Christ, is the only atonement for the sins of the world. And while we represent through an appointed service, and authorized ministry, the sacrifice of Christ in the oblations of bread and wine together with ourselves, our souls and bodies, we must further ourselves be penitent, heart-broken with sorrow for sin, for our hearts must bleed at the remembrance of a life of shame. The sacrifices of God are a broken spirit; "a broken and contrite heart shalt thou not despise." "Offer the sacrifices of righteousness unto the Lord, and put your trust in the Lord; therefore will I offer in his tabernacle sacrifices of joy; and sacrifice the Sacrifice of Thanksgiving, and declare his works with rejoicing, for our sins he hath put away from us and redeemed us.

"In that day there shall be a fountain opened to the house of David and to the inhabitants of Jerusalem for sin and for uncleanness. And it shall come to pass in that day, saith the Lord of hosts, that I will cut off the names of the idols out of the land, and they shall no more be remembered; and also I will cause the prophets and the unclean spirit to pass out of the land. And it shall come to pass that when any shall yet prophesy, then his father and his mother that begat him shall say unto him, Thou shalt not live; for thou speakest lies in the name of the Lord: and his father and his mother that begat him shall thrust him through when he prophesieth. And it shall come to pass in that day, that the prophets shall be ashamed every one of his vision, when he hath prophesied; neither shall he wear a rough garment to deceive: But he shall say, I am no prophet, I am an husbandman; for man taught me to keep cattle from my youth. And one shall say unto him, what are those wounds in thine hands? Then he shall answer, those with which I was wounded in the house of my friends."

That man's broken and contrite spirit may be healed, his uncleanness washed away, sacramental purification and restoration was instituted, by Christ, who has left pledges of his love to prove the reality of his work. He hath instituted a kingdom, his Church, the keeper of his Word, and Sacraments, in which there is a representative priesthood after the order of Melchisedec, who have been constituted, stewards of his mysteries, whom he took for priests and Levites; and as a consequence we find the Saviour, the Redeemer of man, profuse in his mention of these means of grace: and His holy Apostles are equally careful to set forth their importance. This is what is done; but we may be sure that, pride is now as ever an active power in human nature, and expects that, "This man shall surely come and strike his hand upon the place and recover us of the leprosy: are not Abana and Pharpar **rivers of Damascus better than all the waters of Jordan?**" But he who **is the** Creator **and** Redeemer, determines for himself what is best, **and so we discover no other** way of salvation than that which he has instituted. Therefore we appeal to **scripture for the proofs of the reality of man's** restoration in **Jesus** Christ, through faith in **his blood, as a**pplied to our nature in his church through **his Word and in** sacramental celebration, by an authorized ministering Priesthood.

To enable us effectually to approach the throne **of God and sin** not, there ever was shewn a mediatorial way. Uncleanness must be put away, our sins expiated, our dead **hearts** quickened; therefore typical blood-shedding and the offering **up of sacrifice, representing the** great atonement, were from the first the most solemn, because the heaven-appointed **means of access to God's favour.** Lost and ruined, **there can be in man nothing to justify him in the** sight of God. If God's justice is to be satisfied, there must be some mode without man and not in man, to bring about reconciliation. This was **a truth early** made **known.** From the time of Abel to the present hour, Christ **the Redeemer was declared to be our only acceptable way** of approach **to God, and in no other way is man justified in** his appeal **for pardon. The Jew laid his hand on the head of** the victim **to be** slain, **and thus dared to come before** his Father **whom he** had **turned from; and the Christian like** the **Jew, if he be** contrite **and broken in spirit, can come to the same** Father in **no other way but by representing to the Father** that he is **of Christ's redeemed, and by holding in his** hand, as indicative **of the wants in his heart, the** representation of his **redemption,** the appointed **symbols of** " **the Great Sacrifice**" **offered** up and still **in the Person of** Christ being offered for the sins of the **world. Now, as then,** it is the gift of God to man that salvation cometh. **We need** too now, as did they of old time, that the flame of Christ's spirit touch us. "Then flew one of the seraphim unto me, having a live coal in his hand which he had taken with the tongs from off the altar; and he laid it upon my mouth, and said, lo! this hath touched thy lips; and thy iniquity is taken away and thy sins purged."

JUSTIFICATION.

"For when we were yet without strength, in due time Christ died for the ungodly. For scarcely for a righteous man will one die: yet peradventure for a good man some would even dare to die. But God commendeth his love toward us, in that while we were yet sinners, Christ died for us. Much more then, being now justified by his blood, we shall be saved from wrath through him. For if, when we were enemies, we were reconciled to God by the death of his Son, much more, being reconciled, we shall be saved by his life. And not only so, but we also joy in God, through our Lord Jesus Christ, by whom we have now received the atonement."

The sacrifice of the Son of God is the meritorious cause of our justification. God pardons our sins, adopts us into his family, bestows upon us his grace, imparts to us a new principle of life, accounts us as righteous, and admits us into his presence, not because he is well pleased in us, but because Christ has done that for us which we could not do for ourselves,—satisfied the justice of God, paid the penalty of our guilt. That the primitive church received this doctrine in all its fullness, we have the testimony of St. Clement, the fellow-labourer and companion of St. Paul, who, after saying of the Jewish worthies that they all received glory and honour neither through themselves nor their works, nor their righteous dealings which they exercised, but through his will, continues: "In like manner we who have been called by his will in Christ Jesus, are not justified by ourselves, neither by our own wisdom nor understanding nor piety, nor works which we have wrought in holiness of heart, but by the faith by which Almighty God has justified all from the beginning." Since such is the vital importance of justification, it is an interesting question to ascertain at what period of our lives we may reasonably look for it. The 13th Article of the Church of England expressly states that, "works done before the grace of Christ, and the inspiration of his spirit, have the nature of sin." It is a scriptural declaration, for our Saviour says that the tree must be good before it can produce holy fruit; and St. Paul, "that whatsoever is not of faith is sin." In other words, before we can do anything pleasing or acceptable to God, nay, before we can act without sin, we must be justified. Our church then fixes the date of our initiatory justification at our baptism; of which, in the language of the learned Barrow, it "is by St. Paul made the immediate, consequent or special adjunct: therein, he saith, '*we die to sin*,' by resolution and engagement to lead a new life in obedience to God's commandment, and so dying we are said to be justified from sin." It is thus that God not only accounts as righteous through regeneration, those who by nature are unrighteous; but freely and without any merit of your own implants in us, as his adopted children, the power and the desire to do his will and pleasure. If this be not the case, if baptism be not the "seal of justification, and the beginning of sanctification," if the righteousness of Christ be not then imparted to the infant, what ground have we for saying with our church: "It is certain by God's word, that children which are baptised, dying before they commit actual sin, are undoubtedly saved." Justification is or is not necessary to salvation; if it is, how are infants saved if they be not justified? and if they are justified, how are the merits of Christ imparted to them except through "the baptism of regeneration." Our Saviour says, "He that believeth and is baptised shall be saved."

"This," says Cranmer, "is the very plain, ordinary way by the which God hath determined that man, being of age and coming to Christendom, should be justified For as for infants, it is to be believed that their justification is wrought by the secret operation of the Holy Ghost *in the baptism*, they being offered in the faith of the church. And this justification may be called the first justification, that is to say, our first coming into God's house, which is the church of Christ; at which coming we be received and admitted to be of the flock and family of our Saviour Christ, and be professed and sworn to be the servants of God, and to be soldiers under Christ to fight against our enemies, the Devil, the world, and the flesh." Again, St. Paul in Romans, says Barrow, discourseth thus: "Seeing we in baptism are cleansed and disentangled from sin, are dead to it, and so justified from it, God forbid that we should return to live in the practice thereof, so abusing and evacuating the grace we have received; which seemeth plainly to signify that he treateth about the justification conferred in baptism. We may conclude then with the same accurate theologian, "that the justification which St. Paul discourseth of, seemeth in his meaning, only or especially to be that act of grace which is dispensed to persons at their baptism, or at their entrance into the church; where they openly professing their faith, and undertaking to practice their duty, God most solemnly and formally absolves them from all guilt, and accepteth them into a state of favour with him."

This wholesome doctrine of the church of England will be made more clear by a comparison of the 11th and 13th Articles.

In the former, which treats "of the justification of man," we are told "that we are accounted righteous before God, only for the merit of our Lord and Saviour Jesus Christ, by faith, and not for our own works or deservings." In the latter, which treats of " works before justification," the nature of " the works and deservings " intended by the 11th article is expressly stated in the title, while the doctrine of justification itself is formally defined in the body of the article; where, works before justification are explained to be works done *before the grace* of Christ, and the *inspiration of his spirit;* a definition whence it irrefragably follows, that the justification of man, and the reception of the grace of Christ, and the inspiration of his spirit are one and the same thing; in other words, that individual justification consists, not in what has been done collectively for man, but in what is done individually in man by the grace and power of Christ. Behind in every thing, lacking every thing, how can man think even that which is good except God's grace reveal it to him, but as there are diverse gifts from the one spirit so may we not confound them. God's Holy Spirit giveth the unbaptized heathen prevenient grace to receive the truths of Christianity, and believing he will say: "What doth hinder me from being baptized," and being baptized with water in the name of the Father, and of the Son, and of the Holy Ghost, who shall keep back the work of the Spirit in regenerating the soul by the imparting of Christ's nature. "Go ye into all the world and *preach* the gospel to every creature," go and proclaim Christ and his salvation, shew men what I have done for them, let them know that they have been redeemed. I will be with you, my spirit shall work with your spirits, and I will give them the spirit of understanding. But having opened their eyes, and their ears having heard, and their hearts believing the truth that is proclaimed to them, you have another duty to them. Baptize them in the name of the Father, and of the Son, and of the Holy Ghost. They have forfeited all claim on me as their Father, they cannot be inheritors of my kingdom **until** I have sealed and redeemed them in my blood. Tell **them** that this baptism **is a true** work, that they are thereby justified, **and** under **covenant, for so surely as** I have called and **they have answered, so surely do I bury them in** my death, **the** death of their Christ, and elect **them unto all the** blessed privileges that my sacrifice confers. **Their Adam's** guilt or condemnation I put away; and if they **will but** continue to obey my law, and to walk after the pattern of the author of their new birth, the Restorer of fallen humanity, **they shall be mine.** Be not dismayed, I elect them that they may be **saved,** I feed them with spiritual meat, and strengthen them **with** spiritual drink, that they may continue strong in me, **that they** may **be justified before me and** call me their **Father.** Teach **them to hunger** and thirst after righteousness: but having been fed **with that meat** which satisfieth, and having drunk at **the fountain which** allays all thirst, bid them not to crave any other meat, or to **taste of** any other drink, lest lust come upon them and they fall. I will plead with them as I did with Pharaoh, and I will endure with them as with Pharaoh, but if at last they reject my counsel and will none of my reproof, then I will harden their hearts as I did the heart of Pharaoh, for I will not always strive with man:" such is truly the Lord's meaning.

Called of God in baptism, **a** very heavy responsibility **rests** upon us: "I call heaven and earth to record this day against you, that I have set before you life and death, blessing and cursing: therefore *choose* life, that both thou and thy seed may live." Such are the words of God. The regenerated **nature** bestowed upon **the** baptized, endows them with the capacity to grow in the nature of Christ, but the retention of their regenerated nature is conditional, **and is** dependent on their acceptance of those conditions, **the** capacity and ability to perform which are put into them by the washing of regeneration through sanctification by the Spirit. God has manifested his will to be, that *all* should be saved. So a recent apostolic writer* says, "Our merciful Lord seems to have been singularly careful to set at rest any misgivings that might naturally arise in the minds of those, whose consciousness of sinfulness would make them doubt, whether God would vouchsafe to receive them upon their coming to him in repentance and faith. Not only has he given us these parables in succession to set forth his willingness 'to seek and to save that which was lost,' but he has met the question itself in terms too explicit, one would think, to be misunderstood: 'Him that cometh to me I will in no wise cast out." An expression nearly similar occurs in Revelation: "Let him that is athirst come; and *whosoever will*, let him take the water of life freely." St. Paul declares that, "as by the offence of one, judgment came upon all men to condemnation, even so by the righteousness of one, the free gift came upon all men unto justification of life." To the same effect is that remarkable passage in the first epistle of Timothy, in which our Saviour is represented not as one who, according to the supralapsarian scheme, has decreed from all eternity the damnation of some of his creatures; nor as one who, as the sublapsarians tell us, passes over the non-elect as unworthy of his regard; but as a God "who will have *all* men to be saved, and to come unto the knowledge of the truth." Not as a God who decreed his Son to die for a few, who should be saved through his arbitrary election; but as one who "gave himself a ransom for all to be testified in due time." "If any man sin," says St. John, "we have an advocate with the Father, Jesus Christ the

---

* The Bishop of Tasmania.

righteous; and he is the propitiation for our sins." Now it is not a matter of controversy, whether there is any man that doth not sin: "All have sinned and come short of the glory of God," therefore, according to the language of the Apostle, *all* have an advocate with the Father, *all* are privileged to look to him, as the propitiation for their sins. To this the Calvinist says: No! By declaring that the tenor of scripture warrants us in concluding, that God by his immutable counsel has determined whom he should hereinafter call unto salvation, and whom he should devote to damnation: he asserts that there are those for whom there is no propitiation. If we should pause at this point and hesitate for an instant whom to follow, St. John or Calvin, the former decides the matter, for St. John says in the succeeding sentence: "And not for our sakes only, but for the sins of the whole world."

A benevolent, merciful, and just God did not create immortal beings fore-ordained to damnation: such is a dishonouring thought to him who wills that "every man should be saved;" and they who advocate this monstrous doctrine, have never been able to get away from the consequence to which it inevitably leads, viz: the *irresponsibility* of man for his acts, and the reduction of his nature simply to a level with that of the beasts. Fore-knowledge and predestination rightly understood, are compatible with all the attributes of Deity, for it is and must be true that the Almighty does fore-know every thing: "He understandeth my thoughts long before conceived by me." He knew from all eternity that some among the race of man would perish through wickedness, and that some would be workers of righteousness, and to either of these classes he assigned a doom, to the one eternal happiness, to the other eternal misery and death; he placed and places both, in the way of life, he gives to all *capacities* and *powers* to embrace the aid graciously vouchsafed to all who are his, by covenant and grace; and above all His long-suffering is exhibited to the wicked whom he constantly interposes to win back to life in Him. If, therefore, the wicked continue in his wickedness, it is not because God has from all time ordained that this man should perish? No! God has foreseen his course, he has warned and tried to save: and having rejected and forsaken the way of God, the all Holy One at the last leaves him to his fate—to that fate which he has predetermined that the wicked shall receive, but for which he has purposely made no man. He has given us his Word, he has instituted Sacraments, he has established his Church, and by, and in all these ways, he pleads with us and is manifesting himself to us. That our heavenly Father in the employment of means intends to signify a spiritual operation on our spiritual nature may be most certainly gathered from holy scripture, but as a general rule He brings us to himself by a course of instructive discipline, he seldom at once illumines so as to shut out all the stings of sin, we are to grow in grace. Oh! how hard the temptations, how trying the enmity of the "old man," how often the cry, Who will deliver from the body of this death?

THE NEW BIRTH.

"Elect according to the foreknowledge of God the Father, through sanctification of the Spirit, unto obedience and sprinkling of the blood of Jesus Christ: Grace unto you, and peace, be multiplied.

"Blessed *be* the God and Father of our Lord Jesus Christ, which according to his abundant mercy hath begotten us again unto a lively hope by the resurrection of Jesus Christ from the dead."

By revelation from the Creator we learn how strength is to be imparted, and how he designs that it shall ever be imparted to man. First, man must be born again, this second birth as much the gift of God as the first; elected by God's free grace and *called* out of the world, (even before we may have committed actual sin;) by water and the Holy Spirit, Man is buried in Christ's nature and admitted into a society of elected and called people, the citizens of a spiritual kingdom. In this brotherhood are all those necessary conditions to be found, by which the regenerated nature may grow to perfection.

"Lo, he goeth by me, and I see him not: he passeth on also, but I perceive him not. Behold, he taketh away, who can hinder him? who shall say unto him, what doest thou?"

Professor Paget, in his admirable lectures, has not failed to see analogies in the growth and repair of the body under disease, which strikingly set forth the recovery of man's fallen nature, and its repair: "If," he says, "I may venture on so high a theme, let me suggest that the instances of recovery from disease and injury seem to be only examples of a law yet larger than that within the terms of which they may be comprised, a law wider than the grasp of science: the law that expresses our Creator's will for the recovery of all lost perfection. To this train of thought we are guided by the remembrance that the healing of the body was ever chosen as the fit emblem of his work, whose true mission was to raise man's fallen spirit, and to repair the injuries it had sustained, and that once the healing power was exerted in a manner purposely so confined as to advance *like that which we can trace by progressive stages to the complete cure.* For there was one upon whom the light of Heaven first fell, so imperfectly was his vision that he saw 'confusedly' men as trees walking, and then by a second touch of the Divine hand was 'restored, and saw every man clearly.'" And thus does God now ordinarily deal with us, we must daily advance in godliness and be more and more conformed to the image of Christ.

"And he said, so is the kingdom of God, as if a man should cast seed into the ground: and should sleep, and rise night and day, and the seed should spring and grow up, he knoweth not how. For the earth bringeth forth fruit of herself; first the blade, then the ear, after which the full corn in the ear. But when the fruit is brought forth, immediately he putteth in the sickle, because the harvest is come. And he said, whereunto shall we liken the kingdom of God? or with what comparison shall we compare it? It i like a grain of mustard seed, which, when it is sown in the earth, is less than all the seeds that be in the earth; but when it is sown, it groweth up, and becometh greater than all herbs, and shooteth out great branches; so that the fowls of the air may lodge under the shadow of it."

> "For every virtue we possess,
> And every conquest won,
> And every thought of holiness,
> Are His alone."

Guided by the brighter light of revelation, it may be our privilege, while we study the method of cure by which our bodies are renovated to gain by illustration a clearer insight into the oneness of plan by which things spiritual and corporeal are directed. Even now we may trace some analogy between the **conditions of body and** man's intellectual and moral nature. **As in the development of** the germ, so in **the history of the human spirit we may** discern a striving **after** perfection, after **a perfection not viewed** in any present model, **for** the human **model was marred** almost as soon as formed, but manifested to the enlightened reason, in the "express image" of the "Father of Spirits." And so, whenever, through human frailty, amid the violence **of** the world, and the remaining infection of our nature, **the** spirit **loses** aught of the perfection to which it was once admitted, still an *implanted* power is ever urgent to repair **the loss.** The same **power derived and** still renewed from the same parent working by appointed means, and to the same end restores our fallen nature, to the same perfection that it had before. "Then **not unscarred, yet** living"— *fractus sed invectus*—the spirit **still feels its** capacity for a higher life, and passes to its immortal **destiny.**

Truly, **our Lord** in his life **in the flesh on earth did, by** extraordinary manifestation **of** his energy heal the body; **but as Mr.** Paget wisely observes, such *was not* his ordinary **manner of working:** both growth and repair are slow processes reached through **stages.** So Christ in remembrance of our nature, sympathizing with our weakness and fulfilling **his own law,** has left with **man full and perfect** means for the **recovery of his** injured **life, not by miraculous cure,** but by **a gift of power,** enabling him **diligently to** use those means, **and to continue in** the life-long **practice** of all love and obedience. **By implanting into man his own nature** through the gift of regeneration wrought at baptism, by continuing to renew **and feed that** regenerated nature, by imparting Himself as the bread of life, and in the ministry of his

Word, human nature is preparing itself for that fullness of purity which can only be in the presence of God. The effect of this reconstruction in Christ's human nature is thus declared in scripture:

"Know ye not your bodies are the members of Christ? Shall I then take the members of Christ and make them the members of an harlot? He that is joined unto the Lord is one spirit."

"Know ye not that your body is the temple of the Holy Ghost which is in you, which ye have of God, and ye are not your own?"

"Ye are the body of Christ and members in particular. We are members of his body, his flesh, and his bones. We are members one of another."

"We are buried with Him by *baptism* into death. Buried with him in baptism, wherein also ye are risen with him through the faith of the operation of God, who hath raised him from the dead."

"Set your affection on things above, not on things on the earth; for ye are dead, and your life is hid with Christ in God."

"I am the vine; ye are the branches."

All this is God's doing, and we cannot shrink away from the responsibility thereby imposed upon us. No other alternative awaits us, but life or death:—we must, called as we are to salvation, either accept or reject it. Endowed with gifts from on high, supplied with the necessary grace or strength to exercise to the full, the capacity for life which God has given us, the capacity which he has rendered active by our regeneration in Christ's nature, imparted by the Holy Spirit in baptism; we are responsible for the right employment of all those means which God has provided in His Church. Man is free to live up to his true nature, and no authority is given in the sacred word for the belief, that any set of men are by God's *arbitrary* decree alone chosen to ultimate salvation; he calls us to salvation, and bids us, "put on the whole armour of God, that ye may be able to stand;" and again, "Wherefore, take unto you the whole armour of God, that ye may be able to withstand in the evil day, and having done all to stand." For through him we both have access by one Spirit unto the Father.

Now, therefore, ye are no more strangers and foreigners, but fellow-citizens with the saints, and of the household of God, and are built upon the foundation of the Apostles and Prophets, Jesus Christ himself being the chief corner stone; *in whom* all the building fitly framed together groweth unto an holy temple in the Lord. In whom ye also are builded together for an habitation of God through the Spirit. There is one body and one spirit, even as ye are called in one hope of your calling. "One Lord, one faith, one baptism, one God and Father of all, who is above all, and through all, and *in you all*." But unto *every one of us* is given grace, according to the measure of the gift of Christ. We be all dead in trespasses and sin, so how can we live except the life-imparting Body of Christ quicken us? How otherwise could he gather to himself a kingdom, except by "the death of sin and the new birth to righteousness," of which he alone is the author?

"Prophesy unto the wind, prophesy son of man and say to the wind, thus saith the Lord God: Come from the four winds, O breath, and breathe upon these slain that they may live. So I prophesied as he commanded me and the breath came into them, and they lived, and stood upon their feet, an exceeding great army."

Yea! it bloweth where it listeth, and we cannot tell the sound thereof whence it cometh or whither it goeth. We live and we grow, yet we perceive not, nor are we conscious of our growth. So in the act of our regeneration, this is the work of God in our nature at baptism, and by continual renewal in Christ are we kept alive who were dead. Well may we ask, "Can these dry bones live," if we know not the exceeding love of God to-us-ward.

The contemplation of human nature in its weakness, lays open the deep foundation of God's wonderful love, and gives to His word a more awful meaning than is expressed on the mere surface. "Train up a child in the way he should go, that when he is old he may not depart from it," contains the whole moral of education. Passions run riot, desires, appetites unrestrained, all subjugate the loftier faculties of our nature, and raise up, if allowed full license, an almost irresistible antagonism to the exercise of virtue. The heathen affords an illustration of the undeveloped life, the wicked and fallen Christian, is a pitiful and fearful illustration of that more terrible state to which man is reduced, when, with prostrated spiritual reason, he surrenders himself to the guidance of sensual affections. With a conscience free to know the right, and to know the wrong, with spiritual reason enlightened to desire the good, man was surrounded with all those gifts and aids by which he might have fed his holiest affections: and now fallen and degenerate as he is, from whence is he to receive that power unto holiness, without which he cannot see God. Here is the mystery of wonder; this it is which makes us ashamed, and humbles us in the dust. Weak, unconscious, helpless, who is it that takes the wailing infant and embraces it with the arms of mercy; who is it that early into its passive nature infuses that "spirit of life," which even in himself "grew in wisdom and stature and in favour, both with God and man;" and who has expressly declared that his servants are to wage war against sin, that their nature be not again corrupted? And further, who is it that to the unbaptised gives the strength to believe unto repentance, who "enlightens the blind eyes," that they may see? Surely, none other than that Spirit which proceedeth from the Father and the Son! To subjugate desires evil and gross, to crush out the licentiousness of passion, is the work of the Holy Spirit himself operative, and as an operator applying to us Christ's nature. Now, the necessity of the Sacrament of

Holy Baptism, **as a means of** grace, is set forth in Scripture in language **too strong** to be considered as referring to man's mere admission into a **worldly society.**

"Men and brethren, let me freely speak unto you of the patriarch David, that he is both dead and buried, and his sepulchre is with us unto this day. Therefore, being a prophet, and knowing that God had sworn with an oath to him, that of the fruit of his loins, according to the flesh, he would raise up Christ to sit on his throne; He seeing this before spake of the resurrection of Christ, that his soul was not left in **hell, neither his flesh did see** corruption. This Jesus hath God raised up, whereof we are all **witnesses.** Therefore, being by the right hand of God exalted, and having **received of the Father the promise** of the Holy Ghost, he hath shed forth **this, which ye now see and hear.** For David is not ascended into the heavens: but he saith himself **the Lord said unto** my Lord, sit thou on my right hand until **I make thy foes thy footstool.** Therefore, let all the house of Israel know assuredly, that **God hath made that** same Jesus, whom ye have crucified, **both Lord and Christ.** Now when they heard this **they** were pricked in **their heart, and said unto Peter and to the rest of the** apostles; men and **brethren what shall we do?** Then Peter said unto them, repent and be **baptized, every one of you, in the name of Jesus Christ,** *for the remission of sins, and ye shall* receive the gift *of the Holy Ghost.* For the promise is *unto you,* and to *your* children, and *to all* that are afar off, *even* as many as the Lord our God shall call. And with **many other words did** he testify and exhort, saying, **save** yourselves from this untoward **generation.** Then they that gladly received his word were *baptized:* and *the same day* there were added *unto them* about three thousand souls. And they continued steadfastly in the apostles' doctrine and fellowship, and in breaking of bread, and in the prayers."

Can any promise be stronger than this?

Did these people believe St. Peter or not, when he annexed to the act of baptism such promises? or are we to believe with many now a-days, that this baptism in the triune name, means ONLY an admission into a visible Church, and has no direct reference to that body of elect children, whom it is God's purpose to bring unto final salvation if they will but hear. In fourteen places baptism is thus set forth.

I. *St. John's Gospel* iii. 3-5. "Except a man be born again, he cannot see the kingdom of God. Nicodemus **saith unto Him, How can a man be born when he is old? can** he enter the **second** time into his mother's womb, and be born? **Jesus answered,** verily, verily, I say unto thee, except a man be born *of water and of the spirit,* he cannot enter into the kingdom of God."

II. *St. Matthew* xxviii. 19, 20. "Go ye, therefore, and **teach** all nations, baptising them in the name of the Father, and of the Son, and **of** the Holy **Ghost:** teaching them to observe all things whatsoever I have commanded **you:** and lo, I am with you alway, even unto the end of the world."

III. *St. Mark* xvi. 16. "He that believeth and is *baptized* shall be **saved;** but he that believeth not shall be damned."

IV. *Acts* ii. 37-39. **"Men and brethern, what shall we do? Then Peter** said unto them, repent, **and be** *baptised* **every one of you in the name of Jesus Christ** *for the remission* **of** *sins,* **and ye shall receive the gift of the Holy Ghost.** For the promise **is unto you and to your children,"** &c.

Acts xxii. 10 and 16. **"And I said, what shall I do, Lord?** And the Lord **said unto me, arise, and go unto Damascus; and there it shall be** told thee **of things which are appointed for thee to do.** And now, why tarriest thou? **arise and** be *baptised,* and *wash away thy sins,* calling on the name of the Lord."

VI. *Romans* vi. 1, 2, 3, 4. "What shall we say then? **Shall we** continue **in sin,** that grace may abound? God forbid. How shall **we, that are dead to sin,** live any longer therein? Know ye not, that *so many* **of** us as **were baptised unto Christ, were baptised into his death?** *Therefore we are buried with him by baptism into death;* that like as Christ was raised up from the dead **by** the glory of the **Father, even so we also should walk in newness of life."**

VII. *Colossians* ii. 12, 13. "*Buried with him in baptism wherein* also **ye are** *risen* **with him through the faith of the operation of God,** who hath raised him **from the dead. And you, being dead in your sins,** and the uncircumcision of your **flesh, hath he quickened together with him, having forgiven you** all trespasses. iii. 1.—"If ye then be *risen* **with Christ, seek those** things which are **above, where** Christ sitteth **on the right hand of God;** set your affection on things **above,** not on things **on the earth.** *For ye are dead,* **and** your life is hid **with Christ in God."**

VIII. *Ephesians* v. 25, 26, **"Husbands, love your wives, even as** Christ **also** loved the Church, and **gave himself for it, that he** might sanctify **and cleanse** it with the *washing of water* by the word."

IX. *Titus* iii. 5. "Not by words of righteousness which **we have done, but according** to his mercy he saved us, by the *washing of regeneration,* **and** renewing **of the Holy** Ghost."

X. *Galatians* iii. 35, 27. **"For** ye are all the children **of God** by faith in Christ **Jesus. For** *as many of you* as have been *baptised* **into Christ** have put on Christ."

X. *Hebrews* x. 21, 22. "Having an high-priest over the house of God; let us draw near with a true heart, in full assurance of faith, having our hearts sprinkled from an evil conscience, and our *bodies washed with pure water*."

XII. 1 *St. Peter* iii. 21. "The like figure whereunto, even *baptism doth also now save us* (not the putting away of the filth of the flesh, but the answer of a good conscience toward God) by the resurrection of Jesus Christ."

XIII. 1 *Corinthians* x. 1, 2, 3, 4, 5, 6, 11. "Moreover, brethren, I would not that ye should be ignorant, how that *all* our fathers were under the cloud, and *all* passed through the sea; and were *all baptised* unto Moses in the cloud and in the sea; and did *all* eat the same spiritual meat; and did *all* drink the same spiritual drink; for they drank of that spiritual rock that followed them; and that rock was Christ," &c. "Now all these things happened unto them for ensamples: and they are written for our admonition, upon whom the ends of the world are come."

XIV. 1 *Corinthians* xii. 12, 13, 27 "For as the body is one, and hath many members, and all the members of that body, being many, are one body: so also is Christ. For *by one spirit we are all baptised* into one body, whether we be Jews or Gentiles, whether we be bond or free; and have been all made to drink into one spirit. * * * Now ye are the body of Christ and members in particular."

Christ became the son of man, in order that he might give us "power to become the sons of God;" "and this," says Bishop Andrews, "was the chief end of his being 'God with us,' to give us *a capacity, a power* to become the sons of God, by being born again of water and of the spirit: for *originem quam sumpsit ex utero Virginis possuit in* fonte *Baptismatis*,—the same original that himself took in the womb of the Virgin to us-ward, that he placed for us in the fountain of baptism to God-ward, which is well therefore called the womb of the Church."

"The free gift came unto all men;" for as "in Adam all die, so in Christ shall all be made alive." God hath revealed to man that he is a spiritual being; that although he has by nature a connexion with this earth—that he is of the earth, earthy—yet, that he has also a connexion with the heavenly. How has he this golden link? The word of God will tell us that it is through the God-man, through Christ's human nature. The history of baptism and of holy communion, as taken from scripture, shews how Christ gives himself to us in the right celebration and due reception of his sacraments, for St. John saith :

"I indeed baptise you with water unto repentance; but he that cometh after me is mightier than I, whose shoes I am not worthy to bear: he shall baptise you with the Holy Ghost and with fire: Whose fan is in his hand, and he will throughly purge his floor, and gather his wheat into the garner; but he will burn up the chaff with unquenchable fire. Then cometh Jesus from Galilee to Jordan unto John, to be baptised of him. But John forbade him, saying, I have need to be baptised of thee, and comest thou to me? And Jesus answering said unto him, suffer *it to be* so now; for thus it becometh us to fulfil all righteousness. Then he suffered him. And Jesus, when he was baptised, went up straightway out of the water: and, lo, the heavens were opened unto him, and he saw the Spirit of God descending like a dove, and lighting upon him. And lo, a voice from heaven, saying, This is my beloved Son, in whom I am well pleased."

And in St. Luke, c. iii.:

"Now when all the people were baptised, it came to pass, that Jesus also being baptised, and praying, the heavens was opened, and the Holy Spirit descended in a bodily shape like a dove upon him, and a voice came from heaven, which said, Thou art my beloved Son; in thee I am well pleased."

In St. Matthew it is—

"And Jesus came and spake unto them, saying, All power is given unto me in heaven and in earth. Go ye therefore and teach all nations, baptising them in the name of the Father, and of the Son, and of the Holy Ghost: teaching them to observe all things whatsoever I have commanded you; and lo, *I am with you alway, even* unto the end of the world. Amen."

For saith St. Peter—

"As I began to speak, the Holy Ghost fell on them as on us at the beginning. Then remembered I the word of the Lord, how that he said, John indeed baptised with water: but ye shall be baptised with the Holy Ghost. Forasmuch then as God gave them the like gift as *he did* unto us, who believed on the Lord Jesus Christ: what was I, that I could withstand God?"

And who are we, that we should question his power to do as he did then? Are we recipients of John's baptism only? Surely, Christ's baptism was higher than that of John's.

"For it came to pass that while Apollos was at Corinth, Paul having passed through the upper coasts came to Ephesus: and finding certain disciples, he said unto them, Have ye received the Holy Ghost since ye believed? And they said unto him, We have not so much as heard whether there be any Holy Ghost. And he said unto them, Unto what then were ye baptised? And they said, Unto John's baptism. Then said Paul, John verily baptized with the baptism of repentance, saying unto the people, that they should believe on him which should come after him, that is, on Christ Jesus. When they heard this, they were baptized in the name of the Lord Jesus. And when Paul had laid his hands upon them, the Holy Ghost came on them; and they spake with tongues, and prophesied. And all the men were about twelve."*

Here we have the same open testimony as in the baptism of Jesus himself; here are the outward sign and the spiritual gift together, for were these people not baptised, at one and the same time, with the outward sign and the inward grace? Again, in Acts, c. ix., we read of Ananias saying: "Brother Saul, the Lord *even* Jesus that appeared unto thee in the way as thou camest, hath sent me, that thou mightest receive thy sight and be filled with the Holy Ghost. And immediately there fell from his eyes as it had been scales: and he received sight forthwith and arose and (how did he obtain the gift of the Holy Ghost) he was baptised."

---

* If our Lord was *to baptise* with The Holy Ghost, as John had said, the prophecy was fulfilled when Christ began to give The Holy Ghost through baptism, by those whom He hath sent.

THE REJECTION OF CHRIST.

"Look to yourselves, that we lose not those things which we have wrought, but that we receive a full reward.

"Whosoever transgresseth, and abideth not in the doctrine of Christ, hath not God. He that abideth in the doctrine of Christ, he hath both the Father and the Son.

"If there come any unto you, and bring not this doctrine, receive him not into your house, neither bid him God speed:

"For he that biddeth him God speed is partaker of his evil deeds."

The whole object of the Church is to seek and to save the lost, and to bring those who fall into trespasses and sin unto Jesus Christ. That a man may receive the grace of God, and yet receive it in vain, is plainly revealed, for St. Paul says: "We then as workers together with him beseech you also, that ye receive not the grace of God in vain," and, "Moreover, brethren, I would not that ye be ignorant, how that ALL our fathers were under the cloud, and all passed through the sea; and were ALL baptised unto Moses in the cloud and in the sea; and did ALL eat the same SPIRITUAL meat; and did ALL drink the same SPIRITUAL drink; for they drank of that spiritual rock which followed them, and that rock was Christ. But with many of them God was not well pleased, for they were overthrown in the wilderness." Received into the kingdom of God, into His visible church, and enjoying the blessed privileges and protection which that society was capable of diffusing around God's people, they, in a large sense, were partakers of "the spiritual rock which followed them," but some of them refused to acknowledge their indebtedness for these great mercies, they recognised not the protecting hand that led them and fed them; so as we have read, " with many of them God was not well pleased; for they were overthrown in the wilderness," and so St. Paul, using the case of these fallen ones, says to us christians, "Neither let us tempt Christ." Again he addresses the Corinthians, as men who having received the grace of God were committing sin against Him, wherefore he warns them: " Nay ye do wrong, and defraud, and that your brethren. Know ye not, that the unrighteous shall not inherit the kingdom of God," and he counsels the church to discipline its evil members. (See Corinth. 1, ch. v., to the 11th verse.)

Such is the scriptural command to the church, and so is the Church of England, justified in the lamentation uttered in her commination service, and all Christian men must regret that absence of discipline, so necessary to a healthy state of morals and religion, and the want of which allows so much open evil to exist unrebuked.

These, then, are positive declarations from God's holy word; full of goodly promises and comforting assurance to those who are striving to follow the blessed steps of Christ's most holy life, but to the ungodly and despisers of Christ they are a savour unto death. From the express words of scripture learn that,

" Jesus answered and said unto them, Murmur not among yourselves. No man can come to me, except the Father which hath sent me draw him; and I will raise him up at the last day. It is written in the prophets, And they shall be all taught of God. Every man *therefore that* **hath** *heard*, **and** hath learned of the Father, cometh unto me. Not that any man hath seen the Father, **save** he which is of God, he hath seen the Father."

And again:

" Jesus said, I thank thee, O Father, Lord of heaven and earth, **because** thou hast hid these things from the wise and prudent, and has revealed them unto babes. Even so, Father: for so it seemed good in thy sight. All things are delivered unto me of my Father: and no man knoweth the Son, but the Father; neither knoweth any man the Father, save the Son, and *he* to whomsoever the Son will reveal *him*. Come unto me, all ye that labour and are heavy laden, and I will give you rest. Take my yoke upon you and learn of me; for I am meek and lowly in heart, and ye shall find rest unto your souls. For my yoke is easy and my burden is light."

Read this and tremble. We are responsible for the use of our senses, the gates of entrance from the outer world to the spirit. Here then is the stronghold of the missionary, here is his comfort. He is an instrument in God's hands, he is a servant with God's holy word, wielding the sword of the spirit, a Minister IN Christ. Here is he, as an instrument, gathering those whom God elects to salvation. It was the Spirit that moved on the face of the waters, it is by the Spirit that life was given to man, and by the work of the same Spirit man is now taught daily to accept Christ, and after baptism the same Spirit enriches with manifold gifts and daily renews him in the most blessed nature of Christ.

"The Lord said, My spirit shall not always strive with man, for that he also *is* flesh."

Above Jesus says plainly, "No man can come to him, except the Father which sent him draw him; and on this are all our hopes placed, when in God's might we go to the heathen with his word. Man is fallen, God must touch the stony heart; God's prevenient grace, his gift of power unto repentance, must be given to the reasoning man, ere the gift of Christ's nature can be truly imparted. To the unconscious child it is God's free act, and the imparting of Christ's nature an act of free unmerited mercy.

"If ye love me, keep my commandments. And I will pray the Father, and he shall give you another Comforter, that he may abide with you for ever. Even the Spirit of Truth, whom the world cannot receive, because it seeth him not, neither knoweth him: but ye know him; for he dwelleth with you, and shall be in you."

And also:

"It is expedient for you that I go away; for if I go not away, the Comforter will not **come to you;** but if **I** depart, I will send him unto you. And when **he is come he will reprove** the world of sin, **and of** righteousness, and of judgment: Of sin, because they believe not **on me;** of righteousness, because **I go to my Father, and ye see me no more;** of judgment, because the prince **of this world is judged. I have yet many things to say unto you, but** ye can**not bear them now. Howbeit, when he, the Spirit of Truth, is come,** he will guide you into all truth; for he shall not speak of **himself: but** whatsoever he shall hear, *that* shall he speak: and he will show you things **to come.** He shall glorify me; **for he** shall receive of mine, and shall **show** *it* **unto** you. All things that the Father hath are mine; therefore said I, that **he shall** take of mine, and shall shew *it* unto you. A little while, and ye shall not see **me;** and again **a little while,** and ye shall see me, because I go to the Father."

Every good gift, and every perfect gift, is from above. **Man, lost and fallen in his nature, can do** no good thing, **except** God be with **him; so it is** the **great** and merciful work of the Holy Spirit to **lead men to receive** Christ's work. The heathen and the wicked alike **are first** to hear God's law through his **messengers, and then they are** taught by God's **spirit to accept Christianity,** to assent **to its** principles, and **thus a creature is turned** to God by the Holy Ghost. But **this is not** enough—there is yet a further work, this gift of **grace, of** the spirit, must lead to another, we may believe, but—

"He that believeth and is baptised shall be saved; but he that **believeth** not shall be damned."

In holy baptism our fallen nature must be born again, and **have** Christ's nature imparted **to it; for saith Jesus:**

"I am the true vine, and my Father is the husbandman. Every branch in me that beareth not fruit, **he** taketh away; and **every** branch that beareth fruit, he purgeth it, that **it may** bring forth more **fruit.** Now ye are clean through the word which I have spoken unto you. **Abide in me,** and I in you. As the branch cannot bear fruit of itself, except it abide in the vine; no more **can ye, except ye** abide in **me.** I am the vine, ye *are* the branches: he that **abideth in me, and** I in him, the same bringeth forth much fruit: for without me ye can do nothing. If a man abide not in me, he is cast forth as a branch, and is withered: and men gather them, and cast *them* into the fire, and they are burned. If ye abide in me, and my words abide in you, ye shall ask what ye will, and it shall be done unto you."

Also:

"Then said Jesus unto them again, verily, verily, I say unto you, I am the door of the sheep.

"All that ever came before me are thieves and robbers: but the sheep did not hear them. I am the door: by me if any man enter in, he shall be saved, and shall go in and out, and find pasture."

Verily, as in Adam's nature all die, so is it by Christ's humanity that all are made alive. The regeneration of man's nature is the work of Christ, and in baptism is accomplished by the Holy Spirit imparting Christ's nature.

* "The only sure anchor of all our hopes for a joyful resurrection unto the life of glory, is the mystical union which must be wrought here on earth betwixt Christ's *human nature glorified*, and our mortal or dissoluble nature. The divine nature indeed is the prime fountain of life to all, but though inexhaustible in itself, yet a fountain whereof we cannot drink, save as it is derived unto us through the *human nature* of Christ."

Yes, verily, he took our nature that he might raise it; he took it into conjunction with the Divine nature that he might exalt us unto the same place whither he is gone before; he glorified it, that from himself might flow to us his regenerating and renewing spirit, he ascended with it to heaven, with its wounds and sacrificial bruises, there to be the continuous sacrifice, the everlasting manna which he rains down on his church.

In both Sacraments, the same doctrine is discovered. In one, Christ's nature is imparted, in the other by it He sustains our life; in both the Holy Ghost is the wonderworker. Regenerated and daily renewed, thus may we say, that God's holy Spirit must be given to us, to lead us to

---

* Jackson's Works, vol. x., pp. 34-36, Oxford, 1844.

Christ, that in baptism he unites us to Christ, and **that by the Eucharist He renews us in Christ.**

"Jesus answered and said unto him, verily, verily, I say unto thee, except a man be born again, he cannot see the kingdom of **God**. Nicodemus saith unto him how can a man be born when he is old? can he enter the second time into his **mother's womb, and be born?** Jesus answered, verily, verily, I say unto thee, except **a man be born of water and of the spirit, he** cannot enter into **the** kingdom of God. **That which is born of the flesh is** flesh: **and** that which is born of the spirit is spirit. **Marvel not that I said unto** thee, ye must **be** born again. The wind bloweth where **it listeth, and thou** hearest the **sound** thereof, but canst not tell whence it cometh, **and whether** it goeth; **so is every one** that is born of the spirit. Nicodemus answered and **said unto** him, how can these things be?"

And in Romans, c. iv., St. Paul says:

"**I beseech** you therefore, **brethren, by** the mercies of God, that ye present your bodies a living sacrifice, **holy,** acceptable unto God, *which* is your reasonable service. And be not conformed to this world; but be ye transformed by the renewing of your mind, **that ye may** prove what *is* that good, and acceptable, and perfect will of God. **For I say, through the grace given unto** me, **to every man** that is among **you, not to think** *of himself* more highly than **he ought to** think; but to think soberly, according **as God** hath dealt **to** every man the measure of faith. For as we have many **members in one** body, and all members have not the same office. So we, *being* many, are one **body** in Christ, and every one members one of another."

Man that is born of **a** woman hath but **a** short **time to live, and is full of misery. Such is** experience: **nevertheless** we believe in a God who is merciful, and **plenteous in** goodness and truth; an all-perfect, all-holy, almighty **God.** Whence this fullness of misery then in man? Ask thine **own heart; sound** the depths **of** thine **own conscience;** discover the doings and the inclinations of **thine** own nature. God, in holy baptism, has given the capacity to receive and perform the good, but the vile and stubborn will inclines us **to turn** to evil. Disobedience was begotten in the body, and the earth-born strives against **that** which is born of God. We **are not all at once to attain to** the perfect image of

Christ: he does no more for us than for his chosen Apostles; he means that we should grow unto his likeness: we must take up our cross daily, and follow him. No man by searching can find out God; for after that in the wisdom of God the world by wisdom knew not God, it pleased God by the foolishness of preaching to save them that believe,—even so the things of God knoweth no man, but the spirit of God. Now we have received, not the spirit of the world, but the spirit which is of God; that we might know the things that are freely given to us of God. Children by adoption and grace, we are inexcusable: called of God, baptised into the death of Jesus Christ, washed in his blood, and breathed upon by the Holy Spirit, to unite us to Jesus' nature, we have the power to grow in grace, and unto the likeness of Christ. Let us then cling to Jesus. "Except these abide in the ship, they cannot be saved." The storms of sin, of passion, of wickedness, may rage without; yet so long as we continue to live in Christ, will Christ remain with us, to strengthen and sustain. It is only when, like Pharaoh, we set at nought the warnings of God, that he casts us off. Hear what he says:

"Arise and go down to the potter's house, and there I will cause thee to hear my words. Then I went down to the potter's house, and behold he wrought a work on the wheels, and the vessel that he made of clay was marred in the hand of the potter; *so he made it again another* vessel, as seemed good to the potter to make it."

Are we not marred vessels? Were we not in Adam sadly marred? Are we not in baptism again made other vessels, as seemeth good to our potter, Christ and the Spirit, to make us? The free grace of God, thus given to us, not for any merits of our own—for of his own free will begat he us—enables each one who has received the gift "daily to advance in godliness." But "if it do evil in my sight, that it obey not my voice (implying that there is the power to obey), then will I repent of the good wherewith I said I would benefit them."—Is. c. xviii. **The baptised man,** taught to know that the Holy Spirit has implanted in him a capacity to live in Christ, and Christ **promising to feed him with** his **life-giving body** and blood, **and** daily **to renew him by the Holy Spirit, rises refreshed and** strengthened **from every act of** obedience; he knows and feels the awful **responsibility** that **is on** him, and should dread to pollute the garment **of Christ,** which has been put upon him; for if **he** neglect **all these** strivings of the Spirit, and cast away the gift of God, **he is as** Judas **or they of** Sodom.

An American divine observes:

"**It** is asked, **how can I, poor,** weak **creature** that I am, come forward **to** baptism, **and hear the** minister tell the people that **I have been** 'born **again**' **of God's Holy** Spirit, while I am **so** painfully **conscious of indwelling sin?**

"So far from alarming you, this **comparison of the** spiritual to the natural birth ought greatly to encourage **you.** What **is man when first born** into this material **world? A babe. He has life indeed, but little** else: he is feeble, helpless, dependent. **He can neither** walk nor feed himself; and the flame **of** life **burns so** feebly, that **a rude blast would** at once extinguish **it, or** if neglected it would flicker and die of itself.

"**For this** helpless being God **provides a mother. She protects, and** clothes, **and feeds it. Away from** the mother it must **die. God** might sustain its life by other means, but **in the usual** order of his providence it **must** draw strength **from its mother's breast.**

"**Now hear is a little sickly babe;** its vitality is chiefly expressed **by** signs of **suffering and** cries of want. **Shall we** lay it down to die? **Oh, no.** A healthy child might bear neglect for a brief season; but as for this one, pity demands that we seek its mother. And, mother, guard it with a special care; keep it from the wintry blast; give it the support it needs, and let it be most gently dealt with.

"And are we to be born *full-grown men* into the spiritual world, and to begin where St. Paul left off? Are we to be at once teachers, examples, giants in the faith? Is there no nursing-mother needed for us? Think of it then in this light: we can be born again only as *babes in Christ*, and the church is our mother appointed to train us up to manhood. It is quite true that conviction may be sudden; but our Lord once said to a convinced man: 'When thou art converted strengthen thy brethren.'"

Lord! to accomplish the end of my creation, how to work out my destiny I could not have known, unless thou hadst given me a revelation of thy will, and the manifestation of thyself.

Yes, surely God will not do wickedly, neither will the Almighty pervert judgment. Who hath given him a charge over the earth? or who hath disposed the whole world? If he set his heart upon him, if he gather unto himself his breath, all flesh shall perish together, and man shall turn again unto dust.

So we believe according to our Lord's own saying that 'Except a man be born of *water and of the spirit*, he cannot enter the kingdom of God, (for) that which is born of the spirit is spirit,' thus plainly saying to us, 'Marvel not but believe, that when you are baptised with water it is the outward sign that you are receiving AN inward spiritual grace, my life-imparting nature, which causes you to be born again—you were Adam's before, after this, you are planted in my death, and are henceforth spiritual beings. And so with that other gift of myself; you are by baptism in relation to me as spiritual beings, and my quickening spirit shall increase in you to your glory; shall be imparted to you, when in fulfilling righteousness you eat of that bread and drink of that cup."

"For neither pray I for these alone, but for them also which shall believe on me through their word; That they all may be one; as thou Father, art in me, and I in thee, that they also may be one in us; that the world may believe that thou has sent me. And the glory which thou gavest me I have given them; that they may be one, even as we are one; I in them, and thou in me, that they may be made perfect in one: and that the world may know that thou hast sent me, and hast loved them, as thou hast loved me.

How to walk and to live perfectly we could not find, had no manifestation of sinless life, and perfect holiness, been vouchsafed to degenerate man. Revelation and manifestation are to man essential, they are both concessions to the wants of his nature, and grants of mercy by a merciful God. God manifest in the flesh is to man at once a God known, satisfying to his understanding, and the evidence of his creation for a spiritual life. In him there is not only ideal perfection, not only a conception of the good and the beautiful, and the true, but Christ is to him the perfect living pattern of holiness. There, is the sinless life, the exemplar, in whom there is no guile, holy Jesus! the same yesterday, to-day, and for ever. By the cravings and wants of man's spiritual nature is revealed the perfect adaptation of God's revealed Word to his necessities; it is the system of philosophy, of ethics, which alone is satisfying. In that blessed book, the Word of God, is there alone found the history of a faultless life, and a code of moral and religious duty to be observed and practised; there alone can man find how best he may serve and worship God, how surely be saved.

The life of Jesus is the light of the world; in that smitten rock is there indeed the gushing font of living water, which can alone flow on unto eternal life;

> "Rock of ages, cleft for me,
> Let me hide myself in thee;
> Let the water and the blood,
> From thy wounded side which flowed,
> Be of sin the double cure—
> Save from wrath and make me pure!

> "Nothing in my hand I bring,
> Simply to thy cross I cling:
> Could my tears for ever flow—
> Could my zeal no langour know—
> All for sin would not atone,
> Thou must save and thou alone!"

Unseen, but ever present, Christ is the life and light of the soul. Who would in some slight degree understand that article of the Christian creed, which sets forth the Son of God as "light of light," may turn to the whole kingdom of organic creation, and see the cold, dark, withering blight which falls on all growth, when the bright pure light of the sun of heaven is withdrawn for length of time, fading, and weak, and dying, things droop day by day, till death overtakes them, or the re-appearing of the life-sustaining beams rekindle their fleeting vitality: or turn we our thoughts in upon ourselves, and call back for solemn meditation the confession of helplessness which freely and spontaneously rushed on the soul, when, lost in the deep recess of the pathless woods, the guiding light of day no longer prevented the stumbling foot, and the loneliness of isolation and despair left us before the great Unseen. Or having gone down to the sea, watch the setting sun sink to rest, enveloped in crimson glare; the pathless ocean, glassy and still, hath not a breath to ruffle its bed; shadowy and grey, the lessening horizon closes around, while dark clouds gather and the departing rays leave us in fear and doubt to the roughening swell. Tossed by the rising wind, angry waves imperil the labouring ship. Amid such scenes of elemental strife, all waged in darkness, how deep the sense of weakness? How alone do we seem? How do we long to say: "Carest Thou not that we perish?" But let the gleam of hope appear on the troubled clouds and a helping hand is felt to be near; the danger lessened by approaching light. Are we as spiritual beings never in danger such as this? Does the soul amid storms of temptation never realize the crushing power of sin which alone subdues when the light of God is withdrawn? No traveller surrounded by night, and awed by the howling of the angry blast, ever felt more keenly the vanity of man's strength, than does the terror stricken sinner, when the wailing of conscience renders evident the demons of sin which hover round him. Let us but realize the ruin and wreck which would soon overspread a world if the sun was turned into sackcloth, and we may somewhat imagine the utter undoing of human nature, if the Sun of Righteousness was to withdraw his shining. Lord God, leave not thy redeemed ones in the wild waste of sin, nor in the sea of trouble; but let thy bright beams of light fall ever upon them.

"Sun of my soul, my Saviour dear,
It is not night if thou art near,
Oh, may no earth-born cloud arise,
To hide thee from thy servant's eyes."

Heavenly Father! we thy creatures now see through a glass darkly, but yet thou hast given us light. For thy law was revealed by signs and wonders! the law which was a rule of life for man, the being whom thou hast made, the link which joins this lower world to that higher one in which spirits dwell. Oh, Father, teach us to see thine immutable truth, in the perfection of that law of order and stability which governs the material world! Thy divine energy, thy creative and merciful providence, which, watching always over the children of men, reveals and manifests eternal power and goodness to them: but teach us by the Holy Spirit to adore and bless thy great name for the revelation of thy will, thy law—the revelation of those higher moral and holy truths, and for the manifestation of thyself to lost man. God, we adore and bless thee in that, in the person of the blessed Son, we have with our eyes seen, and with our hands touched The Life. So, Lord, as thou didst in thy bodily presence speak unto thy servants of old time: so now, to us "life-imparting Christ:" sustain in us, by the Holy Spirit, that nature of thine, which alone is effectual to all our wants and defilements. Cast out our sins, heal our wounded nature: Evermore Jesus! diffuse thyself through our whole nature, "that this corruptible may put on incorruption." Jesus, holy blessed Jesus! our Saviour, and our God, as thou didst humble thyself to take unto thyself man's nature, enable us ever to humble ourselves in true sorrow, to receive thee as thou hast promised. Penitent in heart, contrite, broken in spirit, may we go to thine altar, and there pour out our soul in supplication for pardon; surely believing that thou art there, in the power of thy spirit to speak the word by which thou didst give thyself to thine Apostles. Like the outcast, though we may come to thee in the clothing, the filth-stained rags in which we fed with swine; Jesu, although covered with the leprous skin, with which sin hath clothed us, yet do thou to us now, as thou didst to our brother of old, and heal us by thy life-giving presence. We must offer thee the gift which thou hast commanded, but we will wash our hands in innocency, and so go to thine altar.

 Purged and cleansed by Christ, through the merciful goodness of God; the children of the world converted, and turned heavenward, must loiter not to look on the burning Sodom which they are forsaking. A brighter, a better and a holier country is before them, and Jesus himself walks with them: his rod and his staff supports them. In every act of his church, in every ministration is the flowing forth of his voice: from the blessed scriptures, Jesus, by the ear of faith, is heard to speak; by the eye of faith is seen; and as he was known of old by the breaking of bread, so too now, shall he be ever known to his faithful followers. We are assured of the efficacy of the incarnation and atonement, by the teaching of apostles and prophets, as the Holy Ghost gave utterance, and we have experience in the success of the work in the establishment of Christ's Church: and further, we learn in what sense we are to understand Christ's injunctions by the witness of scripture. Thus the church gathers from the Holy Scriptures, what a long list of confessors and martyrs have testified; that Jesus is even now fulfilling his work—is pleading for men—redeeming them. He is with them now in memorial representation, and he gives himself to them now, and imparts his nature to them now, when, as spiritual beings, they come by his command to commune with him before his footstool, and to receive that strength which he said, " is sufficient for you."

"O, righteous Father, the world hath not known thee; but I have known thee, and these have known that thou hast sent me. And I have declared unto them thy name, and will declare it: that the love wherewith thou hast loved me may be in them, and I in them."

SACRAMENT OF THE LORD'S SUPPER.

"A son honoureth *his* father, and a servant his master; if then I *be* a father, where *is* mine honour? and if I *be* a master, where *is* my fear? saith the Lord of hosts unto you, O priests, that despise my name. And ye say, Wherein have we despised thy name?

"Ye offer polluted bread upon mine altar; and ye say, Wherein have we polluted thee? In that ye say, The table of the Lord *is* contemptible.

"And if ye offer the blind for sacrifice, *is it* not evil? and if ye offer the lame and sick, *is it* not evil? offer it now unto thy governor; will he be pleased with thee, or accept thy person? saith the Lord of hosts.

"And now, I pray you, beseech God that he will be gracious unto us; this hath been by your means; will he regard your persons? saith the Lord of hosts.

"Who *is there* even among you that would shut the doors *for nought?* neither do ye kindle *fire* on mine altar for nought. I have no pleasure in you, saith the LORD of hosts, neither will I accept an offering at your hand.

"For from the rising of the sun even unto the going down of the same my name *shall be* great among the Gentiles; and in every place incense *shall be* offered unto my name, and a pure offering: for my name *shall be* great among the heathen, saith the Lord of hosts.

"But ye have profaned it, in that ye say, The table of the Lord *is* polluted; and the fruit thereof, *even* his meat, *is* contemptible."—*Malachi.*

By revelation we learn that God has established a covenant with his people, and left effectual signs of the reality of His Presence with them, assuring them of the real impartation of those heavenly gifts, which he covenants to bestow.

Thus from the gospel we know of the Eucharistic offering. The Church teaches us that, in a sacrament, "there is the outward and visible sign of an inward and spiritual grace given unto us." In baptism the water and Christ's words of institution, spoken by a ministering servant, are the outward signs, and the inward grace, is the impartation of Christ's human nature by the Holy Spirit. In the most holy Eucharist, the bread and wine, the words of institution, spoken by a ministering Priest, and Christian communicants, are the outward signs, The Spiritual or real presence of Christ (according to his own promise and word given to us), is the inward thing signified. But how can this man give us his flesh to eat?

The Catholic Church when primitive and pure, as when reformed and purified at the Reformation, says that the words of Christ are spirit, and are to be understood as from the Spirit of God, wherefore it is taught, that in the Eucharist He is present with the faithful, and that there is such a re-ordering to a new use of the elements by "The Word," as makes them effectual in conveying to us after a spiritual and heavenly manner, the body and blood of Christ; for says a divine of our church, neither *re-order* nor *re-fashion*, in their etymology or their usage, express or imply, any change of the substance, but the contrary, to re-order, re-fashion, expresses a re-arrangement of that which *is;* an ordering, for some other end, *which is exactly our* belief of the consecrated elements, as truly outward visible signs of the inward substance signified. Thus as the bread and wine by God's appointment are made ordinarily to nourish the carnal body, so the word of the same God may make them, also, the sign that He conveys Christ's Body and Blood to the spiritual man. Whoso eateth this bread and drinketh this cup *worthily*, doth really receive Christ. The wicked receive him not, they drive him away, reject him, and receive that which was an instrument of good, to their condemnation. Virtue goes not out for them: the multitude pressed upon him insomuch that they marvelled, the woman only was healed. Our Lord is now in heaven, in His glorified body,

Humanity glorified; He is there, before the Father's throne, pleading **and interceding** for lost man—*there*, is the only real propitiatory sacrifice. The REPRESENTATIVE SACRIFICE of him here on earth is to set forth the Sacrifice of his Death, that like as they of old did lay their hands on the representative victim to be slain, so we representing IN MEMORIAL the slain Christ before the Father, may receive Christ: for the bread and wine after consecration **are so** re-ordered **to a new use, that they become instruments, whereby, through the power** of the **spirit, to the soul of** the penitent receiver is given the **risen humanity, the spiritual** body and blood **of** Christ, **the Life of** Christ, **like rays from the** great sun of heaven, **to renew and** vivify **the** life of the soul.* The Apostle says, "they crucified The Lord of Glory," which is **the same** as if he had said they crucified God; and therefore the blood which was then shed upon the cross was the Blood **of** God. "Take heed therefore unto yourselves, and unto all the flock, over which The Holy Ghost **hath** made you overseers, to feed **THE CHURCH OF GOD,** which He hath purchased with **HIS OWN BLOOD."** With **His own** Blood! How can **that be?** Hath God any blood in him? No! He hath none **in His own** divine nature, but *He had in that* nature which **He** assumed and united to His own divine person, so as to make it his own nature; and by consequence the blood of IT was his own blood, which otherwise it could not have been: **whereas that it was so is evident,** both from this, where **it is** expressly **called so, and** from many other places of God's own word: as likewise that He is Emanuel, God and Man in one Person; **for** from hence it necessarily **follows, that** although He suffered only as man, yet the person that suffered was also **God;** and therefore his sufferings were properly the sufferings **of God, His** blood THE BLOOD

---

* See Bishop Beveridge, Vol. ii.

of God, as He himself calls it." When therefore we think of the blood of Christ cleansing us, we cannot only think of it as the blood of man, for truly it is also, the blood of God, imbued with and partaking of that divine life which renders it, as The blood of Christ, so effectual in the purification and strengthening and refreshing of our souls and bodies. It is Blood which through conjunction with the divinity of Christ is transfused into the spiritual nature of man to his souls salvation. "The Blood of God." What power, what efficacy, what everlasting life, what presence is there in it. As "The Blood is The Life," here is truly eternal life given to man; as The Blood of the Son of God, here is THE LIFE of the Eternal Son, ever ready to impart itself to the penitent soul of those for whom that Blood was taken into conjunction with Deity, that it may ever be in Him the incorruptible fountain of life, flowing unto all who have hungered and thirsted after righteousness. Here is Life of which we must partake if we would live, for the law which said "thou mayest not eat the blood with the flesh" is repealed, and we are ever by faith to eat of the flesh and drink of the Blood, BECAUSE "THE BLOOD IS THE LIFE."

In such sense, the penitent christian realizes with the eye of faith, "an Object" in the blessed sacrament; to him not a carnal, but a "Spiritual body." Faith translates him to the foot of the cross. The body and blood of Christ, THE LIVING CHRIST are before the spiritual man. In the ribaldry, and blasphemy, that swells up from the deriding crowd surrounding The Crucified, he hears but the echo of the tumult of his own sins; in the agony and out-poured blood, he sees his redemption, the only atonement for his sins. TIME and SPACE are not—the spiritual man sees Christ crucified, he feels the effect of that heavenly, holy presence, which forces him to exclaim, "truly this is the Son of God."

We receive the doctrine of the Eucharist as declared out of scripture to be, The Memorial of THE SACRIFICE of the death of Christ, and not only the memorial of the death of Christ: we accept it as the Saviour instituted it, as a MEMORIAL or REPRESENTATIVE SACRIFICE, and not a REITERATED BLEEDING SACRIFICE. We commemorate, that which Christ did, when he made the OBLATION of HIMSELF on that night, on which he was betrayed, "when he took bread and brake it, and gave it to his disciples, saying, take eat, this is my body," we include as a part of the offering made to God, the man himself; and we look with agony and grief, on the awful guilt and sin by which we nailed him to the cross: for the slaying of the sacrifice was the bloody wicked work of Satan, and a sin-cursed race. We thus from Scripture prove that there is a commemoration of the sacrifice of the death of Christ, in direct contradistinction to the doctrine of a reiterated propitiatory sacrifice, as erroneously taught by the Roman Catholic.

And it is not only at that most awful moment at which we receive the outward elements, that we realize the presence of the Saviour; it is not only then that faith brings to us the substance of things hoped for; it is in the whole celebration of that divine sacrifice of praise and thanksgiving, that we feel that we are in His presence, that he abides with us and is near. It was given to St. John to see with illumined vision somewhat of the adoration given to the Lamb of God:

"And I beheld, and lo, in the midst of the throne and of the four beasts, and in the midst of the elders, stood a lamb as it had been slain, having seven horns and seven eyes, which are the seven spirits of God *sent forth into all the earth.*

"And he came and took the book out of the hand of him that sat upon the throne. And when he had taken the book, the four beasts and four-and-twenty elders fell down before the lamb, having every one of them harps, and golden vials full of odours, which are the prayers of the saints.*

"And they sung a new song, saying, Thou art worthy to take the book, and to open the seals thereof; for thou wast slain, and hast redeemed us to God by thy blood out of every kindred, and tongue, and people, and nation, and hast made us unto our God kings and priests, and we shall reign on the earth.

"And I beheld, and I heard the voice of many angels round about the throne and the beasts and the elders; and the number of them was ten thousand times ten thousand, and thousands of thousands; saying with a loud voice, worthy is the Lamb that was slain to receive power, and riches, and strength, and honour, and glory, and blessing.

"And every creature which is in heaven, and on the earth, and such as are in the sea, and all that are in them, heard I saying, blessing, and honour, and glory, and power, be unto Him that sitteth upon the throne, and unto the Lamb for ever and for ever.

"And the four beasts said amen, and the four and twenty elders fell down and worshipped Him that liveth for ever and ever."

Is the heart of the faithful servant of Christ never elevated by that Spirit, which alone teaches aright, to enjoy with wrapt delight, some dim and distant glimpse, it may be, even of that intensified glory and worship which is given to the Lamb that was slain?

God a is Spirit, and they that worship him must worship him in spirit and in truth, "for our conversation is in heaven." Every act of true devotion, every truthful efficacious prayer, every act of true reverence, must be done in spirit and in truth. No man, no matter what his religious sentiments, enters even God's house, without feeling in some measure subdued: in spirit he feels that he is more immediately before that unseen Presence, "that dwelleth not in temples made by hands," but yet who hath set his name there in the place where his honor dwelleth, and is

---

* The belief that the departed spirits pray to God for the perfecting of his Church, is held by many pious souls of all schools of thought.—*See Dr. Cummins, the Presbyterian author.*

present when two or **three are** gathered together in his Name; **and** can it be supposed that any serious christian will hold a lower estimate of that most real and sublime act **of spiritual** worship, of praise, and thanksgiving, which comprehends a no less mysterious and awe-striking reality, **than the** communion with Christ—the being made one **with** him! Cold and dead must that **heart** be, which in any sense can look upon **such a service as this with fleshly** sight. The true, faithful, **penitent,** contrite, spirit-taught sinner, **can only with the eye of vivid** faith "discern the Lord's body." **Since by the** special appointment of our God these representatives of him, the elements, even **the oblation, are brought** in for his **church, and** among the rest **for us**: we must mind what Israel did when the cloud filled the tabernacle. We will not, indeed, fail to worship God **as soon** as these sacraments, and "*Gospel clouds*" appear **in** the sanctuary. Neither the ark, nor any clouds, were ever adored in Israel, but sure it **is, the** ark **was considered** quite otherwise than an ordinary chest, **and the cloud than a** vapour, as soon as God had hallowed them *to be the signs of* His presence. Therefore, as the former people **did** never see the temple or the cloud, **but that** presently at that sight they used to throw themselves on their faces, so **we will** never behold these surer and better **sacraments of the** glorious mercies of God, but as **soon** as we see them used in his church to that holy purpose, that **Christ has** consecrated them to, we will not fail to **realize** the Saviour whom these Sacraments do represent. **May** such a spirit of fervent contemplation ever **be** vouchsafed to every Christian **brother.**

It will be seen "that the words of Christ ARE SPIRIT AND LIFE, **and are to be** understood AS BY THE SPIRIT, that the eucharist is therefore **a spiritual, not a** carnal service, and that the elements are not changed, but *set apart for a new use*, without ANY CHANGE OF SUBSTANCE; that our Lord in His human body is now in heaven, glorified humanity; *He is there, before* the Father's throne pleading for lost men,— THERE, is the ONLY REAL propitiatory sacrifice that was ever offered, and the faithful receiver doth receive into his spirit, when he takes the elements, bread and wine—*not in them, not under them,* but receives with them, The Divine life, the glorified or risen humanity, the spiritual body and blood of Christ.

That our Lord doth impart his perfect humanity to us fallen beings, is a doctrine despised by many, who are eager to believe that Christ is their Saviour, nor will they receive the truth, that the holy Jesus as the second Adam reclaims mankind through an impartation of his nature, although an apostle declares, that we are "bone of his bone, and flesh of his flesh," very members incorporate.

There is nothing more clear, than that we must not confine our thoughts on the great sacrifice, to the acts and circumstances attendant on our Lord's severe and unjust trial, nor alone to what took place at the pascal feast, nor to the humiliating and bloody spectacle exhibited on Calvary; but we must take in ALL the events of his most holy life. It is ours, to see the just condemned by his own, as unjust; the meek and lowly in heart, derided as a blasphemer, because he said, "I am the Son of God;" the holy obedient devout worshipper called a sabbath-breaker, because he healed the sick on that day: the merciful and considerate dispenser of charity, named the friend of publicans and sinners; a healer of deadly sickness because he cured the fever, the agent of Satan. It is ours to see the man in whom was no guile, buffetted and scourged and spit upon; the Prince who come to his own, rejected and despised and crowned in furious enmity, with a reproachful crown. It is ours to see the son of God in his whole life, acting for men, doing all righteousness, walking blameless, holy, without sin, that in this all holy and sinless life might be hidden the reproaches due to the sinful sin-cursed race of Adam. Here was the Living Sacrifice! In some sort humbly imitating this life of Christ, and endeavouring to follow the blessed steps of His most holy life, we may worthily under the spirit's influence, seek to offer ourselves in Christ a sacrifice to our most merciful God; doing as he did, presenting, as a sacrifice, our bodies and souls and spirits bowed down in contrition, while in our hands and with all our hearts we plead by representation the crucified Jesus.

The most devout interpreters of scripture and the most ancient commentators, hesitate not to see in the new use of the Passover by the adorable Redeemer, all the deep and awful significance of the ancient sacrifice; and in the setting up of the Melchisedeckean, the institution of a better, and more enduring priesthood. There was to be no more blood shedding, since the Lamb of God was slain in very deed: but the meat and drink offering of the sacrifice remaineth, and sets forth the Lamb as slain, and by every true penitent heart who eateth and drinketh of these, is the Lamb of God partaken.

To truly receive the Life of Christ which is given to us in this sublime sacrifice we must do that which Christ did; lead holy devout lives, eschew evil and do good, seek peace and ensue it. We must crucify all evil desires, the lust of the flesh, the pride of the eye, and the pride of life; our stubborn wills must be brought into subjection to the will of God: we must purify *ourselves*, our inclinations, continually mortify all corrupt affections, and daily proceed in all godliness of living. So doing, we may then understand the meaning of that presentation which Christ has commanded "us to make" for a continual remembrance of the sacrifice of his death. Taking the bread, that food which is essential to the life of man, the first fruits of the earth, and wine which sustains the waning life, we in memorial symbolize Christ as our daily food, his blood our life-sustaining drink. On the material, we depend for daily renewal of body, on the spirit, for spiritual life. How humble was the simple child-like confidence of them of old, how sincere the trust, how deep the implicit faith in the power of that awful majesty, which, as the God of nature, he was felt to have over all things; having power to re-order all nature according to his own pleasure. Thus St. Chrysostom says, "Not only do the powers of nature accomplish those things for which they are prepared, but if even he enjoin the contrary. Here too, there is great obedience. He commanded the sea, and not only did it not overwhelm, which was its office, but lulling its waves, it transmitted the Jewish people more safely than a rock. The furnace not only burnt not, but yielded a whistling dew. The wild beasts not only devoured not, but held the place of a body-guard to Daniel. The whale not only devoured not, but preserved its deposit safe. The earth not only bore not, but overwhelmed more grievously than the sea itself, when it opened and swallowed up Dathan, and covered the congregation of Abiram. And many other marvellous works might any one observe; that those who are exceeding senseless, and deify nature may learn, that things are not hurried along by a tyranny of nature, but that all things give way and yield to the will of God. For this is the Creator of nature, and at its good pleasure, it re-orders all things which are, at one time retaining their bounds immoveable; and again, when it wills easily removing them and changing to the contrary." And again, "let us obey God every where, and contradict in nothing, although what is said may seem contrary to our reasonings and to appearances. But let His word be mightier than reasonings or appearances. So also, let us do as to the mysteries, not looking only on what lieth before us, but holding to his words; for *his word is infallible* but, our senses are easily deceived." From the testimony of the early church, we may gather very strong reasons (causes) why divine manifestation of power was reasonably to be expected in the spiritual kingdom of Christ. We have already said that our Lord came to establish for ever a kingdom of grace within, as it were, the kingdom of nature, and he must have included in the whole scheme the laws of both. Now he had sufficiently declared himself the Creator of the latter: He must therefore fully assume his lordship in the former. By his word the world was formed, by the power of the same word the course of nature was directed to the end for which it was created, the manifestation of life again and again re-ordered. Superior power over the physical world, and over nature, is most positively shewn in the records of the natural world, and was in more than one instance in the progress of the human race displayed to credible witnesses; and all these miracles were but the types of that power, which in the kingdom of grace is set forth, for the benefit of the subjects of that kingdom. So St. Gregory of Nyssa illustrates how God makes use of things outwardly of no account, to work by them miracles of Grace and power: thus, baptism is the cleansing of sins, the remission of offences, the cause of renewal and regeneration. Regeneration not seen with the eyes, but beheld by the mind. The author of the "*de sacramentis*" asks, what is the word of Christ? That by which all things were made. (And so made, as in their very nature to be whatsoever he willeth.) The Lord commanded, and the heaven was made—the Lord com manded and the earth was made—the Lord commanded and the sea was made; he commanded and all creatures were brought forth. Thou seest then how powerful in working is the Word of Christ.

Hear how the word of Christ is wont to change all creation, and changes when it will the appointment of nature. Askest thou how? Hear! and first of all take an instance from its generation. It is the wont that a man should not be born save of man and woman, and the use of marriage; but because the Lord willed, Christ was born of the Holy Ghost and the virgin, *i. e.*, the mediator between God and man, Christ Jesus. Seest thou how against its appointments and order, He was born a man — was born of a virgin! So there is no alternative for the disbeliever in God's power to do what he listeth. Either this supernatural work was done or it was not, for if there was no personal Christ born of a virgin, an incarnate Saviour given to our race, then the whole Bible is one huge lie, and religion a state of feeling delusive and vile. We perceive how St. Gregory refers the whole efficacy of the sacrament to its spiritual adaptability to our spiritual nature. But the ordinary operations of nature are not all known yet: day by day new and hidden properties of matter are being brought to light, and it is only when matter is placed under extraordinary circumstances, that some of its latent powers or actions are manifested. Do we yet know and understand all the properties of light or heat or electricity? Wonderful as the known properties of matter are, what man is there bold enough to declare, that in the original constitution of matter, and in the constitution of the whole natural world, the contriver of the universe, physical, and moral, did not include the extraordinary, as well as the ordinary manifestations of his power; who can determine the relation between the material and immaterial. Creation is a miracle, and a miraculous power still in display, *i. e.*, if nature is not God and creation possible. The whole moral world is supranatural; its principles, its government, are all above nature, and often in conflict with nature: the mysterious union of Christ with his church—the enlightenment of the moral nature of man by the HOLY SPIRIT, communicating the power and life of Christ to the members of his holy body, by diverse means and by his direct influence: now by physical means, and now by the employment of human agency, thus involving the establishment of a perpetual priesthood and life-giving sacraments in which He is the great mysterious worker: the proclamation of a code of laws, containing rules of life which use and refer to this present world only as temporary, and but a passing stage to a future one. What has all this to do with material being? Above all there is comprehended a supreme Personal God, dealing with creatures made in his image, endowed with reason, beings who have the power of thought, and who in the exercise of the powers of their own mind, feel a reflection of the mind of the Great I Am, which testifies to their own derivation, and to their own undying nature. The cry of despair which comes from the depths of the utterly powerless soul, is but the declaration by that soul, of an agonizing want, which its very nature seeks to have satisfied. The violence of the wicked, the tyranny of vice over virtue, the perpetual war which the good is forced to wage against the bad, the anxious conflict which religion has never ceased to wage against infidelity, are so many indications of the action of a Spirit which is beyond mere material existence, it implies a work to be done by a personal worker, by one who must be, ever with his work. If we indeed are living in a world governed by a code of laws, which neither admit of modification nor suspension, laws which are so rigid and prefixed, that they can in no way be adapted to the circumstances of a creation, which is still in progress of becoming, and not a creation finished; then the conviction is clear and certain, that neither prayer, supplication nor intercession can be of the least avail, for this God has so made the world and its laws, that they cannot be changed in the future as they have been in times past. How contrary is this, however, to the facts of nature, and to that portion of nature which comprehends the life of man. Look at human nature as engaged in its struggle after the attainment of good, watch it prostrate and fallen in baseness; then, contemplate the ideal good, which the heart yearns after; mark the painful repulses which, in the advances towards the attainment of good are encountered, and find too in the main supremacy over evil secured; then balance in this life the reward which is meted out to good, or can be meted out, and say whether this present can be a satisfying life to man, or that it can be the end of his being. What are the lives of the holy men of old, of saints, and martyrs in the latter days, but supernatural lives, lives fitted not for earthly, but heavenly enjoyment: what but so many witnesses to the operation of a power unseen, but not unfelt. These and such as these are like unto him who was "in a trance but had his eyes open;" these are they who in the means of grace, and in the order and ordinances of the church, are able to discern the Lord, who see neither material thing, nor hear human voice, nor discover human action: but see and hear the commanding, persuasive, beseeching voice, and action, of the Son of God, and who, immediately in the spirit, hear one as the Son of Man saying, "come and see." So has it ever been with the followers of Christ: caught up by his spirit, they do not alone hear him saying, "Come and see things that shall be," but in every call made by Him to them, through the agency of His church, **they audibly, even in** their very ears, hear His voice; **in material** sign and symbol, they discern the **Lord: in the holy font,** no longer bare water, but a gushing fountain of blood, flowing from the wounded **side of the Holy One; and in** that holy, that most sublime **and awful Sacrifice of** the death of Christ, they behold the **Son of God, feeding** the multitude with that **supernatural food,** which His word can alone convey **to the weak** and starving **souls of men. Who** was it ordained **that material bread** should strengthen and refresh **the body? None other than** he, who in the plenitude of **his power was pleased to** ordain that the dying soul **should** be made to feel its renewed strength by diligent preparation for, **and** by eating of that bread and drinking of that cup which he instituted, "for then we spiritually eat the flesh of Christ and drink his blood." "From **all** these things dost thou not understand **how much the heavenly word** operateth?" **It is a most profound** mystery, **a miracle of grace, more wonderful** than any, **that at** the giving of the **elements of bread and wine the** Lord's body should **be** given **to heal my body; not part of, but whole Christ:** yes with S. Cyril, **let us, with fullest** assurance; in **the bread partake of the body of** Christ; and *in* the type **of wine his blood; that by** partaking of the spiritual **body and blood of** Christ we might be made of the same **body with** him; for His Word has declared it, and His **Word giveth it.**

St. Chrysostom, expounding the Epistle to the Hebrews, says: "The priests of old," saith the apostle, "serve to the **example and shadow** of heavenly things. What things speaks **he here** of as heavenly? The things spiritual. For what **if they are** celebrated on earth? For **when** our Lord Jesus **Christ lies** immolated, when the Spirit draweth nigh, when He is here who sitteth on the right hand of the Father, when by the laver men become His children, when they are denizens of the heavenly places, when we are strangers to things here, when we leave then our country, our city, and conversation,—how are not all these heavenly things? Yea, let me ask are not our hymns heavenly? The very strains which the divine choirs of the uncorporeal powers chant on high; do not we also here below utter notes in harmony with them? Is not our altar, too, heavenly? Do you ask how? *It hath nought of flesh:* the things presented there become altogether spiritual, not into ashes, not into smoke, not into sacrificial steam is the sacrifice dissolved, but it renders the gifts set out there bright and glad to look upon. And how are the offices less than heavenly, seeing that unto the persons ministering unto them are still spoken from the time that they were first uttered, the words, ' Whose sins ye retain, they are retained; whose sins ye forgive, they are forgiven?' How is it not all heavenly, when these have the very keys of heaven."—Hom. xiv. Heb. "Those things then we ought to seek, wherein is perfection, wherein is truth. The shadow in the law, the image in the gospel, the truth in the heavenly places. Before-time a lamb was the offering, or a bullock ; now, Christ is offered, that is as man, as capable of suffering; and as priest he offers himself, that he may forgive our sins—here in image, there in truth, where with the Father he interferes for us as an advocate. Here then we walk in an image—in an image we behold; there, face to face, where full perfection is, because all perfection is in 'truth.' 'See thou do all things according to the pattern which was shewed thee in the mount.' Did he refer then as concerning the construction of the temple only, or concerning the sacrifices and all the rest? Nay, you will not be wrong in affirming the latter as well; for the Church is heavenly, yea, it is nothing else than heaven.

GOD A SPIRIT AND MAN A SPIRITUAL BEING.

It seems as if men, in these dark days, were determined to close their eyes to the light. Weak in faith, they are like those whose sight is best at the close of day. If it were possible for God's word to lead astray, how few of the congregation which followed Moses, would have escaped idolatry. When we read of the means which were taken to keep them true to their allegiance, we almost wonder, that, they escaped the sin of setting up the creature for the Creator, seeing as we do now, how grievously misrepresented are the words and acts of the Lord.

In the commands which God gave to Moses on the Mount were the most minute details for the service of the Sanctuary, and when Moses asked for guidance, saying, "If I have found grace in Thy sight, shew me now Thy way, that I may know Thee, that I may find grace in Thy sight; and consider that this Nation is Thy People. God said: My presence shall go *with thee*, and I will give thee rest, ..." "Then a cloud covered the tent of the congregation, and the glory of the Lord filled the tabernacle. And Moses was not able to enter into the tent of the congregation, because the cloud abode thereon, and the glory of the Lord filled the tabernacle. And when the cloud was taken up from over the tabernacle, the children of Israel went onward on all their journeys: But if the cloud were not taken up, then they journeyed not till the day it was taken up. For the cloud of the Lord was upon the tabernacle, by day, and fire was on it by night in sight of all the house of Israel, throughout all their journeyings." Now did the people of Israel even once suppose, that, the cloud which they saw was God! Did they not very distinctly know and remember, when Moses entered in, that the cloudy pillar descended and stood at the door of the tabernacle as the sign that the Lord talked with Moses: for all the people saw the cloudy pillar stand at the door of the tabernacle, and "all the people rose up and worshipped." But did they worship the cloud? No! They perfectly understood that, in compassion to their imperfect faith and sinful nature, God was pleased to "hide Himself," that the full blaze of His glory might not consume them as in a moment. And so under the Gospel; clouds appear in his sanctuary now. When faithful men bow low the knee and veil their sight, is it that they kneel in humble adoration to any earthly veils, or do they not rather with the eye of faith see beyond "the rent veil" The Crucified One, One all Holy, like unto the Son of Man standing in the midst, clothed with a vesture dipped in Blood, whose Name is the WORD OF GOD.

> "Eternal Victim from Thy Side,
> Thy love did pour the crimson tide,
> And still Thy Vesture dyed in Blood,
> Gives token of the cleansing flood;
> The Lamb for ever slain art Thou,
> Pleading Thy Death for sinners now."

Can any traces be found in scripture of a doctrine so monstrous as that which implies the transubstantiation of material elements into spiritual substance? Did the Israelites propagate the equally untenable proposition the transubstantiation of the Deity into a cloudy pillar. What these scriptures do really teach is, that God is pleased to draw near to men, and in mercy to their weakness comes to them in such way, that they sink not. Verily thou art a God that hidest thyself; said Isaiah, and yet a very present God.

> "O God unseen yet ever near,
> Thy presence may we feel,
> And thus inspired with holy fear,
> Before Thine altar kneel."

Throughout the whole Scriptures the nearness of God to man is revealed with a clearness that is most remarkable. The faithful in all ages, and at all times, have dwelt securely because they were conscious of the truth of the Word of the Living God. (See Isaiah, xliii.) Through the mouth of the Prophet He bids all the weary and heavy laden to come unto Him; and in order effectually to come He has instituted a way of coming. On the foundation of Apostles and Prophets, Himself the chief corner stone, He has built up and is ever enlarging His church, into which all who are called by the Spirit are sacramentally gathered. No mere assembly of learned men, no gathering of clean and unclean souls to see and to hear great and wonderful things, but a gathering together of spiritual worshippers, that they may, through the power of the Holy Spirit, enlightening their spirits, "see the King in His beauty and behold the land that is very far off." That they may look upon Zion the city of our solemnities, and see Jerusalem, a quiet habitation, a tabernacle that shall not be taken down . . . for there the glorious Lord is unto us a place of broad rivers and streams," "for Christ is the Head of the Church, and He is the Saviour of the body." "He loved it and gave Himself for it; that He might sanctify it and cleanse it with the washing of water by the word, that He might present it to Himself a glorious church." To the true believer the Church of Christ, the solemn assembly of faithful men, stands on holy ground, the holy Mount of Zion from whence they, in faith, see the Heavenly Jerusalem, whither Christ has entered; being come an High Priest of good things to come a Priest for ever, after the order of Melchisedec. A minister of the sanctuary and of the true tabernacle, which the Lord pitched and not man; for every high priest is ordained to offer gifts and sacrifices; wherefore *it is* of necessity that this man have somewhat also to offer."

" In whom we have redemption through his blood, the forgiveness of sins, according to the riches of his grace:

" Wherein he hath abounded toward us in all wisdom and prudence:

" Having made known unto us the mystery of his will, according to his good pleasure which he hath purposed in himself:

" That in the dispensation of the fullness of times he might gather together in one all things in Christ, both which are in heaven, and which are on earth; even in him:

" In whom also we have obtained an inheritance, being predestinated according to the purpose of him who worketh all things after the counsel of his own will."

He hath opened the Kingdom of Heaven to all believers.

> " The saints on earth and those above,
> But one communion make,
> Joined to their Lord in bonds of love,
> All of His grace partake.
>
> " One family we dwell in Him,
> One church above beneath,
> Though now divided by the stream,
> The narrow stream of death.
>
> " One army of THE LIVING God,
> To His command we bow;
> Part of the host have crossed the flood,
> And part are crossing now."

Having, therefore, brethren, boldness to enter into the holiest by the **blood of Jesus, by a** new **and living** way which He hath consecrated for us, through the veil, that **is to say,** His flesh; and having an High Priest over the House of **God, let us** draw near." This language of the Holy Apostle is precise; it speaks of work done by a person, and of work to be done by persons. In the ministration of the Church on Earth there is the pattern close as can be of things heavenly, representations by **effectual signs, of Christ** working in and with His people. The **Priesthood is** representative, for His **Priests are ministers of His** Word and Sacraments, **not theirs.**

They are ministering IN Christ, in His power, in His name, in Him. If then Christ, our most blessed Lord and Saviour, be our High Priest, offering before the Altar of God the Sacrifice which He made of Himself, in ordering the priests and members of His Church on Earth to do as He did, to present themselves, together with an oblation of Bread and Wine, offered to God in remembrance of the Sacrifice of His Death; He is calling upon them to offer themselves a living sacrifice. They are, according to His express promise, made through His sacrifice, partakers of His Body and Blood; "they are one with Christ, and Christ with them." If, in this mysterious service, there be any work wrought in man as a *spiritual being*, it must be a work accomplished by a power outside man. Man must, indeed, subjectively receive the gift; but there must be a worker, who can, into the spirit of man, introduce the Life-sustaining food of the humanity of Christ, for our bodies are made clean by His body, and our souls are washed by His most precious blood. To accept the words of Christ, with child-like faith is to receive implicitly what he promises, neither allowing doubt or cavil to distract our peace. What matters it to us whether men fight about transubstantiation or consubstantiation; the Word of Christ remaineth. Addressing His people as reasoning beings, He tells them to keep Him in remembrance by doing as He did to the end, that they may be united in Him. They are spoken to, not as carnal men, but in the whole Gospel are addressed as SPIRITUAL beings, for the carnal commandment has given way to the power of an endless life. The following quotations, from Hooker, sufficiently explains the doctrine of the Real Presence of Christ, held by the Anglican Church. He thus paraphrases our Lord's words — "This hallowed food, through concurrence of Divine Power, is, in verity and truth, unto faithful receivers instrumentally a **cause of that mystical** participation whereby, as I make myself wholly **theirs, so I give them** in hand, an actual possession of all **such saving grace as my** sanctified body can yield, **and as their souls do presently need,** — this is to them, and in them, **My Body, &c.** "The Bread **which we** break, is it not the communication **of the Body of** Christ?" Hooker continues, "The Body and Blood of Christ are verily and indeed, taken AND received by the faithful. **Let it,** therefore, be sufficient for me, presenting myself **at the** Lord's Table, to know what I there receive from Him without searching or enquiring of the manner *how* Christ **performeth** His promise; let disputes and questions, enemies **to** piety, abatements of true devotion, and hitherto in this cause but over-patiently **heard,** let them take their rest; let curious and sharpwitted men **beat their** heads about what questions themselves will; **the very letter of** the Words of Christ giveth plain **security, that these mysteries do,** as nails, fasten us to the Cross of Christ, that by them **we draw out as** touching efficacy, force, and virtue, **even the** Blood of His gored side; in the wounds of our Redeemer we there dip **our** tongues; we are dyed red both within and without; our hunger is satisfied and our thirst for ever quenched: they are things wonderful which he feedeth, great which he **seeth, and** unheard of which he uttereth, whose soul is **possessed** of this Paschal Lamb, and made joyful in the strength **of the** new wine: this Bread HATH IN IT MORE **than the substance** which our eyes behold; this Cup hallowed **with** solemn benediction availeth to the endless life and welfare both of soul and body, in that it serveth as well for a medicine **to heal** our infirmities and purge our sins as for a sacrifice of thanksgiving: with touching it sanctifieth, it enlighteneth with belief, it truly comforteth us unto the image **of**

Christ. What these elements are in themselves it skilleth not; it is enough that to me which taketh them, they are the Body and Blood of Christ: His promise sufficeth! His word He knoweth which way to accomplish!"

The best commentary on our blessed Lord's words are His acts. What did He? He took an oblation, bread and wine, into His hands; and with these He offered *Himself* to the Father. He then said to His Apostles, "This do (make) in remembrance of me." Every Christian since has done the self-same thing in act. As our Lord offered Himself to God, so He requires that every redeemed child of His should as their Master did, offer himself, together with the oblations of bread and wine, to be a lively sacrifice. But what a difference! We must offer this, our bounden duty and service, and offer simply in obedience, well knowing that that only can make our sacrifice acceptable which is offered by Jesus Christ. As the Jew was to take the blood and strike it on the two side posts and on the upper door posts of the houses, that when the Angel of Death saw the blood he might pass over; so we, representing to our merciful God the holy sacrifice, and being sprinkled with the blood of Jesus, holding in our hands the signs of His sprinkling, and in representation pleading with God the body and blood of His Son, which Jesus Himself as Mediator offers for us, God in His justice is satisfied, and pardons us; He passes over us, hides us from Satan, and blots out our sins. Another fact is here striking: that whereas our sins nailed Christ to the cross—killed Him, it is Christ who slays, *not us*, but our sins, by His own body on the cross.

The withholding from us the truth that our blessed Lord has enlarged and deepened the nature of sacrifice, has been most destructive to full faith in His atonement, and has obscured the perception of our own duty. He never said there was to be *no more sacrifice*, but no more sacrifice *for sin*. And truly, no more blood-shedding, "for a body hast thou prepared." Christ, in the offering of Himself, forever perfected us. Now, throughout the whole scriptures, the redeemed children of Adam are always and everywhere spoken of as "His body." "For now are ye the body of Christ, and members *in particular;*" wherefore, if we are *to do* that which our Lord commanded, or in any sense carry out St. Paul's exhortation, then, although there be no new sacrifice for sin, yet there is *a sacrifice* for sin in the offering, of which we are participators: "I beseech you, therefore, brethren, by the mercies of God, that ye present your bodies *a living sacrifice, holy, acceptable unto God, which* is your reasonable service.". .

"For we being many, are one body *in Christ*, and every one members one of another." When, therefore, the body of Christ on earth, or any member in particular, makes a remembrance of the sacrifice which He made, Christ, our great High Priest, ministers for us, and perfects us in His own nature. Now, granting that the Apostles may not have understood their Lord at the first Eucharistic feast, surely after the second and third celebration they must have comprehended His meaning. "The same day at evening, *being the first day of the week* (and *the second* Eucharist at which Christ was visibly present), *when the doors **were** shut,* when the disciples were assembled for fear of the Jews, *came Jesus and stood in the midst,* and saith unto them, Peace be unto you. And when he had so said, he showed unto them his hands and his side." On the following Sunday, for THE THIRD *Eucharist.* "His disciples were within, and Thomas was with them. Then came Jesus, *the doors being shut,* and *stood* in the *midst,* and said, Peace be unto you. Then said he to Thomas, reach hither thy hand, and thrust it into

my side; and be not faithless, but believing. And Thomas answered, "My Lord and my God!" Here are different occasions on which our Lord was present when His disciples were assembled in Eucharistic worship. Now, we have our Saviour's declaration, "Where two or three are gathered together, there am I in the midst." It is true, the natural eye, because of sin, does not behold Him, any more than it can behold natural things at midnight; but if Faith lighten the darkness, all things are clearly seen. So if it pleased Jesus *now*, we could behold Him at the Feast; but Faith is the eye by which he desires we should behold Him, and welcome Him, "Our Lord and our God." Carnally, we see a man clothed in white, breaking bread and pouring out wine, and blessing them. These he gives to us. *Faith* is roused by familiar Words of Life, and she takes and receives *from Jesus* that which He gave to His Apostles. "And I will come down and talk with thee there; and I will take of the spirit which is upon thee, and will put *it* upon them."*
This is the promise made to us now; for *His* Body and Blood are of a spiritual body, and are His Life, His Spirit. As He gave to them, so to us now. Even so let it be.

Our Lord's words would seem to receive further explanation, from the injunctions for the celebration of some of the Jewish offerings. Levit. xvii. 10, it is written:—"Whatsoever man there be of the house of Israel, or of the strangers that sojourn among you, that eateth any manner of blood, I will even set my face against that soul that eateth blood, and will cut him off from among his people. For the life of the flesh *is in the blood;* and I have given it to you, *upon the altar to make an atonement* for the soul. For *it is* the life of all flesh: the blood of it *is* for the life thereof:

---
* Numbers xi. 17.

therefore I said unto the children of Israel, Ye shall eat **the blood of** no manner of flesh; for the life of *all flesh is* **the** blood thereof." **And in** Deuteronomy xii. 23, " Be sure **that thou** *eat not the blood*, **for the blood** *is the life:* and thou *mayest not eat the life* with **the flesh."** Our heavenly Father here speaks specially of a **sacramental eating.** It is not surprising that the Jews, influenced by **the hard** and narrow Pharasaical doctrines of their teachers, should **have** been offended at an apparently flagrant **violation of their** law, when our Lord said, " This is my blood," **for it was** equivalent to "This is my life." They could not **see that** God had, under the law, set forth before their eyes the shedding of blood as a cleansing from sin, which blood was given to **them** upon the altar, to make an atonement,—an **atonement valid only** for the immediate offerer. They did not see that the blood sacramentally stood for the life, *which life* was the **real** offering. **Such blood, or** such sacrifice of life, may signify **to** them the forgiveness of sins, but it could not make them perfect: they must not eat it, for *no brute* life could even in sacrifice heal the defects of their **nature.** The blood of an inferior life could not impart anything **to a superior life.** But when the true Lamb **came** and offered Himself as the Atonement for the sins of the whole world, then was unveiled the mystery of the Jewish sacrifice of atonement, and the reason made clear why **the blood of** bulls and of goats could not take away sin ; and therefore *could not* be eaten. Their LIFE, *i. e.*, their nature, could in no way influence superior human life; **and God** only permitted it, **to** represent the necessity of bloodshed for sin ; for without the shedding of blood, that is, without the sacrifice of life, there is no remission of sin; and in a **sense, remission of sin to** the Jew was less perfect than **under** the **new** dispensation; for the atonement then **was** operative to the Jew, who offered in his person, not yet for the world; for *we need* now no further shedding of blood. It surely, then, should teach us that what our Lord really meant was, that as hitherto the Jew had only seen on the altar typical blood, which could impart to him no life-giving property, and would only assure him of forgiveness of sin,—so now, when the true blood of atonement is shed, and the River of Life is opened from the side of Christ, they are to come, every one that thirsteth, and buy and eat: "yea come, buy wine and milk without money and without price." The blood *is the life*, for the life of all flesh is the blood, *i. e.*, the source from whence the flesh is nourished, *the liquid flesh.* Jesus Christ *is* the Life of His redeemed; He freely of His own will redeems them, and gives to them His NATURE, His Humanity, that our sinful bodies may be made clean by His body, and that our souls may be washed in His blood—*His nature.* Verily the life of the flesh is in the blood, and the blood is the life* thereof; so it was absolutely essential, in order that there be no more shedding of blood, that the blood of Christ, and the flesh of Christ, should for ever continue on the altar of atonement, a perpetual sacrifice, inconsumable, and yet to be partaken of by every reclaimed soul; for here is the life of the flesh of the God-Man, human nature taken by The Son of God, which can truly impart new life *to us.*

Now, it is clear, that the command *not to eat* the blood, was given, because *it* was the life of the flesh of inferior creatures, and corruptible: it was therefore contrary to God's will, that the life of beasts should be imparted to or taken in by man. Not so, when in His most wonderful, loving kindness, He accepted the sacrifice of the Son of Man.

---

* The life or spirit of man.

Then indeed was the fount of life opened up for **us; then did it** become necessary that Christ should suffer in the flesh, that He may be enabled to say, "Except ye eat the flesh of the Son of Man, and drink His blood, ye have no life in you; for my flesh is meat indeed, and my blood is drink indeed." Nor does this mean *a mere* contemplation of **Christ**—it means a very great deal more; for if our Lord's words have any meaning **at all, they mean, that** the faithful Christian is a partaker of the **Christnature, whenever** in genuine faith he drinketh **of that cup and eateth** of that bread worthily. For the **Jew** touched **not the blood, and why?** The Blood, then **standing for the life of the flesh,** was to be poured out on the ground, **and not touched** on pain of death. Christ's blood, *i. e.,* the Spiritual Body of the God-Man, is to be partaken of by us, for not one drop of **His blood was lost,** for, like His flesh, it could not see corruption. And so it is written: "The first man Adam was made a **living soul: the last Adam was made** *a quickening spirit.*" "For *as in* Adam all die, *even so* in Christ shall **all be** made alive." "And if Christ be in you, the body is dead, because of sin: but the spirit is life, **because of** righteousness. But if the Spirit of Him that raiseth up Jesus from the dead dwell in you, He **that** raiseth Christ from the dead shall also quicken your mortal bodies (*because of*) His Spirit, that dwelleth in you." **And St. Paul** reminds true Christians, that "ye **are not in the flesh, but in** the spirit." **All** which is **in perfect agreement with the teaching of an ancient bishop:**—"He who keepeth **in mind that Christ our Passover** hath been sacrificed for **us,** and that we *must feast, eating* the flesh of the Word, at **all times** keepeth **the** Passover, passing over in thought, and *ever* in *word* **and** *deed,* **from the** things of this life to God, and hastening to His city."

It seems evidently to be our blessed Lord's meaning, that as the Jews had been forbidden to touch the blood of atonement because *it* was the *life* of the animal; so now in the fullness of time, when the Son of Man, the second Adam, had come in man's nature, that as *He* was the true Lamb, the prohibition to drink the blood must be removed, for the blood is the life thereof, and so by partaking of it " our life is hidden with Christ in God." In Genesis ix. 5, the language is very decided: it is there shown, that the blood is spoken of as standing in the place of the Life, and in the sense of the real nature: body and soul and spirit. "Surely your blood of your *lives* will I require." . . . "At the hand of every man's brother will I require *the life* of man." And so, in Romans v. 10, we find St. Paul declaring of our Lord, that " we shall be saved by His life." " For the gift of God *is eternal life*, through Jesus Christ our Lord." And in Acts, He is called " The Prince of Life;" and this explains 1 Cor. xv. 47, where our Lord is declared to be the second Adam, *in* whom we are re-made; for " The first man *is* of the earth, earthy; the second man *is* the Lord from heaven." " For since *by* man *came death*, by man came also the resurrection of the dead; for *as in* Adam all die, *even so* IN Christ shall all be made alive." Christ, therefore, must have become to us the source of actual life; for it is plain that he declared His work to be the rectification of all the ill that Adam had brought upon the race: ill that we to this hour inherit consequent upon our descent from him. Very mysterious words were spoken when our Lord was baptized " with water and the Holy Ghost." He who was sinless, undefiled, yet fulfilled all righteousness, and having *taken our* nature for us, was anointed by the Holy Ghost, and openly accepted as the second Adam by the Father—thus self-anointing his manhood. He is our head; He is the Vine, we are the branches; and we must be grafted in, if we be of Abraham's seed. The sap of life, *i. e.* the very life and essence of *the Christ*, the quickening Spirit,—for He is the second Adam—must flow to us by divine impartation, if we be really heirs of God, and joint heirs with Christ. As death hath passed upon us by Adam, so immortality—*endless life*—by the power of Christ's risen body; we be not then the "untimely fruit of woman;" for all that are baptized into His death are buried with Him, and do rise again: the bad to endless misery; the good to endless life with Him.

The result of the blessed communion of our Lord's risen body to us, is that which St. Paul so fully discourses about; it was *the* consolation which the holy Apostles enjoyed, and the hope they held out to us. The taking part in the *first* resurrection now in this present life begun in baptism: and no doubt it was the same consolation which holy Job enjoyed so fully: "I know that in my flesh I shall see God." So St. Paul hesitates not to say: "It is sown in corruption; it is raised in incorruption: it is sown in dishonour; it is raised in glory: it is sown in weakness, it is raised in power: it is sown a natural body; is is raised a spiritual body. There is a natural body, and there is a spiritual body. And so it is written, The first man was made a living soul; the last Adam was made a quickening Spirit." Now, "THE LORD IS THAT SPIRIT."

In meditating on the nature of our most blessed Lord; we must believe Him to be eternally the Son of God. "The flesh and the conjunction of the flesh with God, began at one instant; His making and taking to Himself our flesh was but one act, so that in Christ there is no personal *subsistence but one*, and that from everlasting. By *taking only* the nature of man He still continueth ONE PERSON, and changeth but the manner of His subsisting, which was before in the mere glory of the Son of God, and is now in the habit of our flesh. Forasmuch, therefore, as Christ hath no personal subsistence but one, whereby we acknowledge Him to have been eternally the Son of God, we must of necessity apply to the Person of the Son of God, even that which is spoken of Christ according to His Human Nature."* And, "Christ is a Person both Divine and Human, not, therefore, TWO PERSONS in one, neither both these in one sense, but A PERSON Divine, because He is *personally* the Son of God. In Christ therefore, God and Man, there is a *twofold substance* not a twofold Person, because one person extinguisheth another; whereas, one nature cannot in another become extinct. For the personal being which the Son of God already had, suffered not *the substance to be* personal which He took, although together with the nature which He had, the nature which He *took continueth*." Bishop Beveridge, in almost identical language, says, "The Word was made flesh or man in general, as the Word always signifies when applied to men. It doth not signify any one, or more particular man, but mankind in general, *the whole human nature*; that which all men are of, that proceeded from the first man Adam, in whom it was all contained. And so it is in the Word made flesh, who is therefore called 'The Last Adam,' 'The Second Man,' because next to the first, who had the whole manhood in him. Hence it is, that when the Word was made flesh, and died in it, 'He died for all men,' and 'for every man;' because He died in THAT NATURE which is common to all, and every man alike. So that all and every man may now be saved by Him whom God sent into the world to be made flesh."

---

* Hooker, p. 225, Book v.

From the very Person of Christ proceeds then for us, all that He came to bestow. Eternally the Son of God, **He has taken humanity to Himself, that,** as the Second Man, the Lord from Heaven, He might quicken from the dead, all and each child of the First Adam who will but receive Him as his Christ. It is the Personality of Christ as the Eternal Son become the God-man, which causes His **Flesh** to be co-operative with His God-head. **It hath by virtue** of being taken into His God-head, power and efficacy which constitutes It for man the living bread which fails not, and which impregnates His Blood with that Life, which He **bestowes on** "whosoever believeth in Him, that they might not **perish but** have everlasting life."

> "Our great High Priest and Shepherd Thou,
> Within the veil art entered now,
> To offer there Thy Precious Blood,
> Once poured on Earth a cleansing flood.
>
> "And THENCE the Church, Thy chosen Bride,
> With countless gifts of grace supplied,
> Through all its members draws from Thee,
> Whate'er they have of purity."

"Forasmuch, then, as the children are partakers **of flesh** and blood, He also Himself likewise took part of **the same;** that through death He might destroy him **that had the** power of death; that is, the Devil. . . . For verily **he took** *not* on *Him* the NATURE of angels, but He took on Him **the** seed of Abraham." "Every spirit **that** confesseth that Jesus Christ is come in **the flesh,** *is* of **God; for** the life was manifested, and we have seen *it,* **and** bear witness, and shew unto you that Eternal Life, which was with the Father, and was manifested unto us." The plain natural meaning of the whole body of Scripture is, that our blessed Saviour took our *human nature* into the divine, that that **nature** may be made a pure, clean, **holy fount of** regeneration to us. In **assuming** man's nature, *all* was taken—the material **body and the** spiritual **soul.** By His divine power, then, He bestows on us that nature, which He as Christ has now **at this very** time. It cannot possibly be, that he bestows **on us** that which was material blood, and material flesh, alone or only. Far, **far** deeper and **more glorious** mystery than this: for it is the **putting away our sinful flesh,** *i. e.* our vile corrupt **nature; by the imparting to us** His own nature, directly **from Himself.** It is *His* Christ-nature, cleansing **and healing** the leprosy by which our nature has been defiled. "I will come and heal him," He said, and the **servant was healed.** So now, we are clean through His **word; for He** hath said, "Whosoever eateth my flesh, and **drinketh** my blood, hath eternal life:" and these words of **His are** SPIRIT, and they are LIFE; *i. e.*, to whomsoever I **shall** give, by the power of my living Word, of **that human** nature, which **in me is** sinless, pure, **holy;** without **spot**— altogether free from **taint of sin—shall have new Life.**

That our **blessed Lord is** to men the source of eternal life, **is again apparent in the raising of Lazarus.** The whole of His **conversation** with **the sorrowing** friends, **whose** hopes and fears **hung so anxiously on** the **very actions and words** of Jesus, indicate **that He was** bringing **them to a know**ledge of that great **truth,** that in Him **men live and** move and have their being. Martha knew **who He** was, and was **willing** to believe, **that** He could, and would, do as He **pleased.** *How* her brother was **to** be restored she could **not know,** until **the Lord had said** unto her, "**I am the resurrection and** the life: he that believeth in me, though **he were dead, yet shall** he live: and whosoever liveth and believeth **shall never die.** Believest **thou this? Yea, Lord;** I believe that thou **art the Christ which** should come into the world." To the dead in trespasses and sins, He has declared Himself the Resurrection and the Life; not only the resurrection, but *the Life* also; so that the life they live is in and from Him. With the humble Christian, who is buried in the baptism of His blood, the like simple confidence and belief draws forth the very same answer. When troubled and grieved at heart for sin, we turn to our Lord for strength, and receive for answer, "Whoso eateth my flesh and drinketh my blood hath *eternal life*." We answer, "Yea, Lord, I believe that thou art the Christ which should come into the world. For God hath given to us eternal life, and this life is *in* His Son." For being reconciled to God by the death of His Son, we shall be *saved by* His life. "For the Spirit of God hath made me, and the breath of the Almighty hath given me life." The mysterious and precious gift of His nature to us in the holy Eucharist, is intended to be for the strengthening and refreshing of our souls; and if so, to keep alive in us an active, vigorous life in Christian faith and works. To really receive Him effectually is to be converted; it is to have the consciousness, even amidst all our shortcomings, that we are still standing in the mercies of Jesus; it is to have the perpetual desire to have Him with us; for, as St. Jerome says, and truly, "Since the flesh of the Lord is true food, and His blood is true drink, the scriptural meaning [of Eccl. iii. 13] is, that in this present life we have only one good, to feed on His flesh, and to drink His blood; not only in the Mystery [the Eucharist], but also in reading of Scriptures: for the true food and drink which is derived from the WORD OF GOD, is knowledge of the Scripture." Clearly one of the greatest blessings, Christ, the Word of God, bestows upon us, is a spirit of discernment to understand the Scriptures through the Holy Ghost. "He who keepeth in mind that Christ our Passover hath been sacrificed for us, and that we must feast, eating the flesh of the Word, at all times keepeth the Passover; passing over in thought, and *ever* in *word* and *deed*, from the things of this life to God, and hastening to His city.*

A great modern divine writes: " **The** Sacraments have **been**, from the first, the natural outwork **of the doctrine** of **the** Incarnation; and from recognising a **true presence** of Christ in **these ordinances, in which He communicates** Himself, both **as God and man, we are carried on to a** genuine **belief that two natures are really** united in His adorable **person. For if Godhead and Manhood** are truly **united in Christ,** *both* **must** co-operate **in those** offices which **He discharges towards mankind. To** this truth many are **unwilling to listen,** because they suppose that the efficacy **of Christ's** manhood can mean only *the natural* efficacy **of** His *material* body." And in another place the same writer says:—" We are assured, **moreover, by our Lord Himself, that the removal of His** bodily substance **into heaven, would be a step** which should lead to that spiritual presence which He has since vouchsafed. After declaring the fact, that His **man's body would be the medium** through which **He would** convey heavenly gifts—' **for** my flesh is **meat indeed, and my blood is drink indeed ;' and ' this is the bread of life, which** cometh down **from** heaven ;'—He proceeds **to** represent His spiritual presence as consequent on his ascension into heaven, ' What, and if ye shall see the Son **of Man** ascend up where **he was** before. **It is** the SPIRIT that quickeneth; the flesh **profiteth** nothing ;' **' for when** the Son of Man,' says St. Leo, **' betook Himself to the** glory of **His** Father's Majesty, He began **in some** ineffable manner to be nearer by His Divine

---

* Origen.

Power, for the very reason that, according to His humanity, He was **removed** farther **off**; and therefore it was,' he adds, 'that **Mary** Magdalene might **not** touch Him before **His ascension**: '**I would not have you come to** Me in bodily **wise, nor recognize Me by** *carnal touch;* I put you off to something higher, **I prepare you for** something greater: **when I am ascended to** my **Father, then you** shall touch **me in** a more true and perfect manner; **when you** shall lay hold of that which you do not touch, and **believe that** which you do not behold."

When, therefore, we speak of our Lord's spiritual presence, **we mean** that as The Christ, His spiritual body is present, or He makes, if you will, the farthest soul present to **His own body,** which therefore is really, truly present; not less really because not visibly **present, but** really present through **the power of the Spirit—a power exerted** through His Deity, in those places, times and **manners to which His presence** *is pledged* in the kingdom of Grace. "**The flesh of the Lord,**" says St. Athanasius, "*meaning thereby* **His HUMANITY,**" is a quickening spirit, because it was engendered **by the Quickening Spirit; for that which is born of the Spirit is Spirit." It is** therefore from **our** blessed Lord's risen body now in heaven, even **from the living Christ,** the only Mediator, that —through the **Holy Ghost—we are partakers of His flesh and blood.**

Again, when the Real Presence is spoken **of, there are two** notions which may suggest themselves. Such presence **may be** supposed **to** result **from** *the action of the mind,* which **receives** an impression; **or, from** *the action of the being* who produces it. The first would be a subjective and metaphorical, **the second is an objective and** real presence. **We** think a spectacle, and **lay hold of it by** internal impulse, **as though it were present to our sight.** But this **is only**

figurative; the movement comes *from within*, irrespective of *any action* IN the *object* thought of. A real presence, on the contrary, is when *there is some* OBJECT, external to ourselves, which produces upon us those effects which result from its nearness. Such presence may be said to be spiritual, as well *as real*, when the medium of communication by which *this external object* effects, or is present with us, *is not material contact*, but spiritual power. Whether we look, then, to the declarations of Scripture respecting the departure of our Lord's body from earth to heaven, or to what He tells us of the source of that influence which He there exerts, we must conclude that the presence of our Mediator, though not independent of his fleshly nature, is brought about by the intervention of that divine nature which is irrespective of material contact, and of contiguity of place."*

"The manhood of Christ may after a sort be everywhere said to be present, from whose Divine substance manhood nowhere is severed." Again: "That Deity of Christ which before His Incarnation wrought all things without man, doth now work nothing wherein the nature which it hath assumed is either absent or idle. Christ as man hath all power both in heaven and earth given Him. Because His human substance is inseparably joined to that PERSONAL WORD which by His Divine Essence is present with all things, the Nature which cannot have in ITSELF universal presence, *hath* it after a manner, by being *nowhere severed* from that which everywhere is present." †

Flesh and blood cannot inherit the kingdom of heaven; nay, but we are spiritual, we have been baptized into His

---

* Wilberforce.   † Hooker, Book v., c. lv. 8.

Name, the ransom has been offered, we have been bought with a price; so Jesus, the God-man, having life in Himself, bestows His human nature, through His divine power, on His faithful people, to whom He is the great and sole object of life, love and mercy. No man can go to the Father except Christ draw him. It is not what *we* imagine; it is what Christ *does*, that saves us. In the celebration of the divine mysteries, then, our blessed Saviour does, in the plentitude of His divine power, impart to our nature—to penitent and faithful human beings—that very nature which He took for them, to the end that the vile children of Adam, who have tasted of the fruit of the tree of the knowledge of good and evil, may now put forth their hands and eat of the Tree of Life, and live for ever. "It is done, I am Alpha and Omega, the beginning and the end. I will give unto him that *is* athirst, of the fountain of the water of life freely." "Yea, we give Thee thanks, O Lord God Almighty, which art, and wast, and art to come; because Thou hast taken to Thee Thy great power, and dost reign. Amen, Amen."

That St. Athanasius truly speaks according to scripture, would seem to be clear, from the reference made by the holy Apostles to our being partakers of the life of Christ; for, says St. Paul, "if any man have not the Spirit of Christ, he is none of His;" and "if Christ be in you, the body is dead because of sin, but the Spirit *is* life because of righteousness. In Him was life; and the life was the light of men." John xiv. 6: "Jesus saith, I am the way, the truth, and the life." Repeatedly, in the older scriptures, innocent blood is spoken of, as standing for the acts of man's life, or for the life; and of many passages, one or two will suffice here. In Jonah i. 14: "Lay not upon us innocent blood; for thou, O Lord, hast done as it pleased thee." In Jeremiah:

"If ye put me to death, ye shall surely bring innocent blood upon yourselves." Hence the fierce remorse and impenitence of Judas—"I have sinned, in that I have betrayed the innocent blood." And when the Apostles were forbidden to use the Holy Name, the high priest said unto them, "Behold, ye have filled Jerusalem with your doctrine, and intend to bring this man's blood upon us." That which endures is the Life; flesh and blood return to the dust, yet the man dies not—God giveth it a body as it hath pleased Him. Christ's body, as a part of His nature, saw not corruption, but was raised again, glorified, and entered into heaven for us, thence ever to be the source of spiritual life for His ransomed people.

Ancient Christians spoke plainly, without being misunderstood, and it is only now, in consequence of Romish corruption, that men speak with faltering lips. But among early Christians, Transubstantiation was unknown. Thus: "In thy visible vesture, there dwelleth an hidden power: a little spittle from thy mouth became a great miracle of light in the midst of the clay. *In* thy bread is hidden the Spirit that cannot be eaten; in thy wine there dwelleth the fire that cannot be drunk."—*St. Ephrem.*

"The skirt of the Lord's garment, and the slightest touch, sanctifieth none but him that hath eaten the flesh of the Lamb, and drank His blood."—*St. Jerome.*

"Two-fold is the blood of the Lord. The one is His natural blood, by which we have been redeemed from destruction; the other the Spiritual, that is, wherewith we are anointed; and this is to drink the blood of Jesus, to partake of the immortality of our Lord."—*St. Clement of Alexandria.*

They who spake thus, did but follow the Apostles. St. Paul, to the Corinthians, writes:—"For I have received of the Lord that which also I delivered unto you. That the Lord Jesus, the *same* night in which He was betrayed took bread; and when He had given thanks, He brake *it*, and said, Take eat, this is my body *which is broken* for you: this do in remembrance of me. After the same manner also He took the cup, when He had supped, saying, This cup is the New Testament of My blood: this do ye, as oft as ye drink it, in remembrance of Me. For *as often* as ye eat this bread and drink this cup, YE DO SHEW the Lord's death till He come." Shew to whom?

The sacrifices under the law, were not a whit more sacrifices than is the Christian Sacrifice of Praise and Thanksgiving. "The blood of bulls and of goats, and the ashes of an heifer, sprinkling the unclean, could not take away sin." It was only as they represented "the One All-sufficient Sacrifice," that they were of any efficacy. Christ has desired that we should represent here on earth, before men, His sacrifice; and that we should shew to God, that which He presented, by the oblation of that sacrifice, *together with ourselves, our souls and bodies*, just as He did Himself; to the end that with these pleading memorials in our hands, and with repentant hearts, He may communicate to us His life-giving body and blood, given and shed for us.

We must meet Him, and bow down to Him. He is at His Holy Eucharistic Feast, although with carnal eyes we see Him not. He is the Object of our adoring love. We have more than an intimation, that the Apostles did really understand our Lord's words, as they are interpreted by the Anglican Church; for it is said, that when He had spoken, many said it was a hard—*i. e.* a revolting—saying, and went back. His Apostles remained stedfast. Now, *they* had seen His wonderful power over nature: they had seen Him cure the sick, recover sight to the blind, bring back the spirit and soul into the dead. They certainly do not appear to have understood Him to mean, that they were carnally to eat His body and drink His blood. As the Jews drank of that Rock which followed them, and that Rock was Christ; so in a more clearly understood and real sense, Christians partake of that Rock on which they are built. The Apostles must have believed, that our Lord having come, as a sinless man, to transmake fallen human nature, intended to finish that sublime work of mercy, by rooting out Adam's nature, and imparting to man His own, Christ's nature. Adam ate death into our nature: if we would live, we must eat Christ's perfect humanity into our nature, that we may live. The Holy Jesus draws us to Himself in that hour of deep and adoring worship, in which we present ourselves before God, pleading and representing the Holy Sacrifice, as our only claim to His forgiveness. From Him virtue goes forth to heal: His spiritual body, a real body, is imparted to the faithful man. Thus He is known to us in the breaking of bread; and our hearts burn within us as He talks to us by the way. Faith sees in the midst of the throne "a Lamb as it had been slain;" and hears the new song, "Thou art worthy to take the Book, and to open the seals thereof: for Thou wast slain, and hast redeemed us to God *by Thy blood*, out of every kindred and tongue and people and nation; and hast made us, unto our God, kings and priests; and we shall reign on the earth."

It is because we think it impossible to solve the mystery of—the how—of our blessed Lord's presence, that we, in common with so many, regret the alteration in Mr. Keble's beautiful hymn, although we believe Mr. Keble has been misunderstood. Our Lord and Saviour Jesus Christ was present, as we have shewn, at *the three first* Eucharist celebrations; and we may not be wrong in believing, that in every and all subsequent ones, He is as effectually **present**—our carnal eyes being holden—that the eye of the spirit, through **faith, may see, adore, and** worship our Lord and our God. Yet we know not *how* He is present. Who, at the moment of Holy Communion, thinks of earthly priests, or of bread and wine? Do we not hear the voice of the Son of God saying **to us, " Take eat, this is my body; drink, this is my blood."** Surely, the material representation is to **reveal to** us a real participation. Thus believing, **we are satisfied to** see this highest act of duty **and reverent devotion,** celebrated by a **representative** Priesthood, ministering in our **Lord's stead, clothed in the** emblamatic garb of **pure** white linen, *i. e.* the surplice and stole; and all the more, **if that stole was crimson* or purple† in** place of black, the **emblem of woe.**

That our whole Eucharistic service on earth is representative of a work **that is being done for us, is evidently taught** by St. **Paul, who says, " Now of the things which we have spoken, this is the sum: we have such an** High **Priest, who is set on the** right **hand of the throne of the Majesty in the heavens;** *a minister* **of the sanctuary, and of the true tabernacle which the Lord pitched and not man.** Again, **" Now hath He** obtained a more **excellent ministry, by how** much also **He is the** Mediator of **a better covenant,** which was established **upon better promises." "For Christ is not entered into the holy places made with hands, which are the figures of the true; but into heaven itself,** *now to appear in the presence* **of** God **for us." Therefore we must believe that Jesus is our sole Mediator, a** real personal **Mediator: for "** this **Man,** because he continueth ever, hath

---

* And He was clothed in **a vesture dipped in blood;** and His name is **called the Word** of God.—Rev. **xix.**

† And they put on Him a purple robe.—St. John xix. 2.

an unchangeable priesthood." And consequently it is true that the Holy of Holies is open unto us. In the power of His Spirit, He is with us; and, as one of our recent authors says, " We believe Him to be locally present only in heaven, which he has localised by His ascension in the flesh; but (as has been said by most thoughtful theologians) He is present, both in His Godhead and in His manhood—which He has taken into His Godhead, though without making it, like that Godhead, ubiquitous—according to His own will, wherever and whenever the sacramental conditions which He has laid down are fulfilled;" to our carnal sight, in representation; to faith, truly so. If we would only acknowledge *ourselves* in His Presence we would more easily understand His Presence with us. And as wickedness shuts us out from God's presence, so we are sure that the wicked cannot discern Him, and can have no part in God's service. "They shall not offer wine offerings to the Lord, neither shall they be pleasing unto Him: their sacrifice shall be unto them as the bread of mourners: all that eat thereof shall be polluted; *for their bread for their souls shall not come* into the house of the Lord."—Hosea ix. 4.

If then it be true, as we believe, that our Lord sees *us*, that He is our High Priest touched by our infirmities, and that we are plainly before *Him*, surely it is but fitting, that we worship and adore Him, as we ought to do at all times, but more markedly and openly, when receiving from Him special and peculiar gifts, we kneel before the representation on earth of the heavenly altar, from which Jesus is pleased to give us of the sacrifice. In very spirit and soul, we must adore and worship Him. "For Thou, O God, seest us." If the blessed elements are a sign to us, that at that most holy time Jesus is with us, in the very midst; then let

Faith be active and warm: seeing neither man nor material substance, and knowing only that Christ hath come in the flesh; let us praise and thank God for His great mercy, lauding and magnifying His holy name, saying, Holy, holy, holy, Lord God of Hosts; heaven and earth are full of Thy glory. Glory be to thee, O Lord most High.—Amen.

Professor Maurice has ably said:—

"I do not seek to get rid of the papal notion respecting a real presence, *merely* by saying that what is spiritual is also most real. I do indeed look upon that proposition as nearly the most important one which a theological student can think of or remember, and also as the one which Romanism is most habitually denying. But I have maintained, that in order to the full acknowledgment of Christ's spiritual presence, we must distinctly acknowledge that He is clothed with a body; that if we lose this belief, we adopt a vague pantheistic notion of a presence hovering about us somewhere in the air, in place of a clear spiritual apprehension of a Person in whom all truth and love dwell; that the spiritual organ therefore does demand an actual body for its nourishment; that through that spiritual organ our bodies themselves are meant to be purified and glorified; that this sacrament meets and satisfies the needs both of the human spirit which is redeemed, and of the body which is waiting for its redemption. But all these admissions only bring out the difference with the Romanist into stronger relief. To enter into fellowship with Christ as He is, ascended at the right hand of God, in a body of glory and not of humiliation, this must be the desire of a Christian man, if he seek the presence of a real, not an imaginary object, if he desire his body as well as his spirit to be raised and exalted. On this ground then he must reject all theories which involve the imagination of a descent into the elements; on this ground, also, he must feel that the intellectual contradiction which such theories contain, and even boast of, is the counterpart of a spiritual contradiction still more gross and dangerous.

"I must say a few words before I conclude upon the difference between my views and those of the Romanists, respecting those who administer this sacrament. The pure Protestant expresses his differences in such words as these. The Romanist, he says, unhappily connecting the idea of sacrifice with the Eucharist, necessarily supposes that the Christian Church must have its priests as well as the Jewish; we rejecting the first idea, of course reject the second. Now as I have so carefully connected the idea of sacrifice with the Eucharist, it follows from this statement, that if I suppose it to be administered by human hands at all, I must suppose those hands to be, in some sense of the word, sacerdotal. Nay, it would seem to follow by almost necessary inference, that if I suppose the Jewish sacrifice to have passed into something higher, I must suppose the Jewish priesthood to have passed into something higher. And this in fact is my belief. I do think a Melchisedec priesthood has succeeded to an Aaronical priesthood, even as the power of an endless life has succeeded to the law of a carnal commandment. I do think that he who presents the perfect sacrifice before God, and himself and his people as redeemed by that sacrifice, has a higher function than he had who presented the daily offering, or made the yearly atonement before God. I do think he who is permitted to feed the people with this bread and wine has a higher work to do than he who came out of the holy place to bless the people in God's name. And I complain of the Romanists for lowering this office, for depriving it of its spiritual and Catholic character, for reducing it to the level or below the level of that which existed before the Incarnation. No honour which is put upon the person of the priest can make amends to him for the degradation which he suffers by being treated as if he were without the veil, pleading for admission into the presence of God, not claiming the privilege for himself and his people of being admitted into it. No emblems which exhibit his own mysterious glory and beauty can be any compensation for the loss of the belief that he is permitted with open face to behold the glory of his Lord. Above all, the differences which are made between him and his flock, especially that most gross and offensive one, by whatever arguments it may be palliated, of permitting him alone to receive the sacramental wine, do but show that he is not like his Lord, that he is not one of many brethren, but has only the melancholy delight of fancying that there are blessings reserved for him in which other men are not sharers. Herein he is far below the Jew. The high priest believed that he was one of a kingdom of priests; that he received his garments of beauty and his holy mitre because he was their representative. A Jew would have answered to the complaint of Korah, "Ye take too much upon you, seeing that all the congregation are holy, every one of them." "We take this upon us which has been put upon us, *because* the congregation is holy, and because it would not be holy if we were not consecrated to be witnesses and preservers of its holiness." A Jew could see that the oil upon Aaron's head went down to the skirts of his garments. It is not surely for Christians and Catholics to set up an office in the Church against the Church itself, to set at nought the ascription which they are appointed to offer up in the name of the whole body: "Unto him that loved us and washed us from our sins in his own blood, and hath made us kings and priests unto God and his Father; to him be glory and dominion for ever and for ever."

CONCERNING THE SACRAMENTS.

Hooker (p. 256, v. 2, p. 3) says, concerning sacraments, that "their chiefest force and virtue consisteth in that they are heavenly ceremonies, which God hath sanctified and ordained to be administered in His Church, *first*, as marks whereby TO KNOW when God doth impart the vital or saving grace of Christ unto all that are capable thereof; and, *secondly*, as means conditional which God requireth in them unto whom He imparteth grace. For this God himself is invisible, and cannot by us be discerned working, therefore when it seemeth good in the eyes of His heavenly wisdom, that men, for some special intent and purpose, should take notice of His glorious presence, He giveth them some plain and sensible token whereby to know what they cannot see." Again: "We take not baptism or the Eucharist for bare resemblance or memorials of things absent, neither for *naked* signs and testimonies assuring us of grace received before, but—as they are indeed and in verity—for *means effectual*, whereby God, when we take the sacraments, delivereth *into our hands* that grace available unto eternal life, which grace the sacraments represent or signify." It is most likely that it was this view of the matter which the venerated and dearly beloved Keble had in his mind when he determined to alter that beautiful hymn to which we have referred, and which contains or implies doctrine which, unless read by the light which Hooker's clear and judicious mind throws upon it, is very likely to be misunderstood and to mislead. The original was—

> "O come to our Communion Feast,
> There present in the heart;
> *Not* in the hands th' Eternal Priest,
> Will His true self impart."

The altered verse runs—

> "As in the hands th' Eternal Christ
> Will His true self impart." *

At p. 355: "If we doubt what these admirable words import—"Take eat, this is my body"—let him be our teacher for the meaning of Christ, to whom Christ was himself a schoolmaster; let our Lord's Apostle be His interpreter; content we ourselves with his explication—My body, *the communion* of my body; My blood, *the communion* of my blood. Is there anything more expedite, clear and easy, than that as Christ is termed OUR LIFE, because through Him we obtain *life*, so the parts of this sacrament ARE His BODY and BLOOD, for that they are so to us, who, receiving them, receive that by them which *they* are termed. The Bread and Cup are His Body and Blood, because they *are causes instrumental*, upon the receipt whereof the participation of His body and blood ensueth. For that which produceth any certain effect is not vainly nor improperly said to be that very effect whereunto it tendeth. Every cause is in the effect which groweth from it. Our souls and bodies quickened to eternal life are effects the cause whereof is the Person of Christ; His body and blood are the true wellspring out of which this life floweth. So that His body and blood are in that very subject whereunto they minister life, not only by effect or operation, even as the *influence of heaven is in plants, beasts, men, and in every thing which they quicken*, but also by a far more divine and mystical kind of union, which maketh us one with Him, even as He and the Father are one. The *real* presence of Christ's most blessed Body and Blood is not therefore to be sought for in

---

* We believe that the venerated writer meant to say that, the elements being pledges of a covenant, as surely as they are in the hand so is that they represent in the heart of the faithful.

the sacrament, but in the worthy receiver of the sacrament."
..... "Take, therefore, that wherein all agree: it is on all sides confessed, first, that this sacrament is a true, real participation of Christ, who thereby imparteth Himself, even His whole, entire person, as a *mystical Head*, unto every soul that receiveth Him, and that every such receiver doth thereby incorporate or unite himself unto Christ as *a mystical member of Him*, yea, of them also whom He acknowledgeth to be His own; secondly, that to whom the Person of Christ is thus communicated, to them He giveth by the same sacrament His Holy Spirit, to sanctify them as it sanctified Him which is their Head; thirdly, that what merit, force or virtue soever there is in his SACRIFICED body and blood, we freely, fully and wholly have it by this sacrament; fourthly, that the effect thereof in us is a *real transmutation* of our souls and bodies from sin to righteousness, from death and corruption to life and immortality; fifthly, that because the sacrament, being of itself but a corruptible and earthly creature, must needs be thought an unlikely instrument to work so admirable effects in man, we are therefore to rest ourselves altogether upon *the strength of His glorious power*, who is able and will bring to pass, that the bread and cup which He giveth us shall be truly the thing He promiseth." Why distress ourselves about the manner of our dear Lord's presence? Is it not enough to know that He is *really* and *truly present* at His own most holy feast; and can we believe that He makes His resting place anywhere in man, but in the spirit of man, cleansed and made a temple fit for the Spirit of Christ through the Holy Ghost. The mouth of the spirit is FAITH, whereby we eat the Body and drink the Blood of Christ.

Augustin contra Maximin., 4 b. 3, c. xxii.—"In sacraments we must consider *not what they be*, but what *they signify.*" Again: "The sacrament of Christ's body is **one thing, and the substance of the sacrament—or Christ's body represented by the sacrament—is another thing.**" Again: "To take **the signs instead of the *things themselves*** is the miserable bondage **of the soul.**"

Chrysost. in Genes. hom. 24 (iv. 228).—" The EYES OF OUR FAITH, when they behold these unspeakably good things, they do not so much as mark these outward things that we see with our bodily eyes; *so great is the difference between these things.*" And does not all this agree with the teaching of St. Paul, who saith, "Faith is *the substance of things* hoped for, *the evidence* of things *not seen;*" for if by faith Abraham offered up Isaac, and yet slew not his son, so we by faith offer up ourselves in an oblation of bread and wine, representing the sacrifice of Christ, pleading by faith the body of Christ given for our salvation, and which we see as St. Thomas saw, wounded and bleeding.

Augustin saith, "The grace of Christ is not consumed by Morsels."

St. Basil—"There is a spiritual mouth of the inner man, by which he is nourished by receiving the Word of Life, which is the Bread that came down from heaven." Again he saith, "Taste and see that our Lord is gracious. We have often marked that the powers of the mind have their names from some likeness of the parts of the body. Therefore seeing our Lord is bread indeed and His flesh is verily meat, it cannot be chosen, but the pleasure and sweetness of that bread, must be wrought in us by the spiritual taste of the SOUL." St. Augustine—"Christ is the Bread of our heart." Again Chrysostom—"Their bodily eyes, that see things visible cannot do so much, as the eyes of the spirit; for these eyes are able to see the things that be not seen." Again—"The eyes of the mind notwithstanding they find walls, or mountains, or the bodies of the heavens to stand against them, yet will they easily pass through them all. With these eyes, we see the most worthy and most glorious body of Christ: therefore let us believe and we see Jesus presented before us." And St. Heirom saith—" There is a spiritual understanding wherewith Christ is seen." For concludes St. Ambrose—" By faith Christ is touched: by faith Christ is seen." Indeed all the most devout and faithful men have in all times taught out of the scripture, that by the federal rite implied in baptism, men are adopted and become sons of God, through that new relation which they have to Jesus Christ: they are no longer carnal but *spiritual*.

" Whereas in our infancy we are incorporated into Christ and by baptism receive the grace of His Spirit without any sense or feeling of the gift which God bestoweth; in the Eucharist we so receive the gift of God, that we know by grace what the grace is which God giveth us, the degrees of our own increase in holiness and virtue we see and can judge of them, we understand that, the strength of our life begun in Christ is Christ, that His flesh is meat, and His blood is drink, not by surmised imagination but truly, even so truly, that through faith we perceive in the body and blood sacramentally presented, the very taste of eternal life, the grace of the sacrament is here as the food which we eat and drink. This was it that some did exceedingly fear, least Zuinglius and Oscolampadius would bring to pass, that men should account of this sacrament but only *as a shadow*-destitute, empty, void of Christ. But seeing that by opening the several opinions which have been held, they are grown for aught I can see on all sides at the length to a general agreement concerning that which alone is material, namely, the *real participation* of Christ and OF LIFE in His body and blood by means of this sacrament; wherefore, should the world continue still distracted and rent with so manifold contentions, when there remaineth now no controversy saving only *where* Christ *is?* Yea! even in this point no side denieth but that the soul of man is the receptacle of Christ's presence."

The fruit of the Eucharist is the participation of the body and blood of Christ. There is no sentence of Holy Scripture which saith that we cannot by this sacrament be made partakers of his body and blood, except they be first contained in the sacrament, or the sacrament converted into them. "This is my body" and "this is my blood" being words of promise, still we all agree that by the sacrament Christ doth really and truly *in us* perform his promise, why do we vainly trouble ourselves with so fierce contentions, whether by consubstantiation or else by transubstantiation the sacrament itself be first possessed with Christ or no?— a thing which no way can either further or hinder us, however it stand, because our participation of Christ in this sacrament dependeth on the co-operation of His omnipotent power which maketh it His Body and Blood to us, whether with change or without alteration of the element such as they imagine, we need not greatly care to enquire.

As part of our human nature the body of flesh is intended to be benefited by the participation which we have of Christ; yet it is to our spirit, that the adorable Son of God imparts Himself directly; it is with us as spiritual beings that He dwells; and it is to elevate and presently to transform our nature, to assimilate it to His own, that He so mercifully and lovingly pleads with us for a resting place in our hearts. "Behold I stand at the door and knock:" such are His own words, let us then open our hearts freely to Him, so that the influence of His most precious body and blood be upon us to transform us into His likeness.

The repeated injunction of the sacred word is, that we should no longer fix our minds on earth. The shadows of earth are but the reflections of heavenly things and not the things themselves: they are but signs to awaken us to high and holy truths, not seen by carnal eyes. He only who has received the gift of faith hath eyes for those glories which are beyond the sphere of mortal vision. He who possesses faith hath the realization which it alone gives; for faith is the substance—not the shadow—of things hoped for, the evidence of things not seen. Wherefore, the holy apostle St. Paul did very earnestly pray, "that the God of our Lord Jesus Christ, the Father of glory, may give unto us the spirit of wisdom and revelation in the knowledge of Him; the eyes of our understanding being enlightened; that we may know what is the hope of his calling, and what the riches of the glory of his inheritance in the saints, and what is the exceeding greatness of His power to us-ward who believe according to the working of His mighty power, which He wrought in Christ when He raised Him from the dead, and set Him at His own right hand in the heavenly places, far above all principality and power and might, and dominion, and every name that is named, not only in this world, but also in *that* which is to come; and hath put all things under His feet, and gave Him to be head over all things to the church, which *is His body the fullness of Him that filleth* all in all. And you *hath He quickened*, who were dead in trespasses and sins; wherein in time past ye walked according to the course of this world, according to the prince of the power of the air, THE SPIRIT that now worketh in the children of disobedience. . . . . . But God who is rich in mercy, for His great love wherewith He loved us, even when we were dead in sins HATH QUICKENED us together with Christ—by grace ye are saved—and HATH

RAISED us up together, and *made us sit* together in heavenly places in,—not by or through,—Christ Jesus.

"*There is* therefore now no condemnation to them which are in Christ Jesus, who walk not after the flesh, but after the Spirit.

"For the law of the Spirit of life in Christ Jesus hath made me free from the law of sin and death.

"For what the law could not do, in that it was weak through the flesh, God sending his own Son in the likeness of sinful flesh, and for sin, condemned sin in the flesh:

"That the righteousness of the law might be fulfilled in us, who walk not after the flesh, but after the Spirit.

"For they that are after the flesh do mind the things of the flesh: but they that are after the Spirit the things of the Spirit.

"For to be carnally minded *is* death; but to be spiritually minded *is* life and peace."

"Where high the heavenly temple stands,
The house of God not made with hands,
A great High Priest our Nature wears,
The guardian of mankind appears.

"He who for men their surety stood
And poured on Earth His precious Blood,
Pursues in Heaven His Mighty plan,
The Saviour and the Friend of Man.

"Jesus, who suffered here below,
Feels sympathy with human woe,
And still remembers, in the skies,
His tears, His prayers, His agonies."

The Epistle to the Ephesians is truly a marvellous production, its whole aim and object is to declare to Christians the elevation of their nature through Jesus Christ: the glories of redemption are unfolded, and man is taught to look upon himself, as already dead to all fleshly lusts and desires, and through the imparted life of Christ, to know that His spirit is alive to God, nay, actually now in communion with God. The earthly tabernacle of wood and stone may be all ablaze with the splendour of earth, but what God requires is, that His true Church shall be lighted by the fire of the Holy Spirit, each stone shining white, the sun of righteousness shining in it, and on the true altar, *i. e.*, the hearts of His purchased; Christ the clean, pure offering of purchased souls.

The late Cardinal Wiseman, in his second lecture on "the Eucharist," affirms that "the phrases which occur in the first part of the discourse (John, c. 6, v. 18) were calculated to convey to the mind of those who heard our Saviour, the idea of listening to his doctrines and believing in Him, the more so, as he positively explained them in that sense. But after the transition pointed out, a totally diferent phraseology occurs, which to *his hearers could not possibly convey that meaning*, NOR ANY OTHER, save that of *a real eating of His flesh, and drinking of His blood.*"

Now we entirely agree with the learned Cardinal, that our Lord's words can mean nothing else, and that He intended His apostles to believe that He gave them nothing less than His flesh and blood; but the question is, what did our Lord mean by the words "flesh and blood," "take eat this is My body," "drink, this is My blood," and, what is meant by "*real* eating?" Did He mean to convey to His apostles and to all men that His human flesh and blood was the essence of His nature—that that which was of His body, taken of the substance of the Virgin, constituted His higher nature—that His mere flesh and blood was to be isolated or separated from His other nature, and given to man? The whole voice of Scripture affirms the very opposite. Even in man, his flesh and blood, material substance, is only spoken of as material: the "life of his flesh," the blood, is as constantly put for his spirit, in order to convey the truth of the reality of that spirit or life which dwells in the body, and which is really the man, and without which the flesh were nothing. The Jew was told that the blood represented the life. Our Lord meant to convey the truth, that, as the Quickening Spirit, He did, by or through the power of His essential nature as Christ, bestow on man that which He took for man—pure, sinless humanity; *not only bare* flesh and blood, as it was in His muscles and in the vessels of His undefiled body. Cardinal Wiseman could not surely have meant the latter; and if he did not mean it, then his whole argument falls to the ground; for unless we receive Christ, as Christ, we pretend to receive *only* that part of His nature which is not the highest. We shall now endeavour to shew that our Lord meant to convey to His disciples, that as they were not animal beings, but spiritual, it was to them, as spiritual, He addressed himself, and that as He was the Quickening spirit, so would He quicken their bodies, souls and spirit.

"God," He had taught, "is a Spirit, and they that worship Him, *must* worship Him in spirit and in truth." St. Paul, following his Master, everywhere proclaimed the entire superiority of the spirit over the flesh, which we were to mortify and keep down, lest by any means the spirit be overborne by it. Through all the New Testament teaching, the spiritual nature of human beings is brought prominently out, that man might understand that he had another nature than that of the brute, in whose midst he now lived, and from whose nature he was now more widely being separated. When, then, our Lord said, "Take eat, this is my body," "this is My blood," He meant us *by faith* to receive into our deepest nature His glorified nature as the Christ.

Cardinal Wiseman has endeavoured to fasten on the Church of England, that the expression, "to eat the flesh of Christ," is to be taken figuratively. We do not at all deny some individual writers may have so expressed themselves; but the Church Catechism, the Communion office, and the teaching of the Service Book, as well as the formal declaration of the soundest and best, and more numerous body of English Fathers and Divines speak the same mind, and borrow almost the language of the ancient Fathers. The Anglican Church distinctly teaches, that there is nothing *figurative* about our Lord's language, and she objects to the doctrine as stated by Cardinal Wiseman, because it is a miserable contraction of the meaning of the blessed Jesus. "Take eat, this is my body," has a most important meaning: —the Roman teaching limits the reception of our Lord's body and blood, to that part of His nature which hung on the cross *after* He had yielded up His Spirit. Rome bids us remain waiting at the tomb, and forbids our following on His footsteps as He "walks by the way," or to partake with Him of the bread which He breaks as He makes himself known. The Anglican Church affirms, that our most blessed Redeemer *meant us to understand*, that He gave us *not only* that part of His nature which reposed in the new-made sepulchre, but that whole nature which was His, when at the Paschal Feast He made men partakers of true flesh and blood, the essential Humanity, the whole Spirit of Christ, which incorporates or includes His whole nature, and which He imparted to those for whom He broke bread, after that he had risen from the Dead. It is the Roman divine who mutilates the doctrine of Christ, and perverts the teaching of Christ; for it was Christ *alive* in the flesh, and ministering for men, who took bread and blessed, and brake it, and gave it to them, saying, "Take eat, this is my body." It was Jesus who, standing in the midst of His chosen ones, made the oblation of Himself to God, and who, as in the faith of Abraham, offered up Himself a sacrifice; it was He who bade them take eat of the sacrifice. Therefore, as the Jews drank of that Spiritual Rock, and did all eat the same Spiritual Meat, so now apostles and baptised men eat of the same meat and drink of the same spiritual drink; for they drink of that Rock on which they are built, a spiritual House, and that Rock is Christ.

All the early Fathers speak, even when they use the severest language, of *Eucharistic* eating and not of *ordinary* or *common* eating. If it is spiritual worship which we engage in, then all our acts are spiritual, *i. e.*, it is as spiritual beings, that we enter into the service of God, not to the exclusion of any part of our nature, but to the inclusion of all that is human in us. St. Irenæus in a remarkable passage says, "the body is nourished by that, which is the body of Christ. It is not nourished by the body of Christ itself, *for that is spiritual and incorruptible;* but our Lord gives through His body, that virtue to the consecrated elements, that they impart to the body THE LIFE which He himself is. Since we are His MEMBERS, and are nourished through the creature, and He himself gives us the creature, making His sun to rise and raining as he willeth, He owned the cup, which is from the creature, to be His own blood, from which he increaseth our bodies. When, then, both the mingled cup and the created bread receive the word of God, and the Eucharist becomes the body and blood of Christ, and from these the substance of our flesh is increased and consisteth, how do they say, that the flesh is not capable of receiving the gift of God, which is eternal life—it (the flesh) which is nourished by the body and blood of Christ, and is His member, as the apostle saith—" for we are all members of His body, of His flesh, and of His bones (that is, are of the humanity of Christ), not speaking this of some essential and invisible man, but of the constitution as to the very man which is nourished both from His cup and from the bread, which is His body. And as the wood of the vine laid in the earth bears fruit in its own season, and the corn of wheat, falling into the ground and dissolved, is raised manifold, through the spirit of God, which holdeth all things together, and afterwards, through the wisdom of God, comes to the use of man, and receiving the word of God becometh an Eucharist, which is the body and blood of Christ; so also our bodies, being nourished from it (the Eucharist), and placed in the ground and dissolved in it, shall rise again in their due season, the word of God granting them the resurrection to the glory of God the Father."

St. Clement of Alex., explaining Gen. xlix., ii., in reference to the Holy Eucharist, says, " The vine bears wine, as THE WORD blood; but both to meat and drink unto salvation: the wine for the body, the blood for the spirit." Again he says, "Twofold is the blood of the Lord: the *one* is His natural blood, by which we have been redeemed from destruction; the *other* SPIRITUAL, *i. e.*, wherewith we are anointed. And this is to drink the blood of Jesus, to partake of the immortality of our Lord. But the virtue of the Word is the Spirit, as blood is of the flesh. Analogously, then, the wine is mixed with the water, *and the Spirit with the man*. The one, the mingled drink, feasteth unto faith; the other, the Spirit, leadeth to immortality. And the mingling of both again, of the draught and the Word, is called Eucharist, an admirable and beautiful grace, whereof they who partake, according to faith, are sanctified both as to body and soul, the will of the Father mingling together mystically the divine mixture, man with the spirit and the Word. For truly is the Spirit united with the soul, which is borne along by it, and the flesh with the Word, for which the Word became flesh." Throughout the ancient Fathers, a singular consistency runs through all their teaching, which is entirely opposed to that of the Roman divines, and as entirely accordant with the writings of the large majority of the soundest divines of the Anglican Church.

There are numberless instances in the material world, in which matter acts on matter simply by " presence," *i. e.*, one body being brought within the presence of a second, an influence is exerted which causes the one so brought into presence, to manifest powers which were not previously exhibited, and yet the substances are not changed either one into the other or perceptibly at all, either of them. Christ, by the operation of the spirit, has been pleased to intimate, that in the due use of the bread and wine, *set apart for a special purpose*, He is pleased to communicate to the human spirit, and consequently to man, the spiritual food of His own most blessed body and blood. How can our Lord do this, except by the Holy and Eternal Spirit, who translates into the virtue of the flesh and blood of Christ the duly constituted elements of bread and wine, and who makes the spirit of man a fitting abode for the Life of Christ the Lord. Surely the Lord Almighty may by His word re-order substances to new uses. What if ordinarily He hath ordained, that bread shall sustain the body? Is it impossible for Him to do what He will with His own, and to also ordain that this bread, re-ordered by blessing, and set apart to another use, should be an effectual sign, that thereby He is imparting to the spirit of man, prepared by the Holy Spirit for new life, His own body and blood, His own quickening spirit.

The gift we receive, as the blessed Body and Blood of Christ, is " Life." " Verily, verily, I say unto you, except ye eat the flesh of the Son of man, and drink His blood, ye have no life in you." Life-giving, then, is the body and blood of Christ, for saith St. Cyril, "Since IT is the Body of Life, It is life-giving. For, therefore, IT infuseth LIFE into our mortal bodies: as also IT destroyeth the power of death." It matters not then whether the body and blood of Christ are close at hand, or a great way off, as regards the effect upon us of the power of His body. No one who is a disciple of Christ disbelieves that he is in the presence of Christ in a very special manner whenever he is adoring his Saviour: the very idea of prayer implies that prayer is heard; why then think, that He before whom we kneel in worship is too far off to impart to our nature the Life-giving substance, the spiritual food of His own most precious body and blood by which we are united to Him, becoming very members incorporate of His mystical body. The language of Scripture is too strong, the words of the Saviour, too explicit to allow us to believe, that He does not really impart to us, that nature which He took of the Virgin and which united with His Divinity is the real body of Christ. It cannot be that He only willeth us to be *like* Christ, but that, really and truly, not by an energy imparted, but by the *power* of the body and blood of Christ He gives to man that Life which imparted, leads to union with His own adorable Person. So may the Lord Jesus Christ *be* with thy spirit. Grace *be* with you. Amen.

There can be no manner of doubt, that, the Anglican refuses to receive the declaration of the Roman Church with regard to the transubstantiation of the elements of bread and wine into the flesh and blood of Christ. But she as strongly maintains that "the spiritual food of His most precious body and blood are verily and indeed, taken and received by the faithful, *in the Lord's Supper*, after a spiritual manner. If so, this giving, taking and receiving of spiritual food must mean a higher and different sort of eating to that of common or ordinary eating. Surely it can only mean, that as man in the highest exercise of His nature, as a spiritual being, is engaged in the performance of a spiritual work, that it is by the Spirit he receives and takes to His health of body and soul, the Life-giving body and blood of the Quickening Spirit.

That spirit is real, *i. e.*, is substance, we are distinctly taught. "There is a natural body and there is a spiritual body," our natural, will be changed as Christ's body was, into a purely spiritual body. But in order to this, in order to Christ's existence, He must be a Person, wherefore, in the creed of the church we acknowledge that:—

"The right Faith is, that we believe and confess that our Lord Jesus Christ, the Son of God, is God and Man;

"God, of the *Substance* of the Father, begotten before the worlds: and Man, of the *Substance* of his Mother, born in the world;

"Perfect God, and perfect Man: of a reasonable soul and human flesh subsisting;

"Equal to the Father, as touching his Godhead: and inferior to the Father, as touching his Manhood.

"Who although he be God and Man: yet he is not two, but one Christ;

"One; not by conversion of the Godhead into flesh: but by taking of the Manhood into God;

"One altogether; not by confusion of Substance: but by unity of Person.

"For as the reasonable soul and flesh is one man: so God and Man is one Christ."

Here the scripture as the Church affirms, teaches that The Holy! Holy! Holy! Lord God Almighty is Substance; really, truly, Personally is; and as we are made after the likeness or image of God, so when this mortal shall have put on immortality, then shall all that is in us of matter be done away; and our life, *i. e.*, our spirit, that which we truly are, be revealed a spiritual body. When, then, we are asked, what is it that our adorable Saviour imparts to us by virtue of His Sacramental Bread and Cup? are we not to believe, that He is *uniting our **nature to His***, as He had done in His own Person, not His to ours, and so imparting the influence and power of His nature to ours by His Presence, that we have thereby the assurance of "a glorious resurrection;" our rising to eternal life, effected **by *no*** power in ourselves, but by the power of the perfected, glorified, Spiritual Body of Christ by which we have **been touched**. We are made like unto the **Son of Man by the impartation of the nature** of the **Second Adam, and not the putting away thereby** of that of **the first Adam, but its regeneration in Christ**.

"Then said I, Woe *is* me! for I am undone; because I *am* a man of unclean lips, and I dwell in the midst of a people of unclean lips: for mine eyes have seen the King, the LORD of hosts.

"Then flew one of the seraphims unto me, having a live coal in his hand, *which* he had taken with the tongs from off the altar:

"And he laid *it* upon my mouth, and said, Lo, this hath touched thy lips; and thine iniquity is taken away, and thy sin purged."

At all events this is the doctrine taught us by St. Paul; for he does not leave us to believe that man can in any other way put off his sinful nature as derived from Adam, but by renewed life and that by derivation of the pure life-giving nature of the Second Man—

"Let no man beguile you of your reward in a voluntary humility and worshipping of angels, intruding into those things which he hath not seen, vainly puffed up by his fleshly mind.

"And not holding the Head, from which all the body by joints and bands having nourishment ministered, **and knit together, increaseth with the increase** of God.

"Wherefore if ye **be dead** with Christ **from the** rudiments of the world, **why, as** though living in the world, are ye subject to ordinances,

(Touch not; taste not; handle not;

"Which all are to perish with the using:) after the commandments and doctrines **of men?**

"Which things have indeed a shew of wisdom in will worship, and humility, and **neglecting of the body;** not in any honour **to the** satisfying of the flesh."

17.

The burying of our nature in that of Christ's is the hiding away, the putting away our weakness, and the illuminating, and transforming us into the perfect image of Christ by the imparting to us the Life or Nature of Christ:—

"If ye then be risen with Christ, seek those things which are above, where Christ sitteth on the right hand of God.

"Set your affections on things above, not on things on the earth.

"For ye are dead, and your life is hid with Christ in God.

"When Christ, *who* is our life, shall appear, then shall ye also appear with him in glory.

"Mortify therefore your members which are upon the earth; fornication, uncleanness, inordinate affection, evil concupiscence, and covetousness, which is idolatry:

"For which things' sake the wrath of God cometh on the children of disobedience:

"In the which ye also walked some time, when ye lived in them.

"But now ye also put off all these; anger, wrath, malice, blasphemy, filthy communication out of your mouth.

"Lie not one to another, seeing that ye have put off the old man with his deeds;

"And have put on the new *man*, which is renewed in knowledge after the image of him that created him:"

The words of institution of the Eucharist were addressed in the first place to the chosen Apostles who were present. They were not, as is too commonly asserted, "ignorant men:" so far were they above all other men in true knowledge, that they have left us evidence too strong to be refuted, that the light which was in them had nothing whatever of darkness in it. What had mere intellect to do with such Truth as Christ revealed? Taught by the Spirit, they received our Lord's words in implicit faith and understandingly. They knew that under the law the shedding of blood was typical; they knew that it represented or stood for the life of the creature, and was not to be eaten. Our Lord had all along been warning them against the viciousness of Pharisaical teaching, telling them to look to the spirit and intent of the law or commandment, and not to the letter; so that when He, the still living Jesus, reversed the command, or fulfilled the spirit of the Jewish law, and said, as he stood before them, "Take, eat, this is my Body," so in a figure giving to them His Nature, must not the Apostles, as "ENLIGHTENED" men, (not as babes in Christ, not as ignorant,) have seen the accomplishment of the law in the making plain its spirit and intent? The living Christ could then, as He does now, through the power of His Word as the Christ, give His human nature to the cleansing of ours; and the Apostles must have known, that it was not part of, but whole Christ the Son of Man, which was imparted to them, to their spirits, *i. e.*, Christ working on the spirit or truest part of man's nature, to the salvation of soul and body, giving that soul His body and His blood.

It may be argued that our Lord's words are direct, and are not to be twisted in any way to mean less than they mean as they stand.

"This *is* my Body."—"It *was* Bread."
"This *is* my Blood."—"It *was* Wine."

Very positive, very clear, unmistakeable words: nevertheless without departing one jot from the full, prime meaning of them, we are forced to look into their spirit as well as to the letter. It had, from the time of Noah to the sacrifice of Christ, been said, "The blood is the life," this not once, but over and over again. Will our friends of the Roman branch of the Church gravely assert that the blood is verily and truly THE life, or do they not with us admit, that like as *it* furnishes the flesh with means of increase, so is itself maintained, *living* by that which it partakes of in common with the bones, muscles, nerves, ligaments, bands and joints; so it resembles, but is not that substance which is the spiritual soul, and therefore it is the figure of the life, but yet is not the life? If Almighty God hath been pleased in crowning his creation, to elevate material substance in the body of man, and so to correlate matter with spiritual substance; if He is teaching that out of the union of body and spirit the former is to be merged, transelemented into spiritual life, and that, by the efficacy of the superior nature of the Son of Man, the whole nature of man is re-made in Him, then this supra-natural work which is being wrought in us by the God-man, the putting off of the old man and putting on of the new, is a real work of regeneration and renewal, accomplished by Christ in our spirits, and therefore also in our bodies.

A learned divine has written, "The question as to the elements themselves is not whether they are a figure of His body broken and His blood shed for us. The very creation of the Holy Eucharist *shows that they are*. The question so far is, whether they are figures of what is present, or what is absent. But in these words of our Lord, 'This is my Body,' the question is, whether our Lord meant to express A SPIRITUAL REALITY, or whether, while He appeared to be speaking of a gift which He was bestowing, He meant that He gave to His Apostles and to us only a shadow, a rite, as outward as any of the law which He Himself came to fulfil. He Himself was the substance of the shadows of the law."

It is as if we only looked on our Lord's blessed Body and Blood as alone constituting His human nature, instead of accepting Him as He is and was, the Saving Christ, God and Man, of a reasonable soul and human flesh subsisting: He hath life in Himself "that He might bestow it upon men." Did our Lord yield up nothing when He expired on the Cross? Did the thief, who had partaken of the promise of eternal life, partake of nothing as he asked of

Christ agonized on the altar, **of The Cross the** living **Bread? Did** he **as a person, go into the Paradise of** God, **or was** there **nothing to go into** Paradise? **How** are we to understand this scripture, **if our** whole nature consisteth only **of our** material parts?

"And he said unto Jesus, Lord, remember me when thou comest into thy kingdom.

"And Jesus said unto him, **Verily I say unto thee, to-day** *shalt thou* be with me in paradise.

"And it was about the **sixth hour, and there was a darkness over all the** earth until the ninth **hour.**

"And the sun was **darkened, and the veil of the temple was rent in the** midst.

"**And when Jesus had cried with a loud voice, he** said, Father, into thy hands **I commend M**y S**pirit: and having said thus,** he gave up the G**host**."

But once **again** are the **words** "It is done" used, and **they are used** to testify to man his adoption *in* Christ, the consummation of the union **of** our nature with Christ's:

"And he said unto me, It **is done. I am Alpha and Omega, the beginning** and the end. I will give unto **him that is athirst of the fountain of the water of life freely.**

"**He that overcometh shall inherit all** things; and I will be his God, and he shall be my son."

St. **Athanasius** plainly says, in speaking **of our Lord's words,** "The **Bread** which I will give is my **flesh, for the life of the world."** For the Lord's flesh is life-giving spirit, because he was conceived of the life-giving spirit, that which is born of the Spirit **is spirit.**

St. Ambrose says,—"This **is the** Bread of Life; whoso then eateth life **cannot die. For** how should *he* die whose food is life? How shall **he fail who** has a living substance? Approach **to Him and** be satisfied, because He is Bread; approach **to Him and** drink, because He is a fountain; approach to Him and be enlightened, because He is light:

approach and be free, because where the Spirit of the Lord is, *there* is liberty. Approach and be absolved, for He is the remission of sins."

St. Paul, in his second epistle to the Corinthians, calls our attention to the true relationship which we now have with Christ as the risen Saviour; for He died for all, that they should not *henceforth* live unto themselves, but unto Him which died for them, and rose again. *Wherefore* HENCEFORTH know ye no man after the flesh; yea, though we have known Christ after the flesh, yet now henceforth know we Him no more. "It is the Spirit that quickeneth, the flesh profiteth nothing. The words that I speak unto you, they are Spirit."—John, c. vi. v. 63.

Atonement for sin is made by a Personal Mediator, the work is still going on, the sacrifice alone efficacious for man's redemption has been made, and must continue in offering. Men are by virtue of the incarnation, raised up in the manhood, not of Adam, but of Christ the Second Adam, who is the quickening spirit; and by virtue of that union, are no longer left in their carnal nature to sink into misery, but are re-made alive to God by the spirit of Christ dwelling in them. It is of necessity that the gospel be addressed to men as spiritual beings, who are freed from the law of a carnal commandment, and who are living under the power of an endless life. Already, there is in the true believer a knowledge of his calling in Christ Jesus, "for we that are in *this* tabernacle do groan, being burdened; not for that we would be unclothed, but clothed upon, that mortality might be swallowed up of life. . . . . . We are confident, *I say*, and willing rather to be absent from the body, and to be present with the Lord." Here is a positive declaration of the spiritual nature of man, a voice from the heart. The body profiteth nothing, it is I who desire to be with Christ. It is I who worship in my **body,** but with my spirit, *i. e.*, it is I who **worship;** not only my body. To be carnally minded is death. **Wherefore, they** that worship God must worship **Him** in spirit and in truth. If this be true; then it follows, **that** the Church on earth, the house of God, the place where **His** honor dwelleth, both the temple of wood **and** stone as well the earthly house, as our flesh, are abodes **of** spirit: and it is to build up a spiritual **house for eternal habitation,** and not for temprorary rest, **that, men meet to worship and** adore. In God's **house on earth we** are at **the gate of** heaven, the **veil is taken away and we enter the Holy of** Holies: here the faithful **in Christ are in** possession of **a wonderful** privilege, they do draw nigh unto Christ, they **look, with** faith illuminating them, on that which was to the **Jew death,** they are "in the spirit" when with firm faith **they bow down** before the throne of God; they **see the seven** Golden Candlesticks, and in the midst one like **unto the** Son of Man, clothed with **a** garment down **to the foot, and girt** about the paps **with a golden girdle.** "It is He **that liveth and was dead, and is alive for ever** more, and who **has the keys of** hell and of death." "It is He, who in **the midst of** the throne and of the four beasts, and in the midst of **the elders,** is standing, The Lamb **as it had been** slain, having seven horns and seven eyes which **are the** seven spirits of **God** sent forth into all the earth." **Who** then shall climb up into heaven **to bring** Christ down? Nay, **He** is very nigh, ever knocking **at the door of** our hearts that He may enter in. He is very nigh unto all who call upon Him faithfully, and if **His** nearness be such as to **render** Him a very present **help in** trouble, is He not near **enough** to impart to the perishing souls of men, to trusting, but **weak** servants, that heavenly blessing which he has promised **to bestow,** the impartation **of** His own most blessed body and blood; now become to man a source of spiritual life as proceeding from the risen body of Christ. There is a spiritual body and there is a natural body, the one as real as the other; the former never dying, ever living. When therefore it is said, that Christ is spiritually present, it is not meant that we are to imagine Him present, but that as a Personal Divine Being, the Quickening Spirit, He is truly, verily present, at such times and under such circumstances as He promised to be present to His own people. "I perceive" He said to the woman, "that virtue hath gone out of me," are we to believe, that the virtue of His risen body and blood, goeth not out to heal the broken *spirit*. It is the contrite heart of the spirit of man, not his fleshly heart, that Christ heals; it is the wounded spirit into which He pours balm, not the wounded body; it is the spirit that is sanctified so that the body may be saved, albeit changed. He has instituted *effectual* signs of His Presence, shall we cavil and dispute whether He be in the sign or out of it, so long as His rest is in the faithful heart. Did the children of Israel dispute as to whether the cloud was God or a sign of God's presence with them. Let it be enough for us, that in the holy celebration of the most blessed Eucharist, instituted and ordained by Christ himself, as a means for sacramentally joining Himself to His people and they to Him; that the service is of His appointment and the promise made is His. In making a remembrance of the sacrifice of His death, we are shewing forth that sacrifice to God, and pleading for union with Christ through that one sacrifice. We present ourselves in Him, having about us the marks of the dying of the Lord Jesus; we represent to God, that which Christ does in heaven, that there is no other salvation, that there is none other Name, that there is no other sacrifice which can take away the sins of the world, but the offering of Jesus Christ the Lamb which was slain and **is alive again** for **evermore.**

Everywhere throughout the New Testament man is taught **to forget his carnal** or animal life, and to think of that which **is far** higher and more truly his nature, viz., his spiritual **life.** The baptized disciples of Christ **St. Paul** urgently implores to consider, that in Christ Jesus, they **are** dead to all carnal things, and are alive, *i. e.*, are living in **Christ.** Nay, they are so highly privileged, that they **are to consider** themselves as **already** entitled to the fellowship **of spirits.** "But ye are **come, he says, unto Mount Sion,** and unto **the** city of the **living God, the heavenly Jerusalem, and to an inumerable company of Angels, to the** general assembly **and church of the** first-born, **which are** written in heaven, **and to God the Judge** of all, and to the spirits of just men **made perfect, and to** Jesus the mediator of the new covenant, *and to the blood of sprinkling* that speaketh **better things than the** blood **of Abel."** For as he tells **the Galatians, "Jerusalem which is above is free, which is the mother of us all."** And St. John has revealed the promise of Christ, that, "Him that overcometh will I make a pillar in the temple of my God, and he shall go no more out, and I will **write** upon him the name of my God, which is new Jerusalem which cometh down out of heaven **from my God, and I will write upon him my new Name."** "**If** *there* **be** therefore any consolation in Christ, if any comfort of love, **if any** fellowship of **the spirit, if any bowels** and mercies, fulfil ye my joy, that ye may be like-minded, having the same **love,** being of one accord, **of one** mind."

To those who believe in the power of the Son of God, it is **impossible not to** think of Him as a Person who both can, and **does draw His servants to** Himself. It is impossible, having faith in His **Word,** not to feel, **when** we fall down before His footstool, that we are not before Him; we **cannot get rid of the belief** that " Thou, O God, seest us." **For** we are not only in the flesh, but in the Spirit, if so be that the Spirit of God dwelleth in **us; for if** any man have not **the Spirit of Christ, he is none** of His; and if Christ *be* in us the body *is* dead because of sin; **but the Spirit** *is* life because of righteousness. But if the **Spirit of** Him that raised up Christ from the dead dwell **in us,** He that raised **up** Christ from the dead shall also quicken **our mortal** bodies by His Spirit that dwelleth in us, ... **and if** we through the Spirit do mortify the deeds of the body, we shall live, ... for we have received the Spirit of **adoption** whereby we cry Abba, Father.

> " Lord I believe Thy precious Blood,
> Which at the Mercy Seat of God
> Forever doth for sinners plead—
> For me, e'en for my soul was shed.

> " Thou God of power, Thou God of love,
> Let the whole world Thy mercy prove!—
> That all, who to thy wounds will flee,
> May find eternal life in Thee."

It is true—observes Jackson—that in the Sacrament **of** Christ's Body and Blood there is a propitiation for our sins, because He is really **present in** it, who is the propitiation for our sins. But it **in** no way hence follows that there is any propitiatory sacrifice for sins in this sacrament. **He becomes** the propitiation for our sins; he actually remits our sins, not directly and immediately by the elements of bread and wine, nor by any other kind of local presence or mispresence with these elements, than is in baptism. The orthodoxal accounts use the same language for expressing His presence in baptism and in the Eucharist; they stick **not to say** that Christ is present or latent in the water, as well as in the elements of **bread and wine.** Their meaning is, that **neither of** these elements, **or** sensible substances, **can** directly **cleanse us from** our sins by any virtue communicated unto them; or inherent in them; but *only* as **they are** *pledges* or *assurances* of Christ's peculiar presence in **them,** and of our true investiture in Christ by them. We are not then to receive the elements of bread and wine *only* in remembrance that Christ died for *us*, but in remembrance or assurance likewise, that His Body, which **was once given** for us, doth **by its everlasting virtue** preserve **our bodies** and souls unto **everlasting life; and** that His Blood, **which** was but once shed **for us, both** still cleanse us **from** all our sins, **from which in this life we are cleansed or** can hope to be **cleansed.** If we, then, receive remission of our sins, or **purification** from our sins, in the Sacrament of the Eucharist,—**as we** always do when we receive it worthily,—we receive it, not immediately by the sole serious remembrance **of His** death, but by the *present efficacy* or *operation* **of His Body** which was given for **us, and** His Blood which was **shed** for us.

The reason why the blood of **bulls and** of **goats** had no longer force or efficacy to cleanse **men,** though but **from** sins against the law of ceremonies, than when they were offered, was because *their blood was corruptible blood*, **and** did perish with **the** using. *But we are not redeemed—saith St. Peter—with corruptible things as silver and gold, but with the precious Blood of Christ, as a Lamb without blemish and without spot.* One **part** of the preciousness of **His** blood is, that it is far more incorruptible than any silver **or gold.** Though Christ was truly mortal when he died for **us; yet** the blood that He shed forth for us, did not become like **water** spilt upon the ground, which cannot be gathered again; **it did** not vanish or consume **as** the blood of the legal sacrifices did; as His body, so His blood was not to see or feel corruption: not a drop which was shed for us, whether in the garden or on the cross, *but was the blood of* THE SON OF GOD; but was shed by Him, as willing at this price, to become the everlasting High Priest of our souls: and not a drop of blood which was so shed did cease or shall ever cease to be the blood of the Son of God. This self same blood which was then shed is still united to the Fountain of Life, to the Godhead in the Person of the Son of God. And being united to this Fountain of Life—who dwelleth in it, as light within the body of the sun—it is of efficacy everlasting: it hath an immortal power or force to dissolve the works of Satan in us. The virtue of it to cleanse and purge us of our sins, is at this day as sovereign as if it had been sprinkled, in or upon our souls whilst it issued out of His body." To the same end Hooker saith: "His body being part of that nature, which whole nature is presently joined unto Deity, wheresoever Deity is, it followeth, that His bodily substance hath everywhere a presence of true conjunction with Deity. And forasmuch as it is by virtue of that conjunction made the body of the Son of God, by whom also it was made a Sacrifice for the sins of the whole world, THIS GIVETH IT a *presence* of *force* and *efficacy* throughout all generations of men." Through the resurrection of the Blessed Saviour of man, His body is to us a source of ever flowing Life. As the fount and spring of incorruption, it was not possible that His flesh should see corruption. "It was sown a natural Body free from all taint of corruption and It was raised a Spiritual Body. The first Adam was made a living soul; the last Adam *was made* a quickening Spirit. The first man is of the earth, earthy; the second Man *is* the Lord from heaven. As is the earthy, such are they also that are earthy; and as *is* the heavenly, such are they also that *are* heavenly." If then Christ is the Quickening Spirit it is by the power and efficacy of His risen Body, that we are united to Him, it is through His incorruptible Flesh and Blood, that "this corruptible must put on incorruption." There be those who cannot understand any form of substance other than that which their dull senses lay hold on: carnal ideas alone fill their mind; in the flesh, and living not in the freedom of the spirit given to them, they degrade the Manhood of Christ, and look not to the supreme dignity of that Nature which was His; perfect Man and perfect God. They see not that into His death all are buried, that they may rise from the baptism of His incorruptible blood, purified and gifted with Life:

> "The flesh begotten of the dead,
> For us He rose, our glorious Head,
>   Immortal life to bring;
> What though the saints like Him shall die,
> They share their Leader's victory,
>   And triumph with their King."

Our Lord rose from the grave in that very Body which was His when on the Cross He poured out His Blood for us; as risen, it is revealed that It was changed, for as He had borne the image of the earthly, He was also the image of the heavenly, yea, the heavenly itself; and by His resurrection swallowed up death in victory: therefore thanks be to God which giveth us the victory through Jesus Christ our Lord. "To all things," says Hooker,* "He is life, and to men, light, *as the Son of God;* to the Church both light and life eternal, by being made the Son of Man for us, and by being in us a Saviour, whether we respect Him as God or as Man. Adam is in us as an original cause of our

---

* Ed. by Keble, V. 2, p. 230.

nature, and of that corruption of nature which causeth death; Christ as the cause original of restoration to life; the *person* of Adam is not in us, BUT HIS NATURE; and the corruption of his nature derived into all men by propagation; Christ having Adam's nature as we have, but incorrupt, deriveth not *nature* but incorruption, and that immediately from His own Person into all that belong unto Him. As therefore we are really partakers of the body of sin and death received from Adam, so except we be truly partakers of Christ and as really possessed of His spirit all we speak of eternal life is but *a dream*. That which quickeneth us is the Spirit of the second Adam, and His flesh that wherewith He quickeneth. That which in Him made our nature uncorrupt was the union of His Deity with our nature."

The Apostolic writings repeatedly warn us to acknowledge the Human Nature of Christ, to confess that "He has come in the flesh:" and inasmuch as He was the God-man, taking Flesh of the Virgin and fulfilling all the conditions of human life from birth to death, He through the grave and gate of death carried Humanity to its final destiny, its glorification in the Presence of the Father. Our Lord Himself veiled His Godhead, and bade His hearers look on His Humanity, Why callest thou Me good? And probably it was in order, that we might keep His Humanity in mind, that He used the elements of Bread and Wine, the common food of the body, by which to signify the impartation or communion of His whole nature by which our regeneration and renewal is effected.

But the Holy Spirit has taught us that His flesh and blood are really, truly, and essentially *His Life* as the Son of Man and Son of God, *i. e.*, the Life of Christ; it is It which is imparted to human hearts by the Spirit, through the Faith which is given us of God. When we pray, that the Holy Spirit may descend on the creatures of Bread and Wine, that they may be to us the Body and Blood of Christ, we in effect pray too, that the Holy Spirit may make our spirits a fit abode for the Body and Blood of Christ, which the taking and receiving of the blessed elements insures to the faithful man.

> "O Lamb of God! Thy Precious Blood
> Shall never lose Its Power,
> Till all the ransomed Church of God
> Be saved to Sin no more."

The Body and Blood of Christ have power to work in us a change from death to Life. Throughout the whole Scriptures, both in the Old as well as in the New Testament, we are taught to believe, that it is the Spiritual Life of Man which is to be nourished in all virtue and godliness, to the end that man may be saved in body, soul, and spirit. Having received of God the "breath of immortality," thereby becoming "a living soul," the very life of the soul and body, the Spirit given to man, must have its root in the Eternal Nature of Christ in whom we live and move and have our being. As the blood is the source from whence the body immediately receives the food necessary for its maintenance, it is in a peculiar sense "the life of the body," and therefore in scripture is constantly spoken of as "the Life" or in the place of the Life: but whenever it is so used it is employed to signify the true Life or Spirit, which indwells in the body and by which even the blood is alive. It was on this account, that, from the very first offering of sacrifice when Noah offered of every clean beast, and of every clean fowl, that God accepting the offering, commanded, even in eating of food, that "the flesh with the life thereof, *which* is the blood thereof, shall ye not eat."

"And surely your blood of your lives will I require; at the hand of every beast will I require it, and at the hand of man; at the hand of every man's brother will I require the life of man.

"Whoso sheddeth man's blood, by man shall his blood be shed: for in the image of God made he man."—*Gen.* ix.

Here the blood stands for the life and is spoken of as the life.

"And he shall kill the bullock before the Lord; and the priests, Aaron's sons, shall bring the blood, and sprinkle the blood round about upon the altar that *is by* the door of the tabernacle of the congregation.

"And if his offering be of the flocks, *namely*, of the sheep, or of the goats, for a burnt sacrifice; he shall bring it a male without blemish.

"And he shall kill it on the side of the altar northward before the Lord:* and the priests, Aaron's sons, shall sprinkle his blood round about upon the altar."—*Levit.* c. i.

"And he shall lay his hand upon the head of the sin offering, and slay the sin offering in the place of the burnt offering.

"And the priest shall take of the blood thereof with his finger, and put *it* upon the horns of the altar of burnt offering, and shall pour out all the blood thereof at the bottom of the altar."—*Levit.* c. iv.

"And he shall sprinkle of the blood of the sin offering upon the side of the altar: and the rest of the blood shall be wrung out at the bottom of the altar:† it *is* a sin offering."—*Idem.*

"And if he bring a lamb for a sin offering, he shall bring it a female without blemish.

"And he shall lay his hand upon the head of the sin offering, and slay it for a sin offering in the place where they kill the burnt offering.

"And the priest shall take of the blood of the sin offering with his finger, and put *it* upon the horns of the altar of burnt offering, and shall pour out all the blood thereof *at the bottom of the altar.*"

These strict injunctions not to eat the blood because it was the life of the flesh, are very clear and decided. It was to be poured out under the Lord's Table or Altar, but could not be presented on The Altar, could not be drunk.

---

* Here again the north side of the Altar is spoken of as the most holy part.
† The hiding or putting out of sight under Christ, the true Altar of our sins.

"And Moses said, This is the thing which the Lord commanded that ye should do: and the glory of the Lord shall appear unto you.

"And Moses said unto Aaron, Go unto the altar, and offer thy sin offering, and thy burnt offering, and make an atonement for thyself, and for the people: and offer the offering of the people, and make an atonement for them; as the Lord commanded.

"Aaron therefore went unto the altar, and slew the calf of the sin offering, which was for himself.

"And the sons of Aaron brought the blood unto him: and he dipped his finger in the blood, and put it upon the horns of the altar, and poured out the blood at the bottom of the altar."—*Levit.* c. ix.

Again:—Jehovah denounces the drinking of blood, because it is the life:

"And whatsoever man *there be* of the house of Israel, or of the strangers that sojourn among you, that eateth any manner of blood; I will set my face against that soul that eateth blood, and will cut him off from among his people.

"For the life of the flesh *is* in the blood: and I have given it to you upon the altar to make an atonement for your souls: for it *is* the blood *that* maketh an atonement for the soul.

"Therefore I said unto the children of Israel, No soul of you shall eat blood, neither shall any stranger that sojourneth among you eat blood."— *Levit.* c. xvii.

Here it is fully affirmed that "the life of the flesh" was for an atonement for the life or soul of man, it must not be touched, as it was the life of an inferior animal.

"Even as the roebuck and the hart is eaten, so thou shalt eat them: the unclean and the clean shall eat *of* them alike.

"Only be sure that thou eat not the blood: for the blood *is* the life; and thou mayest not eat the life with the flesh.

"Thou shalt not eat it: thou shalt pour it upon the earth as water."

The 24th verse is very emphatic, and implies an intense anxiety lest the blood should be taken.

"Only thy holy things which thou hast, and thy vows, thou shalt take and go unto the place which the Lord shall choose:

"And thou shalt offer thy burnt offerings, the flesh and the blood, upon the altar of the Lord thy God: and the blood of thy sacrifices shall be poured out upon the altar of the Lord thy God, and thou shalt eat the flesh."

Thus, under the law, it is manifest that the blood of animals, although shed and poured out in atonement for the sins of men, was, in consequence of its being "the life" of corruptible creatures, utterly unfit to be consumed, and was incapable of taking away sin. When, therefore, we mark the change in the commandment, and learn under the covenant of grace that we must no longer abstain from drinking of the blood of the sacrifice, we can only account for the change by remembering that the Blood of the Victim once for all offered for the sins of the world was "the life," not even of a holy and good man, but the life of the Son of God and Man. It was to regenerate human life that He came and suffered—it was to give man of the Water of Life freely. By the hand of St. John has been transmitted to us His own most precious words, from which we know that in pouring out His Blood, He gave His Life a ransom for many.

"I am the door: by me if any man enter in, he shall be saved, and shall go in and out, and find pasture.

"The thief cometh not, but for to steal, and to kill, and to destroy: I am come that they might have life, and that they might have *it* more abundantly.

"I am the good shepherd: the good shepherd giveth his life for the sheep.

"But he that is an hireling, and not the shepherd, whose own the sheep are not, seeth the wolf coming, and leaveth the sheep, and fleeth: and the wolf catcheth them, and scattereth the sheep.

"The hireling fleeth, because he is an hireling, and careth not for the sheep.

"I am the good shepherd, and know my *sheep*, and am known of mine.

"As the Father knoweth me, even so know I the Father: and I lay down my life for the sheep.

"And other sheep I have, which are not of this fold: them also I must bring, **and they shall hear my voice**; and there shall be one fold, *and* one shepherd.

"Therefore doth my father love **me, because** I lay down my life, that I might take it again.

"No man taketh it from me, **but I lay** it down of myself. I have power to lay it down, **and I have** power **to take it again.** This commandment have **I received of my Father."**

It was His life that He laid down, **and which He took again.** It was His nature, that which **is His as the** second Adam, and in consequence of which **He is** the quickening Spirit. It was not only the material substance **of** blood which He had as Man, but **it was the life which is His, and** which, as in us, **maintained the life of His Blood.** Of this Blood **we are** to drink, and on the Flesh derived from this Blood we are **to eat.**

"For in the flesh and blood of Christ, the human soul receiveth *nothing loody,* but a *life-giving saving substance* by the bread and wine."—*Theophylact.*

If we rightly interpret Scripture, then our Blessed Lord **must** have intended us to understand that it was an impartation of His Spirit or Life, of that which in its essence **is truly His** Flesh and Blood, that with which **He** regenerates and renews man's **nature. It is His** Spirit, *i. e.*, H Life, true **real** substance **of His risen** Body, which is bestowed, **when in the spirit of obedience, and in** full reliance on **the efficacy of the** Atonement, **the** repentant **child** of man by the **mouth of faith takes of** the sacramental elements.

"Lift up your eyes on high, and behold who hath created **these** *things,* that bringeth out their host by number: he calleth them all **by names by the** greatness of his might, for that *he is* strong in **power; not one faileth.**

"Why sayest thou, **O** Jacob, and speakest, **O Israel, My way is hid from the** Lord, and my judgment **is passed** over **from my God?**

"Hast thou not known? **hast** thou **not** heard, *that* the everlasting God, the Lord, the Creator of the ends of the earth, fainteth not, neither is weary? *there is* no searching of his understanding.

"**He giveth power** to the faint; and to *them that have* no might he increaseth **strength.**

"Even the youths shall faint and be weary, **and the young** man shall utterly fall:

"But they that wait upon the Lord shall renew *their* strength; they shall mount up with wings as eagles; they shall run, and not be weary; *and* they shall walk, and not faint."

"Moreover, brethren, I would not that ye should be ignorant, how that all our fathers were under the cloud, and all passed through the sea;

"And were all baptized unto Moses in the cloud and in the sea;

"And did all eat the same spiritual meat;

"And did all drink the same spiritual drink: for they drank of that spiritual Rock that followed them: and that Rock was Christ."

It will be said that our Lord Himself directed the Apostles to remark that He was not a Spirit, for said He, "a Spirit hath not flesh and blood as ye see me have," but the assertion of our blessed Redeemer is but a declaration of the truth afterwards enunciated by the holy Apostle St. Paul, that "there is a natural body and there is a spiritual body." Our Lord would not have fulfilled His office of Mediator as the Man Christ Jesus, if He had laid aside His humanity, and He would not have perfected or completed human nature if He had not risen from the grave a spiritual body, that *into which* humanity is intended to be developed. Jesus Christ could not have come forth victor over Hell and Death, precisely in that state of body which He had before He went into the Paradise of the Saints. He returned from the dead a spiritual body, *i. e.*, His humanity was endowed with the quality of Spirit, allied to Spirit, so intensely spiritual that the flesh was subdued to the Spirit, insomuch the Saviour no longer veiled His spiritual power, but openly manifested Himself to His people. He made Himself known "in the breaking of bread." He warmed their hearts as "He walked with them by the way." H came to them in the hour of adoring worship "when they were assembled for fear of the Jews." In all those forty days of communion with His disciples, He was revealing to them death swallowed up in immortality. As was the risen Jesus, the second Adam, so shall they be who are of His body, His blood, His flesh, and His bones. Men have pierced the blackness of the tomb; they have looked across the dark ocean of time and have gazed on eternity. The Son of Man and the Son of God has not only risen from the dead, but He brought with Him from the chambers of death many dead bodies of the saints which slept. As the risen Saviour in His spiritual human body He moved among men as the Spiritual Christ, and shewed forth the power of Spirit.

"But some man will say, How are the dead raised up? and with what body do they come?

"Thou fool, that which thou sowest is not quickened, except it die:

"And that which thou sowest, thou sowest not that body that shall be, but bare grain, it may chance of wheat, or of some other grain:

"But God giveth it a body as it hath pleased him, and to every seed his own body.

"All flesh is not the same flesh: but there is one kind of flesh of men, another flesh of beasts, another of fishes, and another of birds.

"There are also celestial bodies, and bodies terrestrial: but the glory of the celestial is one, and the glory of the terrestrial is another.

"There is one glory of the sun, and another glory of the moon, and another glory of the stars: for one star differeth from another star in glory.

"So also is the resurrection of the dead. It is sown in corruption; it is raised in incorruption:

"It is sown in dishonour; it is raised in glory: it is sown in weakness; it is raised in power:

"It is sown a natural body; it is raised a spiritual body. There is a natural body, and there is a spiritual body.

"And so it is written, The first man Adam was made a living soul; the last Adam was made a quickening spirit.

"Howbeit that was not first which is spiritual, but that which is natural; and afterward that which is spiritual.

"The first man is of the earth, earthy; the second man is the Lord from heaven.

"As is the earthy, such are they also that are earthy; and as is the heavenly, such are they also that are heavenly.

"And as we have borne the image of the earthy, we shall also bear the image of the heavenly.

"Now this I say, brethren, that flesh and blood cannot inherit the kingdom of God: neither doth corruption inherit incorruption.

"Behold I shew you a mystery; We shall not all sleep, but we shall all be changed.

"In a moment, in the twinkling of an eye, at the last trump: for the trumpet shall sound, and the dead shall be raised incorruptible, and we shall be changed.

"For this corruptible must put on incorruption, and this mortal *must* put on immortality.

"So when this corruptible shall have put on incorruption, and this mortal shall have put on immortality, then shall be brought to pass the saying that is written, Death is swallowed up in victory.

"O death, where *is* thy sting? O grave, where *is* thy victory?

"The sting of death *is* sin and the strength of sin *is* the law.

"But thanks *be* to God, which giveth us the victory through our Lord Jesus Christ."

Can any doubt after the declaration of these scriptures, but that our Lord Jesus Christ in rising again in the Flesh fulfilled or completed human destiny. As man lies in the womb of his mother awaiting the completion of his body for terrestrial life, so does he lie down in the grave, the womb of Eternity, waiting in Paradise until he shall be prepared for that final change which shall transform him into a spiritual being. For this has Christ taken our whole nature. If the birth of the Saviour of men filled the hearts of Patriarchs and Prophets with joy, the melodious voice of those who were chosen into the New Covenant, bursts forth in praise and glory to God, for that triumphant victory over the grave effected by the resurrection of Christ. To the Corinthian Christians St. Paul declared: that if Christ had not risen, then was his preaching vain. He openly declared that, the consequence of the resurrection of Christ was immediate, revealing not only the certainty of all men being raised from the dead; but the fact of the *instant* burial of our Adam's nature, and our resurrection in Christ. "Wherefore my brethren, ye also are become dead to the law by the body of Christ;

that ye should be married to another even to Him who is raised from the dead that we should bring forth fruit unto God. For when we were in the flesh, the motions of sins, which were by the law did work in our members to bring forth fruit unto death: but now we are delivered from the law, that being dead wherein we were held; that we should serve in newness of *spirit* and not in the oldness of the letter. For I through the law am dead to the law, that I might live unto God. I am crucified with Christ: nevetheless I live: yet not I, but Christ liveth in me: and the life which I now live in the flesh I live by the faith of the Son of God, who loved me and gave Himself for me." "Ye are all the children of God by faith in Jesus Christ: for as many of you as have been baptized have put on Christ." "And because ye are sons, God hath sent forth the Spirit of His Son into your hearts, crying Abba, Father." "For we are His workmanship, created in Christ Jesus unto good works, which God hath before ordained that we should walk in them." "Now, therefore, ye are no more strangers or foreigners, but *fellow citizens* with the saints and of the household of God." "Buried with Him in baptism, *wherein* also *ye are risen* with Him through the faith of the operation of God who hath raised Him from the dead. If ye then be risen with Christ seek those things which are above where Christ sitteth on the right hand of God. Set your affections on things above, not on things on the earth. For ye are dead, and your life is hid with Christ in God." "For Christ also hath suffered once for sins, the just for the unjust that He might bring us to God, being put to death in the flesh but quickened by the Spirit." "What shall they do which are baptized for the dead, if the dead rise not at all? Why are they then baptized for the dead? And why stand we in jeopardy every hour? I protest by your rejoicing which I have in Christ Jesus our Lord, I die daily." "That which thou sowest, thou sowest not that body that shall be. . . . . . It is sown a natural body; it is raised a spiritual body, and so it is written, the first man Adam was made a living soul: the last Adam was made a Quickening Spirit." "Now is Christ risen from the dead, and become the first-fruits of them that slept. For since by man came death, by man came also the resurrection of the dead. For as in Adam all die, even so in Christ shall all be made alive."

In all these several scriptures we are taught to consider that our nature is elevated by the baptism of Christ; gifted with a better life than that which we had before, for through Christ's incarnation, His death, and His resurrection, we who have been baptized, have put on Christ; to the end that the nature derived from our forefather Adam may be renewed; and that the New Man may be perfected in us. It is as the Risen Lord, that Christ now imparts to us, "that thing which by nature we cannot have;" it is the spiritual food of His risen body and blood, even the Life of Christ which in the Sacraments is derived to us. It is the most blessed food of the Quickening Spirit, which renews our bodies, souls, and spirits, and which is given to us in the Holy Eucharist.

"I will magnify thee, O God, my King: and I will praise thy Name for ever and ever.

"Every day will I give thanks unto thee: and praise thy Name for ever and ever.

"Great is the Lord, and marvellous, worthy to be praised: there is no end of his greatness.

"One generation shall praise thy works unto another: and declare thy power.

"As for me, I will be talking of thy worship: thy glory, thy praise, and wondrous works;

"So that men shall speak of the might of thy marvellous acts: and I will also tell of thy greatness.

"The memorial of thine abundant kindness shall be shewed: and men shall sing of thy righteousness."

The heat of controversy has kept our minds too intent on what our Lord said and did at the Passover, but if we look to His ways and acts, after that He had risen from the dead, we may see how truly He explains His words, and sets forth His intentions, in the service of the most blessed Eucharist.

"Then he said unto them, O fools, and slow of heart to believe all that the prophets have spoken: ought not Christ to have suffered these things, and to enter into his glory? And beginning at Moses, and all the prophets, he expounded unto them in all the Scriptures the things concerning himself. And they drew nigh unto the village whither they went; and he made as though he would have gone further: but they constrained him, saying, Abide with us, for it is towards evening, and the day is far spent. And he went in to tarry with them. And it came to pass, as he sat at meat with them, he took bread, and blessed it, and brake, and gave to them.* And their eyes were opened, and they knew him, and he vanished out of their sight. And they said one to another, Did not our heart burn within us, while he talked with us by the way, and while he opened to us the Scripture? And they rose up the same hour, and returned to Jerusalem, and found the eleven gathered together, and them that were with them, saying, The Lord is risen indeed, and hath appeared to Simon. And they told what things were done in the way, and how he was known of them in breaking of bread."

The eleven disciples went away, into a mountain where Jesus had appointed them. St. Matthew, says Burgon, gives a remarkably prominent place to the appearance of our Lord to His disciples in Galilee. It is recorded as the great event, almost the only event, after His resurrection. Nothing else is said concerning the mysterious forty days which followed the first Easter. The very ascension of our Lord into heaven does not obtain the slightest notice. On the other hand, the Angel in the Sepulchre said, "Behold He goeth before you into Galilee: *then* shall ye see Him."

---

* Here then, again, did our Lord Himself celebrate the Holy Eucharistic Sacrifice.

Christ repeated the same assurance, "Go tell My brethren that they go into Galilee, and there shall they see me." "And the *eleven* went away into Galilee, into a mountain where Jesus had appointed them." Here, therefore, He is now, with His glorified body, where *He had been so often* in His humiliation. And Jesus said, "All power is given unto Me in heaven and on earth." This dominion thus given unto Christ in His human nature, was a direct and plenary power over all things: but was not actually given at once, but part while He lived on earth, part after His death and resurrection. For though it be true that "Jesus knew" before His death that the Father had given all things into His hands; "yet it is observable that in the same place it is written, that He likewise knew that He came from God, and went to God." And part of that power He received when He came from God, with part He was invested when He went to God; the first to enable Him, the second not only so, but also to reward Him. For to this end Christ died, and rose, and revived, that He might be "Lord of the dead and the living." It is now that Christ claimed the kingdom, and exercised royal authority, instituting, ordaining, regulating all things necessary for the good government and safety of His own ransomed people. He sitteth a King for ever be the earth never so unquiet. As Man, He has entered for man into the presence of God: before His Father He pleads for His people; and over His people He throws the mantle of His grace, that they may be hid in Him, so that an offended God may once more look on His once lost children, and seeing only the spotless life of His Son resting on human souls redeemed and saved through Christ's most precious body and blood, may be reconciled to man, and be enabled to restore to him that favour which he had lost.

> "Ascending to the **Father's throne**,
> **Thou** claim'st the Kingdom as **thine own**;
> Thy days of mortal weakness o'er,
> All power is Thine for evermore.
> In awe and wonder angels see,
> How changed is man's estate by Thee,
> **How** Flesh makes pure as flesh did stain,
> And Thou true God in Flesh **dost reign.**"

From birth to death, from Advent to Easter, what a change! For eighteen hundred years and more, the earth has been full of the goodness of God, and songs of jubilee have been sung in exultation of man's deliverance from the bondage of a worse than Egyptian slavery. This death, over which human hearts rejoice, differs from all other deaths, since by it, springs from the grave light and immortality. Death is vanquished, overcome, put away, so that it has no longer force or power over men. There is no more death to man. The hiding in the grave, the putting away our mortal flesh, is but the keeping out of sight the corruption incident to material substance. That which thinks, and feels, and knows, and perceives; that which came from God and goes to God, is that which I am. He bid the earth, by the power of His word, bring forth herb and beast; He, out of the material world, made man, and breathed into *him* the spirit of life. Even as Lazarus awaked out of his corruption by the presence of God, so Adam rose a living soul, lifted up before he saw corruption by the breath of the Almighty. Man cannot die, for he has the breath of God in his spirit; and although "after my skin worms destroy this body, yet in my flesh shall I see God, whom I shall see for myself, and mine eyes shall behold, and not another." No wonder that the resurrection from the grave fills so large a place in the hearts of the holy Apostles. How can we be surprised that the whole tenor of their pleadings, is the coming of Christ to reign with His own redeemed, and to take them to Himself, to be partakers of those good things which it hath not entered into the heart of man to conceive? The terrors of the chamber of death have been for ever removed, because death itself is abolished. "I am the resurrection and the life, saith the Lord; he that believeth in me, though he were dead, yet shall he live; and whosoever liveth and believeth in me shall never die." The forty days' communion with His blessed Apostles, their handling the Bread of Life, their souls drinking in the new wine of His spiritual communion with them, were so many hallowed blessings poured upon them, to lift up their hearts in adoring love to Him, who had in His own person made open the way which leads to the throne of God.

> "Chime on, ye bells; again begin,
> And ring the Sabbath morning in;
> The labourer's week-day work is done,
> The rest begun,
> Which Christ hath for His people won."

It is REST, and not the stillness of death, which remaineth for man. To enter upon that rest, is to be in joy and felicity; it is to be with Christ, and to be witnesses of His glory, and doers of His will; it is to be glorified, purified, sanctified, made holy, Christ-like. We know enough of Him already to understand, however imperfectly, the glory of that life which we shall enjoy with Him. If on this earth as man, His is the life to which all men betake themselves as to a source of endless, exhaustless virtue, how shall it be when with purified eyes they see the King in his beauty! Millions on millions of white-robed saints bow down before the throne, and sing the song of the Lamb. They wait upon Him, they adore Him, and, living on in the pure light of their Lord and of their God, who alone giveth them light, they wait in patience till "the marriage of the Lamb is come, and His wife shall have made herself ready." The resurrection of Christ, his second advent, is the joy and hope of all the ends of the world. "The souls of the righteous are in the hand of God, and there shall no torment touch them. In the sight of the universe they seemed to die, and their departure is taken for misery, and their going from us to be utter destruction; but they are in peace."

The Holy Ghost, speaking by St. Paul, has declared to us that "there is a natural body, and that there is a spiritual body;" that the former is sown in corruption; and that as we have borne the image of the earthly, so also we shall bear the image of the heavenly. It is then revealed to us that the body of our blessed Lord, although before His crucifixion spotless and pure, was nevertheless that truly natural body which He had been pleased to take of the Blessed Virgin, His mother; that by death He completed or attained perfect manhood by that change in His body, through death, which it is necessary that the human body should pass through before it can be received into the Paradise of God.

The body of the risen Christ is therefore no new body; it is the very body which was His when walking and living with men. But as the seed is not the tree, nor the germ the animal, but both are developed into the perfect form of their being, so it is the destiny or end of the human body to be developed into that spiritual body which God has declared is natural and proper to it, after it shall have passed through those necessary changes which He in his wisdom and justice has apportioned to it. Our brethren of the Roman community would change the elements of bread and wine into the natural flesh and blood of Christ; our adorable Redeemer bids us to come to Him with these effectual memorials of a broken body and poured-out blood, that through the power of that **body**, risen, glorified, perfected through suffering, the **sinful body** of man might be made pure, even as Christ is pure. **If, in His ministry on** earth, he exhibited to the **world the effectual working of His Word;** if the clay did, **through the power of His own word and** will, open the eyes of the blind **man; if,** through the same effectual operation **of** His word, holy Apostles exhibited the power of Christ, **after** His resurrection, over the bodies and spirits **of. men;** how are we to doubt that the same sovereign Lord **worketh** on our blindness, and brings back from the dead, souls that **are reanimated** by the efficacy which is from the body and **blood** of Christ risen: transformed after the pattern and likeness of **Him who is the Author** and Giver of all good. How then are we to receive the words of Christ Jesus when He says, "Take, eat, this my Body?"

The Anglican Divines **enforcing the teaching** of the early Fathers of **the** Church, point **out to us the** true meaning of their blessed Lord's words to be: that **as surely as** we taking **bread and wine into** our mouths, consume **these elements and assimilate them to our** bodily **substance; so certainly do we** by the act of Faith, which is the door of the Spirit, receive **the** body and blood **of** Christ, which by His own divine will He has promised **to** impart to us, and which we must believe He does so impart. If neither His body nor His blood could see corruption, then they are still **in union** with His person as the eternal Son. It is still the very body and blood of **Christ** which now worketh in us to the effectual saving of our souls; no longer carnal, but life-giving substance. The incarnation of Christ has unfolded to man his true nature. No longer dreaming of immortality, or dreading the entering on the shoreless sea of an unknown future; He by the quickened eye of faith looks on that happy home where naught but what is beautiful and good and true may be found.

Made to lift his eyes to heaven whither His spirit would soar, the child of Christ living by the Spirit which is in him already, learns to bring into subjection the movements of the flesh. How deeply did the Apostle yearn to speak to spiritual and not to carnal followers. The whole burden of the call to Christ is, that we recognise the power we possess as spiritual beings, to subdue the flesh.

"And they that are Christ's have crucified the flesh with the affections and lusts.

" If we live in the Spirit, let us also walk in the Spirit.

" Let us not be desirous of vain glory, provoking one another, envying one another.

" *This* I say then, Walk in the Spirit, and ye shall not fulfil the lust of the flesh.

" For the flesh lusteth against the Spirit, and the Spirit against the flesh: and these are contrary the one to the other: so that ye cannot do the things that ye would.

" But if ye be led of the Spirit, ye are not under the law."

" The burden of the word of the Lord for Israel, saith the Lord, which stretcheth forth the heavens, and layeth the foundation of the earth, and formeth the spirit of man within him.

" I said, Days should speak, and multitudes of years should teach wisdom.

" But *there is* a spirit in man: and the inspiration of the Almighty giveth them understanding.

" What? know ye not that your body is the temple of the Holy Ghost *which is* in you, which ye have of God, and ye are not your own?

" For ye are bought with a price: therefore glorify God in your body, and in your spirit, which are God's.

" Quench not the Spirit.

" Despise not prophesyings.

" Prove all things: hold fast that which is good.

" Abstain from all appearance of evil.

" And the very God of peace sanctify you wholly; and *I pray God* your whole spirit and soul and body be preserved blameless unto the coming of our Lord Jesus Christ.

" Faithful *is* he that calleth you, who also will do *it*.

" Brethren, pray for us."

Having taught that Christ has opened the Kingdom of Heaven to all believers, we are necessarily reminded that we have been by baptism made spiritual beings, and that having the gift of the Spirit, we must no longer live under the dominion of the flesh. We are reminded that all our worship is spiritual, and must be, to be worship at all.

"O foolish Galatians, who hath bewitched you, that ye should not obey the truth, before whose eyes Jesus Christ hath been evidently set forth, crucified among ye?

"This only would I learn of you, Received ye the Spirit by the works of the law, or by the hearing of faith?

"Are ye so foolish? having begun in the Spirit, are ye now made perfect by the flesh?

"Have ye suffered so many things in vain? if it be yet in vain.

"He therefore that ministereth to you the Spirit, and worketh miracles among you, *doeth he it* by the works of the law, or by the hearing of faith?

"Even as Abraham himself believed God, and it was accounted to him for righteousness.

"Know ye therefore that they which are of faith, the same are the children of Abraham?"

The essential difference between the Anglican and Roman branches of the Church lies in this: that, whereas the Roman divines have declared that bread and wine are transubstantiated into the Body and Blood of Christ, and so are carnally taken and received; the Anglican affirms that the faithful Christian does really take and receive Christ, whenever in faith he takes and receives the effectual signs of His presence; *i. e.*, together with the bread and wine blessed; Christ's Body and Blood enter the spirit or heart of man to the purification and renewal of his body, and soul, and spirit. Christ dwells in him, and he in Christ: for the Flesh and Blood of Christ are, by the Spirit of Christ, and are of the risen Christ. What is the true doctrine, then, of the presence of Christ with His people at the Eucharist?

It may, I think, be at once admitted, that the difference in the two great schools in the Church of England lies in this, that **the one** party **believes** that our blessed **and** only Redeemer **is only** present *subjectively* in the mind of the **receiver: the other** holds, **that** he **is** objectively present, **and is taken and** received subjectively **by the** faithful receiver. Now we, who are of this latter **school, may** safely express our belief in the very fitting **language of Dr. Monsell: "Believing, as we do most** firmly, **in** the **Real Presence of the Body and Blood of Christ in the Holy Communion, we still feel,** *that in so great* **A MYSTERY,** it **is** taking too much upon **us to assign** ANY *place* to that **Presence, of** which **we** only **know, that THE SACRAMENT** being rightly **celebrated,** *it is there,* **where all** rightly receiving may verily **and indeed partake of it. But** where *that there is,* save **that its ultimate rest is in** the faithful heart, *we dare not say."*

Again, **Mr. Liddon** observes: **" Mr.** Hubbard **is** perfectly right **in** assuming that Transubstantiation *is denied* **on both sides** of the controversy. Mr. **Keble's language on the subject is sufficiently explicit.** He describes the doctrine as '*an error,* **a one-sided formula, a half-truth;' and** urges '**that it must be an exceeding calamity for any** portion of the **Church to have** committed **itself to it;' and** he **maintains that, '** looking to the **average of** believers, **it must be** judged **on the whole to have borne very evil fruit,** both where it **is received, and** *where it is not.*' **It may** then be affirmed, that in argument between ourselves, in the Church of England, the erroneous dogma 'Transubstantiation' is excluded, as being foreign to the **belief of any section of our** Church. Well, then, the possible **error that** *we* **would** guard **against is, the** belief that the celebration of the Eucharist is **a** *mere* **memorial service. We** never, in our present state, **can explain a mystery.** The fact of our using the Scriptural term *Mystery,* **implies** something **to be** taken on FAITH;

19

and the language of our Service enables us *in Faith* to declare that we 'eat the flesh of Christ and drink His blood,' and truly to teach in the Catechism that 'the Body and Blood of Christ are verily and indeed TAKEN AND RECEIVED *by the faithful* in the Lord's Supper.' We must believe, that when we are taking and receiving the outward sign, that, *in a way that is mysterious and unknown to us*, our blessed Lord is communicating to us *supra-naturally* Himself; and, to use a recent writer's language, 'it matters not *to Faith* whether the Presence be close at hand with the Sacramental, as in the Upper Room, or be as far from it as Heaven from Earth, as in all subsequent Eucharists: the impossibility of conceiving the manner of this, is no objection, any more than it would be to any other, the most undeniable aspect or result of the mystery of the Holy Incarnation.'"

What His rising from the dead accomplished we are told by the witnesses of His resurrection, for it is recorded for the consolation and confirmation of the hope of the Israel of God, "that after His resurrection many bodies of the saints which slept arose, and came out of the graves, and went into the holy city and appeared unto many." This, not at His *crucifixion*, but after His RESURRECTION. Even so now they that are in the grave of sin and who hear His voice do come forth; the Eternal Word brings them forth clothed and in their right mind. They leave "the linen clothes" that be of this world, wrapt and lying in the tomb, being clothed upon by the spotless robe of Christ's righteousness. Resurrection from the grave is one of the articles of our christian belief, that article which St. Paul so constantly preached, and which he affirms to be at the very basis of the faith. In the Acts of the holy Apostles the attention is at once directed to the re-appearance on earth of our blessed Lord after His crucifixion, when "He shewed Himself alive after His passion by many infallible proofs; being seen of the apostles forty days, and speaking to them of the things pertaining to the kingdom of God. Of those things to which the apostles thought it necessary to give immediate heed, was the election to the Apostolic office of one who had been a *witness* of the Lord's *resurrection*, to fill the place of the traitor. St. Peter having declared the history of the treachery of Judas concludes his address with the declaration, "Wherefore of these men, which have companied with us all the time that the Lord Jesus went in and out among us, beginning from the baptism of John unto that same day that he was taken up from us, must one be ordained to be a witness with us of His resurrection." St. Peter, therefore, by the Holy Ghost, declares from the very depth of his soul the purport of the Holy Penticostal outpouring. "Men and brethren let me freely speak unto you of the Patriarch David, that he is both dead and is buried, and his sepulchre is with us unto this day. Therefore being a prophet and knowing that God had sworn with an oath to him, that of the fruit of his loins, according to the flesh, he would raise up Christ to set on His throne; he seeing this before spoke of the resurrection of Christ, that His soul was not left in hell, neither His flesh did see corruption; this Jesus hath God raised up whereof we all are witnesses."

The Apostles, in this that they did, only followed their Master's teaching. He had declared Himself to be "the resurrection and the life." He had himself, before tasting death for all men, shown his power over death; He had confounded the Sadducees, who denied that there was any resurrection; and He sent forth his ministering servants to proclaim the glad tidings of the resurrection to eternal life. He declared himself to be eternal King and Priest over a

Kingdom not of this world. He is Sovereign Lord, supreme in and over spiritual men, now indeed compassed about by many infirmities, hereafter to be with Him, freed from all the fetters of the flesh. He has conquered, and hath gone up on high, having led captivity captive, and received gifts for men, yea, even for his enemies, that the Lord God might dwell among them.

It was this glorious truth that instantly drew down upon the Apostolic missionaries the fury and malice of the Jewish priests, who stirred St. Peter to the bold declaration that "If they be examined of the good deed done to the impotent man, by what means he is made whole, be it known unto you all, and to all the people of Israel, that BY THE NAME of Jesus Christ of Nazareth, whom ye crucified, whom God raised from the dead, EVEN BY HIM doth this man stand here before you whole." Here St. Peter, by the Holy Ghost, affirms that although Christ be not visible to mortal eyes, yet that the risen Jesus of Nazareth hath the same power now to raise the sick and dead, as He had when He was visible to men. And what is it but lamentable declension of faith which prevents one part of the Church from following the injunction of St. James in anointing the sick, while another, from a more serious declension of faith, applies the anointing oil, the outward sign of grace in answer to the prayer and act of faith, to the cleansing of the soul? If we needed any illustration to convince us, what Christ, as the risen Lord, does for the spirits and souls and bodies of men, surely there cannot be a mightier proof of His power than is afforded, first, by the success of the Apostolic ministrations and next the progressive establishment, in the face of Satanic hate, of His truth upon earth. We believe that "He sitteth at the right hand of God." If so, we believe not only that He hath risen, but that *He lives* even in the oneness of the Father and Holy Spirit, our Priest and King, bestowing those gifts which He has received for man.

The Latin Church, by its one-sided statement of truth, has not only so obscured it as to render the truth difficult to be seen, but has rendered the discussion of the question so painful and unpleasant, that a sensitive mind naturally shrinks from entering upon it. Constituted as we are, we cannot shut out from the perception of truth whatever light we may derive from the exercise of any one gift we possess. As God's workmanship we must be constituted for the work He has given us to do. Therefore in the consideration of any question put before us, we must examine it by every faculty or power, mental and otherwise, with which we are endowed. We cannot then, even in the instance of the Holy Commemoration refuse the evidence which our senses may afford touching the nature of any change in the elements of bread and wine. It is difficult to define the limits to be assigned to the senses as witnesses to the truth, or to express the extent of their capacity to reveal to us the truth of all that is brought within their sphere: but of this we may be sure, that, when they are engaged in combination with the faculties and power of the mind in the investigation of objects, they are not likely to go astray. The holy scriptures sufficiently attest the real value of the senses, and explain how far and under what circumstances we may rely upon their testimony. When St. Stephen "saw the heavens opened, and the Son of Man standing on the right hand of God," we believe that he did see what he describes as having seen. When they who were fed, "had eaten and were satisfied;" they were not deceived as to the nature of the food of which they partook.

Tertullian* says: "We may not call in question those

---

* De Anima, c. 17.

senses, lest their truth should be questioned in Christ Himself, lest it should be said, perchance, that He saw untruly Satan cast down from heaven: or heard untruly the voice of the Father bearing witness of Him; or was deceived when He touched Peter's mother-in-law; or perceived, as other than it was, the breath of the ointment which He accepted for His burial: or afterwards, *the taste of the wine,* which He consecrated to be a memorial of His blood."

St. Chrysostom in arguing the Real Personality of Christ, draws from the natural substances in the Eucharist his proofs for the unity of two substances in the one Person of Christ. He says: "We call the bread before it is sanctified bread: but when Divine grace has, through the intervention of the priest sanctified It, it is set free from the name bread, and is thought worthy to be called the Lord's body, *although the nature of bread remains,* and we proclaim not two bodies, but the one body of the Son: so too here, THE DIVINE NATURE having come to indwell in the body, they have together formed one Son, ONE PERSON." The power of the LIVING WORD consecrating bread and wine, leaves them to the natural senses both bread and wine, but in efficacy they are the Spiritual Body and Blood, just as the conjunction of the human with the Divine destroyed not the human, but resulted in the Person of Christ. Faith seeing a right perceives that which is inward and unseen, although to carnal sense there be only bread and wine. Theodoret says: "His very Body we call the Divine Body and Life-giving, and the Body of the Lord, teaching *that it is not common with any man,* but is OF OUR LORD WHO IS GOD AND MAN."

Again: "Neither after consecration do the mystic symbols depart from their *own nature.* For they remain in their former *substance* and figure and form, and can be seen and touched as before; but in thought they are conceived and believed and adored, as being those things which are believed. Compare then the Image with the Archetype and thou wilt see the likeness." Again: "Certainly the Sacrament of the Body and Blood of Christ which we receive is a Divine Thing; wherefore, also, we are by THE SAME made partakers of the DIVINE NATURE, and yet *the substance and nature* of Bread and Wine *ceaseth not to be.*"

St. Ambrose says: "This is the Bread of Life: whoso then eateth LIFE cannot die. For how should *he* die whose food is Life? How shall *he* fail who hath a LIVING SUBSTANCE? Approach to Him, and be satisfied because He is Bread, approach and drink because He is a Fountain." . . . Hear Himself saying, "I am the Bread of Life."

There is a passage in St. Ambrose, which, while shewing the true meaning of the Sacrament, also **gives** sanction to Bishop Beveredge's opinion as to the position of the celebrant at the altar-table, being properly at the north end as commonly assumed in the Anglican Church. "The angel appeared to Zechariah on the right hand of the altar of incense, because he brought a token of the Divine mercy. For 'the Lord is on my right hand, therefore I shall not be moved,' and elsewhere, the Lord is thy protector on thy right hand." Again: "Would that, to us too burning incense at the Altar and offering Sacrifice, the Angel would stand by; yea, rather would permit Himself to be seen. *For thou canst not doubt* that the Angel stands by, when CHRIST STANDETH BY, when Christ is offered." "In that Sacrament Christ is: because It is the body of Christ; It is not therefore bodily food, but Spiritual." Again: "For the Body of God is a Spiritual Body; the Body of Christ is the Body of the Divine Spirit." Since Christ is Spirit, as we read, "The Spirit before our face is Christ the Lord."*

---

* Ambrose 55, p. 340; ib. 57.; 58. ib.

How did Divine Bread come down from heaven? Because our Lord Jesus Christ partaketh both of Divinity and a Body: and thou who receivest flesh, dost in that Food partake of His Divine Substance.

The conditions under which our Lord vouchsafes His Presence are not secret. He has made known to us that FAITH in Him is *the work* which God hath given us to do. When the Jews asked Him, "What sign showest thou?" His answer was, "This is the work of God, that ye believe on Him whom He has sent." Wherefore the holy Apostle St. Paul taught as he was moved by the Holy Spirit, that

"Without faith *it is* impossible to please *him:* for he that cometh to God must believe that he is, and *that* he is a rewarder of them that diligently seek him."

And again:

"The scripture, foreseeing that God would justify the heathen through faith, preached before the gospel unto Abraham, *saying*, In thee shall all nations be blessed.

"So then they which be of faith are blessed with faithful Abraham.

"For as many as are of the works of the law are under the curse: for it is written, Cursed *is* every one that continueth not in all things which are written in the book of the law to do them.

"But that no man is justified by the law in the sight of God, *it is* evident: for, The just shall live by faith.

"And the law is not of faith: but, The man that doeth them shall live in them.

"Christ hath redeemed us from the curse of the law, being made a curse for us: for it is written, Cursed *is* every one that hangeth on a tree:

"That the blessing of Abraham might come on the Gentiles through Jesus Christ; that we might receive the promise of the Spirit through faith.

"Brethren, I speak after the manner of men; Though *it be* but a man's covenant, yet *if it be* confirmed, no man disannulleth, nor addeth thereto.

"Now to Abraham and his seed were the promises made. He saith not, And to seeds, as of many; but as of one, And to thy seed, which is Christ.

"And this I say, *that* the covenant, that was confirmed before of God in Christ, the law, which was four hundred and thirty years after, cannot disannul, that it should make the promise of none effect.

"For if the inheritance be of **the law,** *it is* no more of promise; but God gave *it* to Abraham by promise."

And he continues:

"**Before** faith came, we were kept under the **law,** shut **up** unto the faith which should afterwards be revealed.

" Wherefore the law was our schoolmaster *to bring us* unto Christ, that we might be justified by faith.

" But after that faith is come, we are no longer under **a schoolmaster.**

" For ye are all the children of God by faith in Christ Jesus.

" For as many of you as have been baptized into Christ have put on Christ.

" There is neither **Jew nor Greek, there is neither bond nor free, there** is neither male nor **female: for ye are all one in** Christ Jesus.

" And **if ye** *be* **Christ's, then are ye** Abraham's seed, and heirs according to **the promise."**

He that hath been baptized, has **come to** that baptism in **faith, believing** that Christ is, that He is the Son of God, and that He died to redeem mankind. He that hath **been** baptized into Christ's death is risen in Him. Therefore **we are** debtors, not to the flesh, **to live** after the flesh. For if ye live after the flesh, **ye shall die:** but if **ye through the Spirit do mortify** the deeds of the body, **ye shall live.** For as **many as are** led **by the Spirit of** God, **they** are the sons **of God. For ye have not** received the spirit **of bondage** again **to** fear; **but ye have received** the spirit **of adoption,** whereby we **cry,** Abba, Father. **The** Spirit **itself** beareth witness with **our** spirit, that **we are the** children of **God:** And if children, then heirs; **heirs of God, and** joint-heirs with Christ; if so be that we suffer with *him*, that we may **be** also glorified together. To such the Lord vouchsafes, by **the** power of His Divinity, to communicate **His** Body **and Blood, not** only because of covenant made in baptism, **but as the conditions** of that covenant on our part have been complied with.

" If there be found among you, within any of thy gates which the Lord thy God giveth thee, man or woman, that hath wrought wickedness in **the** sight of **the Lord thy** God, in transgressing his covenant,

" And **hath gone and served other gods, and worshipped** them, either the **sun, or moon, or any of the host of heaven, which I have not** commanded;

" And it be told thee, and thou hast heard *of it*, and enquired diligently, and, behold, *it be* **true**, *and* **the thing** certain, *that* such abomination is wrought in Israel:

" **Then shalt thou** bring forth **that man or that woman, which** have committed that wicked thing, unto thy gates, *even* **that man or that woman,** and shalt stone them with stones, till they die.

" At the mouth of two witnesses, or three witnesses, **shall he that is** worthy of death be put to death; *but* at the mouth of one witness he shall not be put **to** death.

" The hands of the witnesses shall be first upon him to put him **to death,** and afterward **the** hands of all the people. So thou shalt put the **evil away from among you."**

"**Thus he that** despised **Moses' law died** without mercy under **two or three witnesses: of how much sorer** punishment suppose **ye, shall he be thought worthy, who** hath trodden under **foot the Son of God, and counted the Blood of the covenant** wherewith *he was sanctified* **an unholy thing, and hath** done despite **unto** the Spirit of Grace."

See how faith operated:

" And behold, **a woman, which was diseased with an issue of blood twelve** years, came behind him, and **touched the hem** of his garment; for she said within herself, If I may **but touch his** garment, I shall be whole. But Jesus turned him about, and, when **he saw** her, **he** said, Daughter, be of good comfort, thy faith hath made thee whole. **And** the woman was made **whole from that hour."**

And in **later** times the same living faith worked **in those who believed, for in** the pious souls of the early Church, Faith **was in them;** sight, hearing, smell, taste, touch. The **great St. Isaac could say:** I beheld that her cup was mingled, **and instead of wine it was** full of blood, **and instead of bread a body was placed for her in** the midst of her **table. I saw the blood and trembled; and** the body, and fear seized me: and she, FAITH, made to me a sign, "Eat and be silent; drink, child, and scrutinize not." She shewed me a body slain, and placed thereof between my lips, and cried to me sweetly, "See what it is thou art eating." She gave me the pen of the Spirit, and bade me subscribe; and I took, I wrote, I confessed, "This is the Body of God;" so again, I took the cup, and I drank in her feast, and from the cup the scent of that body of which I had eaten struck me; and what she said of the body, that, "That this is the Body of God;" that again I said of the cup, That this is the Blood of my Redeemer."

St. Ephraim could say, "The fire threateneth my limbs, O Lord, and Thine atoning blood, O my Saviour, is hidden in me." "From hateful desires free me, through THY SAVING BODY AND BLOOD, which thou givest me."

"O help us, through the power of FAITH,
  More firmly to believe;
For still the more the servant hath,
  The more shall he receive.

"O help us, Jesus, from on high;
  We know no help but Thine;
O, help us so to live and die.
  As thine in heaven to be."

Herbert says of FAITH:

"Hungrie I was, and had no meat;
I did conceit a most delicious feast;
I had it straight, and did as truly eat,
As ever did a welcome guest.

"Faith, makes me anything, or all
That I believe, is in the sacred storie:
And when sinne places me in Adam's fall,
Faith sets me higher in His glorie.

"If I go lower in the book,
What can be lower than the common manger?
Faith puts me there with Him, who sweetly took
Our flesh and frailtie, death and danger."

The good Herbert, has further also left us the outflowing of his **soul**, thankful and full of love for the heavenly Visitant who shed such comfort in his heart.

> "Not in rich furniture or fine array,
>   Nor in a wedge of gold,
>   Thou, who from me wast sold,
> To me dost now Thyself convey;
> For so thou should'st without me still have been,
>   Leaving within me sinne.
>
> "But by the way of nourishment and strength,
>   Thou creep'st into my breast;
>   Making Thy way my rest,
>   And Thy small quantities my length,
> Which spread their forces into every part,
> Meeting sinne's force and art.
>
> "Only Thy grace which with these elements comes,
>   Knoweth the ready way,
>   And hath the privie key,
>   Opening the soul's most subtile rooms:
> While those to spirits refin'd at the door attend,
> Despatches from their friend."

It is impossible to read the ancient Fathers of the Church and not perceive the importance attached by them to the words of our most blessed Lord. They do not forget to consider the whole of the teaching conveyed by Him, when He said, "The words I speak unto you, they are Spirit and *they are Life.*" These latter words are too often now-a-days passed over, even by thoughtful exponents of scripture, and yet they are words not in any sense less important than the former words, which commentators dwell so forcibly upon. "They are life." So says Jesus Himself; hence in every part of the Christian Church the words of life, the living words, "Take, eat, this is my Body,"—living because still the words of the living Jesus—are held to be necessary to the valid consecration or blessing of the elements. The ancient Fathers, therefore, ever taught that those living words, **words** of life, accompanying the elements, **are the force and efficacy** of the sacrament. They are not the echo of the voice which once spake them, they come not to us reverberating through time and space, *they* ARE the very true words of the Living Christ who now speaks, and it is done. Mark the construction of **our Holy Office** for this great work of Christ feeding His **flock. It is not only sufficient** that there **shall be bread and wine set forth, but** that **bread is to be taken into the hands, as Christ took it; it is** to be broken **and exhibited to the Father; it is then to have** spoken **over it the words of Christ. And so with the cup:** the **wine is to be poured out, and there is then to be said over it the words of the Living Christ.** This is not enough. **Each Christian soul must now act his part** in the new nation **of Priests; each soul is to** draw near and offer itself with the **representative** pledges **and** symbols, of the sacrifice **of the death of** Christ; to the end that the words of **the Living Lord, accompanying** the due **taking of the hallowed food, may guide to the spirit of penitent man to the home where loves to rest the Glorified Humanity, the Body and Blood of the Spiritual Christ. Mark the language of St.** Ephraim, **quoted above: "How should He die who is Life?"** How **should He fail who hath the** Living Substance?

The question **whether there be any, and what the** nature of the change **in the elements of bread and wine by the** solemn act of consecration, **is not to be answered, we admit, by** an appeal **to the** senses **alone. All we contend** for is, **that in** considering the nature **of** any material change, the **ability** which the **senses have of** guiding **us to** a correct **judgment as to the change, be not** neglected or ignored. **On many occasions our Lord** appealed to the senses of His **disciples and the** multitude whom He addressed, as sufficient **to determine the truth of that** which **was done.** "Ye seek me not because ye saw the miracles." "The star which they saw went before them." "Stephen saw the glory of God and Jesus standing," &c. In St. Matthew, c. xiv. v. 36—"They brought unto Him all that were diseased, that they might only touch the hem of His garment." "Then said He to Thomas, reach hither thy finger, and behold my hands, and reach hither thy hand and thrust *it* into my side: and be not faithless, but believing."—Heb. i. 2. "How long shall I cry, and thou wilt not hear?" "If they hear not Moses and the prophets, neither will they be persuaded, though one rose from the dead." "My sheep hear my voice." "When the ruler of the feast had tasted the water that *was made* wine, ... he said, 'Thou hast kept the good wine until now.'" "Then took Mary a pound of ointment of spikenard, very costly, and anointed the feet of Jesus, and wiped His feet with her hair; and the house was filled with the *odour* of the ointment." Thus far the senses are by the scriptures stated to be sufficient witnesses. The Almighty Father hath not constituted them for us blind guides, but has given them to His creatures as helps to be employed, and to co-operate with other good gifts bestowed on man. We are not considering the question as to any change consequent on the new use, or the re-ordering of the elements to a purpose other than that which they ordinarily possessed: we are not discussing the possibility of material elements being employed as symbols or signs of gifts of spiritual life: we are not considering the possibility or impossibility of material substance being endued with efficacy to impart spiritual blessing.

"And as he lay and slept under a juniper tree, behold, then an angel touched him, and said unto him, Arise and eat.

"And he looked, and, behold, *there was* a cake baken on the coals, and a cruse of water at his head. And he did eat and drink, and laid him down again.

"And the angel of the Lord came again the second time, and touched him, and said, **Arise** *and* eat; because the journey *is* too great for thee.

"And **he arose,** and did eat **and** drink, and went in the strength of that meat forty days and forty nights unto Horeb the mount of God."

It is not, therefore, impossible for God to endow with extraordinary power, material substance.

We are speaking against the possibility of a substantial change taking place in a particular sort of matter—a change which is said entirely to alter the entire physical character, and yet be to all the senses, that which it was before; nay further, remaining also amenable to the accidents and changes, incident to the material substance which it was before the reputed change. A change by spiritual significance and power is a different matter: here faith is called in, and leads us to the foot of the Sacrificial Cross. Christ is near, very near: we may lay hold on Him. With such presence the Spirit of God given to man must take cognizance; carnal senses are indeed here not to be rudely intruding themselves, but performing their true office they enlighten us, and help us to a correct understanding of the Spirit's meaning. My senses truly tell me here is bread, holy bread, significant of something which *it* is *not*. Reason and Faith conjoin to explain the import of the sign, and to know Him by a sign, as angels were guided to the place where He lay. Of what great value are my senses? I might have erroneously, if *distrusting them*, consented to impanate the Lord in a morsel of cake; or *by trusting them*, blindly have denied His real true Presence at His own appointed place and at His own Feast. By a reasonable Faith in His Word, I accept Him, and in humble spirit bow down at His feet and adore Him, a very present God.

In "The Catholic Christian Instructed," as also in Cardinal Wiseman's Lectures, the senses are taught to be unworthy of trust, except they give impressions conformable to the Papal mind. The only sense not astray on the matter of the Eucharist, it is said, is "Hearing:"—

"*Q.* But are we not sufficiently authorized, by the testimony of the senses, to make a judgment of a thing's being in effect, that which it has all the appearance of?

"*A.* Regularly speaking we are, when neither reason nor divine authority interpose itself, to oblige us to make another judgment. And thus the miracles and the resurrrection of Christ were demonstrated to the apostles by the testimony of their senses. But the case would have been altered had God himself assured them that what appeared to be flesh and bones, was indeed another thing: for in such a case they ought certainly to have believed the testimony of God, rather than their own senses."

Is the Roman divine correct in his declaration that the sense of hearing is the only sense not deceived in the case of the Eucharist? We certainly hear words which come to every ear correctly. Every one who hears them will agree that they hear the very same sound, or form of words. Is their Spirit the same to every ear? Among those to whom they were first addressed, they only went back, who understood Him to speak of carnally eating Him. They who believed on Him, and had Faith, were immovably firm, and hanging upon His words as very life, eat Him into their souls, and spirits, and bodies. Where is the hearing if there be no understanding spirit? "Hear ye, indeed, but understand not." And again: "See ye, indeed, but perceive not." "And He called the multitude and said unto them, Hear and understand." And correcting His disciples who had heard and had not understood, He said, "Are ye also yet without understanding? Do *not ye* yet understand that whatsoever entereth in at the mouth goeth into the belly, and is cast out into the draught? But those things which proceed out of the mouth come forth from the heart, and *they defile the man.* There is not an instance in our

Lord's **ministry** which **leaves** His people in doubt **as to His** meaning. He ever takes them from the letter to the spirit. **He always** teaches them to consider themselves as spiritual **beings, and** Himself as ever referring **to their** spiritual **life.** " **Why do** ye not understand my speech? Even because ye cannot hear my word!" And our Lord declares who they are which hear rightly, for, saith He, " He **that is** of God heareth God's words. Ye hear them **not because ye are not** of God."

"Also I heard the voice of the Lord, saying, Whom **shall I send, and who** will go for us? Then said I, Here *am* I; **send me.**

"And he said, Go, **and tell this people, Hear ye indeed, but understand** not; and **see** ye indeed, but perceive **not.**

"Make **the** heart of this people fat, **and** make their ears heavy, and shut their eyes; **lest** they see with their eyes, and hear with their ears, and **understand** with their heart, and convert, and be healed."

When then we hear distinctly the words of Christ: " **Take** eat, this is My body," are we to take the words as they are in the letter, or are we to understand with the understanding, **what** the import **of such awful** words of God are. Surely, **even the most** ultramontane follower of Pius IX., will not deny that he professes to understand the words which are addressed to him. He will **not** insist upon it that his **hear**ing the words is sufficient without adding another **word** " correctly." " Bring forth the blind people that have eyes, and the deaf **that have ears.**" **If any man** have ears **to** hear let him hear, was the injunction of the Lord; He also added, " Take heed what ye hear." " Take heed, therefore, *how* ye hear, for whosoever hath, to him shall be given," here then is the promised reward to him who heareth **correctly.**

" In the vi. of St. John, our blessed Lord furnishes us with an **illustration of** hearing without the understanding. He **had been explaining to them in** the **deep** anxiety of His heart for their conversion, that He was the true Paschal Lamb of which they were henceforth to eat. They understood Him to mean a carnal eating of Him. Many, therefore, of His disciples when they heard this, said, *this* is a hard saying, who can *hear* it*." Jesus then explained Himself to them and points out that He was speaking to them of Spiritual eating, true, real participation of Him as Christ, concluding with the words, "It is the Spirit that quickeneth the flesh profiteth nothing. THE WORDS that I speak unto you, THEY are Spirit and THEY are Life." From that time, many of His disciples went back and walked no more with Him. These had not heard with the understanding, like those who believed and had heard; they had not heard as they should have heard: like the deaf adder they stopped their ears and perverted the teaching of God.

St. Paul, writing to the Romans, tells them, that, it is impossible for them to hear unless the word be preached unto them, as also had said the Eunuch, "how can I understand unless some man explain it to me;" so then says the Apostle, "Faith cometh by hearing, and *hearing* by the Word of God." Now, does the Apostle, by this mean, the mere hearing of certain words, or does he mean, that inner hearing by the Spirit of Man, by which *he learns* what is meant by the sounds which he apprehends; *i. e.*, hears and understands.

The question is not as to the infallibility of the senses, but as to our being in the particular case sufficiently authorized to receive their supplemental testimony. Now Cardinal Wiseman has shewn in another case that the senses were quite trustworthy, and did not deceive as to the change of substance; and so in all our Lord's miracles. Here is what the most Rev. Archbishop says:—

---

* Obey and do.

We read, v. 9, "And when the chief steward had tasted the *water made wine*, and knew not whence it was; but the waiters knew, who had drawn *the water*." Here it is called water, though transubstantiated into wine. From which examples we may fairly conclude, that it is usual in scripture to continue to call substances, after they have been changed into others, by the name which they bore before the change occurred." Nevertheless, there was no deception of the senses here. It was wine, which before was water.

In Dr. Challoner's work, appeal is made to the Schools of Philosophy, and he closes his instruction, to discredit the senses, not by any reference to the Word of God, but by pointing out, that modern philosophy regards what are called the senses, smell, taste, colour, "as affections of the senses." This unfair sporting with the aims and work of philosophy, unworthy a great mind, may be answered by a quotation from the writings of a leader of modern thought. It is quite true that God has not left us entirely to our senses for satisfying proof of all that may even be given to us by them.

I think, says Locke, "It may not be amiss to take notice, that however faith be opposed to reason, faith is nothing but a firm assent of the mind; which, if it be regulated, as is our duty, cannot be offered to any thing but upon *good* reason, and so cannot be opposite to it." And of positive Faith, *i. e.*, revelation, He says: "In propositions, contrary to the clear perception of the agreement or disagreement of any of our ideas, it will be in vain to urge them as matters of faith. They cannot move our assent under that or any other title whatever. For Faith can never convince us of any thing that contradicts our knowledge. Because, though faith be founded on the testimony of God—who cannot lie—revealing any proposition to us: yet we cannot have an assurance of the truth of its being a divine revelation greater than our own knowledge; since the whole strength of the certainty depends upon our own knowledge *that God revealed it:* which, in this case, when the proposition supposed revealed, contradicts our knowledge or reason, will always have this objection hanging to it, viz., that we cannot tell how to conceive that to come from God, the bountiful Author of our being, which, if received for true, must overturn all the principles and foundations of knowledge which He has given us; render *all our faculties useless;* wholly destroy the most excellent part of His workmanship, our understanding."

And approving of this, Cousin observes, "Attributes, accedents, phenomena, being, substance, subject, are the generalisations drawn from the source of the two incontestible facts of *belief* in my personal existence and the *belief* in the existence of the exterior world. If we seek the origin of the idea of phenomena, of quality, of attribute, it is given us by the senses, if *the object of search be an attribute* of external substance: by consciousness, if the object of search be an attribute of the soul. As to substance, whether it be *material* or *spiritual*, it is given us neither by the senses, nor by consciousness: *it is a revelation* of reason in the exercise of the senses and the consciousness, as space, time, the infinite and personal identity, are revealed by reason in the exercise of sensibility, consciousness, and memory." "That which moveth man's will, is *the object* or thing desired. That which causeth it to be desired is either true or apparent goodness: the goodness of things desired is either manifest *by sense*, gathered *by reason*, or known *by faith*. Many things good to the judgment *of sense, are in the eye of right reason abhorred as evil,* in which case the voice of reason is the voice of God. So that they, who, being destitute of that

Spirit which should certify and give reason, follow the conduct of such sensual direction, termed *the wisdom of the flesh*, must needs thereby fall into actions of plain hostility against God." Such wisdom neither is, nor can be, subject to His law, because, perpetually the one condemneth what the other doth allow, according to that in the book of wisdom, "We fools thought the life of the just madness." Again, as the wisdom of the flesh, man's corrupt understanding and will, not enlightened nor reformed by God's Spirit, is opposite and cannot submit itself unto His law, but followeth the judgment of sensuality, contrary to that which reason might learn by the light of the natural law of God: *so in matters above the reach of reason*, and beyond the compass of nature, where only faith is to judge by God's revealed law which is right or good, the wisdom of the flesh, severed and divided from that Spirit which converteth man's heart to the liking of God's truth, must needs be here as formal adversaries to him, and as far from subjection to His law as before.

Faith has a firm basis to rest on, from the necessary conception we have of Infinite Wisdom, a notion positive fixed in the mind. We cannot grasp all knowledge of the Infinite, but we do realise Infinite Wisdom. It is revealed to us in the notion of the order in nature in time and space; and the idea of infinite time and space brings us to an understanding of infinite being. From the conception of infinite space we rise to the conception of a God who fills all space, and from the conception of infinite time we rise to the conception of a God who has ever existed and ever will exist. By the necessity of our nature we must think of a First Cause as the originator of all other objects. This is revealed as a fact in consciousness. Having a knowledge that God *is*, we determine by our moral nature the fitness of moral law, the adaptability of that law to human wants, and by the exercise of that deep emotion of the soul which impels man to worship, **we know that the God** who has **made himself known to us is the God of Wisdom, and** is the **Supreme Moral Governor.** In consciousness, then, finding **the** Infinite **God, the reason guided** by **the moral nature** of **man,** and by his fitness and capacity for **religious** life, and by the suitableness of that life to his condition, **knows that** whatever Faith reveals or presents to the **mind is sure,** because of the relation which whatever is truly revealed has to Almighty God, who is infinitely wise, holy, just, good and true. **St. Peter says,** "Sanctify the Lord God in **your hearts;** and be ready always to give an answer to every man that asketh you a *reason* of the hope that is in you, with meekness and fear." If whatever is presented to us be in conformity with the knowledge we have of Christ, and is agreeable to the word of God, then we act against reason in rejecting it, even should we not **comprehend** fully.

"There is no respect of persons with God.

"For as many as have sinned without law shall also perish without **law**: and as many as have sinned in the **law shall** be judged by the law;

"(For not the hearers of the law *are* just before God, but the doers of the law shall be justified.

"For when the Gentiles, which have not the law, do by nature the things contained in the law, these, having not the law, are a law unto themselves:

"Which **shew** the work of the law written in their hearts, **their** *conscience* also bearing witness, and *their thoughts* the mean while accusing **or else excusing one another);**

"In the day when God shall judge the **secrets of men by Jesus Christ** according to my gospel."

Our blessed Lord himself, reasoning with the Jews, said, "**If I do not the** works of my Father, *believe me not.* But if **I do,** though ye believe not me, *believe the works;* that ye may *know* and *believe* that the Father is in me, and I in Him." The psalmist of old had followed this inductive **reasoning,** and **was** comforted:

"O give thanks unto the Lord; call upon his name: make known his deeds among the people.

"**Sing** unto him, sing psalms unto him: talk ye of all his wonderous works·

"**Glory ye** in his holy name: let the heart of them rejoice that seek the Lord.

"Seek the Lord, and his strength: seek his face evermore.

"Remember his marvellous works that **he hath done; his wonders**, and the judgments of his mouth;

"O ye seed of Abraham his servant, ye children of Jacob his **chosen**.

"He *is* the Lord our God: his judgments *are* in all the earth."

Again:—

"I remember the days of old; I meditate on all thy works; I muse on the work of thy hands.

"I stretch forth my hands unto thee: my soul *thirsteth* after thee, as a thirsty land. **Selah**."

And:—

"**The** heavens declare the glory of God; and the firmament sheweth his handywork.

"Day unto day uttereth speech, and night unto night sheweth **knowledge**·

"*There is* no speech nor language, *where* their voice is **not heard**.

"**Their line is gone out through all the earth, and their words to the end** of the world. In them hath he set a tabernacle for the sun.

"Which *is* **as a bridegroom coming** out of his **chamber,** *and* rejoiceth as a strong man to run a race.

"His going forth *is* from the end of the heaven, and his circuit unto the ends of it: **and there** is nothing **hid** from the heat **thereof**.

"The law **of the Lord** *is* perfect, converting the soul: **the testimony of the** Lord *is* sure, making **wise** the simple.

"The statutes of **the Lord** *are* right, rejoicing the heart: **the** commandment of the Lord *is* pure, enlightening the **eyes**.

In all this the Scripture is unfolding to us Eternal Wisdom, even God **as** He has revealed himself to **us in** His **works,** "which have ever been of **old.**" Not only are we taught to meditate "on the works of His fingers, **the** moon and **the** stars, which He ordained;" **but** we are bid to look **to the** whole life-history of man, and in all its painful yet deeply checquered course, **to** study the relation which God has to him, and to His other creations. In drawing our conclusions as to the meaning of what has been spoken for our guidance, shall **we be** wrong in insisting on the use of prayerful meditation, **and** deep, searching study of **the** Word, **comparing scripture with scripture, before we** accept as true **that which is presented to us for acceptance?** Knowing as we do the corruptions **which the Word** underwent by the Pharisees, ought not all lovers of truth to see to it, that **they** have the spirit of the Word as well as the **mere letter of the Word?** How **dare** we, as religious beings; how **can we, as** beings morally accountable for our time, our talents, and **all** our thoughts **and** acts, abstain from the study of the Word of **God?** When the Author of **our** salvation said, "Search the **Scriptures," what did He mean?** When Dives was told, in answer **to the bitter cry for the** salvation **of his** brethren, "they have **Moses and the prophets,"** what **was** the lesson intended to be **conveyed to us? Was it not that man was** to exercise his mind in the acquisition of that revealed truth **which** had been entrusted **to** divinely constituted **men, and to** engage **in** the study **of all** God's works as speaking of Him. There **must** then **be** of necessity harmony in creation, **and creation must be in harmony with the** great Creator, revelation itself not contrary to the revelation of His Being.

"Thy hands **have made me and fashioned me;** O give me understanding, that I may learn thy commandments."

In his examination of the method by which we apprehend "substance," M. Cousin, in opposing Locke, observes, "Touch gives the idea of solid; sight and the other senses give the idea **of** other qualities, primary and secondary. But what! is there nothing **but** these qualities? Whilst **the senses give you** solidity, color, figure, softness, hardness, &c., do you not BELIEVE that these qualities are not in the air, but that they **are** rather **in** something which really exists, which is solid, hard, soft, &c.? You would not have had the idea of this something, if the senses had not given you the idea of these qualities; but you cannot have the idea of these qualities without the idea of something existing; this is the universal and NECESSARY BELIEF, which the distinction between qualities and the subject of these qualities implies, the distinction between accidents and substance. Whilst the senses and the consciousness perceive such or such a form, such or such a sensation, more or less agreeable, *the understanding conceives the beautiful as well as the good and true,* by the primitive and spontaneous judgment, the whole force of which resides in that of the understanding and its laws, and of which the only dictum is an exterior perception."

"All points of doctrine,"—says Bishop Hooker,—"are either demonstrable conclusions or demonstrative principles. Conclusions are invincible proofs, as well in the school of Jesus Christ as elsewhere. And principles be grounds which require no proof in any kind of service, because it sufficeth if either their certainty be evident in itself, or evident by the light of some higher knowledge, and is itself such as no man's knowledge is ever able to overthrow. Now the principles whereon we do build our souls have their evidence where they had their original, and as received from thence we adore them, we hold them in reverent admiration, we neither argue nor dispute about them, we give unto them that assent which the oracles of God require. We are not, therefore, ashamed of the gospel of our Lord Jesus Christ, because miscreants in scorn have upbraided us, that the highest point of our wisdom is *believe.* That which is true and can neither be discerned *by sense,* nor concluded by *mere natural* principles, must have principles of revealed truth whereupon to build itself, and an habit of faith in us wherewith principles of that kind are apprehended. The mysteries of our religion are above the reach of our understanding, above discourse of man's reason, above all that any creature can comprehend. Therefore the first thing required of him which standeth for admission into Christ's family is *belief.* Which belief consisteth not so much *in* knowledge as in acknowledgment of all things that heavenly wisdom revealeth: the affection of *Faith* is above her reach—her love to Godward above the comprehension which *she hath* of God." Again:—"We find by experience that although faith be an intellectual habit of the mind, *and have her seat in the understanding*, yet an evil moral disposition obstinately wedded to the love of darkness dampeth the very light of heavenly illumination, and permitteth not the mind to see what doth shine before it." "There are lovers of pleasure more than lovers of God." Their assent to His saving truths is many times withheld from it; not that the truth is too weak to persuade, but because the stream of corrupt affection carrieth a clean contrary way. That the mind, therefore, may abide in the faith, there must abide in the will* as constant a resolution to have no fellowship at all with the varieties and works of darkness." In all this we are conscious of our own weak and dependent state, and reason points out to us the necessity of seeking aid from the only true Source of all real power. God does not desire superstition; He will not receive from us, as acceptable worship, the rhapsody of a soul willing to address Him as the

> "Father of all, in every age,
> In every clime adored,
> By saint, by savage, or by sage,
> Jehovah, Jove, or Lord."

No, He will not be recognised as any other than the Triune

---

* See Locke.

Eternal God, revealed to us by the Holy Spirit in His own Word, and immediately known in the person of the Eternal Son. We must not only have "judgment," but "a right judgment in all things" if we wish to rejoice in His holy comfort. And to receive Him aright, we must also have a right faith. He hath not left us without witness that He is. Man is not merely an intelligent being; he is not merely a moral being; he is by his very nature a religious being. Not only must he account for the existence of all things, and thus rise from the creation to the First Cause which is true Power; not only is he conscious of moral judgments and a sense of obligation, which must be accompanied by a knowledge of the Supreme Moral Governor, but there are also emotions of reverence and adoration passing through the mind, which have for their immediate object the one true God.* It is, then, the moral and religious quality of the mind which is concerned in all that relates to worship and to God, and necessarily the senses act but a relatively subordinate part. The consciousness of our relation to the adorable Deity is the result of emotions of veneration and awe which spring up within us; *frequently* the emotions are awakened by impressions made on the senses by sensible objects, and if any very moving ideas are associated, with the object, the impression made on the memory by the sight of such, will be all the more acutely preserved by the *mind*. In short, sight is lost in the deeper vision of the soul, all carnal sense in the apprehension of Spirit. But in all this succession of events the intervention of MEMORY is necessary, and memory has for its direct object nothing external, it is related to us, not to things: hence, the importance of external objects is to arouse or fix our attention.

---

* Calderwood on the Infinite.

The will governing our acts, we voluntarily *attend* to whatever has consciously aroused us. If, then, consciousness is the condition of memory, as memory is the condition of the idea of succession, it follows, that the first succession is given us *in ourselves,* in consciousness, in the proper objects and phenomena in consciousness, in our thoughts, in our ideas. Our senses are very necessary to our nature, and the sensations awakened in us through them are most important; but after all, that which is concerned most in ideas called to mind, is memory, which has been awakened by an external object or internal emotion or idea. It is not a little remarkable that our Lord, in instituting sacramental signs of His love, should have left them, with the affectionate appeal, "this do in remembrance, or memory of Me." He knew, that the awakening of the memory, by a sign rendered sacred by His own spoken words, must have the effect of directing the will of man consciously to an apprehension of that which He desired man should apprehend; therefore, to aid the reason and help the judgment, He took as a symbol of spiritual food, that which was the essential stay and nourishment of mankind, and giving to these elements of His creation a new significance, and annexing to them a specially determined use, they are intended to be sure and certain pledges of that gift, which in the due use *of them,* He covenants to give.

The Hallowed Feast all ready prepared for the nourishment of humble hearts, is made known to memory by sight and hearing: but what do we realise in the mind by inward sight, *i. e.*, by faith? To what is my *attention* given? On what is my mind fixed? A thousand impressions may assail my sensibility, if I do not give them attention I have no consciousness of them. It is the same with my thoughts. Memory awakened to all that my Father and Friend has done for me, forgets or heeds not the awakening cause of my thoughts, but I fondly seize at once all that is present to memory, not heeding the sign. The immortal Spirit, by a power superior to that of any ability of sense, realises in the depths of consciousness, all that memory brings before the mind. Our blessed Lord did not borrow, as He had done more than once, sayings of the prophets, He did not say, "taste, and see, how gracious the Lord is:" but appealing to their affection for Him, and exhibiting His love for them, He said, "Do this in memory of Me;" thus leaving with them, not only a memory of that His precious death till His coming again, but a memorial of the real gift of His precious life. How little has all this to do with carnal sense, how has it a direct relation to the spirit of man. God requires of us, the employment of all He has bestowed: all our gifts are in relation to each other. But this much may be said, that God did not intend that there should be a schism in the body, which He has made one whole. "According to M. de Biran, as well as according to Locke, the idea of cause is not given to us in the observation of exterior phenomena, *which considered solely with the senses*, do not manifest to us any causative power, and appear simply successive: it is given from *within* in the reflection, in the *consciousness* of our operations and of the power which produces them, to wit, the will. I make an effort to move my arm, and I move it." "Let us not forget, says Cousin, that the belief in the world and in external causes is universal and necessary, and that the fact which explains it must itself be a necessary and universal fact: if then, our belief in the world and in external causes resolves itself into the assimilation of these causes to our own, this assimilation must be a universal and necessary fact. The character of a necessary and universal fact is that, it must unavoidably exist; and the necessity of an idea, of a law, implies the domination of that idea, of that law, in the whole extent of its duration, and so long as the human mind subsists." We have all the most perfect conviction that God exists, that He is Omnipotent, Omnipresent, All-wise, All-holy, the Just, the Good, the Merciful God, the Truth, the Maker of all things created either in heaven or earth. We, as Christians, necessarily believe, that by His Word, by His Will are all things: we arrive at this not from any power of the senses. Why should we not, with the Roman divine, accept at once without cavil, Words which we *hear*, and which come to us from lips agonised with love for us, "Take, eat, this is My body." Why do we not bid our senses "get thee behind me" and fall down in fear and trembling? For this reason, that we dare not trust to our hearing alone as infallible, when it contradicts the other senses and our reason. We are told that ours is "a reasonable service;" that we are to "pray with the understanding" and "with the spirit;" that the whole man, the body, soul and spirit, are sanctified, regenerated, renewed; that the whole man is to, and as to all natural gifts, must apprehend and serve God. I cannot, therefore, become blind, dumb and deaf; I cannot paralyse my sentient limbs, and trust everything to my imagination. God helping, ALL our gifts are to be enlisted in His service, each correcting the wants of other, all and each one aiding the reason to yield to and act with that great gift, which is from the Eternal Giver of all good gifts, the gift of A LIVELY FAITH. "If our senses supply the media by which we are put on trial, by which we are all brought together, and hold intercourse with each other, and are disciplined, and are taught, and enabled to benefit others, it is enough. We have an instinct within us impelling us, we have external necessity forcing us to trust our senses, and we may leave the question of their substantial truth for another world—'till the day break, and the shadows flee away.' And what is true of reliance on our senses, is true of all the information which it has pleased God to vouchsafe to us, whether in nature or in grace." * The same spirit breathes through the following lines:

> "Lead, kindly Light, amid th' encircling gloom,
>   Lead Thou me on;
> The night is dark, and I am far from home;
>   Lead Thou me on;
> Keep thou my feet; I do not ask to see
> The distant scene; one step enough for me.
>
> "I was not ever thus, nor pray'd that Thou
>   Shouldst lead me on;
> I loved to choose and see my path, but now
>   Lead Thou me on:
> I loved the garish day, and spite of fears,
> Pride ruled my will: Remember not past years.
>
> "So long Thy power has blest me, sure it still
>   Will lead me on,
> O'er moor and fen, o'er crag and torrent, till
>   The night is gone;
> And with the morn those angel faces smile,
> Which I have loved long since, and lost awhile."

The Very Rev. Dean Mânsell, of St. Paul's, observes: "We may indeed believe, and ought to believe, that the knowledge which our Creator has permitted us to attain to, whether by revelation or by our natural faculties, is not given to us as an instrument of deception. We may believe, and ought to believe, that intellectually as well as morally, our present life is a state of discipline and preparation for another; and that the conceptions which we are compelled to adopt as the guides of our thoughts and actions now, may

---

* J. H. Newman's University Sermons.

indeed, in the sight of a higher Intelligence, be but partial truth, but cannot be total falsehood. But in thus believing, we desert the evidence of Reason, to rest on that of Faith; and of the principles on which Reason itself depends, it is obviously impossible to have any other guarantee. But *such a faith*, however well founded, has itself only a regulative and practical, *not* a speculative and theoretical application." Again, the same writer illustrates the right use of Reason and its province in aiding Faith: "Here then is the issue which the wavering disciple is bound seriously to consider. Taking into accout the various questions, whose answers, on the one side or the other, from the sum total of evidences for or against the Christian Faith: the genuineness and authenticity of the documents; the judgment and good faith of the writers; the testimony to the actual occurrence of prophecies and miracles; and their relation to the religious teaching with which they are connected; the the character of the Teacher Himself, that one portrait, which in its perfect purity and holiness and beauty, stands alone and unapproached in human fiction or history; those rites and ceremonies of the elder Law, so significant as typical of Christ, so strange and meaningless without Him: those predictions of the promised Messiah, whose obvious meaning is rendered still more manifest by the futile ingenuity which strives to prevent them; the history of the use and progress of Christianity, and its comparison with that of other religions; the ability or inability of human means to bring about the results it has actually accomplished; its antagonism to the current ideas and age of the country in which it had its origin; its effects as a system on the social and moral condition of mankind; its fitness to satisfy the wants and console the sufferings of human nature; the character of those by whom it was first promulgated and received; the sufferings which attested the **sincerity** of their convictions; the comparative trustworthiness **of ancient** testimony and modern conjecture; **the mutual contradictions of** conflicting theories of unbelief, **and the** inadequacy of all of them to explain facts for which **they** are bound to account. Taking all these **and** similar questions into full consideration are you prepared to affirm, as the result of the whole inquiry, **that Jesus of Nazareth** was an impostor, or an enthusiast, or a mythical figment; and His disciples crafty and designing, or well-meaning, but deluded **men. For be assured, that** nothing short of this is **the conclusion which** you must maintain, if you reject one jot or one tittle of the whole doctrine of Christ."*

Here is an exemplification of the Apostolic teaching, "Give a reason of the faith that is in thee." Reasoning **then** about those things which are of Christ, remembering **how** He was pleased, Himself to come among men in **the form of** a Servant, that we may both know how to serve God acceptably, and **know somewhat of** Him who cannot be wholly **known; remembering that** He hath said, "*I come* that they **may have** *life* **and that they may have it** more abundantly, *i. e.*, more abundant life, eternal life; seeing it **is He** who hath **fulfilled** the Law in all righteousness; recollecting **that the shadows** of that **Law** were dispersed when He who **was** foreshadowed came: **we as of the household of** Faith walk no more in the lust of the flesh, **but in** the spirit; "Looking to Jesus **the author and finisher of our** Faith;" who living a Mediator between God and man, **sitting a** King for ever, and **a** High Priest over **the House of** God, draws all men unto Him, that, through **the influence,** on our bodies, souls, and spirits, of His own body and

---

* **Mansell,** Bp., Lec. viii.

blood, we may be made partakers of that eternal life which is in Him and of Him. As this was signified under the Law in rites and sacrifices; **so under the** New Covenant, Christ Sacramentally gathers **to Himself all** in whom the in-dwelling **Life has been received to the salvation of their** immortal souls.

Faith coöperating with reason induces the belief, **that** He separates not Himself from His grace. All power is of and from *Himself*, who is the Way, the Truth, and the **Life; how** then can we reasonably believe, that He enters into union with Bread and Wine; when reason and faith alike induce the belief that His Word, which is the Living Word, causes His Flesh and Blood to be in us, whenever we partake of that Bread and drink of that Cup. The waters of Jordan were made **the means** of bodily healing, the brazen Serpent was a **sign of** healing **power, the** hem of His garment was touched **and virtue went out of Him,** yet were neither of these God or His Christ. The waters of Jordan were better than the water either of Abana or Pharphar; the hem of His garment was savingly touched by faith.

Knowing that THE WILL of God operateth to make **holy** bread and wine signs **of His presence;** that **His** will is, that I, and each redeemed child of Christ, should **take eat** of that Body which Christ has, **and** which is a spiritual body, and not *spirit only,* but *a body* which is the body of the God-man; I most firmly and faithfully **believe,** that in the eating **of** that Bread and in the drinking of that Wine, which, the living Word of the living Christ hallows, I am **by** the power of the Word of **the same** living Christ, possessed in my most inmost spirit of **the very** Humanity, the body and **blood of** the Son of God. I taste bread by carnal taste, **see it by** carnal sight, handle it by fleshly touch, and smell of the cup of the vine. Faith being by me **and in me,**

Faith leading me to the foot of the cross, Faith awakening in me a terror, for all I see brought Him there, lays me down and strengthens and refreshes me with that Life-sustaining drink which no other water may become, and puts between the lips of my feeble spirit, the living food which no other bread may be. I correct my senses by reasonable Faith, which is the gift from God to bring me to the knowledge of truth in Him. I believe; and believing that Christ can and does do all that He said He would do; I rest in full assurance, that, I am strengthened and refreshed by the body and blood of Christ which is given to me and for me. We can neither trust to our senses alone, not even the hearing, nor to our reasoning faculty alone. All that we are, must be equally employed in knowing the will of God; the one power of the mind correcting the information brought to it by the other.

St. Paul, 1 Cor. c. xii. vs. xiv. to v. xxvii.:

"For the body is not one member, but many.

"If the foot shall say, Because I am not the hand, I am not of the body; is it therefore not of the body?

"And if the ear shall say, Because I am not the eye, I am not of the body; is it therefore not of the body?

"If the whole body *were* the eye, where *were* the hearing? If the whole body *were* hearing, where *were* the smelling?

"But now hath God set the members every one of them in the body, as it hath pleased him.

"And if they were all one member, where *were* the body?

"But now *are they* many members, yet but one body.

"And the eye cannot say unto the hand, I have no need of thee: nor again the head to the feet, I have no need of you.

"Nay, much more those members of the body, which seem to be more feeble, are necessary:

"And these *members* of the body, which we think to be less honourable, upon these we bestow more abundant honour; and our uncomely *parts* have more abundant comeliness.

"For *our comely parts* have no need: but God hath tempered the body together, having given more abundant honour to that *part* which lacked:

"That there should be no **schism in the** body: but *that* the members should have the same **care one for another.**

"And **whether one member suffer, all the** members suffer **with it; or one member be honoured, all the members rejoice** with it."

And as the body of Christ:—

"Our blessed Redeemer, ere He breathed
His tender, last farewell,
A Guide, a Comforter bequeathed,
With us to dwell.

He came sweet influence to impart,
A generous, willing Guest,
While He can find one humble heart
Wherein to rest."

We are not left to ourselves. The Holy Spirit is with the contrite spirit, and **reveals to him, by** Faith, that which Jesus wills that he should perceive **and do.**

The early fathers, and very many **of the divines of the** Anglican Church, draw the distinction between "*distrusting* our senses" and the being "*misled* by them." If we, trusting **to** our senses only and alone, should say, "there is nothing in the Eucharist but common bread and ordinary wine," for our senses tell **us so! would we not** err, not *knowing* the power of God? Equally, then, when I am called **upon to say,** "**Bread** is no longer there where bread was," and yet my senses force me to admit that it is bread, "because it still retains the qualities **and all the** accidents of bread, and has all the outward appearance of bread;" so must I say that my senses do not mislead me, but teach me that bread *is there,* **which the** spirit that is within me informs me is *more* than bare bread, for it is the hallowed sign that the Christ is near, and will be in me when I eat and **drink** in faith.

" Yet stay, before thou dare
 To join that festal throng,
 Listen and mark what gentle air
 First stirred the **tide** of song."

'Tis not

———" The Saviour born **in** David's **home**,
To whom for power and health **obedient worlds should come."**

'Tis not

"'The Christ the Lord;'—
 With fixed, adoring look,
 The choir of angels caught the word,
  Nor yet then silence broke;
  But when they heard the sign where
   Christ should be,
  In sudden light they shone, and
   Heavenly harmony."

We, too, by Faith, eagerly look for the signs of His appearing who was pleased to hallow special signs, to the end that in the breaking of bread He might be known unto His brethren. "Is not My word like as fire, saith the Lord, and like a hammer that breaketh the rock in pieces?"* "**For** this they willingly are ignorant **of,** that by the Word of God the **heavens were of old, and** the earth standing out of the water and in the water; whereby the world that then was, being overflowed with water, perished: but the heavens and the earth, which are now, *by the same word* are kept in store, reserved unto fire against the day **of** judgment and perdition of ungodly men." Speaking **of** Christ, the Apostle says: "Who being the brightness of *His* glory, and **the** express image of His Person **and** upholding all things **by the** word of His Power, when He had by Himself purged **our** sins, sat down **on** the right hand of the Majesty on **high.**" "For the word of God is quick and powerful, and **sharper than any** two-edged sword, piercing even to the

---
* Prophet **Jeremiah.**

dividing asunder of soul and spirit, and of the joints and marrow, and is a discerner of thoughts and intents of the heart." Wherefore, this being true, the Holy Ghost has declared that, as regards the Church of the Living God, that our most blessed Lord gave Himself for it, in order

"That he might sanctify and cleanse it with the washing of water by the word.

"That he might present it to himself a glorious church, not having spot, or wrinkle, or any such thing; but that it should be holy and without blemish."

In the Sacrament of Baptism the element used is **water** conjoined with the Word, and to its use is attached in scripture precisely the same importance as has been attached to the use of bread and wine. By the washing of **water BY THE WORD a great spiritual work is done.** Why has it never been taught, that the water is transubstantiated into the Blood, as it is said is **the case** with **the wine in** the Eucharistic sacrifice? If, following **the teaching of Holy Writ, we keep our minds attent, we cannot avoid plainly** discerning **the** truth to be, **that THE WORDS** of the **Lord, which "are** Spirit and Life," truly cause the Sacraments to **be what they are. He who was** able to bring them into material existence, and to bestow on **them properties** fitting **them for ordinary** bodily food; has **certainly** the power, by **the** power of His Word, likewise **to render** them effectual **when employed by** Him **in, or set** apart by His Word for, a spiritual work: and this extraordinary power He may give **without in any way transforming the** mode of existence of the thing so employed. **Under the** old dispensation we find the **same employment of** means **to** accomplish God's will, **and** in no case **is a hint** thrown out that the thing was changed **as** to its own **essence.** The case of Elijah is instructive:—

"So he departed thence, and found Elisha the son of Shaphat, who was plowing **with** twelve yoke *of oxen* before him, and **he** with the twelfth: and Elijah **passed by him, and** cast his mantle upon **him.**

"And he **left the oxen,** and ran after Elijah, and said, Let me, I pray thee, **kiss** my father and my mother, and *then* I will follow thee. And he said unto **him,** Go back again: for what have I done to thee?

"And he **returned back from** him, and took a yoke of oxen, and slew them, **and** boiled their flesh **with the instruments** of the **oxen,** and gave unto the people, and they did **eat. Then he arose,** and went **after** Elijah, and ministered unto him."

In the 2nd Book of The Kings we read:—

"And Elijah said unto him, Tarry, I pray thee, here; for **the Lord hath sent me to Jordan.** And he said, *As* the Lord liveth, and *as* **thy soul liveth, I will not leave thee. And they two went on.**

"And fifty men of the sons of the prophets went, and stood to view afar off: and they two stood by Jordan.

"And Elijah took his mantle, and wrapped *it* together, **and** smote **the** waters, and they were divided hither and thither, so that they two went over on dry ground.

"And it came to pass, when they were gone over, **that Elijah said unto** Elisha, Ask what I shall do for thee, before I **be taken away from thee. And Elisha said, I pray** thee, let a double portion of thy spirit be upon me.

"And he said, **Thou hast asked a hard** thing: *nevertheless,* if thou see me *when I am* **taken from thee, it shall be so** unto thee; but if **not,** it shall not **be so.**

"And it came to pass, as they still went **on, and talked, that, behold,** *there appeared* a chariot of fire, and horses of fire, and parted them both **asunder;** and Elijah went up by a whirlwind **into** heaven.

"And Elisha saw *it,* and he cried, My father, **my** father, the chariot of **Israel,** and the horsemen thereof. And he saw **him** no more: and **he took hold** of his own clothes, and rent them **in two pieces.**

"He took up also the mantle of Elijah that fell from him, and went back **and** stood by the bank of Jordan;

"And he took the mantle of Elijah that fell from him, and smote the **waters,** and said, Where *is* **the Lord God of** Elijah? and when he **also** had **smitten the waters, they parted hither** and thither: and Elisha **went** over.

"And when the sons of the prophets which *were* **to** view at Jericho saw **him, they said, The** spirit of Elijah doth rest on Elisha. And they came to **meet him, and** bowed themselves to **the ground before him."**

Although Elisha smote with the mantle of Elijah did he believe, that, **the** parting of the waters was by the mantle or by the **power of** God. Why God is **pleased** to employ material **agencies** in accomplishing that which His Word effects is not for us to dispute about. He pleases to do so, and it is enough for us.

In the case of Elijah the Prophet, **the word of God endued the ordinary meat** given for bodily sustentation with **the peculiar** property of sustaining for unusual length **of time, that** material body which it is the wont **of ordinary** food **to** nourish for a short time. On another occasion Moses **sustained** without food his bodily strength for forty days, by the power of God. When our Lord fed the multitude He sensibly increased the quantity of the food eaten by them, entirely by the power of His **Word**. He spake as **afore and it was done.** He by **the Word of His** mouth made clay and spittle, instruments **for executing** His will without either being other in substance **than they were before. The** Hem of His garment was to her who **touched in faith,** healing! His Word was to him who desired life for his **child,** effectual to his most earnest desire. Accepting the statement as true, that in every case where there is the condition, "Faith," there also will there be realized the presence **of** Christ according **to** promise; **we** can understand the nature of the difference between **those** cases, **in** which extraordinary results **followed** on the touching his garments or the operations of His Word, and those instances **in the** which the multitude pressed upon **Him, and on whom His** presence had no effect. If St. Paul's definition of Faith **is** correct, " That we **must** believe that God *is* and that he is a rewarder of persons;" then **our** Lord's appeal to those who came to Him not only is not unnecessary, but most necessary, for except upon the ground that they believed in Him, and willingly desired to accept Him, virtue went not out of Him. If then Faith be present, if Faith hold the **soul of man open,** Christ will manifest Himself.

It is quite clear that the hallowed food is still as to all **its** sensible qualities what it was before consecration; but as to spiritual significance, and as **a means** accompanied by the Word of Christ in the due and faithful **reception,** it is effectual in uniting the spirit, soul, **and body of the** faithful receiver to the Blessed **Body of Christ. The Bread hallowed** by the **Word of Christ, is here an instrument of assurance,** that Faith **being in the** Heart Christ, is necessarily present. In the **Holy of Holies Himself** locally, He by His own **divine power,—having thrown** down the veil,—brings all men within His Presence, and to them He vouchsafes that **influence of** His Presence which derived from Himself into **every** redeemed spirit is the communion of His Spiritual **Body** and Blood. St. Paul, therefore, full of Faith, did **in the** Cup discern the Blood and **in** the **Bread the Body of God.** He has not said that, the **Wine is changed into the blood; he has not** so taught, nor **has he in any wise led us to infer, that there is any** material change **in the Bread. He does** most positively affirm, that, by the faithful **reception of the Wine and of the** BREAD that the Body and **Blood of Christ** are communicated to the faithful. **But in no one** case, does the Apostolic teaching, any more than the acts and teaching of the Lord, set **forth the** notion of a physical change in the elements. **There is** one change which Christian men far more readily overlook, there is, there must **be,** *transubstantiation,* but not with reference to the sacramental **symbols.** THE CHANGE which the adorable Christ desires to **accomplish,** is the change **of** the hard obdurate heart of **man** into the likeness of His undefiled sympathising Spirit. He is only too anxious **to let His own most** blessed Body and Blood be in us a power unto life: and nothing can keep Him from His merciful work of the renewal of our bodies, souls, and spirits, but the willing slavery which binds us to Satan. Christ Jesus will not enter by force into our hearts; "Behold I stand at the door *and knock;*" He visits us, He exhibits to us signs of His approach, **He has appointed means by which He communicates** Himself to us, thereby **bringing us** into union with Himself; **how then, can we** substitute the *means*, for Him, or think it necessary, **that** He should *dispense with means instituted by Himself*, by the conversion, of what He tells us by the Holy Spirit are means of grace, into Himself. If transubstantiation be true, **then, there** are no longer "any means of grace" in the Holy Eucharist so **far as the** elements are concerned; for if **they** are themselves **converted** into the body and blood of Christ, then *to speak of them as means*, when they have become that, which **they were not and only represented, is** contradictory in terms. But when St. Paul says, "THE BREAD which we break, IS IT NOT the communion of the body of Christ." We understand him to teach, that the Holy Communion bread, *i. e.*, **consecrated** bread, is **the** appointed **means by which** the faithful are assured **of the communion** of the Body and Blood of Christ.

There is one passage in the writings of Saint Paul which is very remarkable. He does not with any arbitrariness lay **down** the law to his hearers, he appeals to them, "I speak as **to wise men:** *judge* ye what I say," think how reasonable the doctrine is, mark the simplicity **of the truth, remember** what Christ has effected for you by the Sacrifice of His Death, think of **this, and hear what I** say; "The cup of blessing which *we* bless, **is IT not** the communion of the blood of Christ? THE BREAD which we break, is IT not the communion of the body of Christ? for we being many, are one bread, and one body, for we are all partakers of that one Bread, for he that is joined unto the Lord is one spirit.

> "O most Blessed Light Divine
> Shine within these hearts of Thine,
> And our inmost being fill:
> If Thou take Thy grace away,
> Nothing pure in man will stay,
> All our good is turned to ill."

The effect then of sacramental eating, is a *spiritual union* with Christ, through His Body and Blood; for "he that is joined unto the Lord, is one Spirit." It is then, that the union of our blessed Lord's Spiritual Body with ours, *i. e.* with the spirit of each redeemed soul, is not only to cleanse and renew in strength and godliness our immortal souls, but the influence of immortality extends even to our bodies. St. Paul does not mystify his hearers with abstruse propositions, he nowhere raises the question as to the matter of the elements, but he at once and straight to the point says what Christ said, "THE BREAD *which we break is it not the* communion of the Body of Christ." Just as in baptism, the water IS THE *washing* of regeneration *through* the Holy Ghost.

According to the Roman doctrine of transubstantiation, the sacraments as means of grace are destroyed, and are not the means whereby we receive, but become the thing signified. Objectionable as the doctrine is on many grounds, there is this objection which outweighs all others; it causes us to lose sight of the great truth, that, the Presence of the Lord Jesus is to raise our nature to His, not to bring His to a level with ours. The effect of the Lord's words is to cause us to appear before Him, or to be present immediately to Him wherever He has set His name. Unseen but ever near, He at the appointed time and in the appointed way, causes us to be especially and for a special purpose, in His Presence.

"Take heed, brethren, least there be in any of you an evil heart of **unbelief**, in departing from the living God.

"But exhort one another daily, while it is called To day; least any of you be hardened **through the deceitfulness of sin.**

"**For we are made partakers of Christ, if we hold the** beginning of our **confidence steadfast unto the end;**

"While it is said, To day if ye will hear his voice, harden not your hearts, as in the provocation."

If full faith in Christ, as the Saviour and Restorer of all that it yearns to possess, fills the spirit; if there is the deep conviction that nothing can restore, not only lost purity, but can alone give to the soul the unsullied virtue which it beholds in the Son of man; then it is a matter of no consequence at all to that spirit whether Christ be locally inhabiting the right hand of the Throne of the Majesty on High, or whether He be at the Holy Feast as with His Apostles, His Word remaineth, Lo! I am with you always! The power which issued from His presence on earth to heal the blind or raise the nobleman's son, is not curtailed, because of His ascent into the immediate presence of the Father. Our Lord Himself declared that He would continue a Priest for ever over His Body The Church, against which even the gates of Hell should not prevail.

"I have yet many **things to say unto you, but ye cannot bear** them now.

"Howbeit when he, **the Spirit of truth, is come, he** will guide you into all truth; for he shall not **speak of himself; but** whatsoever he shall hear, that shall he speak; and he **will shew you things** to come.

"He shall glorify me: **for he shall receive of** mine, and shall shew *it* unto **you.**

"All things that the Father hath are mine: therefore said I, that he shall take of mine, and shall shew it unto you."

The illuminating Spirit has for all these years guided and directed the unruly wills of sinful men: to the elect He has and does ever shew unto them the things of Christ. Our Lord, as the Minister of the Sanctuary, the Great High

Priest, still having somewhat to offer for us, does effectually renew our nature by the divine power of His own body and blood, in the presence of which no child of Abraham by promise and of faith can remain unrenewed or be sent away unhealed of those infirmities and deadly ills which drove him into the presence of the Eternal Word made Flesh.

What power has the Word of God! It is the realization of His will only to speak. His Word spake all created things into existence. Do we meditate sufficiently on the power of the Word of God in sending His Son into the world.

"The angel came in unto her, and said, Hail, *thou that art* highly favoured the Lord *is* with thee; blessed *art* thou among women.

"And when she saw *him*, she was troubled at his saying, and cast in her mind what manner of salutation this should be.

"And the angel said unto her, Fear not, Mary, for thou hast found favour with God.

"And, behold, thou shalt conceive in thy womb, and bring forth a son, and shalt call his name JESUS."

With God all things are possible. He who is omnipotent made to himself an habitation of flesh, that he might in it prepare a place for those whom He wills to take unto Himself. His mystical body on earth, co-extensive with earth, is but a type of that union of Christ with His redeemed ones, which ten thousand times ten thousands saints rejoice in. The WORD OF GOD hath said that He maketh us "one with Himself," that we "are members of His Body," that "He is in us." For, says Hooker: "Thus much no Christian man will deny, that when Christ sanctified His own flesh, giving as God and taking as man the Holy Ghost; He did not this for himself only but for our sakes, that the grace of sanctification AND life which was first received in Him, might pass *from* Him to His whole race, as malediction came from Adam to all mankind." Again: "Christ is whole with the whole Church and with every part, as touch-His person, which can in no way divide itself, or be possessed by degrees and portions. But the participation of Christ **importeth**, besides the presence of Christ's person and besides the mystical copulation **thereof with** the parts and members of his whole **Church, a** true *actual influence* of grace whereby the **life which we live according to** Godliness **is His, and from Him we receive those perfections wherein** our eternal happiness consisteth.

While, therefore, it be perfectly true here, according to **Art. IV.,** "**of the** resurrection of Christ," " Christ did truly rise again **from death, and took again** His body, with flesh, **bones, and all** things appertaining to the perfection of man's nature; wherewith He **ascended into** heaven, and there sitteth, until He return to judge all men at the last day," yet this in no way limits the **Presence of Christ, for** "He that descended is the same **also that ascended up far above all** heavens, that He might fill **all things."** His Word *abideth;* the Lord still dwells with His people, for **as it was impossible** that the grave should be holden of Him, so is it equally impossible that His Divinity should be limited by His Humanity. Nay, how much rather that, **manhood** being conjoined to His Divinity inseparably, should, in **partaking of** that conjunction, **be** inseparably joined with it wherever He may specially **please to be; so** that **by** virtue **of** His Divinity is the power and efficacy of that human substance **which** He took by the power of His Word, **and which** Word **causeth His** Flesh and Blood **to** be in **us.** Again, St. Paul says:—

"Beware* **lest any man spoil you** through philosophy and vain deceit, after the tradition of men; after the rudiments of the world and not after Christ. For in Him *dwelleth all the* FULNESS OF THE GODHEAD BODILY."

---

* Col. II. v. ix.

To the Ephesians, speaking of the mighty work wrought by God in Christ, whom he says God gave,

"To be head over all things to the Church, which is His body, THE FULNESS OF HIM THAT FILLETH ALL IN ALL."

And again:

"God, who at sundry times and in divers **manners spake** in time past unto the fathers by the prophets,

"Hath in these last days spoken **unto us by** *his* **Son, whom he hath appointed heir of all things, by whom also he made the worlds;**

"Who being the brightness **of** *his* **glory, and the express image of his person,** and upholding **all things by the word of his** power, **when he had** by himself purged **our sins, sat down on the right hand of** the Majesty on high.

"Being **made so much better than the angels, as he** hath by inheritance obtained a more excellent **name than they.**

"For unto which of the angels said he at any time, Thou art my Son, **this day have I begotten thee?** And again, I will be to him a Father, **and he shall be to me a Son?**

"And again, when he bringeth in the first begotten into the **world, he saith, And let** all the angels of God worship him.

"And of the angels he saith, Who maketh his **angels spirits, and his ministers** a flame of fire.

"But unto the Son *he saith*, Thy throne, O God, *is* for ever and ever: a sceptre of righteousness *is* the sceptre of **thy kingdom.**

"Thou hast loved righteousness, and hated iniquity; therefore God, *even* thy God, hath **anointed thee with the oil of gladness above thy fellows.**"

In the Person of Christ Jesus, Godhead cannot be limited, for **He is** equal **to** the Father **as** touching His Godhead, although inferior to the Father **as touching** His Manhood. We cannot, therefore, understand those **writers who would deny** to the Son of **God** a Presence **whithersoever He wills to be.** What way does it effect the **gift of Jesus to us, whether** He be with us, **as with His Apostles in the upper room, or** whether He be **at the right hand of God?** He ruleth **by His** power, His eyes behold the nations. Is He who created all things and by whom are all things, too far off to **bestow on** us that which He gave to His holy Apostles, and which He voluntarily promised should pass to every soul which needs the redeeming life of Christ, for He promised to redeem us, "In the body of His flesh through death, to present us holy and unblamable and unreprovable in His sight." Is He limited by place? Are not all things naked before Him?

The intention of the "continual remembrance of the sacrifice of the death of Christ" is, among other reasons, to keep us in mind that, His death was the voluntary surrender of Himself for the redemption of man; which sacrifice was for each one who should believe in Him, and who so believing and accepting this needful work of redemption for his soul, might have Christ to offer, and in whom and by whom he might offer himself to God "a reasonable lively sacrifice."

> "Worthless and lost our offerings seem,
>   Drops in the ocean of His praise;
> But mercy with her genial beam
>   Is ripening them to pearly blaze,
> To sparkle in His Crown above,
>   Who welcomes here a child's as there are angels love."

"Now therefore why should we die? for this great fire will consume us; if we hear the voice of the Lord our God any more, then we shall die.

"For who is there of all flesh, that hath heard the voice of the living God speaking out of the midst of the fire, as we have, and live?

"Go thou near, and hear all that the Lord our God shall say: and speak thou unto us all that the Lord our God shall speak unto thee; and we will hear it, and do it.

"And the Lord heard the voice of your words, when ye spake unto me; and the Lord said unto me, I have heard the voice of the words of this people, which they have spoken unto thee: they have well said all that they have spoken."

We have seen Him and are not dead, nay, we live!

For God has not only spoken to man, He has also taken flesh and lived with man. He who was very God of very God has talked with and has been with us as our friend and brother. How entirely do we seem to forget that we have beheld "the glory of God" in His only Son. How do we forget the mount which burned with fire in which His disciples were not consumed, but from the midst of which, came the words of the living God, "This is My beloved Son, hear Him." Yet, how wide the difference with us? No longer are we to send Moses to draw near, no longer is Christ transfigured before us, but each one is to draw near by Faith; there is no more outward revelation to the vision of sense, but by inward illumination, which is by the Spirit, we are to behold "the Lamb of God which *taketh* away the sins of the world." We must hear His voice, as He still calls to us from the altar of Sacrifice,—

> "The Spirit and the Bride say come,
> And let him that is athirst come,
> And let him take of the waters of life freely."

How is it, that, we seem to doubt, whenever, by Christ's command we draw near to Him that we are actually not in His presence, not really near Him. Yet, He says, He is near by; and if so, there cannot but be an influence to us by that nearness. See what happened in time of old. In all their religious services the Jews were made to feel and to know, that they were in the Holy Presence, that every act was in relation to God who was very near.

"Moses said unto Korah, Hear, I pray you, ye sons of Levi:

"*Seemeth it but* a small thing unto you, that the God of Israel hath separated you from the congregation of Israel, to bring you near to himself to do the service of the tabernacle of the Lord, and to stand before the congregation to minister unto them?

"And he hath brought thee near *to him*, and all thy brethren the sons of Levi with thee: and seek ye the priesthood also."

Moses reminding the people of the appearance of God on the mount, bids them recollect what a dread reality it was. And to us to-day the words with all their deep spiritual significance are " tongues of fire " resting upon us. If we ever journey to the holy mount of Calvary, the church where Christ wills to meet His people, then, truly are we in His presence, and by that very Presence are we made to live, who but for Him must perish. "Master it is good for us to be here," let us erect a tabernacle in our hearts where Thou mayest dwell. We pray to Thee because Thou hearest! We worship Thee because Thou art near! We lift up our eyes to Thee because Thou dost lift up the light of Thy countenance upon us.

THE EUCHARIST A SPIRITUAL SACRIFICE.

"The Bread which we break *is* IT *not* the communion of the Body of Christ."

Not inferior in our privileges to the Jew, we have access to God through our High Priest, who ever liveth to make intercession for us. We can no longer,—nor need we desire it,—slay a lamb without blemish, but we do need to pray that there may be applied to ourselves all the benefits of Christ's sacrifice, and to confess to God our need, and to acknowledge our entire and only salvation in Christ, and we are under the obligation openly and honestly to confess this to the God of heaven. We can, therefore, without doubt, bring forth our meat-offering of "fine flour," and our drink-offering of "wine," and with these oblations of Christ's appointing, and penitent in heart, present ourselves to God, shewing forth the Lord's death: and then spiritually eating His flesh and drinking His blood, obtain all the benefits of His Passion, even the pardon of our sins and continued union with Him.

In a commentary on Joel by a learned divine, it is shewn that "the meat-offering and drink-offering were part of every sacrifice, as they were made part of the sacrifice of Christ by Himself. If the materials for these, the corn and wine, ceased, through locusts or drought, or the wastings of war, the sacrifice must become mangled and imperfect.

The priests were to mourn for the defects of the sacrifice; they lost their own substance, since the altar was to them in place of all other inheritance. The meat and drink-offerings were emblems of the materials of the Holy Eucharist, by which Malachi foretold, that when God had rejected the offering of the Jews, there should be a peace-offering among the heathen. When, then, holy communions become rare, the meat and drink-offerings are literally cut off from the house of the Lord, and those who are indeed priests, the ministers of the Lord, should mourn."

But let us examine into the nature and meaning of the Jewish elements of sacrifice:—

MEAT-OFFERINGS, MINCHA or *unbloody sacrifices*, were composed of wheaten or barley flour, or parched grain, and frankincense, mixed with oil, and with or without wine; *they usually* accompanied burnt offerings and peace-offerings; *but they could not* be presented as sin-offerings, except by those who were too poor to buy two pigeons or two turtle-doves.

DRINK-OFFERINGS were the constant accompaniments of sacrifices. They were never used separately; and consisted of wine, part poured on the brow of the victim, or upon the meat-offering to consecrate it, and part allotted to the priests.

OBLATIONS were without the shedding of blood—such as vegetables and fruits—whence they were termed unbloody offerings. There were also drink-offerings and meat-offerings.

The PASSOVER, the solemn sacrifice to which our Lord gave a new significance, in that it was to continue in His Church under a new and very much enlarged signification, is the one to which we Christians look with lasting interest. It was instituted four days before the infliction of the last plague, on the tenth of the month. The Israelites were commanded "to prepare for a *feast* of the Lord," and to take every man *a Lamb* according to his house, without spot or blemish, and keep it until the fourteenth of the month, and to kill it in the evening (at 3 o'clock, p.m.); not a bone was to be broken; they were to take a bunch of hyssop and dip it in the blood that was in the basin, and sprinkle the blood on the two side-posts, and on the upper door-posts of the houses wherein they were to eat it, and were to eat the flesh with unleavened bread, and with bitter herbs; and not to eat of it raw, nor sodden with water, but roast with fire. And that which remained of it until the morning was to be burned with fire: and thus were they to eat it, with the loins girded, the shoes on the feet, and the staff in the hand; and to eat it in haste; it was the Lord's Passover. And "the blood shall be to you for a token upon the houses where ye are, and when I see the blood I will pass over you." The feast of Unleavened Bread was but a continuance of the Passover.

Now, as our Lord, in fulness of time, came as the true Lamb, so there was no longer to be any other offering of bloody sacrifice for sin, for in that he offered up Himself, he ceases not to be offered, but is still the Lamb which taketh away the sins of the world. What then is necessary for us to do, is to bring the oblation, *i. e.*, the meat-offering, and the drink-offering which no more belongs to the paschal feast, and with ourselves present them as representing to God that bloody sacrifice which can no more be reiterated, but which is still effectually offered. That this is truly the meaning of the Christian Passover is more strongly implied by the subsequent events. Thus the feast of Pentecost was celebrated fifty days after the feast of the Passover. It was instituted in order that the Israelites should acknowledge the goodness of God, and offer Him in His temple the first fruits of the wheat harvest, accompanied with certain sacrifices. On this day, in a later age, the Holy Ghost descended on the Apostles in the shape of fiery cloven tongues, and it is now kept by Christians, as Whit-Sunday, fifty days after Easter, or the resurrection of the Lord. The first fruits of the Spirit were thus gathered in an offering to the Redeemer. If, however, we compare the requirements for the due celebration of the Christian Passover, we shall find a close agreement with, although there is a deeper spiritual purpose in it than in that Passover, in the stead of which it remains. The Jew was to eat it with his staff in his hand, and his shoes on his feet; he was to eat it in bitterness, and in haste to flee from his bondage. The Christian is told, that he must be clothed with righteousness, to lean only on Christ, "for his rod and his staff shall comfort him," that he is to be shod with the preparation of the gospel of peace, having on the breast-plate of righteousness, and the armour of salvation on the right hand and on the left:—he is to flee from the wrath to come, and to be in bitterness for his sins, and that he must ever keep this feast in commemoration of his great deliverance, from a greater than Egyptian bondage, and his admission into a new fellowship. If to the Jew all these things had a spiritual meaning, how much more to the Christian whose call is to a Spiritual Kingdom.

If we reflect on the changed nature of the Paschal feast as reconstituted by our blessed Lord, we find the following to be the clear and definite meaning of this service.

First the Passover, in its material form, consisted of the Lamb without blemish, of unleavened bread and bitter herbs, and the drink offering and the offerers. The Lamb without spot was a figure of the Lord.

Now, the adorable Jesus, Himself the Lamb at the last Jewish Passover, was also high priest as well as the "living sacrifice," so when the hour was come, He took into His most sacred hands, not a portion of, not the whole Lamb, but he took into his hands the bread and the mingled wine, the memorials of the sacrifice, and with these He made the oblation of Himself to God, the Father, dedicating Himself a perpetual Lamb, to be in perpetual offering for his people; adding in the power of his own words, that he, as the Sacrifice, should be spiritually eaten by his people, as the lamb under the law had been carnally eaten by the Jew. It is surely true, then, that we Christians are to do in a higher sense what the Jew did: we must continue to make this offering of ourselves, and bread and wine, a representation "of the sacrifice of the death of Christ," and in making it, we must do all that our Lord did relative to his death, in order that the benefits of his death may be applied to us. We must use the oblations of bread and wine as he used them, as representative of himself slain, to be the heavenly food of his people, that by faith, when partaking of them, we might receive the Lamb as our true food. For in offering the oblations of the Sacrifice, we are offering to God the one only Sacrifice of which they are still the oblations, inasmuch as He has not ceased to be offered. The really sacrificial nature of the Eucharist is most certainly set forth in the very act of its Institutor taking the memorials of the Paschal sacrifice, and *delivering them* to His Church to be offered, at the same time declaring that He was the Lamb slain, by the participation of which all true believers were to be restored to life. While, therefore, it is impossible for us to offer to God any other sacrifice than that which our Lord Himself offered, nevertheless whensoever we offer the oblations of bread and wine with ourselves, we clearly and unmistakably do offer IN Christ the Saviour, for we having been made members of His Body, of His Flesh, and of His

Bones, are UNITED IN HIM, and must therefore of necessity share with the Eternal Victim the offering of Himself which He is ever making to the Father for us. If we are very members incorporate of His Body, joint-heirs with Him, if He is the Vine and we the branches, if He is the second Adam and we His children, through the operation of faith, then Christ, having become the Head over all and the Eternal High Priest, does most certainly make us now participators of those high gifts which He received for men. Nothing can be acceptable to God which is done *out* of Christ. He is the Way, the Truth, and the Life, and except as members of His Body, the eye of the Father sees us not as redeemed sons.

> "For ever here my heart shall be,
>   Close to Thy bleeding side;
> This all my hope, and all my plea,
>   For me the Saviour died!
> My dying Saviour and my God,
>   Fountain for guilt and sin,
> Sprinkle me ever with Thy Blood,
>   And cleanse and keep me clean!
> Wash me, and make me thus Thine own;
>   Wash me, and mine Thou art!
> Wash me, but not my feet alone;
>   My hands, my head, my heart!"

This deep conviction of the ever-abiding virtue of the life of Jesus, which by the Spirit of Grace is given to us in the holy commemoration, fills the heart of man with undying love to God for so undeserved mercy; the Spirit is kept in the presence of Christ, and full of hope, is comforted by the assurance that He is both willing and able to save all who come unto Him, pleading their only claim for pardon in the blood of the Lamb of God.

> "Standing now as newly slain,
>   To Thee I lift mine eye:

> Balm of all my grief and pain,
>   Thy Blood is always nigh;
> Now as yesterday the same
>   Thou art, and wilt for ever be;
> Friend of sinners! spotless Lamb!
>   Thy Blood was shed for me."

The last words of the late Archbishop of Canterbury are these:—

"The Romish notion of a true, real, and substantial Sacrifice of the Body and Blood of Christ, as it is called in the Council of Trent, entailed the use of the word *altar*. But this term appears nowhere in the Book of Common Prayer, and was no doubt omitted lest any countenance be given to the sacrificial view. The notion, therefore, of making in *the material elements* a perpetual offering of the Body and Blood of Christ, is as foreign to the spirit and the letter of our Service as I hold it to be to the doctrine of the early Fathers, as well as of the leading divines of our Church. This latter point also I shall endeavour to establish hereafter.

"Meanwhile, it cannot be denied on the other hand, that the doctrine of the Real Presence is, in one sense, the doctrine of the Church of England. She asserts that the Body and Blood of Christ are "verily and indeed taken and received by the faithful in the Lord's Supper." And she asserts equally that such presence is not material or corporal, but that Christ's Body "is given, taken, and eaten, in the Supper, only after a heavenly and spiritual manner." (Art. XXVIII.) Christ's presence is effectual for all those intents and purposes for which His Body was broken, and His Blood shed. As to a presence elsewhere than in the heart of the believer, the Church of England is silent, and the words of Hooker therefore represent her views: "The real presence of Christ's most blessed Body and Blood is not **to be** sought in the Sacrament, but in the worthy receiver of the Sacrament."

"All agree in believing that the Holy Eucharist is a commemoration of the Sacrifice **of our blessed Lord** upon the Cross; a representation of it, a pleading of its merits before **the Throne** of Grace. **Some of our divines also** have **applied the word** *Sacrifice* **to** it, **but in some part of their writings** or other have explained **their meaning to be a** Representation **of the** one Sacrifice, and not a real Sacrifice in itself.

"In the general view which I have briefly sketched of the mind of our Church on this subject, I am firmly convinced that she fully harmonizes with the Primitive doctrines as stated by the early Fathers. They are very consistent in the opinion that *spiritual* sacrifice was the real and true sacrifice, that duties **and** service are the offerings which the Christian has to offer to God, that in **this sense the** whole **act** of celebrating the Holy Communion **is a spiritual sacrifice, and that it requires no other** offering **on our part to** make it more acceptable. In truth, this was **a favourite topic with them** when arguing **in** behalf **of** spiritual sacrifices, **that such** offerings **were most** suitable **to** spiritual beings, **to God, and to the souls of men.** And they **constantly** maintained **the dignity of the** Holy **Eucharist by** supporting the dignity of spiritual services."

It is to be observed that the Archbishop is writing against the Romish view **of** the Eucharistic Sacrifice; "*the notion of making in the material elements a perpetual offering* **of** *the Body and Blood of Christ.*" Against such **doctrine** every loyal Anglo-Catholic is bound to protest.

It is not at all surprising that some should manifest considerable reluctance to the employment of the term "Sacrifice," when **it is recollected that** the Romish doctrine of the sacrifice of the mass, sets forth **that** which the true follower **of** the word of God shrinks from; and which constitutes the Holy Eucharist a reiteration of the *bloody* sacrifice of our Lord: but if there is Roman error in this matter, that can be no justification for our rejecting the truth. Now, we have no right to restrict the **term sacrifice** to the immolation of a living animal, because it **is also** applicable to many **other** offerings, and as Bishop Jolly remarks, there were more unbloody than bloody sacrifices. Besides, the paschal feast **did not consist** merely of the lamb **which was to** be slain, but there were its meat-offering and drink-offering; **and in the Christian sacrifice, we learn that the** Lamb which was offered and **slain,** *is still in offering,* **and is before the** heavenly altar yet, a continuous sacrifice **for sin,** while the offerer offers *the memorial of* that, which the High Priest himself continues to present **and to make his** people partakers of. Thus, the **command of old was,** "When any will offer a meat-offering unto **the Lord, his** offering shall be of fine flour; and he shall pour oil **upon it,** and put frankincense thereon. And he shall bring **it to Aaron's son,** the priest, and he shall take thereout his **handful of** the flour thereof; and the priest shall **burn THE MEMORIAL OF IT** upon the altar, to be an offering **made by** fire of a sweet savour unto the Lord. **And if thou bring an** *oblation* of a meat-offering, baken in **the** oven, it shall be unleavened cakes of fine flour, mingled with oil: thou shalt **part it in** pieces: it is a meat-offering."—Levit. c. xi. v. **11,** But if he be not able to bring two turtle doves or two **young** pigeons**, then he** that sinneth shall bring his offering, the **tenth part of** an ephah of fine flour for a sin-offering; he shall **put no oil** upon it, neither shall he put any frankincense thereon for it is a sin-offering. Then shall he bring it **to the priest,** and the priest shall take his handful of it, even *a memorial* thereof, and burn it on the altar according to the offerings made by fire unto the Lord. And the priest shall make an atonement for him as touching his sin, that he hath sinned in one of them; *and it shall be forgiven him*, and the remnant shall be the priest's *as a meat-offering*.

And their meat offering shall be of flour mingled with oil, three-tenths deals for a bullock, and two-tenths deals for a ram.—Numb. c. xxix.

And thou shalt bring the meat offering that is made of these things unto the Lord; and when it is presented unto the priest, he shall bring it unto the altar.—Levit. c. 11, v. 8.

These loaves, says Mr. Scott, one for each tribe, might typify Christ, as the bread of life, and the continued good of the souls of His people. Or they may denote the service of believers presented unto God through Him and accepted for His sake. Or the whole may mean communion betwixt our reconciled Father and His adopted children in Christ Jesus, who, as it were, feast at the same table, whilst he delights in the fruits of the spirit in their hearts, and they are feasted with His love. The frankincense might denote either the advocacy of Christ or the sweet influence of His Spirit, which *are a memorial to the Lord*—they ensure the acceptance of the believer's person and service, as well as to signify the incense of prayer offered." How really applicable is all this to the holy Eucharist, and how completely does it shew that the people of old well knew that there were other sacrifices than those which were bloody, and that in essence they were truly spiritual.

Nevertheless the material symbols were only of value, in that they had a wonderful significance of a spiritual work going on in, and done for man. And it is because all are too poor to offer any thing to God acceptably, that they may only now offer that which is offered for them? Indeed we truly can only offer of our poverty the bread and wine which God has given us, for God has provided the Lamb. The sacrifice also consisted of the offering of the man himself who came to the altar: none knew this better than the true Israelite. Offer, says David, the sacrifice of righteousness and put your trust in the Lord. The sacrifices of God are a broken spirit: a broken and contrite heart, O God, thou wilt not despise. Amos saith: "Bring your sacrifices every morning, and your tithes after three years; and offer unto the Lord a sacrifice of thanksgiving with leaven, and proclaim and publish the free offerings; for this liketh you, O ye children of Israel, saith the Lord." Again, Malachi saith, "A son knoweth his father, and a servant his master: if then I be a father, where is mine honour, and if I be a master, where is my fear saith the Lord of Hosts unto you, O priests that despise my name; and ye say, wherein have we despised thy name? Ye offer polluted bread upon mine altar." We further learn that the shew-bread was to consist of cakes of fine flour, in number twelve, in memorial of the twelve tribes: two-tenths deals, or about six pints in each cake. It was to be placed upon the *pure table before the Lord*. There was also added a libation of wine. It would seem, says La Trobe, that the office of baking and preparing the bread rested with the Levites, though it was presented in offering only by the priests. This offering was accompanied with frankincense and salt, the frankincense being burnt on the golden table.

Again: "To what purpose is your sacrifice unto me? saith the Lord. I am full of the burnt offering of rams, and the fat of fed beasts, &c., &c. Bring no more vain oblations; incense is an abomination unto me. Wash you, make you clean; put away the evil of your doings from before mine eyes; forasmuch as this people draw near **me**, with their mouth and with their lips do honour me, **but have removed** their heart far from me, and their fear **towards** me is **taught** by the precept **of men**: therefore, behold **I will proceed to** do a **marvellous work** and a wonder, for the wisdom **of their wise men shall** perish, and the understanding of their prudent men shall be hid." The christian dispensation demands spiritual worship from those who by **God's free** gift are taken into covenant, and that they should sacrifice to the Lord in righteousness; there must be **no** mere lip service, but in spirit and **in** truth must all **go** before his **footstool. In** obedience to the commands of Christ, we must do those things which he commanded to be **done, and not in external manifestation** only, but in very deed and truth.

The sacrifices under **the law, were not** a whit more so, than the Christian **sacrifice of Praise and** Thanksgiving. "The **blood** of bulls and **of goats, and the ashes of** an heifer, sprinkling the unclean, could not take away **sin.**" It was only **as** they represented "the One All-sufficient Sacrifice," **that** they were of any efficacy. Christ has desired that we should **represent here on earth,** before men, His sacrifice; and that **we** should show to God that **which He** presented, the oblation of that sacrifice, *together with* **ourselves,** *our souls and bodies* **just as He did** himself; **to** the end **that** with these pleading memorials in our hands, and with repentant hearts, He **may** communicate to us His life-giving body and blood, **given and shed for us. His** Apostles had seen his wonderful **power over nature; they** had seen him cure **the** sick, recover **sight to the blind, bring back the spirit** and soul into the **dead. They** certainly **do** not appear to have understood Him to mean, that they were carnally to eat His body and drink **His** blood. **As the** Jews drank **of** that Rock which followed them, and that Rock was Christ, so, in a more clearly understood and real sense, Christians were to partake of that Rock on which they are built. The Apostles must have believed that our Lord, having come, as a sinless man, to transmake fallen human nature, intended to finish that sublime work of mercy by rooting out the corruption of Adam's nature, by imparting to man His own perfect incorrupt manhood. Adam ate **death** into **our nature**: if we would live, we must eat Christ's **perfect** humanity **into** that nature, that **we may live.** The **Holy** Jesus draws **us to** Himself in that **hour of** deep **and adoring** worship, in **which** we present **ourselves** before God, pleading and representing His Holy **Sacrifice** as our only claim to forgiveness. **He** is **known to us in** the breaking of bread, and our hearts **burn within us as He** talks **to us by** the way. Faith sees **in the midst of the throne** "a **Lamb as** it had been slain," **and hears the** new song, "Thou art worthy to take the Book, **and to open the** seals thereof: for Thou **wast slain, and hast** redeemed us **to** God *by Thy blood*, **out** of **every kindred and tongue** and people and nation; **and hast made us, unto our God, kings and** priests; **and we shall reign on the earth."** To effect **the** mysterious gift of **Himself, our considerate** Redeemer left us, or instituted **for us,** *pledges* of **His love, to** ensure **to us the** full and **certain performance of His word.** Not only did he institute **the Eucharistic Feast, with all its** wonderful mystery of goodness **and love, but, to add deeply** to its importance, and **to the necessity for its con**tinuance, our Lord and Saviour **Jesus Christ was** present to His Disciples at *the three first* Eucharistic celebrations; and **are we** wrong **in believing that in every and all** subsequent ones we **are** effectually present to Him, our carnal eyes being holden, that the **eye of the spirit, through** faith, may see, adore and worship our Lord and **our God** without fear?

That our whole Eucharistic service on earth is representative, although real for us, is evidently taught by St. Paul, who says, "Now of the things which we have spoken, this is the sum: we have such an High Priest, who is set on the right hand of the throne of the Majesty in the heavens; *a minister* of the sanctuary, and of the true tabernacle which the Lord pitched, and not man. For every High Priest *is ordained to offer gifts and sacrifices*, wherefore it is of NECESSITY that this MAN have somewhat to offer." And again, "Now hath he obtained a more excellent ministry, by how much also He is the Mediator of a better covenant, which was established upon better promises." "For Christ is not entered into the holy places made with hands, which are the figures of the true; but into heaven itself, *now to appear in the presence* of God for us." Therefore it comes, that we must believe that Jesus is a real personal Mediator: for "this Man, because He continueth ever, hath an unchangeable priesthood."

We cannot but think that the spirit and intent of our services are much obscured by the too great infrequency of the celebration of the Holy Communion. If we truly believe that the visible part of a sacrament is the outward and visible sign of an inward and spiritual grace, *given* unto us; that the outward sign is the means whereby we receive the same, and is also a pledge to assure us thereof; then we should, by more careful living and more earnest seeking, demand that we be not denied the children's bread. We certainly have no more effectual door open to the Throne of Mercy; and although we may not crucify the Lamb of God afresh, yet we may in every act of Communion pray most fervently to God, and plead before Him the one sacrifice of the Lamb of God, as our only claim to mercy and grace. "For ye are not come unto the mount that might be touched, and that burned with fire unto blackness and darkness and tempest, ... but ye are come unto Mount Zion, and unto the City of the living God, the heavenly Jerusalem, ... and to Jesus, the Mediator of the New Covenant; and to the blood of sprinkling, that speaketh better things than that of Abel." *By him*, therefore, let us offer the sacrifice of praise to God continually: that is, the fruit of *our* lips giving thanks to His name; or, as Hosea says, "Say unto Him, Take away all iniquity and receive us graciously." St. Paul says, "To do good, and to communicate, forget not; for with such sacrifices God is well pleased."

When it is remembered that the Holy Eucharist is the very highest act of praise and thanksgiving that men may engage in, it surely is incorrect to confine our view of it, to that side of doctrine which shews us the sacrifice of Christ as saving us. Deeply sensible of this, we yet must truly, with the voice of praise and thanksgiving, chiefly shew forth His glorious Incarnation and Resurrection, and magnify before angels, men, and all created things, the love of God, for such love had He to us-ward, that He gave His only-begotten Son for us. The love of God towards us, the glory of God and of His Christ, in the great work of redemption, are parts of that service and bounden duty which we ought to shew forth in the holy celebration. The Kingdom of Heaven is thrown open to all believers; and no longer are the privileges and promises to a single people, but from the least even to the greatest, all may come to the Holy Mountain. For this, and for that, God in Christ is reconciling us to Himself, and freeing us from the slavery of sin; we gladly join in the chorus of praise, and give " Glory to God in the highest. O Lord, we praise Thee, we bless Thee, we give thanks unto Thee for Thy great glory, O Lord God, Heavenly King, God the Father Almighty."

It has been shown that **our** Lord did not intend **that offering of "Sacrifice" should cease. On the** contrary, He has enlarged and intensified the meaning of it. No longer can an *inferior* **animal represent Christ slain** for *us;* no longer **may we pour out the blood of a brute, as** representing **our deserts** for sin? but **we human creatures are, each of us, in his own** person, **to** go up before the **Lord, and in the** place of the bull, and goat, and heifer, *do* **exactly that** which Christ did, and desired that we should **do; with the** oblations of Bread and Wine, to *present ourselves,* **our souls and** *bodies,* in Him, to be a LIVING SACRIFICE. But inasmuch as we are as unworthy as was goat or bullock, so He, the **Lord,** having taken our nature, and hidden it; put away **and** *concealed all its defects* in His own Christ's nature, and **having** been made the **Head of our** race through suffering, He now bids **us come,** *i. e.,* to bring **ourselves** to Him, holding in our hands the signs of the "blood of sprinkling," and bearing in our bodies "the marks of **His dying;" so** that *dying* daily to sin, **we** may receive of Him "the gift of **eternal** life" that we may live to righteousness: for we are **thereby members** of His **body,** of His bones, and of His **flesh true** members, **very** members incorporate. Here, then *is a sacrifice,* **of which we are** made partakers, more fearfully real, more wonderful **oh! how** much more loving **and** inviting, than any that Jew ever offered or tasted of. **How** awfully solemn! what love, and what deep mysterious **mercy does it** exhibit! "Hath he smitten Him as He **smote those** that smote Him? *or* **is he** slain according **to the slaughter of them** that are slain by Him?"* **Oh! Lord slay our sins; slay not us;** change our corruption by thy **incorruption.**

---

* Isaiah xxvii. 7.

We can scarcely realise that God is so condescending as to permit vile, sinful, disobedient men to *kneel even* in His presence, and offer themselves to Him, "living sacrifices." We can offer Him nothing of ourselves; therefore He bids us to *come*, but *with the marks of the dying Lord about us;* and then, pierced and wounded for our sins, and admitting that we are guilty of death—He says, mercifully, graciously, kindly, "your life is hidden with **Christ in God**; take eat, from henceforth the life that **you shall live in the flesh, shall be in Christ**. . . . "**Thy sins be forgiven thee.**" How can any Christian man say, that the Holy Eucharist *is no sacrifice!* Far from it. It *is* a sacrifice, and one we had better try fully to understand. Let no man presume to eat of that bread and drink of that cup "*unworthily;*" let him not go up to offer himself a sacrifice—to sacrifice *himself* – "*with a lie in his right hand;*" let him not offer also his own body full of uncleanness, a soul full of wickedness, when he offers the memorials of the Sacrifice of Christ;* let him be as the prodigal, "I will go to my Father, and will say unto Him, Father, I have sinned against Heaven and before Thee, and am no more worthy to be called thy son."

"Neither shalt thou suffer *the salt* of the covenant of thy God to be lacking from thy meat-offering: with all thine offerings shalt thou offer salt." Here again, in the salt, is represented the in-dwelling Christ and His people, who were thus typically represented as burned up for their sins by the consuming fire. St. Ephrem, therefore, could properly say, "In Thy bread is hidden the Spirit that cannot be eaten; *in* Thy wine there dwelleth the fire that cannot be drunk;" and St. Chrysostom, "O Thou Coal of double nature, which touching the lips of the Prophet, didst purify him from sin,

---

* Mal. i. 7; Prov. iv. 17; Hosea ix. 4.

touch my lips, who am a sinner, and set me free from every stain, and from the power of sin." Again, *Fire* came down upon sinners and consumed them. The *Fire* of the merciful *in* the bread cometh down and abideth. Fire ate up the oblations, and *we*, O Lord, have eaten *Thy fire* in thine oblation." Instead of that fire which devoured men, ye eat a fire *in* bread, and are quickened." In the New Testament, we are spoken of as " the Salt of the earth ;" and THE SPIRIT, under the Symbol of Fire:

" For every one shall be salted with fire, and every sacrifice shall be salted with salt.

" Salt *is* good: but if the salt have lost his saltness, wherewith will ye season it? Have salt in yourselves, and have peace one with another.

" Withal praying also for us, that God would open unto us a door of utterance, to speak the mystery of Christ, for which I am also in bonds:

" That I may make it manifest, as I ought to speak.

" Walk in wisdom toward them that are without, redeeming the time.

" Let your speech *be* always with grace, seasoned with salt, that ye may know how ye ought to answer every man."

Every sacrifice, therefore, must still be salted with salt, and the hidden virtue of every sacrifice must be "the bread which cometh down from heaven." We must eat of the fire that consumes our sins.

Under this aspect of the Eucharist, we see how well the exclamations of the royal Psalmist fit in. "Give me a clean heart, O God, and renew a right spirit within me." "I will wash my hands in innocency, and *so* will I go to thine Altar." "The sacrifices of God, are a broken spirit, a broken and a contrite heart, O God, thou wilt not despise. . . . . . O give thanks unto the Lord, for *He* is good; for His mercy endureth for ever. . . . . . Let the redeemed of the Lord say *so*, whom He hath redeemed from the hand of the enemy. . . . . . And let them sacrifice the sacrifices of thanksgiving, and declare His works with rejoicing." In our Lord, all sacrifice centres; so Reformers did not hesitate to call the Holy Communion, "The Sacrifice of Praise and Thanksgiving"* which we offer. By our Book of Common Prayer, and from all that we know of the mind of **the Church, the Eucharist is the key-stone of all our services.** We have obscured its pristine beauty by making it an occasional sacrifice. Its true nature is hidden from us. May God, of His goodness, restore it to us, *at least* as our Sabbath food.

By a **natural instinct,** many **keep away** from the Holy Communion, because **they** are conscious of **sin, and** feel distrustful of their ability to lead **better** lives—they shrink from the presence of God. **This interior** conviction, that in some sort *they* are connected **with, or have a part in** the **service, are** peculiarly **in God's** presence, **seen and** known **of Him, is** almost involuntary; they get **it** even from a superficial study **of** Scripture; and it is not right to narrow or lessen this conviction. A direct personal **interest and** responsibility, means also, **a personal and direct interest** *in* the blessing. **When, then, we feel, that** *we*, **in our very** persons, **as members of Christ, are to the Christian Sacrifice** what the Bullock **or red** Heifer **was to** those of the Jewish; **that Christ has** demanded **that we, as very members of** His

---

* **Standing in the** place of the Jewish **Sacrifices of Thanksgiving, and hence may have arisen our rubric.** "And the flesh **of the Sacrifice of his** peace-offerings of thanksgiving shall **be eaten the same day that it** is offered; he shall not leave any of **it until the morning."—Levit. vii. 15.**

"In the month **of Xanthicus, which is by us called Nisan, and is the be**ginning of our year, **on the fourteenth day of** the lunar **month, when the sun** is in Aries,—for **in this month it was that we** were delivered from **bondage under the** Egyptians,—the law ordained that we should every **year** slay that sacrifice which I before told you was slain when we came out **of Egypt, and which was called** *The Passover:* **and so we do celebrate** this Passover in **companies,** *leaving nothing of what* us *sacrifice* till **the day** following."—*Jos. Ant. Livy.*

body, shall make *a personal presentation and sacrifice of ourselves* in Him, as He did to the Father for us; and that in doing so, He ever offers Himself, *mediating* for us, we shall rise to higher conceptions of our duty, and feel a keen and intense personal interest in the atonement. We shall learn more clearly that each man, is sinful, vile, corrupt; we shall feel that, as individuals, *we* need each man, "a new heart, and a right spirit;" and that we have so deep an interest in the Great Sacrifice of the Cross, that, with holy St. Paul, we exclaim, "God forbid that I should glory, save in the cross of our Lord Jesus Christ, by whom the world is crucified *unto me, and I* unto the world. From henceforth let no man trouble me; for I bear in my body the marks of the Lord Jesus."

Bishop Burnett remarks: "In two other respects it may also more strictly be called a sacrifice; *one* is because there is an oblation of bread and wine made in it, which, being sanctified, are consumed in an act of religion: to this many passages in the writings of the Fathers do relate. Another respect in which the Eucharist may be called a *sacrifice* is, because it is a commemoration and a representation to God of the sacrifice that Christ offered for us on the cross; in the which we claim to that, as to our expiation, and feast upon it as our *peace-offering*, according to that ancient notion that *covenants* were by a *sacrifice*, and were concluded in a feast upon a sacrifice." It is a commemorative, not a propitiatory sacrifice.

Waterland has the following: "The plain meaning is, that there is in the Eucharist a real communion or participation of Christ's broken body and blood shed, *i. e.*, of His passion, *i. e.*, of the atonement made by it, in which we actually partake, as often as we worthily partake of this Holy Sacrament. How our Church understands St. Paul

(1 **Cor. x.** 16) may be seen from article xxviii. "The bread which **we** brake is **a** partaking of the body of Christ, and likewise the cup of blessing is a partaking of the blood of Christ." If we look into our older English versions, as **Parker's** and Tindale's, we shall find **there the text thus** rendered: " Is not the bread which we **breake** partakynge of the bodey of Christ. Is not the cuppe of blessynge which we blesse partakynge of the blude of Christ?" at p. 508. Thus far may partly be pleaded, from the nature **and reason** of the **thing, that, the** *service* of the Eucharist—the most proper part of *Evangelical worship*, **and most** solemn act of the Christian **Church—must be understood to ascend up** " for a **memorial before God,"** in as strict a sense **at least as Cornelius' alms and** prayers were said to do, or as "the **prayers of** the saints" go up as sweet odours, mystical *incense* before God. Indeed *incense* and *sacrifical* memorials of the Old Testament were mostly typical of evangelical worship or *Christian services*, and **were acceptable to** God under **that view; and therefore it cannot be doubted** but the true **rational** *incense*, **viz., Gospel** services, rightly performed—and among these more especially the Eucharistical **service—are the acceptable memorials in** God's sight. **Such worship,** rightly performed, has the force and value of *any memorial* elsewhere **mentioned** in Scripture—*sacrificial* or other—cannot be doubted."—at p. 729. The service **of the Eucharist, on the foot of** ancient Church language, is **both** a *true* and a *proper* **sacrifice, and** the noblest we are capable of offering, when considered as comprehending under it **many** true and evangelical sacrifices: 1. The *sacrifice* of alms to the **poor, and** *oblations* to the Church; which, when **religiously intended and offered through Christ, is** a Gospel *sacrifice*. **Not** that the *material* offering **is an** offering to **God, for it goes entirely for the use of man, but the** *service*

is what God accepts. 2. The sacrifice of prayer, from a pure heart, is evangelical *incense*. 3. The sacrifice of *praise* and *thanksgiving* to God the Father, through *Jesus* Christ our Lord, is another **Gospel sacrifice**. 4. The sacrifice of a **penitent and contrite heart even** under the law—and now much more under the Gospel when explicitly *offered through* Christ—was a sacrifice of the **new** covenant, **for the new** covenant commenced from the time of the fall, and obtained **under** the law, but couched under shadows and figures. 5. THE SACRIFICE OF OURSELVES, OUR SOULS AND BODIES, IS ANOTHER GOSPEL SACRIFICE. This is really always included in the Holy Eucharist: "And here we present and offer unto **Thee,** ourselves, our souls, and our bodies to be a lively sacrifice," &c., &c. 6. **The** offering up the mystical body **of Christ, that is, His Church, is** another Gospel sacrifice: **or rather it is coincident with the** former: excepting that there **persons are considered in** their single capacity, and here *collectively* in a body (1 Cor. x. **17**). **7.** The offering **up of** true converts or sincere *penitents* to God, by **their** pastors, &c. 8. The sacrifice of *faith* and *hope* **and** *self-humiliation* in commemorating **the** *grand sacrifice*, and resting **finally** upon it, is another **Gospel** sacrifice, and eminently proper to the Eucharist. These, I think, are all so many true sacrifices, and may all meet together in the one great complicated SACRIFICE OF THE EUCHARIST. Waterland quotes from the ancients to sustain this view. 1st, Saint Barnabas, A.D. 71. " Christ abolished the legal sacrifices, **to** make way for an human oblation;" which he explains soon after, by an humble and contrite heart (Psl. ii. 17). So by human oblation he means free-will offerings of *the heart* **as** opposed to the yoke of legal observances; the offering up *the whole inner man*, instead of the outward superficial performances of *the law*. (See 5th article of preceding account).

Christians offer themselves, their souls and bodies, instead of beasts.

The Right Rev. Bishop Wordsworth, of the diocese of St. Andrew, has admirably vindicated the threefold character of the Christian passover, and very clearly elucidated the three views in which it is presented for our acceptance: 1st, as a sacrafice, 2ndly, as a sacrament, and 3rdly, as a eucharist. With reference to the first, he says: "We are to learn that in this holy rite Jesus Christ is not only preached by word of mouth, but by visible signs "openly set forth, crucified among us." We are to see in the breaking of the bread, "His body broken, and in the pouring out of the wine, His blood shed." But more than this—we are to recognise in the same divine right all the essential properties of a true sacrifice; we are to see done in very deed what Christ did to our remembrance of Him. And what then did He do? when the time of the passover was fully come, He, the great High Priest, the Priest for ever after the order of Melchizedek, took bread and wine, and having sanctified them by His word and heavenly benediction, He offered them to the Father oblations of His Sacrifice. This action, therefore, to be adequately commemorated, requires not only an offering to be made, but a priest to offer it, and an altar to be offered on. And this is the reason why the elements of bread and wine are first placed upon a side table, called a credence table, in order that the priest may solemnly present them on the altar as the minister of Christ, and acting in His stead." Received in this light, we have, as had the Jews, a Lord's table and an altar; an altar-table, at which we present, in memorial, and by representation, the finished but continuous sacrifice, by which God gives us that spiritual gift, even Christ's body and blood. It must be a spiritual sacrifice if there be spiritual partaking of the Sacrifice.

The third Œcumenical Council, that of Ephesus, A.D. 431, gives the full authority of the Church to the following paragraph of **the** remonstrance sent to Nestorius a little before, by St. Cyril and **the Synod of** Alexandria:

"**And there** is **another** point which we must of necessity add, how that, setting forth **the death** after **the** flesh of the **only begotten** Son of God, that **is** Jesus Christ, **and confessing** his resurrection **from the dead,** and ascension into the heavens, we celebrate in the churches the unbloody sacrifice. In **the** fourth Canon of the Nicene Council it is laid down, " Let one of the synods be holden before Lent, that all such ill-temper being done away, *the gift* may be *offered* pure **unto** God." In the eleventh, certain persons are directed, without *offering*, to communicate in their prayers only. The **eighteenth** says, "It hath come before **the** holy and great Synod, that **in some places and cities the** deacons give the Eucharist to the presbyters, a thing transmitted to us neither by canon nor custom, that such as have no authority to offer should give those who offer the body of Christ."

Eusebius says, "Our Saviour Jesus the Christ, in the manner of Melchizedek, **does** indeed now **too** perform, through His servants, the office of the priesthood among **men.** For as he, being a priest of the nations, no where appeareth **to have** used bodily sacrifices, but blessed Abraham, with bread and wine alone, in the manner as did our Saviour, then all the priests from him, throughout all nations, performing the spiritual priestly act according to the laws of the Church, symbolise with bread and wine the mysteries both of his body and blood: Melchizedek truly having foreseen this by a divine spirit, and having forecased the images of the things to come." Again he says, "We offer the show-bread rekindling the saving remembrance, and we offer the blood of sprinkling of the Lamb of God which taketh away the sins of the world, the cleansing of the sins of the world, the cleansing of our souls."

Theodoret, living from A.D. 357 to A.D. 386, says, "Melchizedek was priest not of the **Jews**, but of the Gentiles: so too the Lord Christ offered himself to **God**, not for the Jews only, but also for all men. But he enters on his priesthood in that night after which he suffered; when 'He took bread, and having given thanks he brake it, **and** said, take, eat of it; this is **my body**. Likewise also, having mingled the cup, **he gave it to his disciples**, saying, drink ye all of this, **for this is my blood of the New Testament, which is shed for** many for the remission of sins.'" But we find that Melchizedek was truly both priest and **king;** for **he** was a type of the true Priest and King; and that he **offered to** God no sacrifice of beasts, but bread and wine. **For** these also he offered to Abraham, spiritually foreseeing the archetype of his own high priesthood in the loins **of the** patriarch. If, then, Christ be from David, **according to the** flesh, and David from Judah, **Christ received this priesthood** after the order **of** Melchizedek. So the Levitical priesthood **ceased, and the blessing of the greater** priesthood passed into the tribe of Judah. **But now Christ is The Priest, who hath** sprung from Judah according to the flesh, not offering aught but himself, the head of them who offer. **For** he calls the **Church his body, and** through it and in it by **man** he exercises the priest's office; as God **he** receiveth the offerings. But the Church offereth the *symbols* of his body and blood, hallowing the whole lump through the first fruits."

In the progress of his Church, the blessed Redeemer **elected** certain to be with him, in order that they might be true witnesses of the divine work which he came to accomplish, He as well constituted them the foundation stones of the **new covenant: and they were** instructed and called to represent the Melchizedekean priesthood which our Lord instituted, **in succession to the** Aaronic, as ministers in him and in his stead; as ambassadors from his kingdom to those **summoned into it. As under the old dispensation** particular **persons** were set apart for the performance of religious rites, to celebrate divine praise, and offer prayer to the majesty of **God,** so in the new, a holy office was instituted to accomplish similar purposes. The office that ceased on earth with the setting up of the Melchizedekean priesthood, was that of **High** Priest; but although changed and elevated, the office of the Levitical priesthood remains. Indeed the institution of the Christian Church, with its commissioned officers to carry glad tidings of salvation, to proclaim repentance *and remission* of sins, to celebrate and make the representation of the sacrifice of the death of Christ, and to baptize all nations, plainly testifies that our Lord **intended** "to take them for priests and **Levites.**" "Go, show yourselves to the priests, and offer the gift," is as much a law now as when our Lord spoke of the Mosaic requirements. **Surely the** offering of praise and prayer has not ceased. Have we no **gifts due to** God? Is there no covenanted promise?

The celebration of divine worship in its fullest sense is a duty from which no truly Christian soul dares to abstain. Organised **as** we find the Church of Christ to be by divine authority, **no man can take unto** himself this ministry, **except** he be called of God, as was Aaron. **The** manifest outpouring of the Spirit on the first founders of the Church, satisfactorily shows the sacred nature of the office with which they were **entrusted,** and the care with which the **Apostles** continued to set apart men for the sacred office of the ministry affirms its fixed and holy dignity. As stewards of the mysteries, as ambassadors for Christ, as pastors of the flock, as shepherds of the sheep, as ministers in Christ, they stand indeed in relation to us, not as Aaron, for Christ is our high priest, but as priests, to offer to God spiritual sacrifices, and to reconcile men to God through the ministry of the Word and Sacraments. "They are teachers sent from God," and they are commissioned servants of Christ, to seal in his name the covenant of reconciliation with us, and to minister daily in his temple the bread of life to hungry, perishing souls. The Jewish priesthood was not by any means so exalted; the nature of the office which they filled was, if possible, less spiritual, that is, was more symbolical, while the Christian priesthood is essentially a spiritual one, not after the law of **a carnal commandment but after** the power of an endless life; an office leading men **to walk** by the spirit, by their **spiritual mind, and less by** the eye of carnal sense.

Professor Maurice has well said:—" The main principle of the Presbyterian argument is as directly opposed to the idea of a priesthood as it is to the idea of Episcopacy. **The** doctrine of a priesthood is so much involved with **the** doctrine of sacrifice, that my last section may **be looked** upon as a sufficient statement **of** my views respecting **it.** Still there is so much horror in many minds of that absolving power which I have attributed to the Christian Bishop and to those whom he endows with it, and their complaints involve consequences of so practical a character, **that I** think I should be wrong not to give them a separate consideration. I do not class them under the head of Presbyterian objections, because there are many Episcopalians who appear **to** share in them. They may be expressed **thus:**

"' According to St. Paul, those who believe in Christ are justified from all things from which they could not be justified by the law of Moses. Ambassadors are sent forth to declare Christ's Gospel to men, in order that they may not be prevented from believing by the want of hearing; in order that if they believe they may receive this justification and freedom **of the** conscience. This is the true office of the minister; all **these are accidental and** subordinate to it. He may own orders and governments in the Church, Presbyterian, Episcopal, Apostolical, what you **will; but the** preaching of Christ is his true and essential **function: his commission is to** do this, this first, this above all things. When he pretends that he has some other way of relieving the conscience than this; when he says that **he has the power of** pardoning and absolving,—that he may pronounce men free from their sins,—he is not only committing a fearful usurpation upon the rights of Christ, he is actually misunderstanding and denying **the** true character of his own office. He deprives himself of his true power, in his eagerness to grasp **a power which has never** been given him by God, and can never be of the least **use to man.'**

"There is one point which is very important to **take notice** of in reference to this subject. According to the **idea which** has always existed in the Christian Church, the same person to whom the function of absolving is committed has also the **function of administering the Eucharist.** These two duties never have been separated, and it is most needful that they should be contemplated in their relation to each other; for if the Eucharist be that act in **which the worshipper is** especially brought into direct communion with **his Lord,** that act in which **the** mere human and visible agent **is most** entirely lost and forgotten, or only contemplated as one who bears witness that **He** whom he serves is a living and actual person, we must suppose that this is a key to the whole character of the office, in whatever way it may be **exercised.** If, again, the Eucharist involve at once a confession of sins on the part of the receivers, a thankful acknowledgment of a state of fellowship and blessedness **with their Lord,** into which they have been brought, though they may have walked most unworthily of it, the acceptance **of a** pledge of forgiveness for the past, strength for the present—a strength only to be realized by union with the invisible Lord,—a promise of future blessings, to be attained in the same way and in no other, this would **seem to** determine the nature **of** that particular function which the minister presumes to exercise when **he** pronounces absolution. His **whole object is to present Christ to men and men to** Christ **really and practically.** Suppose him in the congregation, he is there to represent its unity, to offer before God as a whole body, to confess the sins which its members **have** committed by separating themselves from the body. Then **he is a witness** of Christ's continual intercession for the entire Church. Suppose him alone, with any particular member of the congregation, he is with him to **preserve him** in the unity of the Church, **to present before God his tears** and contrition for having lived unworthy **of his** position in it. Then he is a witness of Christ's distinct intercession for every member in his flock. But still this can be but half his duty. The incarnation means very little, the kingdom **of God is a mere delusion, if there** *be not a voice speaking from heaven* as well as one crying from the earth; if **the** one be not an answer to the other, if the minister may **not** say to the congregation, 'God has heard your petitions, **rise** up as pardoned men, with **strength** to offer up praises **and** prayers, with strength to do your work,' the confession is but half real—the Gospel is not real at all. **And if he may not say in** like manner **to the** sick and solitary penitent, **'God accepts thy tears and** pardons thy sins,' I do not see what he means by saying that he has authority **to** *preach* forgiveness of **sins.** He preaches forgiveness to those who will accept it, understanding its nature and purposes; receiving it not as a license to the conscience, as a deliverance of it. He delivers forgiveness under precisely the same conditions. How many of the congregation are in a state of mind to claim their fellowship with Christ and each other, and so to take the mercy which is freely given them—whether the individual man can do this—God only knows. The absolver at all events has spoken the truth; he has acted out his commission; the rest he must leave. His public preaching, his private exhortations, are all intended to remove some stumbling-block out of the way of those to whom he has been sent; to explain to them the meaning of their confession and of his absolution; to prevent their offering the one, or receiving the other in vain; to hinder them from turning either to an evil account.

"Supposing this to be the case, it would seem that there is no greater peril in this doctrine, than in the one which makes preaching the main work and office of a minister. As to misconstruction, there is, at all events, no greater likelihood of it in the case of words which are not our own, which are spoken in the name of God, and on the most solemn occasion, than in the case of words which, under whatever teaching from above, we have composed, which must be mixed with our own peculiar modes of expression and habits of thought. So much I think must be admitted by every one, who considers the subject without prejudice. And the question which such a person might be inclined to ask, would perhaps be this: 'Where is the great difference? You mean by your absolving power just what others mean by preaching the Gospel. Let this be clearly understood, and then no Christian would object to your statements any longer.' My answer is, I cannot make this explanation, because it would not be a true one. I do conceive, there is very great difference between the notion that **the act of absolution** which the minister pronounces in the **name of** the Church is that **act** which interprets the object **of his** preaching, and **the notion** that he is sent to preach, **and that** because he preaches, he may, in **a certain sense,** absolve. The difference seems to me to be **this; in the former** case **the** minister presents Christ actually **and personally to his congregation.** His office is **a witness of Christ's presence** among them, of Christ's relation **to them. It is grounded** on the acknowledgment **of an actual union between the** body and its Head. In **the other case there is much speech,** it may be eloquent, it may be true speech, about Christ, his work, and his offices. But it is

> "A painted ship
> Upon a painted ocean;"

a description of what is very good and beautiful, and what man wants, **but not** the thing itself, not the reality."

Such being the sacred character of the Melchisedekean priesthood which **is now the true character of the Christian priesthood, we not only recognise the servants of the sanctuary** as ministering of holy things *in* Christ, *i. e.*, clothed in His Name and armed with His Word, but as priests, representing the acts done by Christ the Lord for us, in Him, performing those acts and in the unity of the Faith offering, the finished sacrifice to the Father through the Son.

"When **we say** then that our feast, like that of the Passover, is sacrificial, we **do not mean that it does not commemorate a blessing which has** been fully obtained **and** realized; if we did **we should violate** the analogy **in the** very moment of applying it; **for** the Passover did commemorate a complete deliverance and the establishment **of** a national state in consequence of that deliverance. But as that deliverance was accompanied with a sacrifical act, and by a sacrifical act accomplished,—and yet in this passover the act was perpetually renewed,—because in this way the nation understood that by sacrifice it subsisted, and consisted,—and because by such a renewal its members realized the permanent and living character of the good that had been bestowed upon them, so it is here. The sacrifice of Christ is that with which alone God can be satisfied, and in the sight of which alone He can contemplate our race; it is therefore the only meeting-point of communion with Him; but this communion being established, it must be by presenting the finished sacrifice before God that, we both bear witness what our position is and realize the glory of it; otherwise we have a name without a reality, and with the words 'finished and complete' are robbing ourselves of the very thing which makes it so important that we should prize them and preserve them.

"Why these considerations have been overlooked by Protestants I think will be evident from the remarks which were made in the former part. The worth of Protestantism consisted in this, that it asserted the distinct position of each man, affirming that he was a person and not merely one of a mass. This truth had been working itself out into clearness for many centuries, but the process was a strange and painful one. The conscience is that which tells each man he is a person, making him feel that which he has done in past time to be his own, giving him an awful assurance of identity, responsibility, permanence. Overburdened with the sense of evil, it sought for a remedy; it was commanded to perform certain services in the hope of finding one; with each attempt the sense of moral evil increased. The Reformers found that the whole scheme was a delusion. The services presumed that freedom of conscience which men sought to acquire by them; without it they were not true godly services. The emancipation of the conscience was therefore that which they sought as the step to all good; they declared that by faith in Christ, grounded upon acts of complete redemption done on their behalf, they could alone obtain it.

"How true this language was, what a curse had come upon the Church through the denial of it, how necessary it was that, at that time especially but also at all times, it should be proclaimed, I have contended again and again. But it is equally certain that as the Quakers believe self-sacrifice, so the Reformers believed the emancipation of the conscience to be not a necessary condition of our moral being but the end of it. Whatever contributed to this end was necessary, whatever did not contribute to it was worthless. The belief of Christ's sacrifice upon the cross was that which had given peace to their consciences; that it had any purpose save that of giving peace to the conscience was more and more forgotten. And therefore it became necessary to explain how it accomplished this purpose. Then began all the theories about sacrifice, satisfaction, and imputation, which I spoke of as at once so fatal to the principles of the Reformation and to the practical life of Christianity, as affording no comfort to the humble heart, as leading to all disputes and separations, as preparing the way for the infidelity of the eighteenth century. These hungry notions of the understanding being substituted for the clear, simple belief of the Reformers, that we are adopted into Christ by baptism and are therefore children of God and may draw nigh to Him in all duties and services, confessing the sins which have polluted us and separated us from Him, turned every thing into confusion. Men knew that they were not approaching God with pure consciences; the Reformers said that if they did not, the service was a mockery; they therefore sought hither and thither for some better kind of faith which could give them relief; not finding it, they deemed the whole Gospel to be a dream and fable.

"But that which lay beneath all these dark imaginations and sad results was I believe the imperfect apprehension which the Reformers themselves had of the nature of the communion. This feast, says the Zuinglian, is nothing but the memorial of a past transaction. That it is the memorial of a past transaction is of course assumed in every word I have said. If it were not it could have no pretence to the name of Eucharist; it would bear no analogy to the Passover. But the Passover had not merely reference to the past. The Jew had been brought out of Pharaoh's government and brought under God's government. In commemorating the past emancipation of his nation he claimed for himself a privilege which belonged to it then. It would, I think, be insulting the Zuinglian to suppose that he thought the Christian ordinance, in this respect, different from its predecessor. He is particularly practical and rational; he must therefore know well that no men ever did or ever could celebrate with the least heartiness and affectionateness, an event which they did not suppose in some sense to be the cause or the commencement of an improved condition of things, that condition of things being one with which they were in some way connected. The Zuinglian then cannot mean by his words 'Simple memorial' that there is nothing of present continuous interest in it; if he did he would suppose, contrary to all his professions, that our Lord's religion imposes, as a test of obedience, a most dry, dreary, unmeaning ceremony. But if he allows, as of course he will, that certain effects have followed from our Lord's death, in which we are partakers, and that these effects, and not merely the cause which produced them, are recalled to us by this feast, then the question immediately occurs, what are these effects? The great effect which we believe to have proceeded from it, that in which every other is included, is that thereby we are made capable of *entering into the presence of God;* that a mercy-seat is revealed to mankind, where his Maker may meet with him. Supposing this were so, this must surely be one of the effects which is brought to our recollection by the Eucharist. I do not object to the word *recollection;* there is nothing in it which is not applicable to a Living Actual Presence. What I plead for is the duty of recollecting that presence in the Eucharist, *because it is there.**

"But the Zuinglian will ask, why there, and not elsewhere? The question may bear two constructions. It may mean, why may we not feed upon the sacrifice of Christ at all times, and thus enter into the presence of Him who perfectly delights in that sacrifice? Or it may mean, God is omnipresent; why then are we not always in his presence? Evidently these two thoughts are of the most different kind, and originate in most different states of feeling. The first suggests to us the highest standard of perfection which a Christian can propose to himself, and yet a standard which, if what I have said be true, must be a most real and reasonable one: for that the Church *is* brought into the presence of God, is the first principle of the New Dispensation, the one which is especially involved in this Sacrament; and if

---

* When,—says St. **Chrysostom**,—thou art about to approach to the Holy Table think that there the **King of all is present**: for *He is present* indeed, observing the mind of all, and seeth who approacheth with befitting holiness, and who hath an evil conscience, with unclean and foul thoughts and wicked deeds. Let thy coming be to *honour* and *adore* not to spurn the Son of God: only *do this with trembling* and *with joy.*

every one of us ought to consider himself a member of the Church, this wonderful privilege belongs to us, not in proportion as we raise ourselves to some individual excellence, but in proportion as we renounce all such distinctions, and yield ourselves to the Spirit who dwells in the whole body. What then I should say, in reference to this view of the case, is precisely what I have said in reference to the Quaker doctrine. If we acknowledge that the light is somewhere concentrated, that it reveals itself to us in some way which it has chosen; that the revelation is not for us only, but for all; if we make this acknowledgment practically, we are at least in the right road to the realization of that blessing which it is so truly affirmed that we ought to seek. Otherwise we shall fancy that we produce this presence by our acts of meditation or faith: we glorify ourselves for these acts, and for a reality we get a dream; then we gladly betake ourselves to the other doctrine, which comes forth with the boast that it asserts 'the Omnipresence of the Deity.'

"So I believe it has happened with the Zuinglians. An early disciple of the school, attaching an almost superstitious veneration to the Bible, would at once have rejected this phrase as incompatiable alike with its letter and its spirit. He would have asked how it could be reconciled with the words of the book of Genesis, which speak of God as meeting Adam in the garden, as coming down to see the tower which men had builded, as appearing to Abraham at the tent-door? A Zuinglian of the next century would have learnt perhaps to use the phrases, 'figures,' 'eastern allegories,' and such like, in reference to these passages. Still he would have said to himself, 'honest men use allegories and figures for some purpose; they mean something by them; it is a *truth* which they wish to convey. But if I admit these phrases, 'ubiquity,' 'omnipresence,' in their ordinary sense, I must suppose the word of God less **honest and true than the words** of men ; **for** these stories, instead of implying or hinting **a** truth, involve the direct contradiction of one.' But a Zuinglian of the third century will have mastered all these difficulties. He will **at once** dispose of these scriptural expressions, by calling them ' anthropomorphic,' or indications of a low state of civilization ; **or** with less honesty he will pass them **over altogether, only** assuming that the phrase, ' Omnipresence **of the Deity,'** must be good **and true,** whatever else, **either in the early thoughts and feelings of men, or** in the revelations to **which these have been** leading, **should** happen **to** be false.

"Let us consider then for **a moment** the **philosophy of this phrase—Omnipresence. It** has been adopted **to convey the impression that** the limits of space are not applicable to a divine **and** absolute Being. But does **it** convey **this impression to any one who is capable of reflecting upon his own thoughts ? Is** ' everywhere ' less a **word of space than** ' somewhere ?' Did the **ancients** less imprison **the Divine Essence** in forms, **when they spoke of it as inhabiting every tree and flower, than when they viewed it in the person of a Jupiter sitting on the Thessalian mount ? No! in proportion as they attached personal** qualities **to their Jupiter, in proportion as they believed that he was** capable of loving **and hating, and that he had the feelings of a** father, they **were conceiving of him infinitely** *less* **under the** limits of space (and **of time also) than when they were translating his name by ' the air,' and regarding him as a subtile fluid** diffused through **every portion of** the universe. **In the one case** they were dreaming of a SPIRIT with whom **men might** converse ; **a Spirit indeed mixed of good and** ill—their own image—but **still** to be apprehended by **that** which is spiritual in man : in the other case **their** thoughts **were** wholly physical; not the less so for being rarefied and subtilized; or if there was any thing else in them, it was what they derived from the older faith.

"In strict conformity with this principle is that passage of our Lord's teaching which is so often quoted to prove a very different doctrine. He told the woman of Samaria that a time was coming when neither on Mount Gerizim nor at Jerusalem should men worship the Father. He does not give as the reason, 'God is everywhere;' but He rises at once to the higher level; He says, 'God is a Spirit,' and they that worship Him must worship Him in spirit and in truth. And He connects with these words, what would seem to modern thinkers the most direct contradiction of them: 'We know what we worship, for salvation is of the Jews.' Unquestionably such language would have been utterly inconsistent with the Omnipresent doctrine; it was nowise inconsistent with the doctrine 'God is a Spirit.' Every step in the Jewish revelation and history had presumed that truth, and had been preparing the way for the full manifestation of it. Every step of it had been more fully bringing out the idea of God as the Holy One, as the Moral Being, the object of trust, and awe, and reverence. And in nothing had this idea been more expressed, than in those arrangements which seemed to localize the Divine Presence. Because He was the Holy One, He must not be worshipped in all the forms of nature and visible things; He must be viewed as distinct, personal; He must be approached, in the temple, through the priest with the sacrifice. By all these means, now regarded as so sensual, men were taught that it ***was not with*** *their senses* that they were to apprehend God; that it was that in them which desires truth and holiness which must seek Him, which by a wonderful method He was drawing towards Himself. And therefore, though simple people who had sought God without the law, might be far better prepared to welcome Him who brought their sins to their mind, and told them all things that ever they did, than the proud idolater of the law could ever be; yet those who had profited by the law, those who were Israelites indeed, and without guile, those who had served God day and night in the temple, and waited for the consolation of Israel, were far better prepared than any others could be to see the glory of God in the man Christ Jesus; to feel that there was no contradiction in the perfectly Holy One inhabiting a body of human clay; that it was a low, carnal, sensual notion of the Godhead, one which really identified Him with physical things, and therefore subjected Him practically to the laws of space, which made it seem to be a contradiction.

"I maintain, then, that the highest, clearest, most spiritual, most universal idea of God which any creature can attain to, is not that which he receives from a dream about the attribute of omnipresence, but that into which he enters when he contemplates the fulness of truth and holiness and love, the absolute and perfect Being pleasing to identify Himself with a human soul and body, to suffer with them, to raise them out of death, to raise them to glory. We have not here an attempt to merge complete spirituality and distinct locality—each of which is demanded by man's reason, each of which is necessary to the other—in a wretched abstraction called ubiquity, a notion vacant of all substance and reality, only serving to puff up the mind with the vague consciousness of possessing a good idea, which it really needs but has missed altogether. I should be scrupulous about the use of such language as this, in reference to a phrase which is so prevalent among religious people, and which may therefore have some sacred associations connected with it, if I did not see that it had been the means of perplexing the minds of little children, of making moral and Christian education almost impossible, of introducing infinite vagueness and weakness into our pulpit discourses, of preparing men's minds for a settled and hopeless pantheism. That it has also been the means of lowering and confounding our feelings about the Eucharistic feast, is implied in all its other effects. But here it has met with an enemy able to cope with it. The impression that this Sacrament is a reality, in spite of all men's attempts to prove it and make it a fiction, has kept alive the belief *that the presence of God* is a truth and not a dream; and that we may enter it in a better and truer way than by fancying ourselves in it, when we are only indulging pleasant sensations and high conceits.

"But if I maintain so strongly that it is only with the Spirit that we can hold communion with a spiritual Being, how do I differ from the Calvinists, who admit that there is a presence in the Sacrament to those who believe? I do not think that I differ from them except when they differ from themselves. I no more suppose that our spirits can perceive a spiritual object without faith, than that our eyes can perceive a natural object if they be blind. Faith is as much *that exercise in which the spirit is and lives,* AS SIGHT is the exercise in which the eye is and lives. What more does the Calvinist require? He requires that we should suppose there is *no object present* unless there be something which perceives it; and having got into this contradiction, the next step is to suppose that faith is not a receptive, but a creative power; that it *makes the thing* which it believes. We have seen what a tendency to this belief there has been among all Protestants; but we have seen also that there were characteristics in the creed of the Calvinist which ought especially to have delivered him from it. His principle is to refer everything to the will of God, to suppose that nothing originates with the creature. How then has he fallen into an hypothesis apparently so foreign from his deepest convictions? He has been driven into it by his habit of resolving his belief of the Divine Will into his doctrine of individual Election. He cannot suppose that God has any higher end in his manifestations than the redemption and sanctification of particular **men**; the idea, therefore, of the God-Manhood, of God manifesting Himself in the person of his Son, shrinks and **dwindles into a mere expedient for** accomplishing his objects of **mercy towards the favoured members of** the race, **and by** necessary consequence the **belief that He** has **devised** a means whereby men, as members of a body, may apprehend Him who is the head of the body, loses itself in this strange attempt to conceive a presence which is not a presence till we make **it so**. Still it is a curious and interesting fact, that **the form and principle of Calvin's doctrine, as** distinguished **from his system, was mainly** upheld by his faith in this Sacrament; and that when his followers approximated, as **of necessity they did, more** and more nearly to the Zuinglian doctrine on this **subject, the system** became more and **more prominent** and **exclusive.**

"**It is a great transition to** go from either of **these views to the** Lutheran, wherein the actual **presence of Christ as the** ground **of faith, and not as** grounded upon **it,** is so unequivocally asserted. **It** might seem that in doing so I must change **the** character of my statements; that whereas I have hitherto been endeavouring to assert this presence against those **who deny** it, I must now, if I discover any difference **with** this class of Protestants, point out the danger of carrying a true principle to its extreme. But I shall make no such change, and I see no such danger. I complain of the Lutheran, as I do of the Zuinglian and the Calvinist, for seeking the deliverance of the individual conscience as an ultimate end; and therefore for failing to acknowledge the completeness and integrity of the blessing which Christ has bestowed upon his Church. Whatever logical perplexity the Lutheran has fallen into; whatever violence he has done to the understanding by his theory; whatever of confusion he has introduced between the sensible and the spiritual world, is, as I conceive, the consequence of his not taking the language of our Lord and of his Apostles in a sufficiently plain and literal sense. Our Lord says, 'This is my body.' St. Paul addresses the Ephesian converts as sitting in the heavenly places with Christ. He tells the Philippians that their bodies shall be made like unto Christ's glorious body. Surely this is Christianity. It is the Gospel of the deliverance of the spirit and soul and body from all the fetters by which they are held down, and prevented from fulfilling each its own proper function— from maintaining their right relations to each other. And this emancipation is connected with and consequent upon, our union, as members of one body, with Christ, the crucified, the risen, the glorified Lord of our race. Now, if these be the privileges of Christian men, and if these privileges, whatever they be, are in this Sacrament asserted and realized, what a low notion it is, that we are invited to hold communion, not with Christ as He is, not with his body exalted at the right hand of God, but with a body consubstantiated in the elements.

"Think only of the freedom, the fellowship of hope—not only compatible with, but inseparable from, humiliation and fear—implied in intercourse with the Prince and Forerunner who has actually broken through the barriers of space and time, whose body has been subjected to the events and sufferings of mortality, and who is now glorified with the **glory** which He had with the Father before the worlds were, and hereafter to be manifested in the sight of quick and dead. Bring these thoughts before you in connexion with the words, 'This is my body,' and with **the command** that we should show forth his death till **He come; and** then reflect, if you can, upon the **logical dogma of** consubstantiation, the notion **that** all **these blessings do in some way** dwell in the bread and wine. Surely what we need is, that *they* should be made a perfectly transparent medium, through which His glory may be manifested, that nothing should be really beheld by the spirit of the *worshippers*, save He *into whose presence* THEY are brought. For this end the elements require a solemn consecration from the priest, through whom Christ distributes them to His flock; not that they may be clothed with some new and peculiar attributes; not that they may acquire some essential and miraculous virtue, but that they may be diverted from their ordinary uses, that they may become purely sacramental. Morning and evening, the kind looks and parting words of friends, the laugh of childhood, daily bread, sickness and death; all have a holy sacramental meaning, and should as such be viewed by us. But then they have another meaning, which keeps this out of sight. If we would have them translated to us, we need some pure untroubled element, which has no significancy, except as the organ through which the voice of God speaks to man, and through which he may answer, 'Thy servant heareth.' Such we believe are this bread and wine when redeemed to his service: let us not deprive them of their ethereal whiteness and clearness by the colours of our fancy or the clouds of our intellect."

"We Christians who believe in Christ, are taught in the Gospel how we ought to pray to God the Father; in which prayer, among many other petitions we ask for Bread, which Bread is Life, as it is written, this is the Bread of Life which came down from Heaven." This Life both of Christ and God, *i. e.*, eternal, which He Himself calls by the name of ἐπιούσιον ἄρτον, Bread from the same οὐσία—essence,—*i. e.*, from the Life of God. For whence shall we be sons of God, save by participation of eternal life which Christ gave us, bringing it from the "Father." *

In every respect the Eucharistic Sacrifice, *i. e.*, the Sacrifice of Praise and Thanksgiving, is a higher and more true, because a more real and essentially spiritual sacrifice than was sacrifice under the law. With the Jew the carnal commandments were severe and necessary, because the way to the perception of a higher life was not yet made sufficiently clear. When Christ Incarnate came, and died, the Holy of Holies was thrown open, our High Priest entered in calling men unto Him, that He might in His own Person, and through His own Flesh and Blood, offer a Holy acceptable Sacrifice for them once and for ever, and make them partakers of that Sacrifice. As the Jew was ordered to partake of that which he presented to the priest for an offering, so Christ has furnished His people with the oblations of His own Sacrifice, and bids them as baptised into His death and incorporated into His Body, being members of His Body, His bones and His flesh, to offer themselves, *as His corporate members*, to the end, that the members of His Body may live and be kept living members of His Body through the nourishment which is of His own most precious Life. "When the

---

* M. Victorinus, Advers. Arium., ii. c. 8, p. 177.

life-giving Word of God dwelt in *the flesh*, He *transformed* IT into His own proper good, *i. e.*, LIFE."*

We, the members of Christ are in the place of all the carnal offerings of the Jews: we may indeed in a sense be said to "offer Christ," when as very members incorporate of His Body we present ourselves living **sacrifices** unto God. " We then live by Him, eating Him, *i. e.*, receiving Him as that Eternal Life which of **ourselves we had** not."† By effectual signs is shewn forth not only the broken body and poured out blood, but Christ also signifies to His redeemed that He imparts to them the most precious food of His own most precious Body and Blood. We thus, not only as offerers but as partakers of the Sacrifice, are more highly privileged than the Jew; we not only eat and drink the sign but also receive the thing signified.

The establishment of the new priesthood, and the change from the Aaronical to the Melchisedekeal in the headship of Christ the High Priest, the *oneness* and *permanence* of the kingdom of Christ are set forth in the last sayings of the evangelical Prophet: " They shall bring all your brethren, for an offering unto the Lord out of all nations, ... to My holy mountain Jerusalem, saith the Lord, as the children of Israel bring an offering in a clean vessel into the house of the Lord. And I will take them for priests and for Levites saith the Lord: for as the new heavens and the new earth which I will make *shall remain* before Me, saith the Lord, so shall your seed and your name remain." This priesthood which is ministering in Christ, represents what He has done and is doing, pleads with God the one continuous and only Sacrifice, and in an acceptable oblation offers the people committed to their care, together with the memorials of

---

* St. Cyril of Alex., In. St. John, vi. 61, l. iv., c. 2, p. 354.
† St. Augustin, 19, p. 413.

their crucified Lord, receiving Christ and His promises by faith.*

Again: Tertullian, "That we ought not to offer unto God *earthly*, but *spiritual sacrifices*, we may learn from what is written: The Sacrifice of God is an humble and contrite spirit, ... offer unto God the sacrifice of thanksgiving and pay thy vows unto the Most High." Cyprian † says: "Neither your religion nor *faith* can suffer by the hard circumstances you are under, that the priests of God have not the liberty to *offer* and celebrate the *holy sacrifices*. You *do celebrate*, and you *do offer* unto God a sacrifice both precious and glorious and which will much avail your obtaining heavenly rewards. The Scripture says, the Sacrifice of God is a broken Spirit, a broken and a contrite heart God doth not despise. This *Sacrifice* you offer to God, this you celebrate without intermission day and night, being made *victims* to God, and presenting *yourselves* as such, holy and unblemished pursuant to the Apostles exhortations, when he says, I *beseech* you, therefore, brethren, by the mercies of God, that you present your bodies, &c.—Rom. xii., 1. For this is what pleased God: and it is this by which our services are rendered more worthy, for the engaging the Divine acceptance." What we give to God is our own *service*, and *ourselves in* Christ, which is our *sacrifice*. The whole matter is well comprised and clearly expressed in a statement by a judicious Divine of the Anglican Church. Archbishop Sharp: "We offer up our *alms;* we offer up our *prayers*, our *praises*, AND OURSELVES: and all these we offer

---

* In the covenant of circumcision, the wounding of the flesh, or cutting off the part, was significant of the inward blessing of a renewed spirit by the putting away of the lust of the flesh through the blood of Christ the promised Seed. Deut. x. c. 16 v. Jer. iv. c. 4 v. Rom. iv. c. 11 v.

† Epist. to Confessors in Prison.

up in the virtue and consideration of CHRIST'S SACRIFICE represented before us, and before God, by way of remembrance or commemoration; nor can it be proved that, the ancients did more than this: this whole *service* was their Christian sacrifice and this *is ours*." We quote one more, for it would be tedious to enumerate all the old and later writers, so uniform and closely consistent are their views. Eusebius, commenting on Malachi, says: "We *offer* both sacrifice and incense. 1st. Celebrating the *memorial* of the Grand Sacrifice by those mysteries which He has ordained, and presenting our thanksgiving for our salvation by devout hymns and prayers. Next, we offer up OURSELVES to Him and to the Logos, his high priest, resting upon Him with body and soul. Whereupon we endeavour to preserve to Him our *bodies* pure and untainted, &c., and to bring Him minds free from evil affection and take care to honour Him by purity of thought, sincerity of affection and soundness of principles: for these we are taught are more acceptable to Him, than a multitude of sacrifices streaming with blood, and smoke and nidor.*—Euseb. Demonstr. Evang., lib. 1, c. x., p. 40.

We have, says the Apostle, an altar. It is true, the Lord's table is often called an altar, and it is a material table; and the alms and oblations are material: but by prayer of consecration they are re-ordered to a new use, set apart for spiritual purposes, so *the service* is *spiritual*, and such is the sacrifice we offer: and, therefore, the table, considered as an altar, an altar for spiritual sacrifice, is a mystical, spiritual altar. The holy table is called an *altar*, with regard to the *spiritual services* sent up from it, and so it is a spiritual

---

* The legal incense was a memorial, and was burnt over the shew-bread. In like manner, our commemoration service is offered to God by our incense of prayer and of humiliation and dedication offered over the elements.

altar: then, as it bears the symbols of the *Grand Sacrifice* applied in this service, and herein feasted **upon** by every worthy **communicant, it is a** symbolical or mystical Table.

THE PRESENCE OF CHRIST IN **THE HOLY COMMEMORATION.**

"Lord, how is it that Thou wilt manifest Thyself unto **us, and not unto** the world?

"Jesus answered **and said** unto him, if a man love me he will **keep** My words; and My Father will love him, and we will come unto him, and make our abode with him."—John, c. xiv., v. 22, 23.

"Abide in Me and I **in you."—c. xv., v. 4.**

"I am the Vine, ye **are the branches."—v. 5.**

The very idea of sacrifice implies our partaking of the Sacrifice. How **then may the** Anglican Church accept her dear Lord's Words, and say **to her children, "**Take, eat, this is** My body;"** drink, "This is My blood?" **Simply by Faith** in the **ability** of Christ to fulfil His Word, and in **the power of that Word** to accomplish His will. She teaches, that the Lord Jesus Christ did **in** dying **for** lost men, make **a covenant with them, by which He** made certain promises with conditions. The conditions being complied **with, no doubt arises as to the due fulfilment** of the terms. Further, the Anglican **Church does not** confine the meaning of the term "Sacrament," simply **to the elements. By the Sacra**ment She implies the whole celebration **or service; the** ministering **priest, the** spoken Words of Christ, the **con**secrated elements, **and the duly** qualified partakers: **that is, the** Church **in its completeness; as** the corporate body of Christ and through **which we are one** with Him. In this service of praise and thanksgiving, and in this Living Sacrifice, Christ is verily and indeed present. **The** Roman

Divine* argues, "An offender against the blessed Eucharist cannot be described as 'guilty of the Body and Blood of Christ' if these be not in the Sacrament." An offender is guilty, because he insults the Majesty of Christ, who having set bread and wine in honor for His service, to denote His presence to faithful men;† the unfaithful man mocks God in mocking at that, which He has been pleased to say indicates His presence although He is unseen by us. When St. John saw the heavenly vision, He was in the Spirit. When St. Stephen was stoned,

"He being full of the Holy Ghost, looked up stedfastly into heaven, and saw the glory of God, and Jesus standing on the right hand of God.

"And said, Behold, I see the heavens opened, and the Son of man standing on the right hand of God."

Surely it must be a spiritual discernment which is required of us, for it is plainly pointed out how it is men perceive and know spiritual things. The Anglican does discern the Person of Christ, from other and profane food, and does not confound the Body and Blood of Christ with other and even blessed but still material food, to wit, Bread and Wine.

Blessed be God, we have received the Spirit which is of Christ; and by that Spirit's help look up and see Jesus; low on our knees we bend before Him, adoring that mysterious love which brings us into His presence; worshiping Him, present to the spirit, we wash His very feet with our tears. Conformable to this is the language of St. Ambrose, who treats of the elements as effectual signs, viz.: that *by them*, the Body and Blood of CHRIST are *signified*. He says, "Before the blessing of the heavenly Words, another substance is named, after the consecration the Body is *signified*, *i. e.*, denoted by the sign." St. Epiphanius

---

* Wiseman's Letters on the Eucharist, p. 296.
† Malachi, c. i., v. 12.

says: "The Bread indeed is food, but the *might in it* is for giving of Life." St. Clement of Alexandria, says: "Twofold is the Blood of the Lord. The one is His natural Blood by which we have been redeemed from destruction; the other SPIRITUAL, *i. e.*, wherewith we are anointed. And this is to drink the Blood of Jesus, *to partake* of the immortality of the Lord. But *the virtue of the* **Word** IS THE SPIRIT, *as blood is of flesh.* ANALAGOUSLY then, the wine is mingled with the water, *and the Spirit with* **the man**. The one, the mingled drink feasteth unto faith; the other, the Spirit leadeth to immortality." It is thus, that the early Christians generally speak of the elements as "effectual signs" by which Christ signifies His presence to faithful men. The word of man can effect nothing, but the Word of the Everlasting Son everything. It is His will that we shall be united sacramentally to Himself, that our human nature shall be renewed by the impartation of His, taken for us and given to us sacramentally: therefore, in their right and proper use the Eucharistic symbols, *as symbols*, are by consecration translated into *the power* of the Body and Blood of Christ, because they are outward parts of an internal spiritual grace given unto us, ordained by Christ Himself, *as a means* whereby we RECEIVE THE SAME and a *pledge* to assure us thereof. We are not attempting to define the manner or mode of the gift, we simply take the language of the Church Catechism and adopt it, accept it in all its simplicity, as well as in all its fulness. We can no more tell how our blessed Lord and Saviour is pleased to make Himself present to our spirits than we can tell how we live; but this we do know, that He who made man, and knows what man is, has also said, that unless "we eat the Flesh of the Son of Man and drink His Blood we have no life in us." We, therefore, in the simplicity of Faith believe He will accomplish what He willeth to do.

The learned Dr. Pusey quotes a passage from St. Irenæus, and says : "Speaking of the immortality of the body, that it is nourished by that which is the Body of Christ. *It is not nourished by the Body of Christ itself, for that is* SPIRITUAL AND INCORRUPTIBLE ; but our Lord gives through His Body THAT VIRTUE to the consecrated elements, that they impart to the body, THE LIFE, which HE HIMSELF IS." This very precise statement of doctrine by St. Irenæus, is in exact keeping with the doctrine taught by our best divines, who all admit, that IN the *due* and *right use* of the elements and in their reception, the Spiritual food of His Body and Blood are taken. If Spiritual food, then food which is the presence to the spirit of the receiver, of the Spiritual Body and Blood of Christ, THE LIFE of the Son of God and Man.

To the law and to the testimony ; for by the law of the Anglican Church we are willing to stand or fall. The bishop of Quebec is perfectly correct in his appeal to all men, either honestly to abide by the teaching of the Church of England, or to withdraw from her fold. It is the only honest course for men to take, and cost what it may : we should not hesitate a moment about it, we are either to be faithful members of the Anglican Church or else unfaithful, and betrayers of her ; and it is now the stern duty of every man to ask himself the question, " Am I in heart and soul a true loyal disciple of that branch of the Church which reformed itself on the Word and Ancient Customs. Do I take the Catechism of the English Church, and accept in spirit and in very truth, the answers to the questions which she puts to her children :—

" *Question.* **How many** Sacraments hath Christ ordained in His Church ?

" *Answer.* Two only, as generally necessary to salvation, that is to say, Baptism, and the Supper of the Lord.

" *Question.* What meanest thou by this word *Sacrament ?*

"*Answer.* I mean an outward and visible sign of an inward and spiritual grace given unto us, ordained by Christ Himself, as a means whereby we **receive the same,** and a pledge to assure us thereof.

"*Question.* How many parts are there in a Sacrament?

"*Answer.* Two; the outward visible sign, and the inward spiritual grace.

"*Question.* Why was the Sacrament of the Lord's Supper ordained?

"*Answer.* For the continual remembrance **of the SACRIFICE of the death of Christ, and of the benefits which** we receive thereby.

"*Question.* **What** is the outward part **or sign of the Lord's** Supper?

"*Answer.* **Bread and Wine,** which the **Lord hath** commanded **to be received.**

"*Question.* **What** is the inward part, or thing signified?

"*Answer.* **The** Body **and** Blood **of Christ,** which are *verily* and *indeed* **taken** and *received* **by** the faithful in the Lord's Supper.

"*Question.* What are the **benefits whereof we are partakers** thereby?

"*Answer.* The strengthening **and refreshing of our souls** BY THE BODY and BLOOD OF CHRIST, **as our bodies are by the Bread and Wine.**"

We believe that this is the plain teaching of the truth of Scripture. **We accept every word as being the** mind of Christ. We believe **the Church holds that Christ is** present **to the** faithful, and, therefore, that **in a true way, we do receive** the Body and Blood of Christ as the Apostles **teach.** If this be all in accordance with the mind of scripture, if **it be** the Holy Spirit's teaching, **then we** must believe, that **our most** adorable Redeemer is beholding us when we kneel **before His most holy altar** table; **and that He does, in a manner we cannot understand,** give to our bodies, souls **and spirits, by the power and** virtue which is of His own **glorified Body,** the spiritual food of His most precious **Body and** Blood.

If Almighty **God had been pleased to deal with His people without the intervention of "**signs**" of His** dealing, **surely** He could have done **so. We** know **what** happened to those who, in their pride, thought fit **to select means** of **their own.** There are **many Syrians** still, as there are also hundreds who are gainsayers with Dathan and Abiram.

The Son of God has bidden us to take of the Water of **Life freely.** Many there **are who** think that He will surely **heal them** without any material intervention.

"*Are* not **Abana** and Pharpar, rivers of Damascus, **better than all the** waters of Israel? May I not wash in them and be **clean?**"

If Christ had bidden **us do some great thing,** would we not have done **it?** How **much more when He saith,** "Eat and live."

It is very disheartening to find so many minds in the Church of England in hot debate, and so comparatively few, willing to submit to the teaching which her reformed bishops and pastors have written for their guidance, and which her voice by convocation has authorized. One would imagine that in the Catechism and in her Articles of Religion she had spoken plainly enough; and yet how many of her children diligently set themselves to understand the truth as taught by her, in her Articles and formularies?

"XXV. *Of the Sacraments.*

"Sacraments ordained of Christ be not only badges or tokens of Christian men's profession, but rather they be certain sure witnesses, and effectual signs of grace, and God's good will towards us, by the which he doth work invisibly in us, and doth *not only quicken,* but also strengthen and confirm our faith in Him.

"There are two Sacraments ordained of Christ our Lord in the Gospel, that is to say, Baptism, and the Supper of the Lord.

"Those five commonly called Sacraments, that is to say, Confirmation, Penance, Orders, Matrimony, and extreme Unction, are not to be counted for Sacraments of the Gospel, being such as have grown partly of the corrupt following of the Apostles, partly are states of life allowed in the Scriptures; but yet have not the like nature of Sacraments with Baptism, and the Lord's Supper, for that they have not any visible sign or ceremony ordained of God.

"The Sacraments were not ordained of Christ to be gazed upon, or to be carried about, but that we should duly use them. And in such only as worthily receive the same they have a wholesome effect or operation: but they that receive them unwortily purchase to themselves damnation, as Saint **Paul** saith.

"XXVIII. *Of the Lord's Supper.*

"The Supper of **the** Lord is not only a sign of the love **that** Christians ought to have among themselves one to another; **but rather it is a** Sacrament of our Redemption by Christ's death: insomuch that to such as rightly, worthily, and with faith, receive the same, the Bread which we break **is a** partaking of the Body of Christ; and likewise the Cup of Blessing is a partaking of the Blood of Christ."

In this the Church does not deny a quality by sacramental use which the sacred elements have not as bread and wine.

"Transubstantiation (or the change of the substance of Bread and Wine) in the Supper of the Lord, cannot be proved by holy Writ; but it is repugnant to the plain words of Scripture, overthroweth the nature of a Sacrament, and hath given occasion to many superstitions.

"The Body of Christ is given, taken, and eaten, in the Supper, only after an heavenly and spiritual manner. And the mean whereby the Body of Christ is received and eaten in the Supper is Faith.

"The Sacrament of the Lord's Supper was not by Christ's ordinance reserved, carried about, lifted up, or worshipped.

"XXIX. *Of the Wicked which eat not the Body of Christ in the use of the Lord's Supper.*

"The Wicked, and such as be void of a lively faith, although they do carnally and visibly press with their teeth (as Saint *Augustine* saith) the Sacrament of the Body and Blood of Christ, yet in no wise are they partakers of Christ: but rather, to their condemnation, do they eat and drink the sign or Sacrament of so great a thing." *

"XXX. *Of both kinds.*

"The Cup of the Lord is not to be denied to the Lay-people: **for both the parts of the** Lord's Sacrament, by Christ's ordinance and **commandment, ought to be ministered to all** Christian men alike."

The elder **as well as** the more modern divines of the Church **of England** hold **the same doctrine** and express

---

* "They shall **not** offer wine offerings to the Lord, neither shall they be pleasing unto Him: their sacrifice shall be unto them as the bread of mourners: all that **eat** thereof shall be polluted; *for their* **bread** *for their souls shall not come* **into the** house of the Lord."—Hosea ix. 4.

themselves as do the primitive fathers of the Church. They all, with singular unanimity, **set** forth as the doctrine of the Church, that our most **blessed** Lord **and** Saviour is most truly present in the sacrifice of thanksgiving, and is consequently received by the spirit of the faithful communicant. That in THE SERVICE of the Holy Eucharist the Lord Jesus is present, and that the holy bread and **wine** are the effectual signs of His presence, which presence is to the end, that He may be taken **and received in the heart or spirit of the** faithful. The blessed Jesus *is present*, although He **may be neither in the bread nor in the cup.** He is present as He **promised through the** service of praise and thanksgiving, **and is with His disciples now as** He was with them at the **first holy celebrations.** Here is the representative priest ministering in His name with the representative memorials or symbols of His sacrifice. There he stands IN his Master's MINISTRY and IN his Master's NAME, breaking and blessing bread, pouring out and blessing wine. **This** representative priesthood speaking **to baptized men the words of** Christ, the blessed **elements and the assembled faithful** *are* the effectual *signs*, **that no mere human service is being** celebrated, no common human **gift** bestowed; but truly symbolize or figure **a high spiritual** work wrought for man : **and so the elements are in** their *actual* and *right use* **to the receiver, the** signs of the presence **of the body and blood of** Christ. Thus teach English divines :—

HAMMOND, *Practical Catechism*, **lib. vi., sect. iv.**

" This is My body (signifies) this breaking, taking, eating of the Bread;*
this whole action is the real communication of the Body of Christ to me ; that as verily as I eat the bread in my mouth, *so verily God in heaven* BESTOWS on me, communicates to me THE BODY OF THE CRUCIFIED SAVIOUR. . . . . God's part is the accepting **of this our bounden** duty, bestowing **that** Body and Blood of

---

* **This blessing,** giving, and breaking by the hands of a Priest.

Christ upon us, not by sending *it down locally for our bodies to feed upon*, but *really for our souls* to be strengthened and refreshed by it; as when the sun is communicated to us, the whole body and bulk of the sun is not removed out of its sphere, but the rays and beams of it, and with them the light and warmth and influences are really and verily bestowed or darted out upon us."

"For we take not Baptism nor the Eucharist for bare *resemblances* or memorials of things absent, neither for naked signs, and testimonies assuring us of grace received before, but,—as they are in deed and in verity,—for means effectual whereby God, when we take the Sacrament, delivereth into our hands that grace available unto eternal Life, which grace the Sacraments represent or signify." *

"Grace intended by Sacraments was a cause of the choice, and is a reason of the fitness of the Elements themselves." †

"‡ It is too cold an **interpretation**, whereby, some men expound our being in Christ to impart nothing else, but only that the self same nature which maketh us to be men, is in Him, and maketh Him Man as we are. For what man in the world is there which hath not so far forth communion with Jesus Christ? It is not *this* that can sustain the weight of such sentences as speak of the mystery of our coherence with Jesus Christ. The Church is in Christ as Eve was in Adam. Yea, by grace we are every one of us in Christ and in His Church, as by nature we are in those our first parents. God made Eve of the rib of Adam. And His Church He frameth out of the very flesh, the very wounded and bleeding side of the Son of Man. His Body crucified, and His Blood shed for the life of the world, are the true elements of that heavenly Being, which maketh us such as Himself is, of whom, we come. For which cause the words of Adam may be fitly the words of Christ concerning the Church, "Flesh of My Flesh; bone of 'My Bones:' a true native extract out of Mine own Body." So that on Him, even according to His nature as God-man,

---

* Hooker, Bk. v., ch. lvii., 5 6. † Idem., lviii.
‡ Hooker, vol. ii., p. 250.

we according to our regenerated Being, are His branches springing out of that root of which we grow. "To all things He is Life, and to men Light, as *the Son of God*; to the Church both Life and Light eternal by being made the Son of Man for us, and by being in us a Saviour, whether we respect Him as God or as Man. Adam is in us as an *original cause of* OUR NATURE and of that corruption of nature which causeth death; Christ as the cause original of restoration to life: *the person* of Adam is not in us, but his NATURE, and the *corruption* of his nature derived into all men by propagation: Christ having Adam's nature as we have, but incorrupt, deriveth not nature but incorruption, and that immediately from His OWN PERSON into all that belong to Him. As, therefore, we are really partakers of the body of sin and death received from Adam, so, except we be truly partakers of Christ, and as really possessed of His Spirit, all we speak of eternal life is but a dream."

(8.) That which quickeneth us is the Spirit of the Second Adam, and His FLESH that wherewith He quickeneth. That which in Him made our nature incorrupt, was the union of His Deity with our nature. And in that respect the sentence of death and condemnation which only taketh hold upon sinful flesh, could no way possibly extend unto Him. This caused His *voluntary* death for others to prevail with God, and to have the force of an expiatory Sacrifice. The Blood of Christ, as the Apostle witnesseth, doth therefore take away sin, because, "through the Eternal Spirit He offered Himself without spot." That which sanctified our *nature* in Christ, that which made a sacrifice available to take away sin, IS *the* same which quickeneth IT, raised IT out of the grave after death, and exalted IT unto glory.

Seeing, therefore, that, Christ is in us as a quickening Spirit, the first degree of communion with Christ must needs consist in the participation of His Spirit, which Cyprian in that respect well termeth *germanissimam societatem*, the **highest and truest society that can be** between **man and Him, which is both God and Man in one.**

(9.) **These things St. Cyril duly** considering, reproveth **their speeches which** taught that only the **deity of** Christ is the **Vine whereupon** we by **faith** do **depend as** branches, and **that neither his** flesh nor **our** bodies are comprised in this **resemblance.** For doth any man **doubt** but that even from **the flesh of** Christ **our very** bodies do receive *that life* which shall make them glorious at the latter day, for which they are already accounted parts of His blessed body? **Our corruptible bodies could never live the** life they shall **live, were it not that here they** are joined **with His** body which is incorruptible, **and that His is in ours** as a cause of immortality, **a cause,** by removing through the death and merit of **His own flesh, that which** hindered **life in ours.** Christ is, therefore, both as God and Man, **that true Vine whereof we** both spiritually and corporally are branches. **The mixture of** His bodily substance with ours **is a** thing which the **ancient Father's** disclaim. Yet the mixture of His flesh **with ours** they speak of, **to** signify **what our** very bodies through mystical conjunction receive **from** that, *vital efficacy* **which we know to** be in His; **and from** bodily mixtures they borrow divers similitudes rather to declare **the** truth, **than the** manner of coherence, between His sacred **Body and the sanctified bodies of His saints.**

Again, p. 259: "**Even as the Lord doth organize the** body, and give unto every member thereof that substance, quantity and shape, which nature seeth most expedient, so **the** inward grace of sacraments may teach what serveth best **for their** outward form, a thing **in no part** of Christian religion, much less here to be neglected. **Grace** intended by sacraments was a cause of the choice, and is a reason of the fitness of the elements themselves. Furthermore, seeing that the grace which here we receive doth no way depend upon the natural force of that which we presently behold, it was of necessity that words of express declaration, taken from the very mouth of our Lord himself, should be added unto visible elements, that the **one** might infallibly teach what the other does most **assuredly bring to pass."** In the reception of the benefits which flow to us from **our** union with **our most** blessed Lord, **we are to** consider who **he was,** not **forgetting that** he is perfect God **and perfect man, and in the conjunction of** two **natures, but** *one* Christ. **He it is who** thus **being God and man, is able to give** to his children **that** vital **power which, derived** from himself into them, fits **them** for fellowship with the saints in light. Although it is, **by his being** the head of our race, the second Adam, that he saved us, yet as He took the manhood into his Godhead, so it is by virtue of his power **as the Son of God that** he giveth of his spirit **to** the sons of men, **to wit,** his spiritual body and blood, *i. e.*, the body **and blood of** Christ.

Bishop Beveridge, p. 559, v. ii., observes, **in his** sermon on "**The Unity** of Christ with God **the** Father," "As our **Lord** cured some **by** touching **them, so** he cured others by **their** touching him. For as many as touched him were made perfectly **whole.** And some he cured that were at a great distance from him, as the centurion's servant and the nobleman's **son,** whereby he plainly discovered, THAT THOUGH THE BODY HE HAD ASSUMED WAS ONLY IN ONE PLACE, YET HIS DIVINE ESSENCE AND POWER WAS EVERYWHERE, REACHING THOSE WHICH ARE FAR OFF AS WELL AS THOSE WHICH STOOD JUST BY HIS BODY AND TOUCHED IT; and by consequence that He was both omnipotent and omnipresent."

St. Cyril of Alexandria: "Christ gave his own body for the life of all; but again through IT, he maketh *life* to dwell in us; how, I will say as I am able. For when the life-giving Word of **God** dwelt in flesh, He transformed IT into His own proper good, *i. e.*, LIFE, and by the unspeakable character of this union, coming wholly together with IT, made it life-giving, as Himself is by NATURE. Wherefore, the body of Christ giveth life to all who partake of it. . . . . Wholly destitute of all share and taste of that life which is in sanctification and bliss, are they who do not through the mystical Eucharist receive the Son. For He is life by nature, inasmuch as He was begotten of the Father. And since the flesh of the Saviour became life-giving, as being united to that which is by nature life, the Word from God, then when we taste it we have life in ourselves, we too being united to it as it to the indwelling Word. For this cause also, when He raised the dead, the Saviour is found to have operated, not by word only, or God-befitting commands, but He laid stress on employing His holy flesh as a sort of co-operator for this special end, that he might show that *it* had the power to give life, and was as it were already made one with Him; for it was indeed his own body, and not anothers. When, for instance, He raised the little daughter of the chief of the synagogue, saying, 'Maid, arise,' He laid hold of her hand, as it is written. For giving life, as God, by His all-powerful command, and, again, giving life through the touch of His holy flesh, He showed that there was *one kindred operation* through both. When He went into the city called Nain, and one was being carried out dead, the only son of his mother, again, He touched the bier, saying, 'Young man, I say unto thee, arise.' Thus He gave not to His word only power to give life to the dead, but that He might show that His own body was life-giving, He touched the dead, thereby also infusing life into those already decayed. But if by the touch alone of His holy flesh He giveth life to that which is decayed, how shall we not profit yet more richly by the life-giving Eucharist when we taste it!"

It is the Spirit which quickeneth: the flesh profiteth nothing. It is not so unreasonable, He would say, that ye supposed the flesh incapable of giving life; for when the nature of the flesh is considered *alone by itself*, plainly IT IS NOT life-giving. No created thing can give life. Begotten itself, it is in need of Him who can produce life. But when the mystery of the Incarnation is carefully considered, and ye learn thus who it is Who dwelleth in this flesh, ye will then be disposed (to receive it), unless you would impute to the Divine Spirit also that he cannot impart life, although of itself the flesh altogether profiteth nothing. For since it is united to the life-giving Word, it hath become wholly life-giving, rising up to the power of the higher nature, not itself forcing even into its own nature Him who cannot be in anywise subjected. Although, then, the nature of the flesh is in itself powerless to give life, yet it will in-work this, when it has the life-working Word, and will produce the whole operations of that Word. For it is the body of that which is by nature Life, not of any earthly being, as to whom *that* might rightly hold, " the flesh profiteth nothing." For not the flesh of Paul, or Peter, or any other, would alone work this in us, but only and specially that of our Saviour Christ, in whom dwelt all the fulness of the Godhead bodily. Wherefore as to all other things that will be true, that the flesh profiteth nothing ; but as to Christ alone it holdeth not." The whole force of this argument is in the application which is made of the raising the dead by the power of the presence of Christ as the God-man. He has most clearly brought out the truth, that it is from the LIVING Jesus—Christ *manifest in the flesh*, Christ, acting himself as Priest and King, that we are made partakers of His flesh and blood. And in the same way that He by his presence and **by the living power of His** Word and Body, raised **the** dead **and gave sight to the** blind; **so as** by the **clay, so by the bread and wine, the LIVING** WORD raises to life everlasting, **him who is** dead in trespasses **and sins. The word** of Christ stamped upon the elements by his own ministry makes **them** seals of the covenant of promise, that He indwells in the spirit.

Bishop Beveridge, at page 567, speaking of the Incarnation, says: "The expression, 'The Word was made flesh,' implies, that as the Word was the Person that was made flesh, so, when He was made flesh, He was still **one** and the same Person as before. **For in that** He was made flesh, the flesh could have no subsistence **out of Him, so as** to make a Person of itself **distinct from** His, no more than a body can make a human person without being united to a reasonable soul. But as the reasonable soul and flesh together is one man, **so God and man** is one Christ; *the Word and the* Flesh **one** Divine Person. So that whatsoever He did or suffered **in the** Flesh, **was** done and suffered by a Divine **Person.** 'His blood was the blood of God,' and therefore of infinite value and merit. . . . . . The Word was made Flesh, flesh or *man in general*, as the **word** *flesh* always means when applied to men. **IT doth** not signify any one, or more particular man, but mankind in general, THE WHOLE **HUMAN** NATURE; that which all men are of, that proceeded **from** the first man Adam, in **whom it** was all contained. **And** *so it is* in the Word made Flesh, who is therefore **called** 'the **last** Adam,' and, '**the Second Man,**' because next to the first, who **had** the whole manhood in Him. Hence it is, that when the **Word was made** Flesh and died in it, 'He died for all' and 'for every man.'—1 Acts, xx., 28.

Because He died in that nature which is common to all, and every man alike. So that all and every man may now be saved by Him, whom God sent into the world to be made flesh, 'That whosoever believeth in Him should not perish, but have everlasting life.' And in summing up the might and goodness **of** God to us, **the** good bishop concludes, "What shall we render unto the Lord for His wonderful benefits? We will receive the Cup of Salvation and call upon the name of the Lord. We will celebrate the memory of the Word made Flesh, by feeding upon that Spiritual food which **the** Word hath prepared for us OF THE FLESH HE WAS MADE. We will go to His altar, and there offer up **our** sacrifice of praise and thanksgiving."

Bishop Beveridge only utters the mind of Hooker and other divines of the Anglican Church in thus teaching, that **we** do really and in very truth take and receive through the power of the Holy Ghost, the nature which our most blessed Lord and Saviour Jesus Christ took of His mother into union with His Divine, and **which He** was pleased **to dwell** in amongst us. The words ἐσκήνωσεν ἐν ἡμῖν, impart rather, that He dwelt **in us,** *in our* nature: as He is called, Emmanuel, **"God with us;"** God with *our* **nature** united to Him. So He dwelt **in us,** in that flesh or nature, that **we all are** of: He dwelt, or, as the word signifies, He pitched His tent or tabernacle in **it: in** allusion probably to that in the **law,** where He dwelt between the cherubim over the ark, keeping **as it** were, His residence there; which was, therefore, called Shechinah, His habitation, His Divine Presence, and **His** glory, because His glory appeared from thence unto the people." The Holy Thing, τὸ ἅγιον, which was born of the Virgin was the Word made Flesh, God and Man together, and it is because of this union that there is derived to **us** that Body and Blood by which alone we can be united to Christ. We care not whether He is in the bread or whether He is in the wine or no, for this we do know, that we who were dead are made alive by the operation of His nature imparted to us; and by the presence and power of His Body are re-called from the dead saints who were once dead in sin.

Bishop Cosin, History of Transubstantiation, Works (Ed. Lib. **A. C. T.**), **vol.** iv., p. 174, says: "Because *the thing signified is offered and given to us as truly as the sign itself*, in this respect we own the union betwixt the body and blood of Christ and the elements, whose use and office we hold to be changed from what it was **before.** But we deny what the Papists affirm, ... and we also deny that the elements still retain the nature of Sacraments, when not **used** according to divine institution, that is, *given by Christ's ministers*, and received *by his people;* so that Christ, in the consecrated bread, ought not, *cannot be* kept and preserved to be carried about, *because he is present only to the communicants.*"

His meaning he makes more clear in his Notes to the Book of Common Prayer, Works, vol. v., p. 345: "True it is that the body and blood of Christ are sacramentally and really (not feignedly) present when the blessed bread and wine are taken by the faithful communicants; and as true it is also that they are not present, but only when the hallowed elements are so taken, as in another work (the History of the Papal Transubstantiation) I have more at large declared. Therefore, whosoever so receiveth them, at that time when he receiveth them, rightly doth he adore and reverence his Saviour there together with the sacramental bread and cup, exhibiting his own body and blood unto them. Yet, because that body and blood is neither sensibly present, nor *otherwise at all present but only to them that are duly prepared to receive them, and in the very act of receiving them and the consecrated elements together, to which they are sacramentally in that act united*), the adoration **is then** and there to be given to Christ himself, neither is **nor** ought to be directed to **any** external sensible object, such as are the blessed elements."

And lastly (Archbishop Wake on the Catechism, sec. 48): "That which is given by the **Priest** is, as to its **substance**, bread and wine; as to its sacramental nature and signification, it is the figure or representation of Christ's body and blood, which was broken and shed for us. *The very body and blood of Christ, as yet, it is not; but being* **with faith and piety received** *by the communicant, it becomes* **to him**, *by the blessing of God and the grace of the Holy Spirit, the very body and blood of Christ.* As to those who **come unworthily** to it, it is made damnation; that is, it renders them worthy of it, and without repentance it will certainly consign them **over** unto it."

The Bishop of Exeter states the doctrine of the Church of England, with his accustomed precision, thus: "The other sophism rests on the ambiguous meaning of the word Sacrament, a word sometimes, and more strictly, applied to the sign or matter, sometimes *to the whole sacred rite*. Now, it is in the former sense that the Church of Rome holds the real presence of the body and blood of Christ in the Sacrament. It is in the latter sense that the real presence in the Sacrament, maintained by the Church of England, must be sought. The Church of Rome holds that the body and blood of Christ are present under the accidents of bread and wine; the Church of England holds that the real presence of Christ is in the soul of the communicant at the Sacrament of the Lord's Supper."

Again: "It is in this sense that the crucified Jesus is present in the Sacrament of His Supper; not in, nor with the bread and wine, nor under their accidents, but in the souls of the communicants, **not carnally,** but effectually and faithfully, and **therefore most really."**

Bishop Browne, on the **Articles, p. 709, thus sums up** the teaching **of our** best Divines **on this mysterious subject:** " From the time of the Reformation **to the present, all the** great **luminaries of our Church have maintained the doctrine,** which **appears on the face of our formularies; agreeing to** deny **a corporal, and acknowledging a** spiritual feeding **in the Supper of the Lord. It is scarcely** necessary to recount **the names of Mede, Andrews, Hooker, Taylor,** Hammond, Cosin, **Bramhall, Usher, Pearson, Patrick, Bull,** Beveridge, Wake, **Waterland. All these have left us writings on** the subject, **and all have coincided, with but very slight** diversity, **in substance of their belief. They have** agreed, as Hooker says, **that ' Christ is *personally* present,** albeit a part of Christ be *corporeally* **absent;'** that 'the fruit of the Eucharist is the participation **of** the body **and blood of Christ,' but that 'the real presence** of Christ's most blessed **body and blood is not to be sought** for in the Sacrament **(i. e.,** *in the elements*), **but in the** worthy **receiver** of the **Sacraments.' " ***

In the due use of His ordained means, we are certified of His Presence as surely as the **Jew was. "In all places where I** record My name, **I** will come unto thee, **and I will bless thee."** † He must have **very mean** thoughts **of Christ and** His gospel, **who** can **suffer Himself** to be persuaded, **that** the Name **of God is not recorded in our** Christian churches, **as well as it was in the Jewish** tabernacle **or** temple. For **this** is to prefer **the Law before** the gospel, and to make the condition **of the Jews much** better than

---

* These extracts are from the Charge of the Bishop of Quebec.
† Bishop Beveridge, vol. ii., p. 171.

that of the Christians.* " For since God Himself is invisible and cannot by us be discerned working, therefore, when it seemeth good in the eyes of His heavenly wisdom, that men for some special purpose and intent, should take notice of His glorious presence; He giveth some plain and sensible token whereby to know what they cannot see." †

" Seeing that our Lord hath promised to be with His Apostles and their successors to the end of the world; seeing the succession of the office Apostolical, hath without interruption been continued in our Church to this day: and seeing, therefore, that Christ according to His promise, is *always present* by His Holy Spirit at the Word and Sacraments, *to quicken, actuate, and make them effectual* to the salvation of our souls; hence, in His name, and for His sake, and ours too, I beseech you all to meet your Lord and Saviour in the offices of the Church to which He has vouchsafed and promised His peculiar presence.‡

The divines of the Church of England have never concealed their belief of the real presence of Christ in The Sacrament, but have always maintained that He is only present to the faithful; although the teaching of Scripture and the creed of the early Church forbids their saying that He is included in the elements or that they are transubstantiated into His Body and Blood. Looking on the elements as sacred means, they nowhere deny that the Spiritual Body and Blood of Christ the God-man, accompanies the right and due use, *i. e.*, right and due reception of the Sacrament. We receive the Body and Blood of Christ, not the body and blood of a mere man, not the body and blood of the Human Nature of Christ, as something apart and separate drawn away, from His Divine Nature;

---

* Bishop Hooker, vol. ii., p. 257.   † Exod. iii., 2. John 5, 4. Acts ii., 3.
‡ Beveridge's Works, vol. ii., p. 102.

but we receive and **take the** Flesh **and Blood** of that Body, which by reason **of the** conjunction **of the** Human and Divine, was the Body and Blood of **Christ**; and **as** a consequent, a Spiritual Body, "the Quickening Spirit;" gifted with and having *through* the Eternal Word, all those powers and qualities of spirit, which are **of** The Spirit.

Neither the ancient Fathers, nor the venerated doctors **of** the Anglican Church define *how* the Spiritual Flesh **and Blood of** Christ are bestowed upon us, they nowhere **admit the** carnal dogma of transubstantiation. They point **out,** that in the due celebration of the Sacrifice of praise **and** thanksgiving, "The Word" speaks to us with the same *efficacy* and *potency* with which He spoke, when drawing unto Himself **and** imparting the New-Life to His Apostles, transforming them into the perfect image and likeness of Himself. The Sacramental **union** which Christ was pleased **to establish for** our sakes, **is not a** union which contemplates, the possibility of Christ being united to us by any act **or** power in ourselves or of ourselves. The Eternal Word took our flesh; **not** *our flesh* the Eternal Word. So too, also, Christ **condescends** to dwell in us by Sacramental grace, **as He was pleased to** dwell in the flesh which He took for the elects sake. He unites our nature to His. Just as we can the better realise God's Presence by knowing that *we* are **in His Presence**; so we can the better realise Christ's Presence **by** knowing, that *He sees us* and that we are before Him—very near to Him.

No one denies the ability **of** God to do as He pleases with His own. **We admit** that the conversion of bread and wine into human flesh and blood by the word of Christ, is a no **more** impossible work than the conversion of the same elements into our flesh and blood **by the** ordinary process of nutrition within our **living bodies.** God has been pleased, in forming our bodies out of the dust of the earth, to condition those bodies unto spiritual life, to cause their transelementation into pure spiritual existence by the influence of His divine breath, although it be that through the grave and gate of death the ultimate condition of perfect spiritual life is reached. How the spiritual and material are related in us, we know not, we cannot say exactly how even our material food becomes identified with our material flesh; but we do know that the Scriptures declare that our spiritual life is sustained by the operation of the Life of the Son of God in us. As all that lives on this earth would soon wither and die if the sun were to withhold its rays, so all spiritual life would perish from virtue and godliness if Christ were to withdraw His influence, the *direct contact* of His own precious Self in the person of man. It is Jesus, who unites our nature to His, it is the divine presence which comes to us from His own glorified Body, and effectually operates in us, conforming us to the true likeness and perfection of holiness which He is. It is the shining of the Light Divine into us, which illuminates and penetrates our spirits, turning our darkness into light. The language of Scripture is, "He breathed into his nostrils the breath of life, and man became a living soul." The operation of the Spirit of God on the nature of man was to endue him with immortality: "man *became a living spirit*." The whole nature of man is thus filled with life eternal; and although the matter of which his body is formed perishes in the using and is renewed by the daily employment of food, he is conscious of the oneness and unchangeable continuity of himself; he feels that he is not his body, nor is his body all that he is. In the depth of consciousness is the revelation of self; for as in the consciousness of His Divine Majesty, The Lord Jesus without any abatement of majesty, proclaimed His Sonship and oneness with the Father, so it is given to us to know that we live, and that our bodies are of ourselves, but are not ourselves. The unseen is that which is real, the seen is temporal. That which is grasped by sense, is now, and is not; that which is discerned by the spirit, or by faith the act of spirit, is and continues to be. It was to rescue this "living spirit" from eternal misery, that Christ came in human flesh, *i. e.*, in the whole perfect nature of man, in order that this perfect Humanity, as it was dwelt in by the Son of God, might be a source from whence, by the power of THE SPIRIT OF CHRIST, the fallen and corrupt nature of man might receive a perpetual renewing. If St. Paul says that we are members of His body, of His flesh and of His bones, he has also said that "God hath sent the Spirit of Christ into our hearts, whereby we cry Abba, Father." Is Christ divided? Where His Spirit is, there also is His humanity by His divinity. And if Christ be in us, then are we sons and heirs of eternal life with God. The body is saved with the Spirit.

It is sufficient for us to know that Christ has promised to bring us into His presence, and in that He is God and cannot lie, we know Him to be present to His faithful ones. "Even the body of Christ itself although the definite limitation thereof be most sensible, doth, notwithstanding, admit in some sort or kind of infinite unlimited presence likewise. For His body being a part of that nature, which whole nature is presently joined unto Deity wheresoever Deity is, it followeth, that His bodily substance hath everywhere a presence of true conjunction with Deity. And forasmuch as it is by virtue of that conjunction made the body of the Son of God, by whom also it was made *a Sacrifice* for the sins *of the whole world*, this giveth a PRESENCE of force and efficacy throughout all generations of men. Albeit, therefore, nothing be *actually* infinite *in substance* but God only, in that He is God; nevertheless, as every member is infinite by possibility of addition, and every line by possibility of extension infinite, so there is no stint which can be set to the value or merit of the sanctified Body of Christ; it has no measured certainty of limits, bounds of *efficacy* unto life it knoweth none, but is also itself infinite in *possibility of application.*[*] This statement of truth by the judicious Hooker sufficiently answers the objection of the Romanist to the Anglican doctrine of the real presence. Far more clearly than the Roman, the Anglican Church admits Christ to be present in the Sacrament, but defines not how He is present, save that He is so to the spirit of the believer.

To show how erroneous it is to attempt close definition, and how we may keep the truth by the act of faith, nothing can be plainer than Hooker's warning words: "If that be separated which is secret, and that considered alone which is seen, as of necessity it must in all those speeches that make distinction of sacraments from sacramental grace, the *name* of a sacrament in such speeches can imply no more than what the *outward substance* thereof doth comprehend. And to make complete the outward substance of a sacrament, is required an outward form, *which form* sacramental elements receive from *sacramental words*. Hereupon it groweth that many times there are three things, said to make up a sacrament, viz., the grace which is thereby offered, the element which shadoweth or *signifieth the grace*, and *the Word* which expresseth what is done by the element. So that whether we consider the outward by itself alone, or both the outward and inward substance of any sacrament,

---

[*] Hooker, Book **v.**, ch. iv., 9., lvi. 1., p. 245.

there are in the one respect but TWO ESSENTIAL PARTS, and in the other but three, that concur to give sacraments their full being." Hooker further illustrates his meaning of the true nature of a sacrament and the proper use of elements at page 264: "When the letter of the law hath two things plainly and expressly specified, WATER and THE SPIRIT; water, as a duty required on our parts; the Spirit, as a gift which God bestoweth; there is danger in presuming so to interpret it, as if the clause which concerneth ourselves were more than needeth. We may by such rare expositions attain perhaps in the end to be thought witty, but with ill advice. Finally, if at the time when that Baptism which was meant by John came to be really and truly performed by Christ himself, we find the apostles that had been, as we are, before baptised with the Holy Ghost, and in their latter baptism as well a visible descent of fire, as a secret miraculous infusion of the Spirit; if on us He accomplish likewise the heavenly work of our new birth, *not with the Spirit alone, but with water adjoined*, sith the FAITHFULEST EXPOUNDERS of His words are HIS OWN DEEDS, let that which his hands hath manifestly wrought declare what His speech did doubtfully utter." Hence we see the wisdom of the Anglican Church in keeping away from definitions. She simply does as her most dear Lord commands, and, teaching her sons and daughters to walk by Faith and not by sight, puts into their hands the sacred symbols of Christ's Passion, well knowing, that as those symbols are in their hands, so is Christ in their spirits a cause of renewed life in them. To how many renewed hearts has Faith revealed the Lamb of God which taketh away the sins, which cast them to earth? To how many a Thomas and holy St. Paul has the vision of Christ dying for the terror stricken sinner been vouchsafed?

Are they none who have by **Faith felt** Him to be near by, strengthening them by His **merciful fear** subduing power? Hath God forgotten to be gracious? **Has** He never fulfiled His promise, "We will come unto Him and make our abode **with Him?**" **With the** full recognition of Who our blessed **Lord was, that** His humanity was not **separate from** His divinity, but that in Him His Christ's nature **was by the union of the** Human and Divine, **we know that the Spiritual Life-giving** Christ, imparteth Himself **to believing souls, when in full faith they in obedience to His commands, make the representation of the Sacrifice of His Death.** In **the power of His** might, **He came from the abode of the dead, for in the** impossibility **of the grave to** hold **the Lord of Life the sealed stone rolled back** from His **presence.** In **the same** might **He stood** in the midst **of His** assembled **chosen ones, locked in** from the turbulence of Jews. In the same strength **He** manifested Himself to His **own doubting Apostle, dispelling** from his spirit the tide **of** doubt **which** had set in upon **his soul.** Faith **is** the gift of God, it enables the **renewed heart to** open itself to the waiting **Christ who stands at the door and** knocks. More **immovable than the huge sepulchral stone, more impenetrable than the bolted door must our** spirits **be, if the Life-giving Christ cannot enter and pass in, to the cleansing and renewing of** enfeebled **and sin-blighted souls, which have been created** in His own **image.**

The Church of England, in her Articles, and, again, in an assembly of Bishops from **all parts of the** earth **representing her** in most **solemn assembly, has declared that she is of the** same mind **with the Church as represented by her first six Œcumenical Councils. This being so, we as faithful and loyal men,** have only **to bow to Christian teaching, as** expounded by **her and gathered from the general** consent of the Houses **of Convocation, and in the** agreement of her best divines, **whenever** they speak in conformity with Scripture, and with the ancient Fathers, up to the close **of** the sixth Council.

𝔊𝔩𝔬𝔯𝔦𝔞 𝔦𝔫 𝔈𝔵𝔠𝔢𝔩𝔰𝔦𝔰.